lonely planet

San Francisco & Northern California

Alexis Averbuck, Alison Bing,
Celeste Brash, Amelia Mularz, Ryan Ver Berkmoes

FROM LEFT: GEORGINAPAGE/SHUTTERSTOCK, KYLE HEFFERNAN/SHUTTERSTOCK

Golden Gate Bridge (p54)

CONTENTS

Wine tasting, Sonoma Wine Country (p179)

FAST SPEEDS IMAGERY/SHUTTERSTOCK

Bay Bridge, San Francisco (p41)

SAN FRANCISCO & NORTHERN CALIFORNIA

THE JOURNEY BEGINS HERE

Growing up in Oakland, I thought I would never move away from the Bay Area. It's downright perfect: weather, culture, beauty, people. What more could I want? Then life happened. And I became a painter and a travel writer with many years living in places from Greece to NYC, New Orleans and even Antarctica. Yet, whenever I cruise any of the Bay's bridges, not just the heart-soaring Golden Gate, I remember what I've always loved: the sparkle of the water and the promise of the day. Anything can happen here, from a seafront oyster lunch with a local wine and a good friend to a night out dancing to some of the world's best music. Every street is a mix of people and a mix of experiences. No wonder the place remains magnetic – there really is something like a California Dream – and here, we are all welcomed home.

Alexis Averbuck

alexisaverbuck.com

Alexis lives in Sonoma County and on Greece's Hydra Island, where she paints and writes about her adventures – from living in Antarctica for a year to crossing the Pacific by sailboat. Alexis wrote the Napa & Sonoma Wine Country chapter, the Plan section and the Toolkit.

My favorite experience is hiking the **Sonoma County coast** (p210) as the mist clears and the Pacific rolls in, crashing on the rock pinnacles and clean-cut cliffs.

WHO GOES WHERE

Our writers and experts choose the places which, for them, define San Francisco & Northern California.

FROM LEFT: @MANAKIN/GETTY IMAGES, ZACH ZHENG/SHUTTERSTOCK

On a stopover in San Francisco, I wandered through Chinatown into **City Lights Bookstore** (p71). In the basement I noticed a sign painted by a 1930s cult: 'I am the door.' It's true. San Francisco is the threshold between fact and fiction, past and future, body and soul. That was 20 years ago. I'm still here. You've been warned.

Alison Bing

@AlisonBing

Alison survived SoCal sandstorms, NorCal cult potlucks and Bay Area robot wars to tell only-in-California stories. Alison wrote the San Francisco chapter.

The moment when **Mt Shasta** (p284) comes into view from the highway, either welcoming me to California or bidding me farewell to my birth state's natural beauty, I get goosebumps from the great mountain's intense energy. But this hardly compares to the high I get from the otherworldly when up on the mountain itself!

Celeste Brash

@cjbrash

Celeste is a travel nerd, outdoor enthusiast and pearl farmer based in French Polynesia and the USA. Celeste wrote the Northern Mountains chapter.

FROM LEFT: N. F. PHOTOGRAPHY/SHUTTERSTOCK, UVL/SHUTTERSTOCK

Mendocino Village (p232), with its rows of saltbox cottages, distinctive water towers and headland trail perched above rugged rock and roiling Pacific waters, is one of my favorite destinations in all of California. Today it feels simultaneously suitable for a well-journeyed sea captain and a bohemian poet.

Amelia Mularz

@ameliamularz

Amelia Mularz is a California-based writer with a focus on travel and design. Amelia wrote the North Coast & Redwoods chapter.

I may have spent my life traveling the world, but for me the drive between Santa Cruz and Pacifica on **Hwy 1** (p157) will always be the most beautiful in the world. Even now, having driven it hundreds of times, I discover a different beach, explore an unfamiliar tide pool or savor a new angle on a sensational view.

Ryan Ver Berkmoes

@ryanvb

Ryan is a California- and Greece-based journalist. Ryan wrote the Marin County & Bay Area chapter.

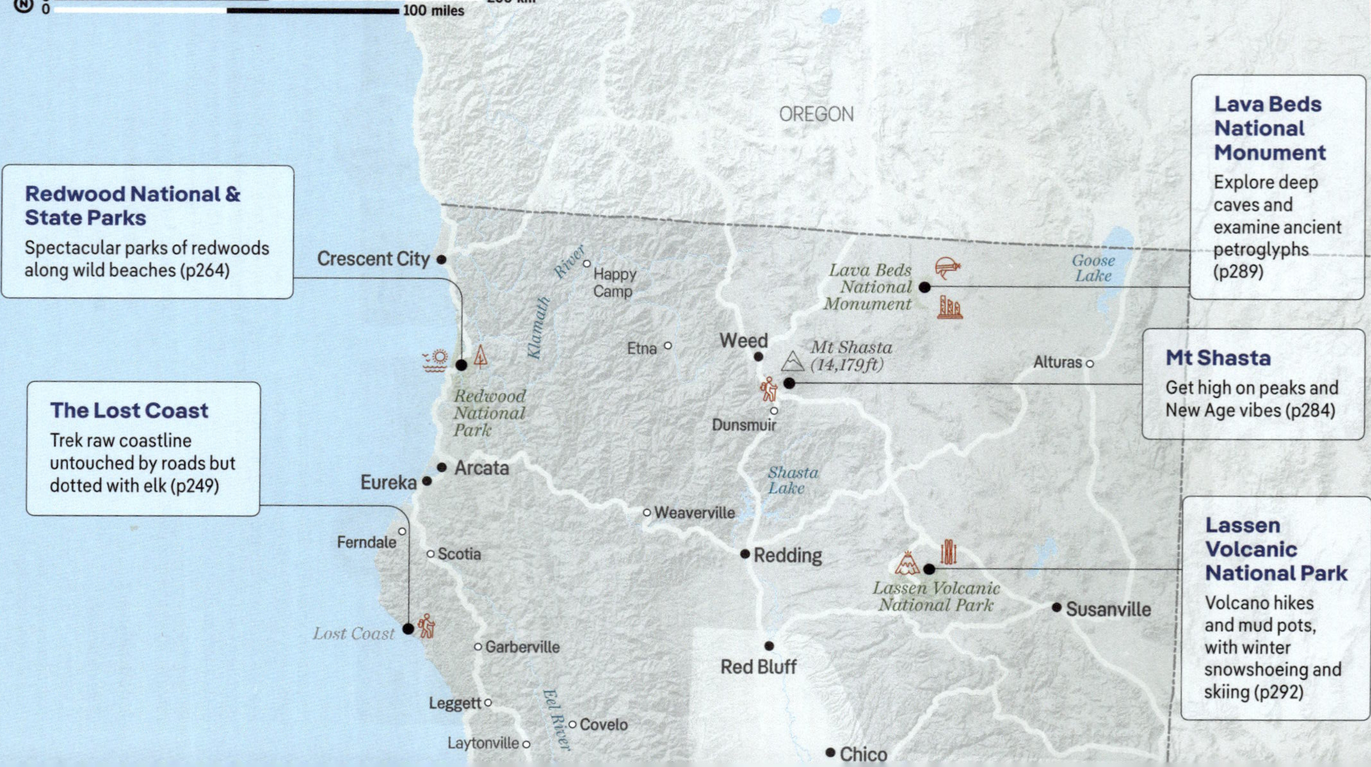

Redwood National & State Parks
Spectacular parks of redwoods along wild beaches (p264)

The Lost Coast
Trek raw coastline untouched by roads but dotted with elk (p249)

Lava Beds National Monument
Explore deep caves and examine ancient petroglyphs (p289)

Mt Shasta
Get high on peaks and New Age vibes (p284)

Lassen Volcanic National Park
Volcano hikes and mud pots, with winter snowshoeing and skiing (p292)

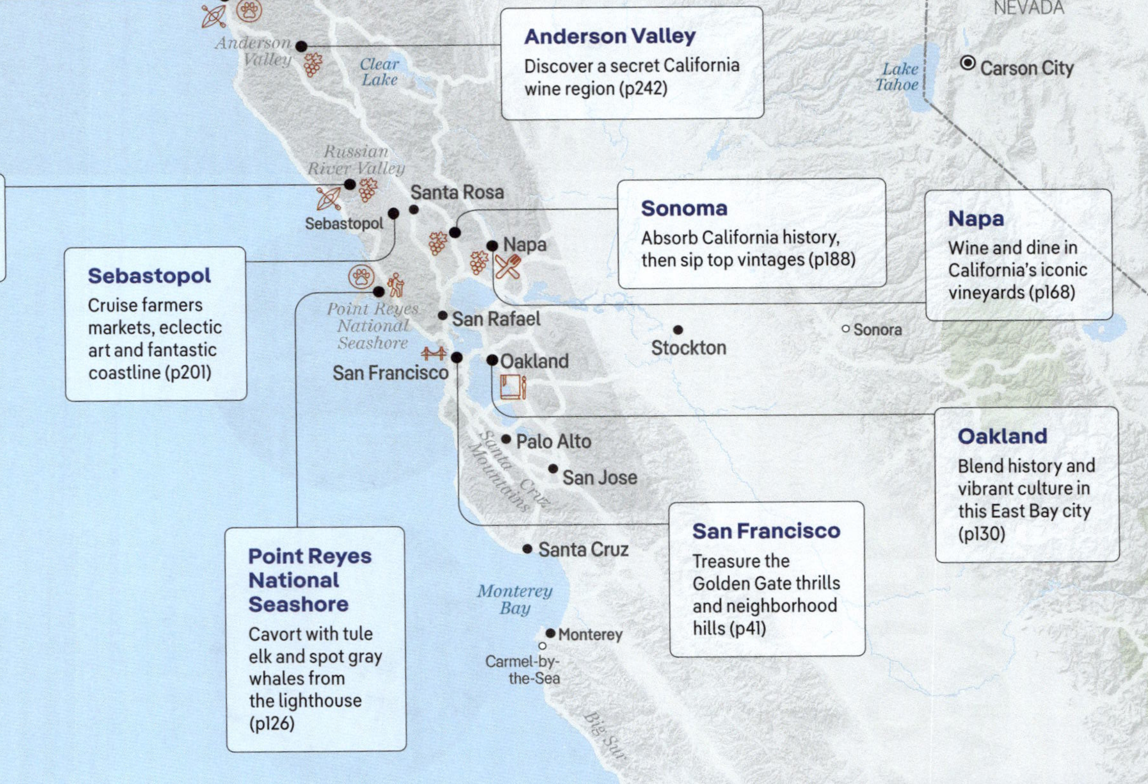
Mendocino
Romantic seaside village, perfect for whale-watching and art (p232)
Anderson Valley
Discover a secret California wine region (p242)
Russian River Valley
Float the river while sipping top vintages (p213)
Sebastopol
Cruise farmers markets, eclectic art and fantastic coastline (p201)
Sonoma
Absorb California history, then sip top vintages (p188)
Napa
Wine and dine in California's iconic vineyards (p168)
Oakland
Blend history and vibrant culture in this East Bay city (p130)
San Francisco
Treasure the Golden Gate thrills and neighborhood hills (p41)
Point Reyes National Seashore
Cavort with tule elk and spot gray whales from the lighthouse (p126)
NEVADA
Carson City
Lake Tahoe
Mendocino
Anderson Valley
Clear Lake
Russian River Valley
Santa Rosa
Sebastopol
Napa
Point Reyes National Seashore
San Rafael
Sonora
Stockton
San Francisco
Oakland
Palo Alto
San Jose
Santa Cruz Mountains
Santa Cruz
Monterey Bay
Monterey
Carmel-by-the-Sea
Big Sur
PACIFIC OCEAN

ADVENTURES OUTDOORS

In Northern California, Mother Nature has created an irresistible combo of blissful beaches, unspoiled wilderness, big-shouldered mountains, high-country meadows, steaming lava fields and trees as tall as the Statue of Liberty – the menu of active options seems inexhaustible. You'll be astonished by Northern California's wild diversity, so step out of the car and get your blood pumping – you'll create memories sure to last a lifetime.

Off the Beaten Path

California has the most national parks in the country. In the north, explore remote Lassen Volcanic National Park's otherworldly lava fields lorded over by a snowcapped volcano.

Redwoods

Northern California is swathed in redwood groves, like the incredible 32-mile Avenue of the Giants (p254), some of which were seedlings during the Roman Empire.

Hot Springs & Swimming Holes

Volcanic mud baths, like Calistoga's, may be exactly what the doctor ordered after a day of wine tasting, or dip into hot springs across the state, like clothing-optional Harbin Hot Springs.

FROM LEFT: ZACK FRANK/SHUTTERSTOCK, JANICE CHEN/SHUTTERSTOCK, ANDRIY BLOKHIN/SHUTTERSTOCK

Mt Shasta (p284)

BEST NATURE EXPERIENCES

Get lost ambling among ancient groves at 1 **Redwood National & State Parks** (p264), home to the world's tallest trees.

Hit the 2 **Lost Coast Trail** (p252), where hardy backpackers tackle 24.6 miles of rugged, unspoiled coastline with Roosevelt elk grazing alongside.

Summit thrilling 3 **Mt Shasta** (p284) before wilding out at Lassen Volcanic National Park with its azure crater lakes.

Paddle a redwood outrigger canoe through the estuary near 4 **Mendocino** (p232) in search of harbor seals and harmony.

Cycle mountain-biking trails or take mellower cruises in Napa and Sonoma Wine Country, like 5 **Dry Creek Valley** (p221) or Sonoma Valley.

EPIC EPICUREAN

Northern California is the epicenter of good eating in the US. Where else is the natural bounty fresher or more varied, the kitchen creativity more boundary-pushing or the flavors and textures more international? New cravings have been invented at California's cultural crossroads for over 200 years, so don't hold back! Get adventurous with anything from roadside food trucks to Cal-Japanese tasting menus, Michelin-starred gastronomic temples and foraged-food cooking – there's something for everyone.

FROM LEFT: FOTOLOGIJA/SHUTTERSTOCK, DANIEL TOH/SHUTTERSTOCK, PHOTOUA/SHUTTERSTOCK

San Francisco Burrito

Burritos are a staple of the NorCal food scene, especially in San Francisco, where the delicious wrap, crammed with fillings, is a local obsession. Get it *dorado:* lightly grilled.

Farmers Markets

Farmers markets abound (check *cafarmersmkts.com* and *cdfa.ca.gov*), celebrating bounties of local veg, seafood, foraged mushrooms, inventive baked goods and more.

America's Cornucopia

California is the top US producer of vegetables and organic foods – expect everything from pistachios to radicchio and olive oil to hillside honey.

Ferry Building (p62)

BEST FOODIE EXPERIENCES

Duck inside SF's ❶ **Ferry Building** (p62), a landmark for good taste, featuring local, sustainable food producers and a legendary farmers market.

Go on a culinary adventure and take a ❷ **wine or cooking class** (p183) in Napa and Sonoma Wine Country.

Slurp up NorCal's best oysters fresh from Tomales Bay at wee ❸ **Marshall** (p128), just north of San Francisco.

Buy a local wine, your favorite farm-fresh food and head to a nearby park, beach or bluff for ❹ **picnic** (p122) bliss.

Taste food right where it's made, on Sonoma County Farm Trails or at ❺ **Pennyroyal Farm** (p242) in Anderson Valley.

COASTAL PLEASURES

Life's a beach in Northern California, and so much more. When the coastal fog lifts, the state's 840 miles of shoreline truly do its 'golden' moniker justice. While summer weather reigns supreme year-round in the south, rock crags, mists and drama define the north. Find family fun and clamber around massive dunes right in San Francisco, mingle with eccentrics in Gualala, cuddle at sunset in a Mendocino cove or find yourself on the stunning Lost Coast Trail.

FROM LEFT: KROPICI/SHUTTERSTOCK, BEN NORTH/ALAMY, UVL/SHUTTERSTOCK

Surfing Along Highway 1

Pick your portion of coast-hugging Hwy 1 with dramatic sea cliffs, playful seals and the Golden Gate Bridge. Leave time to stop and watch (or join) surfers from Ocean Beach to Mendocino and Shelter Cove.

CA Is for Camping

Bed down under a blanket of stars at Northern California's myriad national, state and regional parks, like Sonoma Coast State Park.

Wildlife Encounters

Sharing space with wildlife is just a part of the NorCal way. Sea otters and seals frolic around harbor piers, whales cruise serenely offshore and skies fill with migrating birds.

Point Reyes National Seashore (p126)

BEST COASTAL EXPERIENCES

Hike the Marin Headlands across SF's Golden Gate Bridge to wild, wonderful **1 Point Reyes National Seashore** (p126), spotting free-roaming tule elk.

Commune with aquatic creatures on your way to Tuluwat Island, when you kayak **2 Humboldt Bay** (p261).

Summit the Pomo Canyon Red Hill Trail to behold the wild **3 Sonoma Coast** (p210) unfurl at your feet with beach trails leading onwards.

Listen to the roar of elephant seals at **4 Año Nuevo State Park** (p159) or Drakes Beach.

Search for stones on marvelous Agate Beach in **5 Sue-meg State Park** (p272), then visit nearby redwood groves.

CARY KALSCHEUER/SHUTTERSTOCK

Oakland City Hall (p130)

SPARKLING CITIES

Northern California's towns have more flavors than a jar of jelly beans. They will seduce you with a cultural kaleidoscope that whirls from art galleries and museums, architectural showpieces and vibrant theater to tantalizing food scenes and offbeat local life. San Francisco might hog the spotlight, but you'll find ample charm in smaller towns too.

Quirky Cali

Northern California is full of unusual surprises. The North Coast is a magnet for free spirits, and the SF Bay Area is jam-packed with memorable oddities (look for dinosaurs by the freeway).

Dig Deeper

Northern California cities run deeper than their hipster, technocrat and beach bum stereotypes might have you believe. Ultimately, it's the cultural diversity that can make the biggest impression.

BEST CITY EXPERIENCES

Indulge in the trendsetting food, social movements, art and technology of ❶ **San Francisco** (p41), all draped gloriously around its bay.

Hop between craft breweries, tasting rooms and restaurants in smaller cities like ❷ **Petaluma** (p197) and Santa Rosa.

Blend patchouli aromas at the ❸ **Sebastopol** (p201) farmers market, then tour the recycled sculptures of Patrick Amiot.

Make a stop in ❹ **Eureka** (p257), more town than city, an enclave of street art and seafood restaurants in the midst of North Coast wilderness.

Get a taste of East Bay culture in ❺ **Oakland** (p130), including its historic Grand Lake Theatre, Chinatown, home of the Black Panthers and many excellent eateries.

FROM GRAPE TO GLASS

Wherever you are in Northern California, a vineyard is near. World-class vintages are grown and bottled here, just waiting to be tasted. Raise a toast to these wine-producing regions that are pioneering sustainable practices and brimming with sensory wonders: blooming biodynamic vineyards, lazy bicycle rides to LEED-certified tasting rooms, and restaurants pairing cult wines with seasonal dishes.

FROM LEFT: MICHAEL WARWICK/SHUTTERSTOCK, BRENT HOFACKER/SHUTTERSTOCK

Organic vs Biodynamic

Organic means grapes aren't exposed to chemical fertilizers, pesticides or herbicides. Biodynamic means integrated farming intended to sustain healthy ecosystems (also without chemicals).

Cider & Beer Too

Northern California is tops for more than wine: the state has the most craft breweries in the nation and a killer cider game, with heritage apple orchards throughout the north.

Winery Festivals

Special events abound at individual wineries and during festivals encompassing multiple wineries like **Passport to Dry Creek Valley** *(drycreekvalley.org)* or Napa's **Music in the Vineyards** *(musicinthevineyards.org)*.

BEST WINE & BEER EXPERIENCES

Sample some of the US' best wines in famous ❶ **Napa Valley** (p168), with brilliant appellations from Carneros to Rutherford.

Cruise north from famed Sonoma Valley to off-the-beaten path, excellent Alexander Valley and ❷ **Anderson Valley** (p242) wineries.

Discover one of California's best-kept secrets, the ❸ **Russian River Valley** (p213) – it boasts sparkling wines, pinot noirs and chardonnay.

Spend your days hopping between craft breweries from Petaluma north to stellar brewhouses in ❹ **Santa Rosa** (p206).

Get away from the madding crowds at the laid-back wineries in ❺ **Clear Lake's wine country** (p244).

HIGH ON HISTORY

It's been quite a wild ride for Northern California from the days of mammoths and saber-toothed tigers to the world's fourth-largest economy. Hike to sacred Native American waterfalls, confront the moral complexities of the mission system, reflect upon the frenzied rush for gold and finish up with a martini in Francis Ford Coppola's favorite watering hole.

FROM LEFT: SHUTTERUPEIRE/SHUTTERSTOCK, KARA JADE QUAN-MONTGOMERY/SHUTTERSTOCK

Cultural Crossroads

Native American tribes, Spanish Colonial *presidios* (forts), Catholic missions, Mexican pueblos and mining ghost towns have all left traces here for you to find.

Land Back Movement

California is attempting to return some of the land stolen from Native Americans, from 5 acres in the Oakland hills and 500 acres on the Lost Coast to 14,675 acres to the Tule River Tribe.

Indigenous Ways of Life

Many Northern California museums dive into Native American history, including the Oakland Museum of California, Hiouchi Visitor Center and Siskiyou County Museum.

BEST HISTORICAL EXPERIENCES

Watch Clint Eastwood in *Escape from Alcatraz* before visiting ❶ **The Rock** (p53) – a former military prison and penitentiary – on an islet in the SF Bay.

Visit the garage where Bill Hewlett and David Packard kicked off the Silicon Valley revolution in ❷ **Palo Alto** (p146).

Dive deep in ❸ **Sonoma** (p188) history as far back as the 1820s at an adobe mission and taste the wine that inspired the breakaway Bear Flag Republic.

Witness a painful chapter of the USA's past at ❹ **Tule Lake** (p291), the WWII Japanese American internment camp.

Catch a show at the ❺ **Fillmore Auditorium** (p81), where the psychedelic sounds of Hendrix, Joplin, The Dead, and Sly and the Family Stone blew minds.

IMAGE PROFESSIONALS GMBH/ALAMY

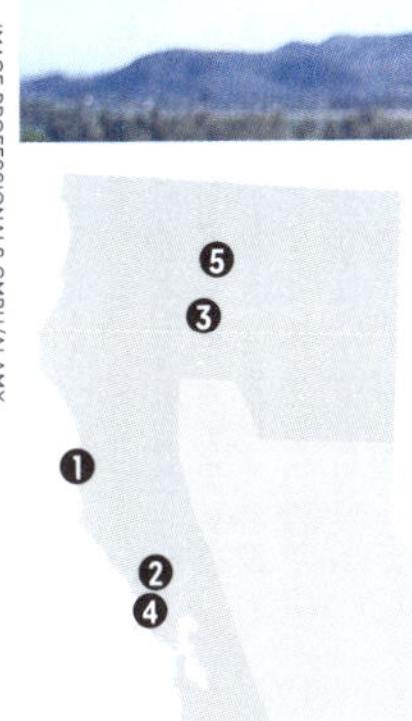

Auberge du Soleil (p186)

BEST ROMANTIC EXPERIENCES

Heed the call of love in ❶ **Mendocino** (p232), a former whaling village with rose-covered cottages and quiet country inns.

Get a designated driver to roll through Napa Valley and along ❷ **Westside Road** (p217), sampling the world-renowned wines of Napa and Sonoma.

Stargaze while houseboating on ❸ **Shasta Lake** (p303) as ospreys and bald eagles soar.

Escape to the coast around ❹ **Point Reyes** (p126), walking the Marin Headlands, watching the sun set from Stinson Beach and slurping oysters in Marshall.

Keep your heads in the clouds in ❺ **McCloud** (p286), where its dreamy inn has a swoon-worthy restaurant and hikes abound.

ROMANTIC GETAWAYS

Whether you're on your honeymoon or simply treating your sweetie, Northern California is tailor-made for romance. Bed down in a Victorian B&B or in a tent under a canopy of stars. Clink glasses in a winery bistro or over a mountaintop picnic, surrender to R&R in a chic spa or hike out to an isolated forest cabin.

San Francisco Charm

SF is all about romance – go ahead and smooch at Pride, cozy up in acclaimed restaurants or drop to one knee beneath the Golden Gate Bridge.

Vineyard Love

Let wine country do the wooing at perfect inns like Napa's decadent Auberge du Soleil (p186) or poetic Beltane Ranch near Sonoma.

REGIONS & CITIES

Find the places that tick all your boxes.

North Coast & Redwoods

PEEK BEHIND THE REDWOOD CURTAIN

Lumber barons wised up and conserved primeval redwood forests along the misty, rugged and wild North Coast. Let your offbeat flag fly in Humboldt County, and swap seafaring stories at spectacular coastal fishing villages like Elk and Mendocino, as you explore some of California's most majestic landscapes.

Northern Mountains

CALIFORNIA'S UNSUNG MOUNTAIN PARADISE

Mt Shasta is a magnet for shamans, New Age poets and ice-axe-wielding alpinists. There's more wilderness as you head north along backcountry byways, passing pristine lakes to the Cascades' chain of volcanoes and Mt Lassen's alien landscape bubbling over with roiling mud pots, multihued sulfur vents and steamy fumaroles.

North Coast & Redwoods p226

Northern Mountains p277

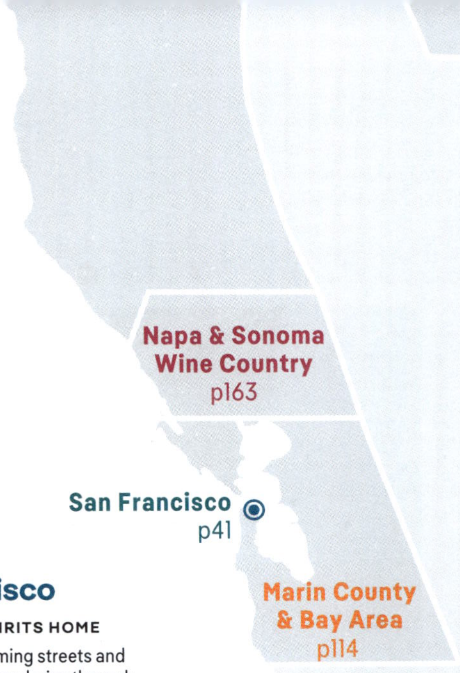

Napa & Sonoma Wine Country

WHERE VINEYARDS, REDWOODS AND OCEAN MEET

The sun-washed valleys and cool coastal fog make Napa and Sonoma Counties the state's most iconic wine-growing regions. But local ranches and hippie free-thinking also thrive, yielding bountiful farm-to-table meals, unusual small towns and interesting blends of luxe and laid-back, with a killer coastline to boot.

Marin County & Bay Area

WHERE THE COAST MEETS THE BAY

Outdoorsy people love Marin and San Mateo Counties for their beaches, forests, wildlife and hiking and cycling trails – but city slickers will appreciate the counterculture hubs of Berkeley and Oakland with their vibrant food and arts scenes, along with the tech culture of world-dominating Silicon Valley.

San Francisco

CALLING ALL FREE SPIRITS HOME

San Francisco, with its charming streets and cable cars, keeps pushing boundaries through trendsetting food, social movements, art and technology. This city is defined by bold moves and rich history, with multicultural influences and its iconic landmarks like the Golden Gate Bridge keeping life fresh and inspiring.

ITINERARIES

North Coast Explorer

Allow: 7 days **Distance:** 430 miles

Cover the Golden State's greatest north coast hits, starting with your head in the clouds in foggy San Francisco with its magnificent bay and ending up over 400 unforgettable miles later with some of the world's oldest redwoods soaring overhead. You'll visit rocky shores, secluded coves, quirky towns and wind-sculpted beaches along the way.

Beach in Bodega Bay

1 SAN FRANCISCO 2 DAYS

Spend two days eating magnificently, riding cable cars and exploring **San Francisco** (p41), from the iconic Golden Gate Bridge to Golden Gate Park. Look at street art in the Mission and stroll the historic North Beach neighborhood. Sail to Angel Island or Alcatraz. Discover the weirdest tech in the west at the Exploratorium and find inspiration at SFMOMA.

Detour: *Hit* ***Half Moon Bay*** *(p154) for surfing and* ***Año Nuevo State Park*** *(p159) for elephant seals. ½ day*

2 SONOMA COAST 1 DAY

Post up in Bodega Bay where you can go whale-watching or tuck into crab sandwiches as you picnic on a stunning beach in **Sonoma Coast State Park** (p210) or Salt Point State Park. Walk along ocean bluffs and, as you drive north to Mendocino, stop to scale Point Arena Lighthouse.

Detour: *Make forays east to float the* ***Russian River*** *(p213) or for vineyards in rural* ***Anderson Valley*** *(p242). ½ day*

3 MENDOCINO 1 DAY

Emerge in **Mendocino** (p232), a postcard-perfect Victorian seaside town that might seduce you into staying longer. The inns are an enticing blend of chi chi and rustic, and nearby Fort Bragg is fun for visits to artists and craftspeople or to ride the Skunk Train. Watch the sunset from a hot tub at your inn, or stroll in beautiful Mendocino Headlands State Park.

Crescent City
END
Klamath River
Redwood National & State Parks 6
Weed
Mt Shasta (14,179ft)
Sue-meg State Park
1h
Arcata
Eureka 5
Shasta Lake
2h
Redding
Humboldt Redwoods State Park
10min
Lost Coast 4
Red Bluff
Leggett
Eel River
PACIFIC OCEAN
3h
Chico
Mendocino 3
Sacramento River
Clear Lake
2h 30min
Dry Creek Valley
Calistoga
Davis
Russian River
Santa Rosa
2
Napa
Sonoma Coast
1h 30min
Sonoma
Point Reyes
San Pablo Bay
San Rafael
Berkeley
San Francisco 1
Oakland
START
40min
Palo Alto
Half Moon Bay
San Jose
Santa Cruz Mountains
Santa Cruz
Monterey Bay
Monterey
Carmel-by-the-Sea
Big Sur
0 100 km
0 50 miles

4

LOST COAST 1 DAY

Swing onto Hwy 101 at Leggett, where your magical mystery tour of the redwood empire really begins. A last outpost of civilization, Shelter Cove is the southern jumping-off point for hikes on the **Lost Coast** (p249), which stretches 24.6 miles to the sandy mouth of the Mattole River at the north end of the King Range Conservation Area. For a taste of the journey, hike to Punta Gorda Lighthouse.

Detour: *On Hwy 101 between Shelter Cove and Mattole Beach, stand in the shadows of the earth's tallest trees at **Humboldt Redwoods State Park** (p254) and Avenue of the Giants. 1 hour*

5

EUREKA 1 DAY

Just before you reach Eureka, Ferndale (pictured below) is one of NorCal's most charming small towns for its distinctive Victorians known locally as 'butterfat palaces.' Spend the night in the candy-colored Victorian harbor town of **Eureka** (p257), with its seafood restaurants and kayaking opportunities, or head north for the outlandish outpost of Arcata (p262).

6

REDWOOD NATIONAL & STATE PARKS 1 DAY

Surround yourself in old-growth redwoods in **Redwood National Park** (p264), which also includes three state parks: Prairie Creek Redwoods State Park, Del Norte Coast Redwoods State Park and Jedediah Smith Redwoods State Park.

Detour: *Make time for gorgeous **Sue-meg State Park** (p272). 3 hours*

ITINERARIES

Marin County & Sonoma-Napa Wine Country

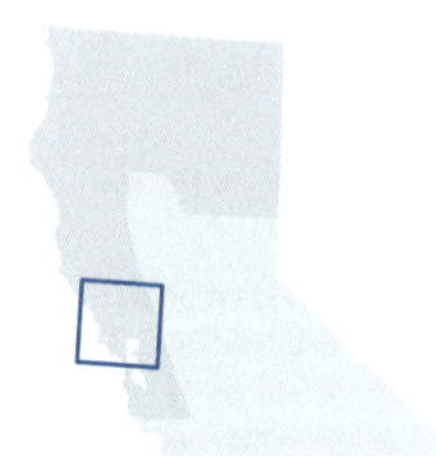

Allow: 6 days **Distance:** 178 miles

Follow coastal highways and country back roads to drink in stunning vistas from 19th-century lighthouses, dizzying ocean lookouts and beaches with marine sanctuaries. Then wind north to the low-key, wine-rich Russian River Valley before looping to the historic Napa and Sonoma Valleys with their charming towns and world-class vineyards.

1 SAUSALITO & MARIN HEADLANDS ½ DAY

Just north of the Golden Gate Bridge, the pretty houses of **Sausalito** (p120) descend neatly to a harbor with stunning bay views. Toward the coast the scenery turns untamed at **Marin Headlands** (p122) with undulating hills and crashing coastline. Stroll along Muir Beach and Stinson Beach, or go to Rodeo Beach for a fascinating marine-mammal sanctuary.

Detour: *Reserve ahead to visit old-growth redwoods at* ***Muir Woods National Monument*** *(p124), the closest to San Francisco.* *2 hours*

2 POINT REYES NATIONAL SEASHORE ½ DAY

The wind-blown **Point Reyes National Seashore** (p126), covering much of the peninsula, shelters free-ranging elk, scores of marine mammals, raptors and wild cats. Its lighthouse, at the base of more than 300 stairs, is one of the best whale-watching spots when gray whales pass during their winter migration.

Detour: *Check out the setting for Hitchcock's* The Birds *in Bodega and* ***Bodega Bay*** *(p210).* *1 hour*

3 RUSSIAN RIVER VALLEY 1 DAY

Bark back at seals along the coast or pass through quirky Occidental, then cruise up the **Russian River Valley** (p213) to gather good vibes in ancient redwood groves at Armstrong Redwoods State Natural Reserve. Float down the river in an inner tube, and join Sonoma County's freethinkers for sunset toasts in organic vineyards – there are 50 wineries within a 20-minute drive of Guerneville.

FROM LEFT: SUNDRY PHOTOGRAPHY/SHUTTERSTOCK, NICK FOX/SHUTTERSTOCK, POCKET CANYON PHOTOGRAPHY/SHUTTERSTOCK

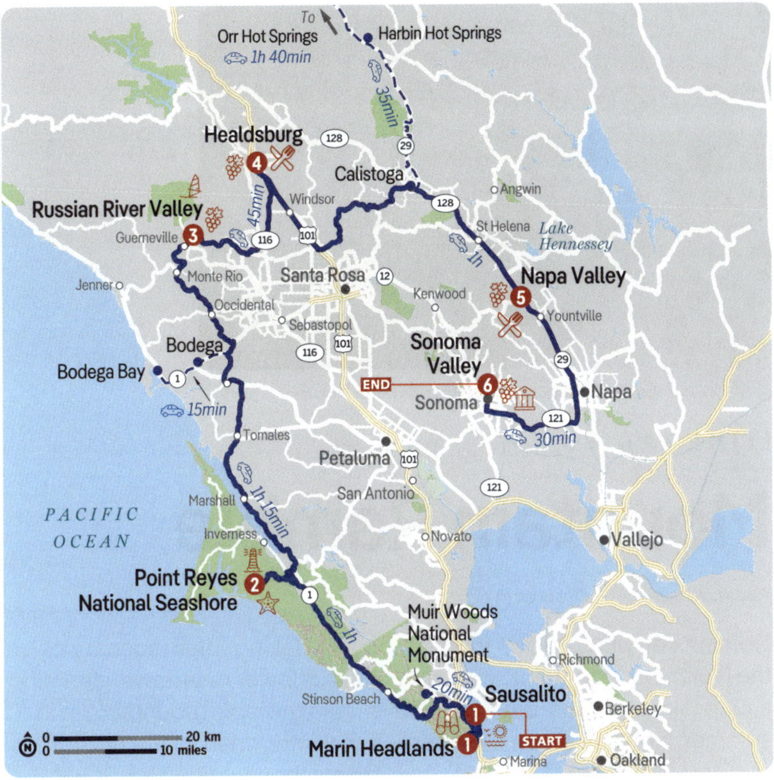

4

HEALDSBURG 1 DAY

Take beautiful Westside Rd north, stopping at wineries along the way. You're in the thick of wine country now. Lunch in happening **Healdsburg** (p218), then unwind in Dry Creek Valley's farmstead wineries, or slightly north at Alexander Valley's many organic vineyards.

Detour: *Hot springs await in* ***Calistoga*** *(p186),* ***Harbin*** *(p247) or, much further north, Orr. 3 hours*

5

NAPA VALLEY 2 DAYS

If your budget can bear it, spend a couple of days exploring the renowned wine capital, the **Napa Valley** (p168) – from the tasting rooms in Napa town, surrounded by vineyards, to the small town of St Helena. Eat and drink like royalty, go cycling and hiking or just laze decadently at a rarefied inn.

6

SONOMA VALLEY 1 DAY

Sonoma Valley (p188) is a 17-mile stretch of pastoral good times. Tour the wineries then stretch your legs at Jack London State Historic Park, the famous author's former ranch (pictured above). Finish up in tiny Glen Ellen or historic Sonoma with its mission and adobe barracks, plus yet more tasting rooms surrounding its welcoming plaza.

ALBERTO LOYO/SHUTTERSTOCK

Golden Dome Cave, Lava Beds National Monument (p289)

ITINERARIES

Mountain Ramble

Allow: 6 days **Distance:** 325 miles

Nothing can prepare you for the monumental mountain scenery of the Northern Mountains, with acres of wildflower meadows, gleaming alpine lakes and sun-catching peaks. Take this epic mountain trip in summer, when all roads are open. Or, in winter, cherry-pick portions and add in snow sports (plus snow chains for your tires).

1 LAVA BEDS NATIONAL MONUMENT ⏱1 DAY

Gaze out across **Lava Beds National Monument** (p289) and spot its dramatic lava formations, cinder cones and bubbling mud pots. Then descend into its caves and lava tubes before you continue on in search of ancient petroglyphs.

Detour: *Bear witness at* ***Camp Tule Lake*** *(p291), where Japanese Americans were interned during WWII.* ⏱*2 hours*

2 SÁTTÍTLA HIGHLANDS NATIONAL MONUMENT ⏱1 DAY

Drive south into the US' newest national monument, **Sáttítla Highlands** (p288). This confluence of 224,676 acres of Modoc, Shasta-Trinity and Klamath national forests surrounds Medicine Lake volcano.

Detour: *Hardcore hikers can spend time in the* ***Klamath Knot*** *(p309) and Trinity Alps Wilderness, west of* ***Trinity Lake*** *(p310).* ⏱*3 hours*

3 MT SHASTA ⏱1 DAY

Choose your charming small town base – Dunsmuir, Weed or McCloud – for forays up **Mt Shasta** (p284). In summer it's hiking, and in winter you can take to skis, sleds and snowshoes. Or just groove out at a crystal shop in Mt Shasta City.

Detour: *On your way to Lassen, bypass Redding and go by way of* ***McArthur-Burney Falls Memorial State Park*** *(p288) with its fabulous waterfalls.* ⏱*2 hours*

FROM LEFT: ALBERTO LOYO/SHUTTERSTOCK, ZACK FRANK/SHUTTERSTOCK, IAN DEWAR PHOTOGRAPHY/SHUTTERSTOCK

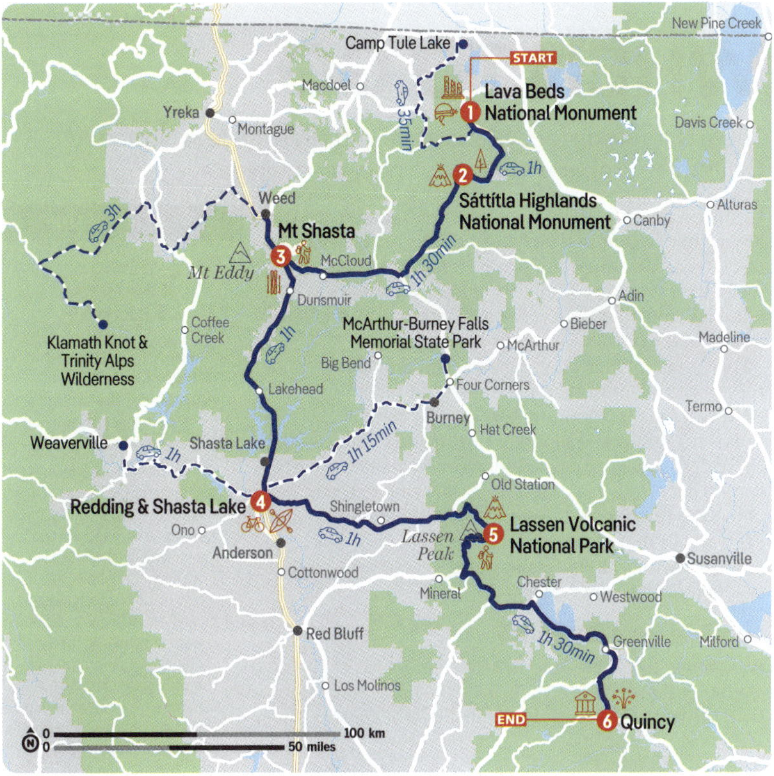

4

REDDING & SHASTA LAKE ⏱1 DAY

Head to deep-blue **Shasta Lake** (p303), where clear, calm waters invite splashing, kayaking and houseboating. Mountain bikers can take on epic single-track trails, on the Redding Trails, then unwind with a craft beer at one of the breweries in Redding (p305).

Detour: *Learn about Northern California's original Chinese immigrant community in **Weaverville** (p309).* ⏱*3 hours*

5

LASSEN VOLCANIC NATIONAL PARK ⏱1 DAY

Spend at least a day in **Lassen Volcanic National Park** (p292) with its myriad hikes up and around magnificent Lassen Peak, the world's largest lava-dome volcano, and out into the vast Lassen National Forest. Or just take a short walk to Bumpass Hell, where steam rises from colorful geothermal pools. In winter, there's skiing, sledding and snowshoeing.

6

QUINCY ⏱1 DAY

Take a dip or go canoeing at Lake Almanor on your way to the laid-back mountain town of **Quincy** (p301). If you time it for High Sierra Music Festival (at the end of June or early July), the town gets hopping. The rest of the year you can explore history museums and nearby gold rush sites at Plumas-Eureka State Park (pictured above) or hike in Lakes Basin Recreation Area.

FROM LEFT: REDWOOD REEF/SHUTTERSTOCK, MARISA ESTIVILL/SHUTTERSTOCK, DREAMART123/SHUTTERSTOCK

WHEN TO GO

There is a season for every climate and every taste in Northern California – pick your region and plan accordingly.

Despite California's sunny reputation, the climate varies across the year and Northern California is decidedly more temperate than the rest of the state. Nonetheless, it's high season from June through August with school holidays and tourists arriving from around the state, nation and world.

Spring in Northern California is brilliant after winter rains, with bright-green meadows and blooming wildflowers. While temperatures are equally comfortable and it can be sunny and cloudless in the fall, increasingly those dry months from September to November have become what's known as 'fire season.' It's vital to be vigilant about the fire danger – light no open flames, ever – and keep an eye on the news.

Winter brings chilly temperatures, rainstorms and, in the mountains, heavy snow.

Looking for a Bargain?

In summer high season (and on the coast on weekends) accommodations prices are 50% to 100% higher on average than the rest of the year. If you can, travel at another time.

I LIVE HERE

MAGICAL SPRING

Bay Area native and writer Carrie Wilkins writes about the thrill of a California spring. *@carrieelysia*

As I grew up, I recognized the undeniable magic of a warm California spring. It arrives like a handwritten letter from a lost love, full of hope – beckoning the young and young at heart to seek the sun again. Now, I wait all year long for the symphony of color: the way the lush, green, rolling hills transform into a shimmering gold and every shade of wildflower imaginable bursts into view.

Wildflowers, California coast

FROM LEFT: ROSCHETZKY PHOTOGRAPHY/SHUTTERSTOCK, CHRIS LABASCO/SHUTTERSTOCK

MOUNTAIN DRIVING

In California's mountains, especially in the Northern Mountains and around Lake Tahoe, winter conditions can demand either snow chains or 4WD with all-season tires. Drivers without these will be turned back. Check driving conditions with CalTrans at *quickmap.dot.ca.gov.*

Weather Through the Year in San Francisco

JANUARY	FEBRUARY	MARCH	APRIL	MAY	JUNE
Ave. daytime max: **58°F** (14°C)	Ave. daytime max: **61°F** (16°C)	Ave. daytime max: **62°F** (16°C)	Ave. daytime max: **63°F** (17°C)	Ave. daytime max: **64°F** (17°C)	Ave. daytime max: **67°F** (19°C)
Days of rainfall: **8**	Days of rainfall: **8**	Days of rainfall: **8**	Days of rainfall: **4**	Days of rainfall: **2**	Days of rainfall: **0**

IT'S GETTING HOT IN HERE

Despite the fog and overall temperate climate in Northern California, increasingly temperatures can spike in summer. The hottest temperature ever recorded in Northern California is 119°F (47.8°C) in Redding on July 6, 2024.

The Big Festivals & Parades

Celebrate **Chinese New Year** (p69) with San Francisco's month-long night markets and parade of dragons, dancers and you. **Spring**

Napa's marquee **BottleRock Music Festival** (p173) is an extravaganza of music, food and wine, and it's followed by the La Onda music festival. **May**

California celebrates LGBTQ+ pride for the entire month of June, with costumed parades, film fests and streets parties. **SF Pride** sets the global parade standard, with over a million people, tons of glitter and ounces of bikinis. **June**

Outside Lands (p107) bring three days of play to Golden Gate Park when headlining indie rockers, rappers, DJs and comedians converge along with gourmet food, beer and wine. **August**

Local & Quirkier Festivals

Settle into the landmark 1926 Grand Lake Theatre in Oakland for the **Noir City Film Festival** (p135), celebrating film noir classics. **January & February**

Napa Lighted Art Festival (p177) transforms normally staid downtown Napa into a mini Burning Man as light projections sparkle and sculptures decorate the streets. **January & February**

Hot rods and hot action fete the classic film at **Salute to American Graffiti** (p199) in Petaluma, where the movie was filmed, with a screening and parade of classic cars. **May**

Head to the hills (specifically Quincy) for the **High Sierra Music Festival** (p302), one of the best laid-back music fests in the state, played over one long weekend. **July**

I LIVE HERE

WINTER WEALTH

Oakland-born fashion designer Amy Brenneman travels between the SF Bay Area, France and Indonesia. *@Hi_rol*

Every winter I come home to the Bay Area and I hit the Berkeley hills for a sunset hike. Saffron-tinted light filters through the redwoods and warms the soft spongy trail, the air perfectly crisp and cool. Upon reaching the top, I look out over the shimmering bay with the Golden Gate Bridge in the distance, calmly perched in winter clarity, promising a golden state of mind.

View of San Francisco from Berkeley hills

COASTAL FOG

Especially in Northern California, summer is marked by coastal fog that doesn't always burn off. So San Francisco can be socked in and chilly, when just inland in Oakland it's a sunny 75°F (24°C). September is the best month for the North Coast.

  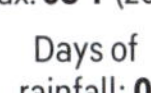  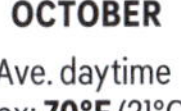

JULY	AUGUST	SEPTEMBER	OCTOBER	NOVEMBER	DECEMBER
Ave. daytime max: **67°F** (19°C)	Ave. daytime max: **68°F** (20°C)	Ave. daytime max: **71°F** (21°C)	Ave. daytime max: **70°F** (21°C)	Ave. daytime max: **64°F** (17°C)	Ave. daytime max: **58°F** (14°C)
Days of rainfall: **0**	Days of rainfall: **0**	Days of rainfall: **0**	Days of rainfall: **2**	Days of rainfall: **6**	Days of rainfall: **8**

FROM LEFT: YAYA ERNST/SHUTTERSTOCK, SUNSET BOULEVARD/GETTY IMAGES

Hiking, Redwood National Park (p264)

GET PREPARED FOR SAN FRANCISCO & NORTHERN CALIFORNIA

Useful things to load in your bag, your ears and your brain.

Clothes

Informal rules Northern California is a laid-back, anything-goes kind of region, especially when it comes to fashion; San Francisco is relaxed, casual chic or iconoclastic, while most other cities are quite informal.

Casual layers Beware the changeable weather. Travelers who've only ever seen California on TV are in for a shock along the coast, where marine fog reprimands anyone in shorts all morning, rolls back in the afternoon to make you wish you'd worn sweat-proof sunscreen, and returns by evening to mock skimpy date-night outfits. The mountains can be cold and deserts blazing hot. Layer up with sweaters, wraps or light jackets over your underlayers.

Comfortable shoes Walking shoes are essential for cities and trails alike. Even on nights out, dressy shoes and heels are not necessary – just dress however you like.

Local Language

In Northern California, language goes way beyond 'dude.' Many Californians are multilingual – more than 200 different languages are spoken here. The top five are English, Spanish, Chinese, Tagalog and Vietnamese. Around 43% of state residents speak a language other than English at home. Dive in and go for it: you may find someone who speaks your native tongue.

READ

Harlem of the West: The San Francisco Fillmore Jazz Era (Elizabeth Pepin & Lewis Watts; 2005) Accounting of SF's 1940s and '50s heyday.

101 Hikes in Northern California: Exploring Mountains, Valley, and Seashore (Matt Heid; 2017) Well-written descriptions of top walks.

Where I Was From (Joan Didion; 2003) California-born essayist shatters palm-fringed fantasies.

If They Come in the Morning (Angela Davis; 1971) Chronicles of the Black Power movement collected by one of its leading figures.

Manners & Rules

Northern Californians are casual by nature, but a few (unspoken) rules still apply.

Attitude Smiles go a long way here. Be friendly, even in a disagreement.

Greetings Shaking hands when meeting for the first time is a tad formal, but it's expected for business dealings and by some older adults.

Bargaining Haggling over the prices of goods usually isn't appropriate, except at outdoor markets and with sidewalk vendors.

Smoking Don't light up indoors (it's illegal, or look around for ashtrays) or anywhere else you don't see others doing it. Some restaurants have patios or sidewalk tables where smoking is tolerated (ask first), but don't expect your neighbors to be happy about secondhand smoke.

Cannabis While people aged 21 and older can buy cannabis, smoking or consuming marijuana in public or on federal land (national parks, Marin Headlands etc) is illegal.

Eating out Northern Californian restaurant etiquette tends to be informal. Only a handful of restaurants require more than a dressy shirt, slacks and shoes that aren't flip-flops. At other places, T-shirts, shorts and sandals are fine.

Tipping (p316) At restaurants, 18% to 25% is expected anywhere you receive table service. Counter service can still rate 10%, though it's not obligatory.

Driving It is illegal to drive under the influence of anything (alcohol, marijuana) or to carry open containers. When wine tasting, have a designated driver and keep any open bottles in the trunk.

WATCH

The Graduate (Mike Nichols; 1967; pictured above) Cue Simon & Garfunkel's 'Mrs Robinson': Dustin Hoffman and Anne Bancroft filmed all over Berkeley.

Vertigo (Alfred Hitchcock; 1958) The famous noir thriller set in San Francisco, starring James Stewart and Kim Novak.

Milk (Gus Van Sant; 2008) The biopic of Harvey Milk, the first openly gay man to hold a major US political office.

Fruitvale Station (Ryan Coogler; 2013) Early film starring Michael B Jordan by Oakland-born director who made *Black Panther* and *Sinners*.

Turn It Around: The Story of East Bay Punk (Corbett Redford; 2017) Dive deep into 30 years of Bay Area music, narrated by Iggy Pop.

LISTEN

All Eyez on Me (2Pac; 1996) Hip hop classic featuring 'California Love' and West Coast stars Dr Dre and Snoop Dogg.

'Estimated Prophet' (Grateful Dead; 1977) Cali psychedelic rock legends (like Jefferson Airplane). Other road trip songs: 'Ripple' and 'Truckin'.'

'I Want to Take You Higher' (Sly and the Family Stone; 1969) Classic funk and soul from album *Stand!*, with 'Everyday People,' too.

Dookie (Green Day; 1994) First major-label release by Bay Area punk band including 'When I Come Around' and 'Welcome to Paradise.'

BRANNON_NAITO/SHUTTERSTOCK

Birria tacos (p33)

THE FOOD SCENE

Northern California cuisine is a team effort that changes with every season – and it has changed the way the world eats.

As you graze the northern parts of the Golden State, you'll often want to compliment the chef – and they will pass it on to the staff, local farmers, fishers, ranchers, winemakers and artisan food producers who make their menu possible. 'Let the ingredients speak for themselves!' is the rallying cry of Northern California cuisine. Most of America's fruit and specialty vegetables are grown somewhere in the state, and you get the pick of the crop year-round. With fruit, vegetables, meats and seafood this fresh, heavy sauces and fussy garnishes aren't required to make meals memorable.

California cooking also reflects the contributions of some of the world's most celebrated food cultures. The state's deep Mexican and Latin American heritage means burritos regularly outshine burgers. And California has some of the best Asian cuisine available outside Asia. The California stew is also peppered with Mediterranean traditions – where the climate and soil are similar to California's – and Afro-Caribbean and southern soul cooking. Thus fusion is not a fad but second nature in California, where international flair blends beautifully with seasonal, local ingredients.

Global Soul Food

California belonged to Mexico before it became a US state in 1850, and almost 40% of the population today is Latinx. It's no surprise, then, that Mexican classics remain go-to comfort foods, and upscale restaurants add novel twists to staple enchiladas and tacos. This blending of local produce

Best California Dishes

CALIFORNIA BURRITO
Mega-meal bursting out of a giant flour tortilla.

DUNGENESS CRAB
November-to-June favorite, eaten whole and in sandwiches.

SALMON
Fresh-caught on menus statewide, prepared in myriad ways.

ARTICHOKES
Giant and springtime delicious, from farms around Castroville.

and international cuisines defines Northern California's great culinary advantage: an experimental attitude toward food. Even in its Wild West days when gold-rush miners and Chinese workers lived side by side, necessity and proximity meant everyone ate adventurously and cross-culturally, pairing whiskey and wine with tamales and Chinese noodles. Similarly, as other groups with distinct cuisines immigrated to the Golden State, they found fertile ground for their food pathways. Learn more in *Tanya Holland's California Soul: Recipes from a Culinary Journey West.*

Vegan & Vegetarian

Seasonal, produce-forward, locavore eating has become mainstream, but Northern California started the movement over 50 years ago when much of the country was eating packaged foods. To all those accustomed to making do with dressed-up side salads: relax, your needs are not an afterthought here. Decades before Billie Eilish championed a vegan diet, San Francisco and North Coast restaurants were already catering to vegans. You won't have to go out of your way to find vegetarian and vegan options: bakeries, bistros and even mom-and-pop joints in the remote mountains are ready for meat-free, dairy-free, eggless requests. Locate vegetarian and vegan restaurants and health-food stores with *happycow.net.*

Regional Styles

Calculate the distance between your tomato's place of origin and your fork: chances are it's shorter than you might think here. So what are your best bets on local menus? That depends where you are and the time of year. Winter may be slim pickings for salad, but ideal for squash and citrus.

Vegetarian Buddha bowl

FROM LEFT: KULKOVA DARIA/SHUTTERSTOCK, FLORIDASTOCK/SHUTTERSTOCK

FOOD & WINE FESTIVALS

Wine & Food Affair (p221) Tour over 100 Sonoma County wineries in November; a specialty dish is paired with their vintages.

Sonoma Harvest Fair (p207) In October, get your spittoon ready for the country's biggest wine-tasting festival.

San Francisco Restaurant Week Sweet deals on special menus from top chefs, once in the spring and again in the fall.

Kelseyville Pear Festival (p247) Things get juicy in Lake County in September as they celebrate their local fruit.

Gravenstein Apple Fair (p203) Tuck into pies galore in Sonoma County in mid-August.

Anderson Valley Pinot Noir Festival (p243) Sample of some of the state's best pinots are found here in May.

FORAGED FOOD

From wild chanterelles found beneath California oaks to hillside miner's lettuce.

OYSTERS

From Hog Island Kumamoto in Tomales Bay to Grassy Bar in Morro Bay.

CIOPPINO

Iconic San Francisco fish stew in a rich tomato broth.

CALIFORNIA ROLL

Sushi roll invented in 1960s LA using crab, avocado and cucumber.

Dim sum

San Francisco Bay Area

You can find literally any world cuisine in the San Francisco Bay Area, with particular emphasis on Asian and Mexican styles. Follow San Franciscans to a Korean restaurant for flavor-bursting *kalbi* (marinated, grilled beef short ribs), a taqueria for *tacos al pastor* (marinated, fried pork), Japantown for homemade ramen noodles and the largest Chinatown outside of Asia for Chinese dim sum. But you'll also find these kinds of restaurants sprinkled around most residential neighborhoods.

Star chefs love a few foraged ingredients these days, too – including wild chanterelles found beneath California oaks, miner's lettuce from Berkeley hillsides, and edible nasturtium flowers from SF backyards.

Napa & Sonoma Wine Country

In 1978 chef Sally Schmitt transformed a 1900s Yountville saloon into an international foodie landmark called The French Laundry, where current owner Thomas Keller dazzles with garden-grown multicourse feasts. The night skies over Napa Valley now shine with seven Michelin stars. In Sonoma County, with farmers as neighbors and seafood and foraged ingredients fresh from beaches and redwood forests, cooks feature sustainable farm-to-table fare.

North Coast

Nature has been kind to this landscape, yielding bonanzas of wildflower honey, berries, wild grains and nuts. Along this rugged coastline, you'll find traditional shellfish collection and Californian-run fishing operations, alongside sustainable oyster farms and fish hatcheries. Fearless foragers closely guard their secret spots for wild morel mushrooms. Seafood is harvested both from the ocean and the many rivers. For help choosing the most sustainable catch, check out Monterey Bay Aquarium's guide at *seafoodwatch.org*.

Northern Mountains

Most of California's produce is grown elsewhere in the state – like the hot, irrigated Central Valley, south of Sacramento, where even some of the agribusinesses have converted to organic methods, making California the top US producer of organic foods. So food in the mountains is simpler, geared toward residents and road-trippers passing through.

NORCAL WINE & BEER

Vineyards are never far away in Northern California, where world-class vintages are bottled and quaffed daily. The region's wine producers are pioneering sustainable production practices (p323) from biodynamic and organic orchards to ecoconscious water and power use and tasting rooms with LEED certification. Key regions include the obvious stars Napa (p174) and Sonoma (p174). But lesser-known but equally delicious vintages come from the Russian River Valley (p213) and Anderson Valley (p242). Wineries also dot Kelseyville and Clear Lake (p244).

Northern California has long been at the forefront of craft beer and artisanal cocktails from microdistillers. At least 400 craft breweries are based in California – more than any other US state. You'll be able to hit the taps at famous brewhouses around San Francisco, Santa Rosa and Petaluma. Even the Lost Coast, small Redding and remote Weaverville and Mt Shasta have excellent breweries. You won't get attitude for ordering beer with fancy food here, either.

Food Trucks

When sit-down meals fail to satisfy, make raids on local food trucks – fleets are standing by across Northern California. The region's legendary food trucks serve up everything from burritos *al pastor* (marinated pork) or Indian curry-and-naan wraps to Chinese buns packed with roast duck and fresh mango.

Come prepared with cash and sunblock: most trucks don't accept plastic cards, and lines can be long at peak hours.

You'll often find batches of food trucks grouped together – sometimes in organized food parks, like in Santa Rosa – or single purveyors in habitual spots, like a supermarket parking lot (as in Guerneville). Ways to locate trucks coming soon to a curb near you include searching for 'food truck' and your location on Google Maps, looking at food-critic picks on local news websites, and checking dedicated food websites such as *eater.com*.

Food-Truck Hits

If you can think of a cuisine, somewhere in the state there's a food truck for it. Expect every type of fusion or comfort food, too – think wood-fired pizza or grilled cheese and Tater Tots.

Food truck, San Francisco

Many food trucks also offer sweets like churros (sweet Mexican fried dough) or fresh-fruit hand pies.

Dim sum Chinese small plates and dumplings.

Kalbi Korean flavor-bursting marinated, grilled beef short ribs.

Jollof rice Spicy West African rice.

Cuitlacoche Corn smut, a sort of mold – a delicacy the world over.

Korean tacos Grilled, marinated beef and spicy pickled kimchi.

Pho Vietnamese noodle soup.

Southern California fish tacos Grilled fish tacos, ideally fresh.

Birria Meat stew from Jalisco, usually using goat.

MEALS OF A LIFETIME

SingleThread (p220) Be dazzled at this celebrated restaurant in Healdsburg where food masquerades as nature.

Benu (p64) Splash out on brilliant wine-paired tasting menus that look like minimalist art in San Francisco.

Chez Panisse (p140) Where it all started – worship at the temple of Alice Waters in Berkeley.

Harbor House Inn (p239) Wee hamlet Elk's stellar 20-seat dinner of hyper-local ingredients sourced from nearby farms, forests and coastline.

San Ho Won (p95) Sample spectacular Korean flavors crafted from farm-fresh ingredients in San Francisco.

Mister Jiu's (p67) Wonderfully innovative Chinese cuisine and a charming banquet-hall ambience in SF.

THE YEAR IN FOOD

SPRING

When the sun comes out, farmers markets fill city streets with salad makings, and lines bend around the block for organic artisanal ice cream studded with just-picked berries.

SUMMER

Beach barbecues are better with wild coho salmon, corn on the cob, fresh salsa made with heirloom tomatoes, and grilled peaches topped with edible lavender flowers.

AUTUMN

Experience your first crush at harvest in wine country, get lost in corn mazes and pumpkin patches, and give thanks for Northern California's bounty of fresh-fruit pies. Many food and wine festivals happen now.

WINTER

Make the most of long winter nights with seafood feasts of Dungeness crab, oysters and sand dabs. Celebrate Lunar New Year with lucky mandarins, and let citrus-spiked craft cocktails with local spirits warm you.

CLOCKWISE FROM TOP LEFT: SVETLANASF/SHUTTERSTOCK, EDDIE-HERNANDEZ.COM/SHUTTERSTOCK, BOCHKAREV PHOTOGRAPHY/SHUTTERSTOCK, OLGABOMBOLOGNA/SHUTTERSTOCK, NEW AFRICA/SHUTTERSTOCK, BAIBAZ/SHUTTERSTOCK

FROM LEFT: TICKTAKUTICKTAKU/SHUTTERSTOCK, SAM EDWARDS/SHUTTERSTOCK

Cycling, Napa Valley

THE OUTDOORS

Hike through desert wildflowers in spring, dive into the Pacific in summer, mountain-bike through fall foliage and ski down wintry mountain slopes.

Northern California is an all-season magnet for outdoor fun, and people come from all over the world for the pleasure. Beach life and surf culture define California's freewheeling lifestyle, so consider permission granted to play hooky and hit the waves. Amble on smooth coastal bluff trails or hike multiday backpacking treks into the backcountry. If you want to get your adrenaline pumping, dive past coastal shipwrecks, scale sheer granite cliffs or go white-water rafting on the rapids.

Water Sports

If your California dream vacation means bronzing on the beach and paddling in the Pacific, Northern California is a trickier proposition than Southern California where miles of warm, sandy beaches keep you living the dream six months of the year. Instead, Northern California is often socked in with fog in summer, and ocean temperatures, while tolerable in July and August, usually call for a wetsuit. A favorite workaround is to kayak or stand-up paddleboard the bays and lakes that fill the region, or float rivers like the Russian River and raft the Feather River.

For surfing, Northern California beaches are blustery and dramatic, with high swells crashing into rocky bluffs – not great for casual swimmers but offering big wave breaks, especially around Half Moon Bay. But smaller breaks dot the coast, from Sonoma Coast State Park to Shelter Cove. If you do surf the north coast, always ask about and respect local wave etiquette.

Action Sports & Wildlife

SNOW SPORTS
Cross-country or downhill ski, sled, snowshoe and snowboard near **Mt Lassen** (p297).

KAYAKING & CANOEING
Paddle Sonoma County's **Russian River** (p215) as it flows by vineyards and redwoods out to the ocean.

KITEBOARDING & WINDSURFING
Let the wind lift you at **Crissy Field** (p51) in San Francisco, alongside the Golden Gate Bridge.

FAMILY ADVENTURES

Kayak with otters and seals on **Humboldt Bay** (p261) or paddle an outrigger on **Big River Estuary** (p318).

Take surf lessons at **Bodega Bay** (p210).

Zipline through the redwoods at **Sonoma Zipline Adventures** (p209).

Go snow-tubing on kid-friendly slopes near **Mt Shasta** (p284).

Explore tide pools along the nature-rich coast at **Point Reyes National Seashore** (p126).

Train through estuaries and forests on Fort Bragg's **Skunk Train** (p240).

Horseback ride near **Lassen Volcanic National Park** (p292).

Look for bison in **Golden Gate Park** (p103) before visiting the California Academy of Sciences.

Skywalk through the towering redwoods at Eureka's **Sequoia Park Zoo** (p259).

Walking & Hiking

With epic scenery, Northern California is the perfect place to explore the state's iconic highlights on foot. Stroll the beach at sunset or trek past cinder cones in Lava Beds National Monument. Summit 14,000ft craggy peaks like Mt Shasta and admire alpine lakes, like Trinity. Walk under redwoods, the world's tallest, largest and oldest trees: from Muir and Armstrong Woods just north of San Francisco, to the massive stands in the parks of Humboldt and Del Norte Counties.

In spring and early summer, the Golden State is touched with a painter's palette as wildflowers bloom down coastal hillsides, across mountain meadows and along desert sands.

ACTION AREAS

For the best outdoor spots, see the map on p36.

View from Marin Headlands (p122)

Legendary long-distance trails cut right through the state, too, including the 2650-mile **Pacific Crest National Scenic Trail** (PCT), which takes hikers from Mexico to Canada. It crosses Plumas County, Lassen Volcanic National Park, skirts Mt Shasta and treks through the Klamath National Forest on the way from Yosemite National Park to Oregon. But there are still more trails to blaze here: the **California Coastal Trail Association** *(coastwalk.org)* is already more than halfway through building a 1200-mile trail along California's shoreline.

Cycling & Mountain Biking

Northern California's outstanding cycling terrain calls for leisurely spins along the beach, adrenaline-fueled mountain rides or multiday road-cycling tours down the coast. Even heavily trafficked urban areas may have good cycling routes, especially around San Francisco. Cycling between wineries in Napa and Sonoma Counties is a life-long memory in the making. You can cycle year-round in most coastal areas, although fog may rob you of views. Avoid the North Coast and the mountains during winter (too much rain and snow at higher elevations) and the slim strips of northeastern deserts in summer (too dang hot).

WHITE-WATER RAFTING

California has plenty of white water, like the **Feather River** (p301), offering beginner and advanced challenges.

WHALE-WATCHING

Spot migrating gray, blue, humpback and sperm whales from viewpoints like the **Point Arena Lighthouse** (p212).

CLIMBING

Rock climbing abounds in the national parks (Half Dome!), the Sierras and other mountains, like **Mt Shasta** (p282).

BIRD-WATCHING

Whip out your binocs and watch birds passing through on the Pacific Flyway at **Klamath Basin National Wildlife Refuge** (p290).

ACTION AREAS

Where to find San Francisco & Northern California's best outdoor activities.

Beaches

1. Baker Beach (p51)
2. Agate Beach (p272)
3. Goat Rock Beach (p210)
4. Stinson Beach (p124)
5. Manchester Beach (p239)
6. Pescadero State Beach (p158)
7. Bodega Dunes Beach (p210)

Walking & Hiking

1. Marin Headlands (p122)
2. Jedediah Smith Redwoods State Park (p264)
3. Lost Coast Trail (p252)
4. Sonoma Coast State Park (p210)
5. Shasta-Trinity National Forest (p282)
6. Mt Lassen Region (p292)
7. Castle Crags State Park (p286)

National Parks

1. Redwood National & State Parks (p264)
2. Lassen Volcanic National Park (p292)
3. Point Reyes National Seashore (p126)
4. Lava Beds National Monument (p289)
5. Muir Woods National Monument (p124)
6. Tule Lake National Monument (p290)
7. Sáttítla Highlands National Monument (p288)
8. Golden Gate National Recreation Area (p106)
9. Whiskeytown National Recreation Area (p307)

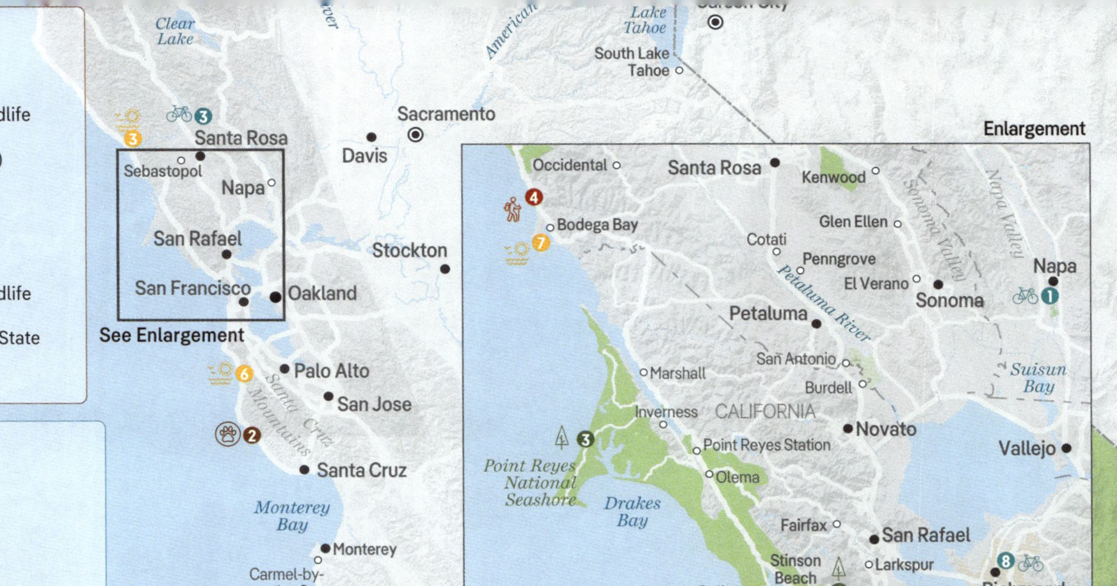

Wildlife

1. Klamath Basin National Wildlife Refuge (p290)
2. Año Nuevo State Park (p159)
3. Arcata Marsh & Wildlife Sanctuary (p263)
4. Sue-meg State Park (p272)
5. Farallon National Wildlife Refuge (p137)
6. Humboldt Bay National Wildlife Refuge (p261)
7. Point Cabrillo Light Station State Historic Park (p236)
8. Shasta Lake (p303)

Cycling & Mountain Biking

1. Napa Valley (p178)
2. Golden Gate Bridge (p54)
3. Dry Creek Valley (p221)
4. Mt Tamalpais State Park (p125)
5. Redding Trails (p306)
6. Avenue of the Giants (p254)
7. Lake Basin Recreation Area (p300)
8. Richmond–San Rafael Bridge (p144)

SAN FRANCISCO & NORTHERN CALIFORNIA

THE GUIDE

Chapters in this section are organised by hubs and their surrounding areas. We see the hub as your base in the destination, where you'll find unique experiences, local insights, insider tips and expert recommendations. It's also your gateway to the surrounding area, where you'll see what and how much you can do from there.

Grapevines, Gundlach-Bundschu winery (p192)

BENJAMIN HEATH FOR LONELY PLANET

For places to stay in San Francisco, see p112

CANADASTOCK/SHUTTERSTOCK

Above: Golden Gate Bridge (p54); Right: The Castro (p99)

THE MAIN AREAS

Researched by
Alison Bing

San Francisco

CALLING ALL FREE SPIRITS HOME

No matter what's going on in the world, know that flowers are blooming year-round along alleyways named after radical poets – if San Francisco didn't exist, you'd have to make it up.

Adventurous food, outrageous entertainment, impossible ideas: your time in San Francisco may seem like a wild dream, except that it's been this way from the start. Oysters and tamales topped the menu in this Mexico-run Ohlone settlement in 1848 – but a year and some gold nuggets later, Champagne and chow mein were served by the bucketload. Gold found in nearby Sierra foothills turned a sleepy 800-person village into a port city of 100,000 freewheeling prospectors, con artists, political dissidents, hard workers and big dreamers from across the globe.

Fast-forward through 175 years, and you'll find San Francisco in another boom/bust cycle – yet its free spirits endure. The city and its grand ambitions came crashing down in the 1906 earthquake and fire – but theater troupes and opera divas performed for free amid the ruins, bringing the city back to its feet and establishing SF's enduring tradition of free public shows. During WWII, soldiers accused of insubordination and homosexuality were dismissed in San Francisco, as though that would teach them a lesson. Instead the gay rights movement took root and SF's counterculture bloomed, inspiring West Coast jazz and Beat poetry. The Central Intelligence Agency tested LSD on local volunteers, who slipped it into punch at SF's 1966 Trips Festival – and the psychedelic '60s took off. The Summer of Love brought free food, love and music to the Haight. The Castro became a symbol of gay liberation, electing Harvey Milk as California's first out gay official. Amid incalculable losses from HIV/AIDS in the 1980 and '90s, San Franciscans wiped their tears and got to work, setting global standards for pandemic prevention and compassionate care.

EDDIE-HERNANDEZ.COM/SHUTTERSTOCK

As in the early days, free spirits from around the globe fit right in here – as the world's first sanctuary city since 1989, San Francisco welcomes all. This is the place to entertain wild ideas. Here, in the proving grounds for the internet, organic cuisine, free speech, biotech, LGBTQ+ rights and self-driving cars, nothing is impossible. So come on in: you're just in time for San Francisco's next act, and it's your turn on stage.

THE HAIGHT & HAYES VALLEY
San Francisco's hippie hotspot.
p83

MISSION, DOGPATCH & POTRERO
Sunshine, murals, books & flavors galore.
p90

THE CASTRO
Welcome to the gayborhood!
p99

GOLDEN GATE PARK & THE AVENUES
SF's wild stretch of imagination.
p103

Find Your Way

Walking and strutting are the preferred modes of transport in this 7x7-mile city – but there are hills to consider. Vintage cable cars summit the steep slopes between downtown and the northern waterfront, and streetcars and buses connect downtown to neighborhoods and beaches.

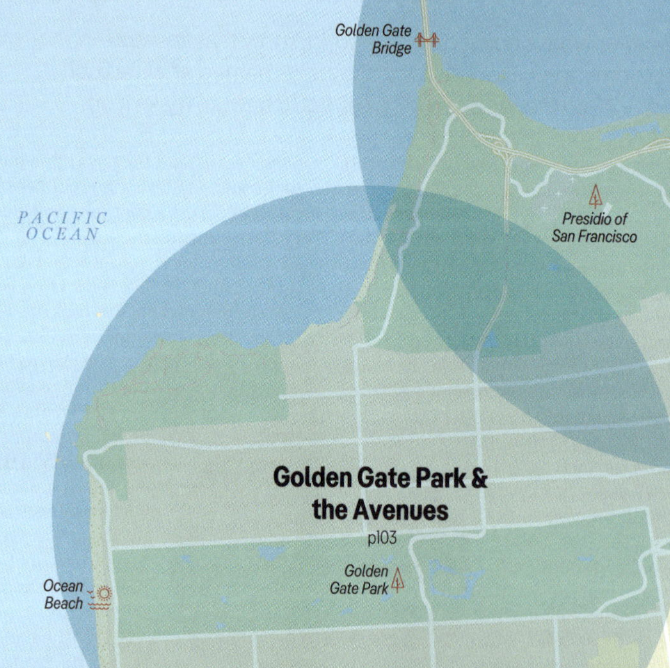

FROM THE AIRPORT

Bay Area Rapid Transit trains get you downtown in 30 minutes *(BART; bart.gov; fare $11.15)*, departing from SFO's International Terminal. Rideshare services including Lyft and Uber depart from Level 5 of the domestic parking garage (*$40–60*). Taxis depart outside baggage claim (*$55–65*).

RIDESHARE & ROBOTAXIS

SF-invented rideshare services Lyft and Uber are widely used – expect waits and/or premium pricing during peak-use times. Robotaxi service is now available in SF from Waymo *(waymo.com)*, aka Google's self-driving car fleet. To try it, download the Waymo One app.

CABLE CARS & MUNI

San Francisco cable cars are total joyrides – grab the wooden bench or hang onto creaking leather straps and brace for downhill slides. Single rides cost $9, or get a Muni Visitor Passport *(sfmta.com; 1-/3-/4-day pass $15/35/47)*. Muni bus, streetcar and metro fares are $3/2.85 *(cash/Clipper card)*.

WALK

Limber up: San Francisco has 40+ hills to summit, with stairway hikes leading to vista points and Golden Gate Bridge views. The Bay waterfront is flat and scenic from Dogpatch to Crissy Field, and Golden Gate Park stretches over 50 blocks to Ocean Beach.

Plan Your Days

A day or two in SF brings breathtaking art, foot-stomping concerts and mouthwatering meals – three days might raise your expectations for peace, love and sourdough.

SERGII FIGURNYI/SHUTTERSTOCK

Cable car (p56)

Day 1

Morning

- Wander Chinatown for **Edge on the Square**'s (p67) art and true stories at the **Chinese Historical Society of America** (p67). Find your fortune at **Golden Gate Fortune Cookies** (p68), and go gourmet with **On Waverly** (p68) cookbooks and **Wok Shop** (p69) kitchenware.

Afternoon

- Sample dumplings at **Osmanthus Dim Sum Lounge** (p67), then cable car to Fisherman's Wharf to meet **Cartoon Art Museum** (p52) comic-book heroes, battle Space Invaders at **Musée Mécanique** (p52) and see **Pier 39** (p53) sea lions.

Evening

- Enjoy waterfront sunsets and SF's seafood cioppino at **Scoma's** (p53). End the day with spur-rattling cocktails at **Comstock Saloon** (p69), comedy at **Cobb's** (p72) or punk rock at **Mabuhay Gardens** (p69).

You'll Also Want to ...

Indulge your curiosity and follow your bliss where it leads. When you find inspiration, act on it: be part of the art, parade, romance, flavor, drama, culture and future.

SEE OFF-THE-WALL ART

Art explodes on mural-covered Mission streets – and you complete the art at **Asian Art Museum's** (p61) immersive installations, **Edge on the Square**'s (p67) participatory shows and **Minnesota Street Project** (p97) gallery openings.

JOIN A PARADE

San Francisco throws extravagant parades to celebrate people being exactly who they are – proud of their immigrant roots, chosen families and civil rights achievements – from **Chinese New Year** (p69) parades to month-long **Pride** celebrations.

HIT PEAK ROMANCE

Your heart beats faster, your knees go weak, your palms get sweaty – either this is true love or you're climbing one of San Francisco's 40-odd hills. Pause to admire the scenery from **garden-lined stairways** (p76) to the sparkling bay.

Day 2

● Get experimental at the **Exploratorium** (p55), where hands-on exhibits dare you to stop time, sculpt fog and dive headfirst into total darkness in the Tactile Dome.

Afternoon

● Go gourmet by the bay at SF's local food showcase: the **Ferry Building** (p62). Explore cutting-edge, multimedia art at **SFMOMA** (p57), or glimpse global art treasures at the **Asian Art Museum** (p61).

Evening

● Get the star-chef treatment with **Benu**'s (p64) multicourse feasts or **Rich Table**'s (p89) seasonal sensations. Cheer for virtuosos at world-renowned **SFJAZZ** (p88), **San Francisco Opera** (p60) or **San Francisco Symphony** (p60). Afterward, head to SoMa clubs to see where the night leads.

Day 3

Morning

● Stroll **Golden Gate Park** (p106), where wonders never cease at the **de Young Museum** (p107). Hang out with penguins at the **California Academy of Sciences** (p107) or beachcomb along **Ocean Beach** (p111).

Afternoon

● Enjoy reinvented Chinese American classics at **Mamahuhu** (p109), then head to the Mission for murals and galleries, disco-naps in **Dolores Park** (p90) and Calle 24's bookstores and **cafes** (p96).

Evening

● Get the definitive Mission burrito at **La Taqueria** (p94). Don't miss showtime at **Chan National Queer Arts Center** (p91), **Roxie Cinema** (p95) or **Oasis** (p64). Follow rainbow-lit sidewalks to Castro clubs or toast to new friends at legendary Mission bars.

FOLLOW YOUR TASTEBUDS

With 46 global cuisines packed into 46 square miles, San Francisco is like a greatest-hits compilation with no skips. SF holds the most Michelin stars of any US city; you might bump into the next great chef at the **Ferry Building** (p62).

HIT A DRAG SHOW

SF drag is outlandishly original at **Oasis** (p64), too wild for TV at **The Stud** (p64) and completely unpredictable at **Aunt Charlie's** (p63). Drag royals keep winning hearts and civil rights victories with false lashes and true courage.

GLIMPSE THE FUTURE

You can see ahead of the curve at **Gray Area** (p91) cyberpunk fests, **Cartoon Art Museum** (p52) sci-fi comic shows and **SFMOMA** (p57)'s futuristic installation art – and join **Exploratorium** (p55) experiments in progress.

DIVE INTO UNDERGROUND CULTURE

Some best discoveries are misleadingly named – ahem, **Free Gold Watch** (p87) and **House of Seiko** (p97) – and smartphones are discouraged at hotspots like **Faight Collective** (p88) and **Noc Noc** (p88).

Presidio, Marina & Fisherman's Wharf

BEYOND THE ICONIC BRIDGE, EXPECT THE UNEXPECTED

GETTING AROUND

The best way to see Fisherman's Wharf and Presidio nature trails is at your own pace, stopping for entertainment and photos. SF's northern waterfront is flat but vast, so walking shoes and buses are handy. Muni buses connect the Wharf, Marina and Presidio with points beyond, Golden Gate Transit crosses the bridge and Presidio GO shuttles cover Presidio parks. Download maps and schedules – especially if you're headed to the Presidio, where cell signal is variable. You can also cover the waterfront on rental bikes – but book ahead on weekends.

Make a grand entrance to San Francisco through the Golden Gate Bridge and follow the waterfront to nature hikes, immersive art, comic-book heroes and a WWII submarine. For centuries, Golden Gate Strait was the main entrance to San Francisco for new arrivals – note the shipwrecks dotting its shores. Luckily, the Golden Gate Bridge now offers easier entry and spectacular views besides. Enter the Presidio military base that's now a coastal preserve to spot only-in-SF sights: rare shorebirds on a former airstrip, priceless sculptures hidden in the woods and goosebumps galore on the clothing-optional end of blustery Baker Beach. To the west, the Marina has chic boutiques on a former cow pasture, deco date-night restaurants built atop old fairgrounds and a waterfront fort creatively repurposed for art. At Fisherman's Wharf, you'll meet local characters: lazy sea lions, legendary cartoonists, pinball wizards, scientific geniuses and actual fisherfolk.

R&R in the Presidio

Go play in an ex-army outpost

Since the Presidio has retired from military duty, civilians can throw strikes at the post's bowling alley, **Presidio Bowl** *(presidiobowl.com; per lane weekdays/weekends from $55/75; shoe rental $7.50)*, or bounce around **House of Air** *(houseofair.com; per hour adult/child $20/28)*, a hangar lined with trampolines. The former PX (provisions warehouse) is a **Sports Basement** *(sportsbasement.com)* stocking bikes and sporting equipment to rent, buy or trade. Presidio's **Outpost Playground** is wildly popular for nature-themed play structures and nearby food trucks.

LYNN FRIEDMAN/SHUTTERSTOCK

Fort Mason Center

TOP TIP

Plan shoes and outfits strategically – coastal weather shifts suddenly and distances are further than they seem on maps. Dress in layers: windbreaker for Golden Gate Bridge hikes, cozy sweater for panoramic Presidio picnics and nice (but washable) shirt for seafood feasts at the Wharf or Marina.

Make Art, Not War, at Fort Mason

Find artistic inspiration in military storehouses

During WWII, **Fort Mason Center** shipped out 23 million tons of supplies – now it supplies creative inspiration to 1.4 million visitors annually. Dockside nonprofit **SF Camerawork** *(sfcamerawork.org; free)* has showcased next-wave photographers since 1974, while **Haines Gallery** *(hainesgallery.com; free)* represents leading global contemporary artists like Ai Weiwei, and **Arion Press** *(arionpress.com; free)* showcases letterpress art-book collaborations. Dockside Herbst Pavilion's arsenal of events includes **FOG Design+Art** *(fogfair.com; admission $35-40)* in winter, **San Francisco Art Fair** in spring, and **Renegade Craft Fair** and **West Coast Craft Fair** *(westcoastcraft.com; free)* in both summer and fall. Capture inspiration with art and craft supplies from well-stocked **Flax Art & Design**. It also hosts a weekly **farmers market** *(fortmason.org/event/fort-mason-center-farmers-market/)*.

Showtime in Waterfront Warehouses

Watch talents launch in Fort Mason

Pushing boundaries since 1967, **Magic Theatre** *(magictheatre.org; tickets $35-75)* stages breakthrough works like *Jerry Garcia in the Lower Mission,* plus freeform jazz services for

(continued on p52)

EATING IN THE PRESIDIO & MARINA: DREAM DINNER DATES

Dalida: *Top Chef* powerhouse Laura Ozyilmaz brings Med flavors to the Bay, like stuffed mussels and Yemeni lamb stew. *11.30-2pm & 5-9pm Fri-Wed, 11am-2pm Thu* $$

Atelier Crenn: Global superstar chef Dominique Crenn creates edible art inspired by SF's seafaring legends and her own Sonoma farmstead. *5-9pm Tue-Sat* $$$

A16: How romantic: James Beard Award–winning wood-fired pizzas, house-cured salami and Italian wine. *5-9pm Mon-Thu, noon-9.30pm Fri-Sun* $$

Greens: Women chefs commandeer Fort Mason's mess hall, inventing flavor-bomb vegetarian dishes with organic ingredients since 1979. *11.30am-2.30pm & 5-9pm Tue-Sun* $$

PRESIDIO, MARINA & FISHERMAN'S WHARF

HIGHLIGHTS
1 Crissy Field
2 Golden Gate Bridge
3 Presidio of San Francisco

SIGHTS
4 Aquarium of the Bay
5 Arion Press
6 Baker Beach
7 Cartoon Art Museum
8 East Beach
9 FOG Design+Art
10 Fort Mason Center
11 Fort Point
12 Haines Gallery
13 Inspiration Point
14 Military Intelligence Service Historic Learning Center
15 Pier 39
16 Presidio Officers' Club
17 Renegade Craft Fair
18 San Francisco Art Fair
19 San Francisco Carousel
20 SF Camerawork
21 Spire
22 Tunnel Tops
23 West Coast Craft

ACTIVITIES
24 Adventure Cat
25 Batteries to Bluffs Trail
26 Ecology Trail
27 House of Air
28 Musée Mécanique
29 Oceanic Society Expeditions
30 Outpost Playground
31 Presidio Bowl
32 Red & White Fleet
33 Sports Basement

SLEEPING
34 Argonaut Hotel

35 HI San Francisco Fisherman's Wharf
36 Hotel del Sol
37 Infinity Hotel
38 Inn at the Presidio
39 Kimpton Alton
40 Lodge at the Presidio
41 Marina Motel
42 Union Street Inn

EATING

43 A16
see 39 Abacá
44 Atelier Crenn
45 Codmother Fish & Chips
46 Dalida
47 Eagle Cafe
48 Fisherman's Wharf Crab Stands
49 Fog Harbor Fish House
50 Greens
51 Palette Tea House
52 Presidio Pop Up
53 Scoma's
54 Surisan
55 Warming Hut

DRINKING & NIGHTLIFE

see 11 Round House Café

ENTERTAINMENT

56 BATS Improv
57 Magic Theatre

SHOPPING

58 Flax Art & Design

INFORMATION

59 Golden Gate Bridge Welcome Center
60 Presidio Visitors Center

OLEG PODZOROV/SHUTTERSTOCK

Baker Beach

TOP EXPERIENCE

The Presidio

Spies, Yoda, Andy Goldsworthy sculptures, Walt Disney drawings: SF's best-kept secrets are revealed along Presidio hiking paths. This retired army base is now a panoramic public park packed with attractions – including sweeping Golden Gate Bridge views previously only seen by top brass and passing commuters.

DON'T MISS

- Tunnel Tops
- Crissy Field
- Fort Point
- Baker Beach
- Andy Goldworthy's *Spire*
- Batteries to Bluffs Trail
- Military Intelligence Service Historic Learning Center

Back to Nature

'Presidio' means fort in Spanish – but in San Francisco, it's a playground. It started in 1776 as a Spanish military post built by conscripted Ohlone people, and was officially retired from military duty in 1996. To the obvious delight of shorebirds, puppies and people, the **Presidio of San Francisco** is now a national park. To allow wildlife to thrive in the park, commuter traffic was rerouted underground – revealing glorious views clear across the bay from driftwood-shaped picnic benches at **Tunnel Tops** park, with the nature-themed **Outpost Playground** downhill.

PRACTICALITIES
Scan this QR code for more information on opening times and entrance passes.

On hot days, race the crowds to **Baker Beach**, the sandy Presidio cove with spectacular views of the Golden Gate framed by wind-sculpted pines – plus nude sunbathing behind the rocks on the clothing-optional, gay-friendly, no-photography-allowed north end. Picnickers and sand-castle architects stick to the sandy south end, near the parking.

Happy Trails

Hiking adventures begin at the **Presidio Visitors Center**, well-supplied with trail maps. For a moderately challenging, inspirational 1.4-mile hike, follow the **Ecology Trail** through redwood groves and spring wildflower meadows to **Inspiration Point** for bird's-eye bay views, then push onward to reach the Presidio's artistic pinnacle: Andy Goldsworthy's **Spire**, made from reclaimed cypress trees. Adventurous hikers take on the 2.7-mile **Batteries to Bluffs Trail**, heading uphill above Baker Beach to splendid Golden Gate Bridge vistas.

Follow San Franciscan regulars to **Crissy Field** to stroll, jog, bike, skate or roll along scenic, flat, wheelchair-accessible paths. The strip where military planes once landed is now a reclaimed tidal marsh, where birders perch on strategically positioned benches. Puppies chase kite-fliers across Crissy Field's grassy lawn, and windsurfers skim bay waters along **East Beach**. Pick up the Bay Trail to reach **Fort Point** (1.6 miles from East Beach) and head over the **Golden Gate Bridge** (p54), or stop at certified-green cafe **Warming Hut** to browse California field guides and warm up with fair-trade coffee.

Military Secrets Revealed

Over two centuries, the Presidio stood armed and ready for invasions that never arrived. At an eye-watering cost of more than $100 million in today's terms, **Fort Point** *(free; 10am-5pm Fri-Sun)* mounted 102 cannons to fight the US Civil War – but Confederate ships never made it this far. **Battery Bluff** guns weren't fired in WWI, and Cold War Nike nuclear missile operations in **Battery Caulfield** were quietly suspended in 1974.

The **Presidio Officers' Club** was long off-limits to civilians – today it houses the **Heritage Gallery** *(free; 11am-4pm Fri-Sun)*, which showcases the Presidio's history as ancestral Ohlone homeland for over 10,000 years and its 250 years of military service for Spain, Mexico and the US. The Presidio's top-secret WWII spycraft school is now the **Military Intelligence Service Historic Learning Center** *(njahs.org/building-640; adult/child $10/free; noon-5pm Sat & Sun)*. Japanese American soldiers lived and trained in this drafty bunkhouse as code-breakers and spies for high-risk WWII intelligence missions, while their families were incarcerated as supposed 'enemy aliens' in accordance with US Executive Order 9066. Fascinating exhibits show how the Japanese American 442nd regiment became the most decorated unit in US history.

GOLDSWORTHY'S NATURAL WONDERS

Above Inspiration Point, you'll spot a natural yet artful formation: **Spire**, Andy Goldsworthy's contemporary sculpture created from 37 reclaimed Presidio cypress trunks. *Spire* was intended to disintegrate, but after it was damaged by fire, San Franciscans volunteered to reinforce it. Follow Lover's Lane Trail past the zig-zagging **Wood Line** and duck into the Officer's Club to view Goldsworthy's **Earth Wall**.

TOP TIPS

- Forgot to pack a picnic? No problem: **Presidio Pop Up** food trucks line the Parade Grounds from 9am to 3pm (to 4.30pm on weekends).

- If you'd rather catch your own lunch, try your luck under the Golden Gate Bridge on Torpedo Wharf. No license is required for fishing here; check posted catch limits. Watch and learn from local anglers, who catch sole and sniggle eels here in season.

- Presidio park rangers tell incredible true stories at 4pm **Tunnel Tops Campfire Talks** *(free)*, introducing legendary locals whose footsteps you're walking in – including indigenous healers, Buffalo Soldiers and Cold War spies.

ROSIE THE RIVETER & FRIENDS

During WWII, women and men came to the SF Bay to serve as shipbuilders. You may recall the poster of muscle-flaunting Rosie the Riveter proclaiming 'We Can Do It' – the model was Bay Area naval worker Naomi Parker Fraley. Bay Area shipbuilders worked long hours to turn the tides of WWII, building an entire ship every day for the duration of the war. Nearly half of all US military cargo ships were built here, plus one in five warships. By the 1950s, Bay Area women were staffing a new local industry: silicon-chip manufacturing.

(continued from p47)
St John Coltrane Church. **Bay Area Theater Sports**, aka **BATS Improv** *(improv.org; tickets adult/student $25/20)* hosts raucous improvised comedy in a range of styles: madcap musicals, SF rom-coms, B-movie sci-fi. Feeling brave? Book improv workshops online.

Game on at Musée Mécanique

Play vintage games at SF's Wild West arcade

Pier 45's massive boatshed can scarcely contain this collection of 300+ vintage mechanical amusements. For a buck at **Musée Mécanique** *(museemecanique.com; entry free)*, you can battle Space Invaders, get your fortune told by robotic wizards, peep at belly dancers through a vintage Mutoscope or get hypnotized by a Ferris wheel made of toothpicks.

Meet Superheroes at the Cartoon Art Museum

Get up close and personal with comic legends

Funded by Bay Area cartoon legend Charles M Schultz of *Peanuts* fame, the **Cartoon Art Museum** *(cartoonart.org;*

EATING AT THE WHARF: BRUNCH

Abacá: Friends become family over Filipino soul food, like fried chicken and pandan waffles. *7-9am & 5-9pm Mon, Tue, Thu & Fri, 8am-1.30pm & 5-9pm Sat & Sun* $$

Palette Tea House: Swanky dim sum – Wagyu potstickers, lobster dumplings – with tea or cocktails. *11.30am-7.30pm Sun-Thu, to 8pm Fri & Sat* $$

Eagle Cafe: Brunch with SF perks: crab Benedicts, sourdough French toast and eagle's-eye views over Pier 39. *8am-3pm* $$

Surisan: Warm up with Cal-Korean specials – savory *pajun* pancakes with shrimp and bacon, matcha mojitos. *9am-2pm & 5-9pm* $

JOSEPH CHRISTOPHER OROPEL/GETTY IMAGES

Pier 39

adult/child $10/4) showcases cartoon classics, including Batman covers, Calvin & Hobbes strips, Edward Gorey's Goth monsters and Trina Robbins' trailblazing feminist comics. At events, mingle with comic legends and local Pixar animators.

Family Fun on Pier 39

Choose your own bayside adventure

Sea lions took over **Pier 39** yacht docks in 1990 and have been making a public display of themselves ever since. Up to 2100 of them lounge here daily *(pier39.com; free)*. Families flock to see them, and for the amusement-park atmosphere without prohibitive entry fees – the antique **San Francisco Carousel** is $6 per ride *(10am-8pm)*. At not-for-profit, Smithsonian-affiliated **Aquarium of the Bay** *(aquariumofthebay.org; adult/child $28/20)*, visit 24,000 aquatic creatures in their habitats – walk through shark tanks, get mesmerized by jellies and join a fish-feeding frenzy.

BEST WAYS TO SAIL AWAY

When the fog lifts and sun shines, only one thing tops waterfront strolls: boating on the bay.

Oceanic Society: Naturalist-led Pacific whale-watching expeditions during migration seasons *(oceanicsociety.org; 7½hr; $300 per person)*.

Adventure Cat: Skim across the bay with the wind in your hair on catamaran trips, including 'Sail and Jail' getaways to/from Alcatraz *(adventurecat.com; 90min cruise adult/child $75/35, Sail and Jail $125)*.

Red & White Fleet: SF's original sunset bay cruises since 1892 – ring boxes keep popping. New triple-decker boats offer full bars and snacks *(redandwhite.com; 1hr cruise adult/child $39/29, 2hr sunset cruise $58/38)*.

EATING IN THE MARINA: PRIME PICNICS

Scoma's: Fishing boats docked out front supply 'pier-to-plate' Cal-Italian classics, from Dungeness crab cakes to SF's definitive cioppio (seafood stew). *noon-9pm* $$$

Codmother Fish & Chips: Crisp, fried-to-order Pacific cod with garlic fries at outdoor picnic tables. *11.30am-6pm Sun-Thu, to 7pm Fri & Sat* $

Fisherman's Wharf Crab Stands: Steaming cauldrons of Dungeness crab at Pier 45 sidewalk stands are ready for feasts. *11.30am-9pm, winter through spring* $

Fog Harbor Fish House: Bay views frame sustainable local favorites like Petrale sole, Pacific cod and Dungeness crab – simply prepared, so flavors shine through. *11am-9pm* $$

TOP EXPERIENCE

Golden Gate Bridge

No other bridge puts on a show like this. Morning mists lift to reveal the Golden Gate Bridge, glowing orange-red against blue skies. Give yourself a couple hours to walk the 1.7-mile span, with time for photo-ops. Stick around for the late-afternoon grand finale: as fog swallows commuter traffic, art deco towers float above the clouds. Magic.

BENJAMINHEATH/LONELY PLANET

TOP TIPS

- Watch acrobatic fog feats over coffee at **Round House Café**, the 1938 diner built by bridge engineer Alfred Finnila.
- If you get cold or tired walking across the bridge, catch any **Golden Gate Transit** bus back from the northern toll plaza.

PRACTICALITIES

- goldengate.org
- Vehicle toll: northbound free, southbound $9.50
- Welcome Center 9am-6pm daily

Iconic Design

It's hard to picture San Francisco without its iconic art deco suspension bridge, but the US War Department almost nixed this design in favor of a chunky concrete bridge with caution-yellow stripes. Local architects Gertrude Comfort Morrow and Irving Morrow realized that ships may pass in the night, but San Franciscans would have to live with the bridge every day. Working with engineer Joseph B Strauss, the Morrows submitted a counter-proposal to harmonize with the natural environment: a sleek suspension bridge painted a signature shade known as International Orange. Even though the War Department owned the land on either side, the City of San Francisco gave the ingenious orange bridge design the green light.

Death-Defying Feats

Stop by the **Golden Gate Bridge Welcome Center** to witness precarious construction work in progress, captured in jaw-dropping vintage photos – riveters balanced atop swaying cables 80 stories high, while divers plunged 110ft underwater with only a rubber hose for air. Take a moment to admire the bridge's signature color, still touched up by a daredevil crew of 34 painters suspended from the 764ft suspension towers.

TOP EXPERIENCE

Exploratorium

Can you stop time, sculpt fog or make sand sing? At San Francisco's living laboratory of science and human perception, you'll discover superhuman abilities you never knew you had – and emerge from the hands-on exhibits with a renewed sense of wonder.

GILBERTO MESQUITA/SHUTTERSTOCK

Mind-Expanding Experiences

Is there a science to skateboarding? How big is your blind spot? Can plankton make art? You have questions about life's mysteries, and the **Exploratorium** helps you find answers. MacArthur Genius–winning designers create 700+ hands-on exhibits to engage all the senses: try static-electricity hairdos, send whispered messages to strangers and dance with your own rainbow shadows in a light-refraction room.

The Tactile Dome

Slip off your shoes and step inside the mysterious geodesic **Tactile Dome**, and suddenly you're enveloped in total darkness. You'll have to rely on your sense of touch to guide you through an elaborate labyrinth – and emerge exhilarated, with hands tingling. Advance reservations and separate ticket required.

A Showcase for Experimental Thinking

The Exploratorium's mind-bending science exhibits are inspired by founder Frank Oppenheimer, a physicist who worked on the atom bomb with his brother Robert – but was blacklisted during the McCarthy era and barred from scientific research. He dedicated the rest of his life to promoting science in the public interest, teaching public high school and founding the Exploratorium in 1969. Today the Exploratorium covers Pier 15, including **Fog Bridge** and other free outdoor exhibits.

TOP TIPS

- At **After Dark Thursdays**, 18+ crowds bond over glow-in the-dark mad-scientist cocktails, technology-assisted sing-alongs and special exhibits. Book ahead.
- The Exploratorium's scenic waterfront **Seaglass Restaurant** serves sit-down, locally sourced meals. It's closed on Monday.

PRACTICALITIES

- exploratorium.edu
- Entry adult/youth $40/30, after dark $23, Tactile Dome $16
- 10am-5pm Mon-Sat, noon-5pm Sun, after dark 6-10pm Thu

Downtown, Civic Center & SoMa

BIG BUILDINGS, BIG CHANGES

TOP TIP

Cable cars are a fun way to get around downtown – unless you get stuck waiting in line at the cable-car turnaround at Powell and Market Sts. Queue for Powell-Mason and Powell-Hyde cars before noon or hop the lesser traveled California St line near the Embarcadero.

Luring San Franciscans downtown after work takes a dazzling museum show, a killer cocktail, fabulous food or a kinky club – and there's plenty to choose from here. After 150 years of entertaining through earthquakes and pandemics, downtown arts venues have something for everyone, including immersive museums, iconic drag and Grammy-winning symphonies. Downtown is a huge swath of eastern San Francisco that encompasses subneighborhoods of Union Square, Civic Center and the Tenderloin, South of Market (SoMa), the Financial District (FiDi) and parts of Mission Bay. Civic Center is a zoning conundrum, with great performances and Asian art treasures on one side of City Hall and dive bars and transitional housing on the other. SoMa's high-tech landscape is fickle – Twitter/X has literally left the building here, but new AI startups keep cropping up in vacant spaces. When work's done, SoMa is where everyone gets down and dirty on the dance floor.

Ride All Three Cable-Car Lines

Max out your day pass

San Francisco's cable cars were invented in 1873 and designated a National Landmark in 1964. Part of the city's Muni system *(sfmta.com; cable car per ride/day pass $9/15)*, SF's three cable-car lines complete 254,000 passenger trips per *(continued on p60)*

GETTING AROUND

To see sights north of Union Square, hop a cable car. Powell-Hyde and Powell-Mason lines link downtown with Chinatown, North Beach and the Wharf; the California St line runs east-west to Van Ness Ave. Muni metro travels swiftly under Market St, while historic F-Market streetcars ambles between the Castro and Fisherman's Wharf above ground. The N line links downtown to the Haight, Castro and Golden Gate Park; the T links Dogpatch and Caltrain to Chinatown. East-west Muni buses 2, 5, 6, 7, 21, 31 and 38 connect downtown and SoMa with western neighborhoods; north-south lines 14, 19, 27, 30 and 45 connect to the Wharf or Mission.

TOP EXPERIENCE

San Francisco Museum of Modern Art

Boggle your mind and refresh your eyes at SFMOMA, where boundary-pushing modern and contemporary masterworks sprawl over seven floors of galleries. See the world-class 3rd-floor photography collection, meditate in Agnes Martin's secluded shrine behind 4th-floor abstract paintings, get an eyeful of Warhol's pop art on the 5th floor and immerse yourself in 7th-floor cutting-edge contemporary installations.

EQROY/SHUTTERSTOCK

TOP TIPS

- During SFMOMA opening hours, lobby and atrium art installations and 2nd-floor Bay Area art shows are free to visit without a ticket.
- Pick up limited-edition exhibition tees, catalogs and jewelry at ground-floor **Museum Store** *(11am-5pm Fri-Tue, noon-8pm Thu)*.

PRACTICALITIES

- sfmoma.org
- Adult/senior/student/youth $30/$25/$23/free free first Thu, ground floor always free
- 10am-5pm Fri-Tue, noon-8pm Thu

1900 to Now: SFMOMA's Collection

Rotating experimental works and masterpieces from its massive collection, SFMOMA encourages viewers to constantly re-examine the contradictions and interpretations of some of the greatest works of our time. Head to the 2nd floor to see how SFMOMA began, with colorful works from Frida Kahlo, Paul Klee and Henri Matisse, and ponder Diego Rivera's radical worker portraits and Georgia O'Keefe's interpretations of nature and the feminine. Recent immersive installations include the disorienting mirrored infinity rooms of Yayoi Kusama, Olafur Eliasson's dazzling social-media sensation *One-Way Colour Tunnel* and Kara Walker's Octavia Butler–inspired lobby installation of robotic black figures transforming trauma.

The Living Wall & Sculpture Garden

Take a breather mid-visit with a quick outdoor detour. On the 3rd floor is the 30-foot-high Living Wall – the largest of its kind in the US, containing more than 19,000 plants. On the rooftop patio of Cafe 5 (5th floor) is a sunny sculpture garden, featuring major modernist works framed by skyscrapers.

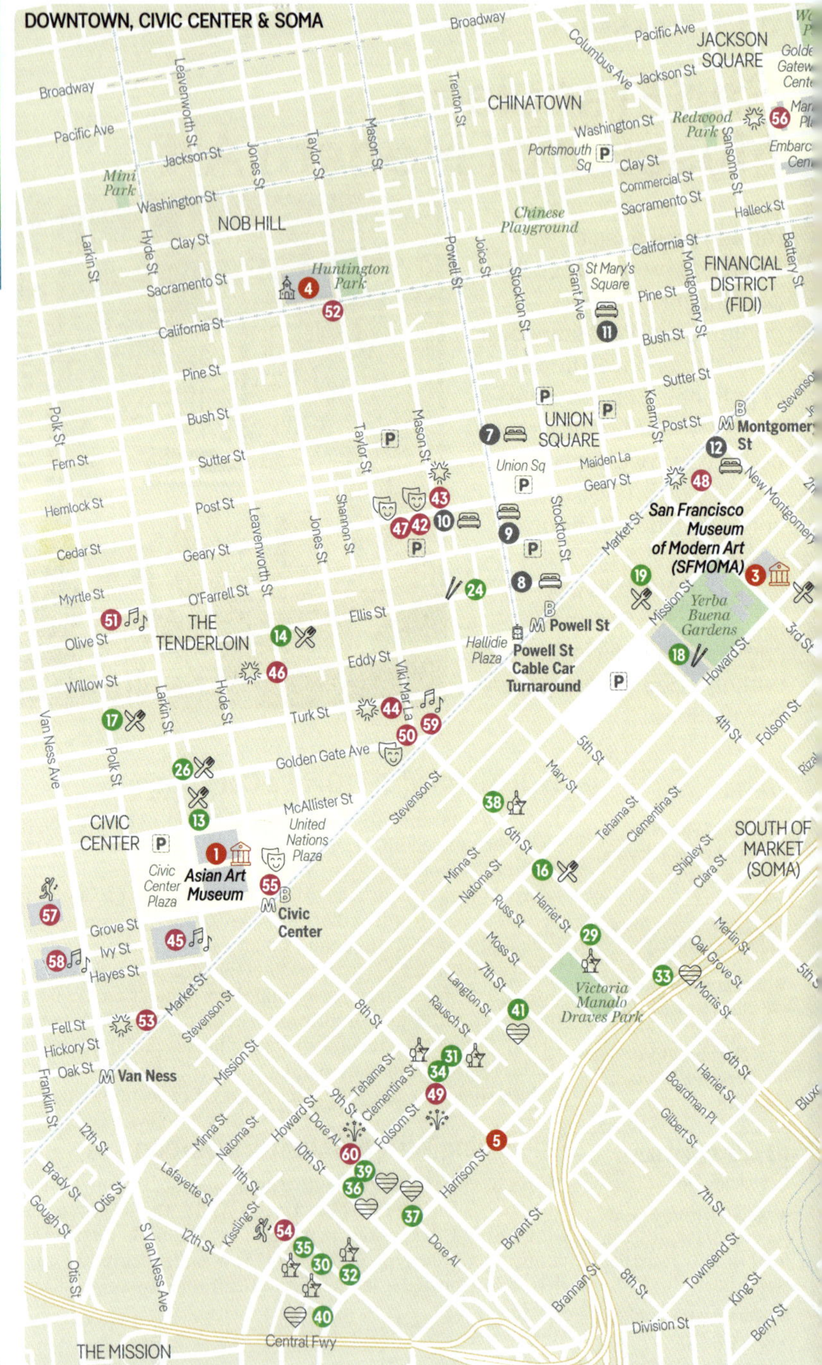
DOWNTOWN, CIVIC CENTER & SOMA
CHINATOWN
JACKSON SQUARE
NOB HILL
FINANCIAL DISTRICT (FIDI)
UNION SQUARE
THE TENDERLOIN
CIVIC CENTER
SOUTH OF MARKET (SOMA)
THE MISSION
Mini Park
Huntington Park
Portsmouth Sq
Chinese Playground
St Mary's Square
Redwood Park
Union Sq
Hallidie Plaza
Powell St Cable Car Turnaround
Powell St
Montgomery St
San Francisco Museum of Modern Art (SFMOMA)
Yerba Buena Gardens
United Nations Plaza
Civic Center Plaza
Asian Art Museum
Civic Center
Van Ness
Victoria Manalo Draves Park
Broadway
Pacific Ave
Jackson St
Washington St
Clay St
Commercial St
Sacramento St
California St
Pine St
Bush St
Sutter St
Post St
Geary St
O'Farrell St
Ellis St
Eddy St
Turk St
Golden Gate Ave
McAllister St
Grove St
Ivy St
Hayes St
Fell St
Hickory St
Oak St
Fern St
Hemlock St
Cedar St
Myrtle St
Olive St
Willow St
Columbus Ave
Trenton St
Halleck St
Maiden La
Leavenworth St
Jones St
Taylor St
Mason St
Powell St
Joice St
Stockton St
Grant Ave
Kearny St
Montgomery St
Sansome St
Battery St
Larkin St
Hyde St
Polk St
Van Ness Ave
Franklin St
Shannon St
Viki Mar La
Market St
Mission St
Howard St
Folsom St
Harrison St
Bryant St
Brannan St
Townsend St
King St
Berry St
Division St
New Montgomery St
3rd St
4th St
5th St
6th St
7th St
8th St
9th St
10th St
11th St
12th St
Stevenson St
Mary St
Minna St
Natoma St
Tehama St
Clementina St
Shipley St
Clara St
Russ St
Harriet St
Moss St
Langton St
Rausch St
Merlin St
Oak Grove St
Morris St
Boardman Pl
Gilbert St
Dore Al
Lafayette St
Kissling St
Brady St
Otis St
Gough St
S Van Ness Ave
Central Fwy

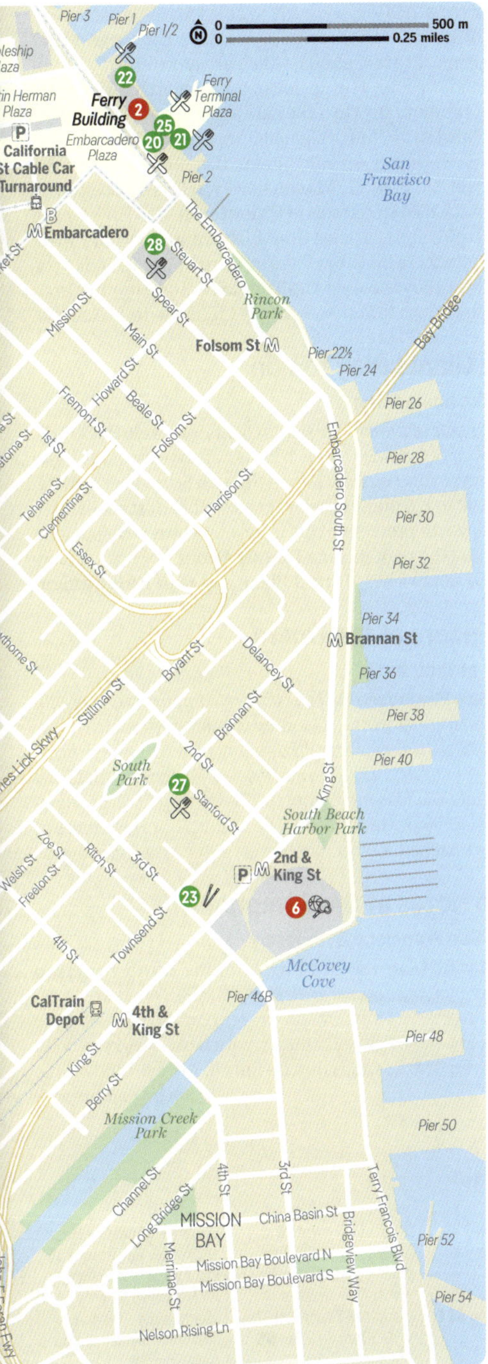

HIGHLIGHTS

1 Asian Art Museum
2 Ferry Building
3 San Francisco Museum of Modern Art (SFMOMA)

SIGHTS

4 Grace Cathedral
5 Leather & LGBTQ Cultural District
6 Oracle Park

SLEEPING

7 Beacon Grand
8 citizenM San Francisco Union Square
9 HI San Francisco Downtown
10 Hotel Nikko
11 Orchard Garden Hotel
12 Palace Hotel

EATING

13 ¡Chao Pescao!
see 2 Acme Bread Company
14 Azalina's
15 Benu
16 Bini's Kitchen
17 Brenda's French Soul Food
18 Dabao Singapore
19 Delarosa Downtown
20 Far West Fungi
21 Ferry Plaza Farmers Market
22 Hog Island Oyster Company
see 22 Humphry Slocombe
23 Kaiyō Restaurant
24 Kin Khao
25 Lunette
see 22 Ocean Malasada Company
26 Outta Sight Pizza
see 22 Peaches Patties
27 Rooh
28 Yank Sing

DRINKING & NIGHTLIFE

29 1015 Folsom
30 Butter
31 Cat Club
32 DNA Lounge
33 EndUp
34 F8
35 Halcyon
36 Hole in the Wall
37 Lone Star Saloon
38 Monarch
39 Powerhouse
see 2 Red Bay Coffee (Ferry Building)
40 SF Eagle
41 The Stud

ENTERTAINMENT

42 American Conservatory Theater
43 August Hall
44 Aunt Charlie's Lounge
45 Bill Graham Civic Auditorium
46 Black Cat
47 Curran Theatre
48 Dawn Club
49 Folsom Street Fair
50 Golden Gate Theatre
51 Great American Music Hall
52 Masonic Auditorium
53 Mr Tipple's Recording Studio
54 Oasis
55 Orpheum Theatre
56 Punch Line
57 San Francisco Ballet
see 57 San Francisco Opera
58 San Francisco Symphony
59 Warfield
60 Up Your Alley Fair

BARGAIN TICKETS

In San Francisco, world-class entertainment isn't just for tycoons. The San Francisco Symphony offers $25 terrace seats, where you can sit right behind the musicians and see the conductor's expressions. At the San Francisco Opera, rush tickets are available for as low as $28 from 11am to midnight the day before the performance, or until sold out – register to be notified when they're available. There are also 200 standing-room tickets ($10; cash only) for mainstage opera performances, which are for the rear orchestra or rear balcony. Tickets go on sale the day of each performance, starting at 10am.

(continued from p56)
month. Why not ride all three lines in a day? The longest part may be waiting at turnarounds, which are more crowded than hopping on mid-route. The upside to the wait is that riders get to watch staff manually turn the cars around on wooden platforms. It's hard work, but seasoned operators make light of it.

Riding north–south up and down the hills on both the **Powell-Hyde** and **Powell–Mason** lines, you'll pass downtown's skyscrapers, the tiled storefronts of **Chinatown**, Nob Hill's **Grace Cathedral** (p75) and end at bayfront **Fisherman's Wharf**. Most visitors stick to these lines, but there's a third line that tends to be less crowded – the east-west **California St** line, running from Market St downtown to Van Ness Ave via Chinatown and Nob Hill.

See the Giants Play to Win

Root for the home team

The official home of the San Francisco Giants is **Oracle Park** *(mlb.com/giants; tickets $16-200),* which hosts events year-round. Baseball season typically runs late March through September, and the park opens 90 to 120 minutes before games, which last about three hours – bring sun protection and a jacket. Crowd-pleasing food options inside the park include **Doggie Diner** hot dogs, **Crazy Crab'z** crab sandwiches, **Tony's Pizza** and **Rah Rah Ramen**.

Shout Encore at the Opera

See divas at their best

Cheer for **San Francisco Opera** *(sfopera.com; tickets from $10)* premieres of original works, including Grammy-winning *The (R) Evolution of Steve Jobs*, Pulitzer Prize–winner Nilo Cruz's *El Último Sueño de Frida y Diego (Frida and Diego's Last Dream)* and Tony Award–winner David Henry Hwang's *The Monkey King*. For modern revivals of classics like *Carmen*, Eun Sung Kim's bold musical direction is matched by spectacular sets and couture costumes.

Hit High Notes at the Symphony

Enjoy the San Francisco Symphony

Hold onto your seat: the Grammy-winning **San Francisco Symphony** *(sfsymphony.org; tickets from $25)* is here to delight and surprise. Symphony programs combine classics like Beethoven, Shostakovich and Mozart, with newer works by John Adams, Xavier Muzik and Gabriella Smith. Always innovating,
(continued on p63)

EATING DOWNTOWN: LUNCH

Dabao Singapore: Emily Lim's Singapore-style hawker stall serves favorites like seafood laksa (spicy noodles). *11am-3.30pm Tue-Thu, to 7pm Fri-Sun* $

Yank Sing: Upscale, classic dim sum served steaming from a rolling cart. *11am-3pm Tue-Fri, from 10am Sat & Sun* $$$

Delarosa Downtown: Consistently excellent Roman-style pizzas pair with Italian spritzes. *11.30am-9.30pm Sun-Thu, to 10.30pm Fri & Sat* $$

Bini's Kitchen: Chef and owner Bini Pradhan inspired SF's cravings for Nepalese *momos* (dumplings) – the turkey and chicken *momos* pop. *11am-3pm* $$

TOP EXPERIENCE

Asian Art Museum

Travel across Asia without ever leaving San Francisco at the Asian Art Museum, surrounded by 18,000 artworks spanning 6000 years. Ground-floor galleries showcase contemporary artists from across the Asian diaspora, and new works interact with timeless masterpieces in upper-floor permanent collections.

ERIC BRODER VAN DYKE/SHUTTERSTOCK

Permanent Collection

Explore one of the most comprehensive collections of Asian art outside Asia from the top floor down, loosely following the path of Buddhism throughout Asia. Start with third-floor collections spanning Persian ceramics, Sikh paintings, South Indian temple sculpture, Javanese shadow puppets, Tibetan mandalas and the museum's beloved unofficial mascot: a 3000-year-old Chinese bronze rhinoceros. The second floor covers 6000-year-old Japanese earthenware, prized Korean moon jars, Chinese scrolls and a minimalist contemporary alcove for meditation.

East West Bank Art Terrace

Second-floor East West Bank Art Terrace is the largest rooftop art terrace in the US (7500 sq ft), featuring large-scale sculptures like Thai artist Pinaree Sanpitak's *Breast Stupa Topiary*, evoking Buddhist domes and the female form. Outdoor 2nd-floor Sun Family Art Terrace Cafe serves weekend afternoon snacks, wine and beer.

Special Exhibits

Ground-floor galleries feature traveling exhibits and special shows focusing on Asian American and Pacific Islander artists from across the Asian diaspora. Recent shows include video artist Yuan Goang-Ming's *Everyday War*, an immersive exhibit about pervasive violence in pop culture, and Sparsh Ahuja's and Sam Dalrymple's *Project Dastaan*, a collection of personal narratives about the impact of the 1947 partition of India and Pakistan.

TOP TIPS

- First-floor Asian Box cafe offers fast-casual, Vietnamese-inspired, locally sourced fare.
- Check the event calendar for upcoming artist talks, concerts and cookbook release parties.
- The Cha May Ching Museum Boutique has museum-exclusive prints, gifts and a kids section.

PRACTICALITIES

- asianart.org
- Adult/senior/student/child $20/17/14/free free first Sun
- 10am-5pm Fri-Mon, 1pm-8pm Thu

TOP EXPERIENCE

Ferry Building

The 1898 Ferry Building is now San Francisco's locavore landmark, featuring the Bay Area's standout restaurants and artisanal food purveyors. Score extra treats on Ferry Plaza Farmers Market days year-round – especially on Saturday, when the farmers market has more than 100 vendors.

BENJAMINHEATH/LONELY PLANET

Bakery, Ferry Building

TOP TIPS

- Bring sunscreen and patience: lines for popular vendors can be a 10- to 30-minute wait.
- Cash is the preferred payment method for many farmers market vendors. ATMs are inside the Ferry Building.

PRACTICALITIES

- ferrybuilding marketplace.com
- 7am-8pm
- Farmers market 10am-2pm Tue & Thu, 8am-2pm Sat

Ferry Building Marketplace

The Ferry Building's stately 240ft-tall clock tower was overshadowed by a freeway overpass until it was damaged in the 1989 Loma Prieta earthquake – and San Franciscans realized the bayfront views they'd been missing. After a four-year restoration, the building was relaunched as SF's monument to food: the Ferry Building Marketplace, showcasing SF's bounty of local, artisanal food. While vendors change, local staples like **Humphry Slocombe** ice cream, **Acme Bread Company** and **Far West Fungi** have held steady. Stop for breakfast at **Ocean Malasada Company** and **Red Bay Coffee**, lunch at **Peaches Patties**, happy hour at **Hog Island Oyster Company** and Cambodian dinners at **Lunette**.

Ferry Plaza Farmers Market

In addition to ready-made food inside the Marketplace, the **Ferry Plaza Farmers Market** run by nonprofit Foodwise takes place outside of the building three times a week – adding even more must-try foods to the checklist. Up to 25 vendors line up in the front of the building on Tuesday and Thursday. California's bounty is showcased at the Saturday market, hosting more than 100 vendors at booths that wrap around the front and south sides, attracting up to 25,000 visitors weekly.

(continued from p60)
the Symphony celebrates Día de los Muertos with Latin American orchestras, collaborates with music legends like Metallica and performs live with screenings of films like *Black Panther*.

Get Mesmerized by the Ballet

See prima ballerinas twirl

San Francisco Ballet *(sfballet.org)* is the country's oldest ballet company, founded in 1933 and still looking sharp in more than 100 shows annually at Civic Center's War Memorial Opera House. The season runs from December through May, with a vast repertoire that ranges from modern originals to the holiday classic *The Nutcracker*, which premiered here in 1944. Score rush tickets 48 hours ahead of showtime online *($35–79)* or $10 standing-room tickets at the box office, which opens four hours before curtain.

Catch Live Shows in the Theater District

See breakthrough acts in historic venues

Curtains are rising across San Francisco's **Theater District**. Touring smash-hit musicals like *Wicked* and *Mean Girls* play the historic **Curran**, **Golden Gate** and **Orpheum** theaters (ticketing & calendars at *broadwaysf.com*). **American Conservatory Theater** *(ACT; act-sf.org)* launches original works by major playwrights, from Tony Kushner's *Angels in America* to Kristina Wong's Pulitzer Prize–nominated *Sweatshop Overlord*. For laughs, hit **Punch Line** *(punchlinecomedyclub.com)*, which launched comedians from Robin Williams to Ali Wong. Music headliners play the baroque former bordello **Great American Music Hall** *(gamh.com)*, grand **Bill Graham Civic Auditorium** *(billgrahamcivic.com)*, rock-legendary **Warfield** *(thewarfieldtheatre.com)*, mid-century-mod **Masonic Auditorium** *(sfmasonic.com)*, and Prohibition-era speakeasy **August Hall** *(augusthallsf.com)*. SF's West Coast cool creds are restored at SF jazz clubs **Black Cat** *(blackcatsf.com)*, **Mr Tipple's Recording Studio** *(mrtipplessf.com)* and 1946-vintage **Dawn Club** *(dawnclub.com)*. Think you've seen it all? Not until you've hit an **Aunt Charlie's** drag show *(auntcharlieslounge.com)*.

Clubbing in SoMa

Hit SF's weekend nightlife hub

Dance parties rage in the club zone around 11th and Folsom Sts, usually going to midnight or 1am on weeknights, and 2am or

WHY I LOVE THE TENDERLOIN

Eric Ehler is chef and owner of Outta Sight Pizza. *(@intheweedz)*

As a local foodie, chef and art lover, I've been visiting and working in the Tenderloin for years. What drew me in was the eclectic urban feel that makes you feel like you're in a city – great restaurants, galleries and people. It's home to folks that are SF's heart and soul, keeping the city going from behind the scenes. Today, the focal point is the UN Plaza, where a world-class skate park is now located. You can watch a local skate like they're in the X-Games, and then go to the farmer's market. Truly a special experience. Truly San Francisco.

EATING IN CIVIC CENTER: DINNERTIME

¡Chao Pescao!: Colorful Cuban-Colombian restaurant serving deep-fried empanadas and signature salty-sour Tajín-fried chicken. *11.30am-8.30pm Tue-Sat* $$

Brenda's French Soul Food: Comforting, rich gumbo and ube beignets by queer Filipina Creole chef Brenda Buenviaje. *8am-8pm Wed-Mon, to 3pm Tue* $$

Azalina's: The breakout food star of the former Twitter building offers Malaysian fine dining, with an affordable $89 five-course tasting menu. *5-10pm Wed-Sat* $$$

Outta Sight Pizza: Grab a slice or commit to a 'hella mortadella' pie or mega-meatball sandwich on ciabatta with craft beer or wine. *11am-9pm* $

THE TENDER LEATHER HEART OF SF

SoMa's Leather and LGBTQ Cultural District has been a hub for leather culture since the 1960s, when local bars boosted business by opening for gay Sunday 'tea dances.' By the 1970s, SoMa had dozens of gay bars, bookstores, restaurants, bath houses and other LGBTQ+ spaces. When the AIDS epidemic hit, SoMa venues adopted safe sex protocols that set global standards for prevention. Today, the district includes legacy LGBTQ+ businesses and new venues that keep queer culture alive and evolving. Since 1984, Folsom Street Fair has been advocating for LGBTQ+ liberation and supporting the AIDS Emergency Fund. The District remains resilient – San Francisco wouldn't be San Francisco without it.

LET GO MEDIA/SHUTTERSTOCK

Orpheum Theatre (p63)

later on weekends. **Cat Club** is urban-legendary for New Wave nights, **Butter** serves rock anthems with soda-pop cocktails, and **DNA Lounge** hosts 18+ dance parties, from goth Death Guild to Latin house. After-hours **EndUp** has hosted gay Sunday tea dances since 1973, and **Halcyon** bumps to techno til dawn. **F8** ranges from hip-hop to dubstep, **Monarch** features multiple DJs with different vibes, and **1015 Folsom** packs out for EDM DJs and hip-hop across five dance floors.

Play in the Leather & LGBTQ Cultural District

Come out to LGBTQ+ bars and clubs

Come out to play in SoMa's **Leather & LGBTQ Cultural District**, SF's legendary queer and kink party hub and home to September's half-million-strong leather street party: **Folsom Street Fair**. At summer spinoff **Up Your Alley Fair**, the sun shines where it usually doesn't in Dore Alley. Both fairs are 18+; request consent and play safe with handy resources, including mpox-vax booths.

For kicks between fairs, drag club **Oasis** mounts outrageous shows and co-op **The Stud** hosts raucous events. **Lone Star Saloon** makes manly men warm and fuzzy at bear happy hour, **Hole in the Wall** draws gay bikers, shirtless gym queens throng **Powerhouse**, and wearing less is more at **SF Eagle**'s all-you-can-drink beer busts.

EATING DOWNTOWN: DESTINATION DINING

Kin Khao: Stellar Californian Thai cuisine with seasonal flair, such as slow-cooked local rabbit in green curry. *11.30am-2pm & 5.30-9pm Tue-Sun* $$$

Kaiyō Restaurant: Go for Nikkei (Japanese Peruvian) cuisine like matcha fettuccine, plus miso pisco cocktails. *5-10pm Mon-Thu, to 11pm Fri & Sat, to 9pm Sun* $$

Rooh: 'Progressive Indian' with seasonal ingredients, including saucy chili garlic crab and dahi puri semolina puffs with avocado. *5-9.30pm Sun-Thu, to 10pm Fri & Sat* $$

Benu: Chef Corey Lee's acclaimed contemporary Californian Asian cuisine is a multicourse celebration of the land and ocean that connect us. *5.30-9.30pm Tue-Sat* $$$

Chinatown & North Beach

COME FOR DINNER, STAY FOR STORIES

Grant St connects San Francisco's historic Chinese and Italian neighborhoods. Over 175 years, these neighbors have swapped epic stories of immigrant ingenuity, radical ideas, daring art and resilience against all odds.

Under Chinatown's pagoda roofs, you'll find noodles, rare teas, temples and Chinese orchestras, just like in the Gold Rush days – but you'll also find the future, with cutting-edge contemporary art, trend-setting restaurants and a packed calendar of cultural events. Wild parrots in North Beach treetops mimic the chatter at local bohemian bars and Italian cafes, serving enough espresso to fuel the next major poetry movement at free speech landmark City Lights.

Whether you're craving Peking duck, pizza or Peking duck pizza, you're definitely in the right place – stick around afterward for breakthrough comedy, raucous punk shows, Cantonese opera and West Coast cool jazz.

GETTING AROUND

Walking is the best way to see scenic Chinatown and North Beach. From downtown or Fisherman's Wharf, take the Powell-Mason or the Powell-Hyde cable car line to Chinatown and North Beach. The California St cable car passes through the southern end of Chinatown. The T metro line links Chinatown and North Beach to downtown and Dogpatch. Key bus routes are 1, 12, 30, 39 and 45.

TOP TIP

There's public parking underneath Portsmouth Sq *(to/after 5pm $4/8 per hour; per day $38)* and at Good Luck Parking Garage *(sfmta.com; $5/hr)*.

Time-Travel at the Chinese Historical Society of America

Follow epic tales inside a living landmark

Picture what it was like to be Chinese in America during California's Gold Rush, the Chinese exclusion era (1870–1943)

EATING IN CHINATOWN: CLASSIC DIM SUM

Good Mong Kok: Chinatown's busiest counter, where shrimp dumplings, pork siu mai and other classics are offered in takeout boxes. *7am-6pm* $

Hang Ah Tea Room: Century-old menus adorn Chinatown's original dim sum hotspot, serving purse dumplings, pillowy pork buns and custard bao. *10.30am-8pm* $$

Dim Sum Bistro: Don't let unconvincing food photos and bargain prices deter you from high-quality takeout, including tender shrimp and chive dumplings. *8am-3pm* $

Today Food: Witness dumpling mastery: dough rolled until translucent, loaded with veggies, shrimp and chicken, pinched and pan-fried or steamed to enjoy. *8am-8pm* $

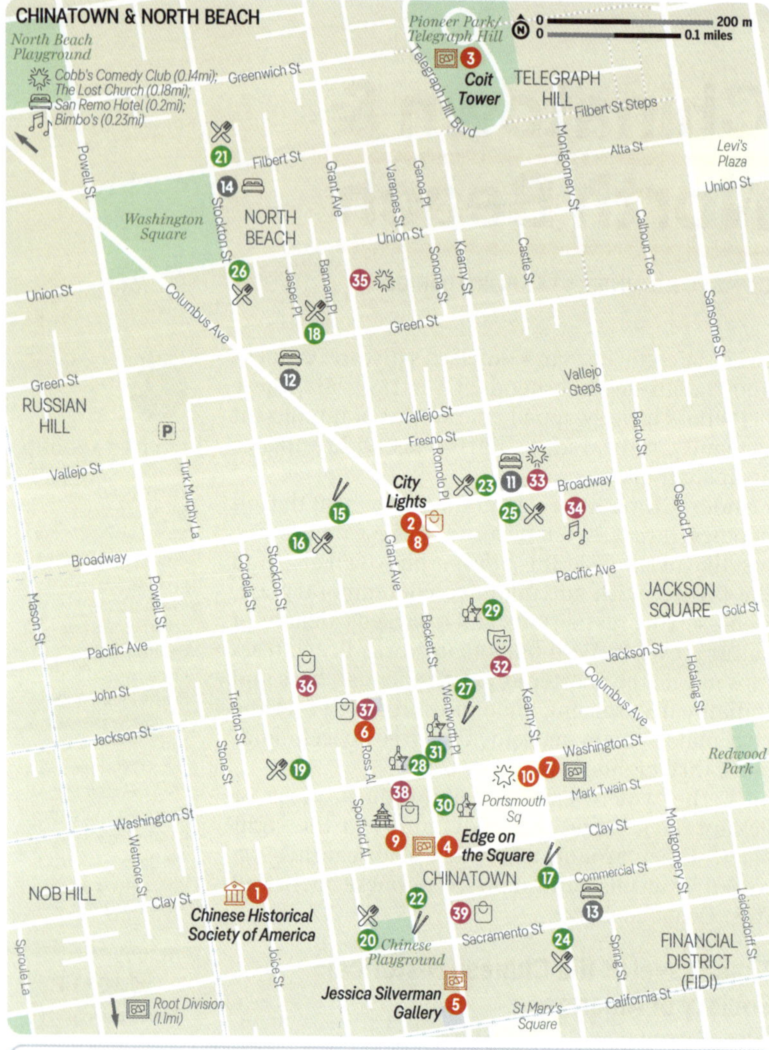

HIGHLIGHTS

1 Chinese Historical Society of America
2 City Lights
3 Coit Tower
4 Edge on the Square
5 Jessica Silverman Gallery

SIGHTS

6 41 Ross Alley
7 Chinese Culture Center
8 Jack Kerouac Alley
9 Tin How Temple

ACTIVITIES

10 Chinatown Alleyway Tours

SLEEPING

11 Green Tortoise Hostel
12 Hotel Bohème
13 Pacific Tradewinds Hostel
14 Washington Square Inn

EATING

15 China Live
16 Dim Sum Bistro
17 Four Kings
18 Golden Boy
19 Good Mong Kok
20 Hang Ah Tea Room
21 Liguria Bakery
22 Mister Jiu's
23 Osmanthus Dim Sum Lounge
24 Today Food
25 Tommaso's
26 Tony's Pizza Napoletana
27 Z & Y

DRINKING & NIGHTLIFE

28 Buddha Lounge
29 Comstock Saloon
30 Empress at Boon Lounge
31 Li Po

ENTERTAINMENT

32 Great Star Theater
33 Keys Jazz Bistro
34 Mabuhay Gardens
35 Savoy Tivoli

SHOPPING

36 Dong Hing Supermarket
37 Golden Gate Fortune Cookies
38 On Waverly
39 Wok Shop

and SF's hippie heyday at the **Chinese Historical Society of America** *(chsa.org; adult/student/child $12/10/5)*, built as Chinatown's YWCA by Hearst Castle architect Julia Morgan. Exhibits in this 1932 landmark spotlight Chinese American culture, from WWII Chinatown nightclub posters to Bruce Lee's martial arts costumes and philosophy library.

Change Your Outlook in Chinatown Galleries

Glimpse the future in the making

Up the block from historic Portsmouth Square is **Edge on the Square** *(edgeonthesquare.org; free)*, Chinatown's cutting-edge cultural hub and arts center. Drop in for fresh takes on current topics with impactful shows like 'All Eyes On Us: Invention & Ingenuity During Artistic Diasporas.' No one is a stranger or spectator here – the art invites you to leave your mark, and music and dance pull you into the groove. Edge events blend art, community and joy, from Chinatown Pride celebrations to live chef demos exploring Asian American identity through food.

Atop the pedestrian bridge spanning Kearny St, a mosaic sun graces the steps to the **Chinese Culture Center** *(cccsf.us; free)*. This landmark art center on the Hilton's 3rd floor has expanded artistic horizons since 1965, sparking conversations through bold collaborations with contemporary Chinese artists from the mainland and across the diaspora.

Visit the Center's satellite gallery at **41 Ross Alley** *(41ross.org; free)*, and gain deeper understanding of the local art scene on the Center's **Chinatown History and Art Walking Tours** *(1½ to two hours; four-person minimum; $45 per person)*.

Between international art fairs, contemporary art stars converge at the **Jessica Silverman Gallery** *(jessicasilverman gallery.com; free)*. Beyond frosted glass doors lie stunning parallel universes, featuring Ruby Tut's cosmic gardeners, Judy Chicago's world-birthing quilts and David Huffman's history-repairing Traumanauts.

Go Gourmet in Chinatown

Collect secret ingredients, tools and tips

Stockton St is a gourmet dream, lined with dim-sum takeout joints like **Good Mong Kok** (p65) and grocers like **Dong Hing Supermarket** selling gourmet condiments. If you've scored

CHINATOWN'S CONTEMPORARY ARTS SCENE

Candace Huey is head curator at **Edge on the Square** and co-chair of SFMOMA's SECA prize council.

At Edge on the Square, we celebrate Chinatown as an immigrant gateway and a touchstone for Asian American experience. Our programs are free and family-friendly, and expand what it means to be American. The Chinese Historical Society of America bridges past and present, and the **Center for Asian American Media Film Festival** launches new voices. Great Star Theater (p72) introduces younger audiences to Cantonese opera, and On Waverly (p68) curates Asian American authors and artists. Independent nonprofits like Southern Exposure (p97), Gray Area (p91) and Root Division give artists space to explore.

EATING IN CHINATOWN: FAMILY-STYLE FEASTS

Mister Jiu's: Brandon Jew's acclaimed Californian Chinese banquets feature lamb with plum sauce and roast Sonoma duck. *5-9pm Tue & Wed, to 10pm Thu-Sat* $$$

Z & Y: Spicy banquets guaranteed to make faces shine: Sichuan pork dumplings, flaming cauliflower and chili-oil-poached fish. *11.30am-3pm & 4.30-9pm Wed-Sun* $$

Osmanthus Dim Sum Lounge: Gourmet rule-breaker adds brandy to blistered beans, spinach to shitake dumplings and *pu-erh* tea to Old Fashioneds. *10.30am-8pm* $$

China Live: George Chen showcases modern Chinese dishes including kumquat-glazed Peking duck, plus top-notch tea and cocktails. *noon-9pm Mon-Fri, 4-9pm Sat & Sun* $$

TOP EXPERIENCE

Chinatown Alleyways

Chinatown's 41 historic alleyways have seen it all since 1849: gold rushes and revolution, incense and opium, fire and icy receptions. Local and national exclusion laws restricting Chinese immigration, employment and housing lasted for 73 years – but the community held its ground. Today, Chinatown's alleyways are cultural touchstones and places of possibility, through art, mutual aid and shared celebrations.

ADELE HEIDENREICH/SHUTTERSTOCK

TOP TIPS

- Teenage historians guide epic two-hour nonprofit **Chinatown Alleyway Tours** *(chinatownalleywaytours.org; adult/student/child $50/20/10)*, covering Sun Yat-sen's revolutionary plotting at 36 Spofford Alley to martial-artist Bruce Lee breaking down racial barriers.
- Respect people's privacy in their homes and workplaces when taking photographs.

PRACTICALITIES

- Free
- Between Grant Ave, Stockton St, California St & Broadway

Waverly Place

Through earthquakes, world wars and Prohibition gunfights, Waverly Place changed the culture around it. You'll spot the flag-festooned balcony of **Tin How Temple** *(9.30am-3pm Fri-Wed)*, where prayers have been offered since 1852 – even after the 1906 earthquake and fire, when altars were still smoldering. To pay your respects, follow sandalwood-incense aromas upstairs. Entry is free but offerings customary; no photography inside. Readers may remember Waverly as the namesake of one of the narrators in Amy Tan's novel *The Joy Luck Club*, and find new favorites at **On Waverly** *(onwaverly.com)*, which showcases Asian American authors and artists.

Ross Alley

You might recognize colorful **Ross Alley** from its cameos in ho-hum Hollywood blockbusters – *The Karate Kid Part II*, *The Pursuit of Happyness* – and its star turns in indie gems like *Who Is Michael Jang?* and *Chan Is Missing*. Stop by the Chinese Culture Center's contemporary art shows at **41 Ross** *(41ross.org; free)*, then seek your fortune at **Golden Gate Fortune Cookies** *(goldengatefortunecookies.com)*, where cookies are stamped from vintage presses, just as they were in 1909, when fortune cookies were invented in San Francisco.

reservations at wildly popular **Four Kings** *(itsfourkings.com; book 29 days in advance)*, you can savor ingeniously reinvented Chinatown classics, like Sichuan peppercorn-spiked mapo spaghetti.

At **China Live** (p67; *chinalivesf.com*), browse the gourmet shop while you wait for chef George Chen's modern Chinese feasts. Get equipped to make five-star meals at the **Wok Shop** *(wokshop.com)*, where owner Tane Chan jokes that she's sold 'woks for all walks of life' since the 1970s.

Celebrate Lunar New Year

Welcome spring with celebrations

Chinatown celebrates Lunar New Year for a month, with **night markets** *(bechinatown.weebly.com)* along lantern-lit Grant Ave. Stock up on lucky bamboo, red envelopes and miniature mandarin trees. Chase the 200ft dragon, legions of lion dancers and fierce tiny-tot martial artists at the **Chinese New Year Parade** *(chineseparade.com)*.

By the end of the night, everyone's happy and hoarse from exchanging best wishes for prosperity: *Gung hay fat choy!* (Cantonese) or *Gōng xǐ fā cái!* (Mandarin).

Rock Out in North Beach

Catch live shows at iconic underground venues

You're right on time for the revival of legendary North Beach clubs. **Bimbo's** *(bimbos365club.com)* is an iconic 1931 speakeasy known for danceable indie bands (Zap Mama, Dandy Warhols) and marquee talent (Adele, Van Morrison, Lizzo).

Keys Jazz Bistro *(keysjazzbistro.com)* features rotating residencies by international jazz talents and raucous classics by SF's Jazz Mafia. Punk's not dead at **Mabuhay Gardens** – the 1970s Filipino supperclub that took a chance on loud local acts, including the Dead Kennedys and an unsigned Metallica.

At quaint, mural-lined 1907 **Savoy Tivoli** *(savoytivoli.com)*, the tiny stage that survived earth-shaking shows by the Ramones, Muddy Waters and SF drag phenomenon Beach Blanket Babylon, is reinforced – ready when you are.

GRANT AVENUE'S BRILLIANT NEON

Grant Avenue became America's brightest street 100 years ago, as part of Chinatown's brilliant redesign. After the 1906 earthquake, developers schemed to push Chinatown outside SF, on the pretext that this thoroughfare was a red-light strip – never mind that white landlords profited. Savvy Chinatown leaders led by Look Tin Eli lobbied to rename shady DuPont St 'Grant Avenue,' and consulted architects to design its modern, pagoda-roofed Chinatown deco style. Dim lanterns were replaced with dazzling neon and dragon-wrapped street lamps. The image overhaul worked like a charm: photographers, partiers and celebrities flocked here, establishing neon-lit **Li Po** and **Buddha Lounge** as signature SF attractions.

DRINKING IN CHINATOWN: ICONIC BARS

Li Po: Enter the 1937 faux-grotto doorway for baiju-spiked mai tais under the Buddha. Brusque bartenders, cellar bathrooms, random dance-offs. *2pm-1.30am*

Comstock Saloon: Authentic Wild West saloon, complete with the trough where cowboys once relieved themselves. Cocktails remain potent. *4pm-midnight Tue-Sat*

Buddha Lounge: The vintage neon Buddha promises dangerously enlightening nights, featuring an eclectic jukebox. *1pm-2am*

Empress at Boon Lounge: Chinatown's 1966 landmark is crowned by this swanky octagonal lounge, featuring top-shelf cocktails and Cantonese bites. *5-10pm Mon-Sat*

TOP EXPERIENCE

Coit Tower

The exclamation mark atop Telegraph Hill is Coit Tower, dedicated to SF first responders by firefighting millionaire Lillie Hitchcock Coit, who raised eyebrows in the 1860s for smoking cigars, gambling, drinking and wearing men's gear like other firefighters. The 1930s lobby murals celebrating workers were initially denounced as communist, but are now landmarked.

RIGUCCI/SHUTTERSTOCK

TOP TIPS

- For a parrot's-eye panoramic view of San Francisco, take the creaky 1930s elevator to the tower's open-air **viewing platform**.
- For a challenge, hike up 13 flights of stairs to the Viewing Platform.

PRACTICALITIES

- sfrecpark.org
- Elevator adult/student/child $10/7/3
- Mural tour from $5
- 10am-6pm Apr-Oct, to 5pm Nov-Mar

Secret Treasures in the Stairwell

Book a tour up the narrow 2nd-floor **stairwell,** where recently revealed murals were hidden for 80 years. The seven murals show San Francisco in the 1930s – the showstopper is Jane Berlandina's strikingly modern egg-tempera mural *Home Life*, showing San Franciscans baking pies and kicking back.

Lobby Murals

Publicly funded **1930s lobby murals** show what daily life was like here during the Depression: San Franciscans organized dockworkers' unions, lined up at soup kitchens, partied despite Prohibition and read books – including Marxist manifestos – in Chinese, Italian and English. When they were completed in 1934, the artworks were so controversial that the opening of the tower was delayed by censors. Authorities called the 26 artists that painted them communists and demanded that radical elements be removed. The artists refused, and in a last-minute compromise, park employees painted over a hammer-and-sickle symbol in a union logo. Public opinion overruled the censors: San Franciscans embraced the murals as symbols of the city's openness. In 2012 voters passed a measure to preserve them as historic landmarks, and today the murals are freshly restored – and as bold as ever.

TOP EXPERIENCE

City Lights

Free spirits and free speech have found refuge at City Lights since 1957. Words were dangerous business back in the '50s, when library books were often banned, Hollywood screenwriters were blacklisted and comedians got arrested for swearing in North Beach nightclubs – but poet Lawrence Ferlinghetti founded City Lights Books anyway.

BENJAMINHEATH/LONELY PLANET

'A Kind of Library Where Books Are Sold'

As Ferlinghetti's hand-lettered sign says, idle browsing is highly encouraged. Wax poetic in the upstairs Poetry Room, load up on 'zines on the mezzanine and entertain radical ideas downstairs in the Pedagogies of Resistance section. On the main floor, City Lights publications include titles by Angela Davis, Diane di Prima and Noam Chomsky, proving the point on another of Ferlinghetti's signs: 'Printer's Ink Is the Greater Explosive.'

Poetry Room

City Lights' affordable Pocket Poets series brought poetry to the people, sparking the Beat poetry movement. Number four was Allen Ginsberg's epic *Howl and Other Poems* (1956), an instant sensation that got Ferlinghetti and City Lights manager Shigeyoshi Murao arrested for publishing poetry with homoerotic content. They fought charges of publishing obscenity not on technicalities but on artistic merits, and won a landmark free speech victory. Celebrate your freedom to read freely in the upstairs Poetry Room overlooking **Jack Kerouac Alley**, in the designated **Poet's Chair** with your choice of 60 Pocket Poets books – including *Howl,* available in 24 languages.

TOP TIP

- Duck into Jack Kerouac alley, a poetry-paved shortcut between Chinatown and North Beach.
- Visit Kerouac's favorite haunts: City Lights, neighboring Vesuvio and a stool by the golden Buddha at Li Po (p69) – he was a true believer in literature, Buddhism and beer.

PRACTICALITIES

- citylights.com
- 10am-10pm daily
- Free

THE OTHER BROADWAY

When San Franciscans reminisce about Broadway shows, they're not talking about Disney musicals. North Beach's Broadway strip has seen it all since the 1930s: the nation's first openly lesbian bar (Mona's, 1936), dedicated drag venue (Finocchio's, 1936), uncensored comedy acts (Jazz Workshop, 1961), topless strip club (Condor Club, 1964), and unionized strip club (Lusty Lady, 1997). Some shows here actually changed history: Carol Doda was arrested for going topless but won her case, and Lenny Bruce was arrested and acquitted of obscenity charges. SF Broadway shows continue to push buttons and boundaries, honoring almost a century of fearless performers.

JON BILOUS/ALAMY

Great Star Theater

Catch North Beach Comedy

See bold, breakthrough standup acts

Comedy and drag acts have packed North Beach clubs since the 1930s – comedian Lenny Bruce got arrested here for cursing in 1961 and won a landmark free speech victory. Today **Bimbo's** (p69) and **Cobb's Comedy Club** keep launching and relaunching careers – John Oliver, Mo Amer, Michelle Wolf – at cozy showcases with a two-drink minimum *(18+; tickets from $25)*. At tiny nonprofit **The Lost Church** *(thelostchurch.org)* and Chinatown's **Great Star Theater**, comics work up material for **SF Sketchfest** *(sfsketchfest.com)* – you saw it here first.

EATING IN NORTH BEACH: PIZZA AND FOCACCIA

Liguria Bakery: Bleary-eyed rockers and Italian grandmothers queue by 8am for cinnamon-raisin focaccia hot from the 100-year-old oven. Takeout only. *7am-noon Tue-Sat* $

Tony's Pizza Napoletana: Pizza-slinger champ Tony Gemignani ends coastal rivalries with Jersey tomato pies and Cal-Italia pizza. *noon-9.30pm Mon-Thu, to 11pm Fri-Sun* $$

Golden Boy: Punks have politely queued since 1978 for the Sodini's focaccia-crust pizza – try clam-and-garlic slices. Takeout only. *11.30am-9pm Sun-Thu, to 11pm Fri-Sat* $

Tommaso's: Charming North Beach since 1935 with wood-fired brick-oven Neapolitan pizza, cozy booths and communal tables. *5-10.30pm Tue-Sat, 4-9.30pm Sun* $$

Nob Hill & Russian Hill

VIEWS FROM SUCH GREAT HEIGHTS

Summit San Francisco's twin downtown hills and you'll discover everyone's heads are in the clouds up here – billionaires and penniless poets, rock stars and rock-star chefs, urban hikers and spiritual seekers. There's no getting around these peaks if you really want to see the city – Nob Hill stands between downtown and Chinatown, and Russian Hill rises between North Beach and Fisherman's Wharf. But first you have to get here: hop a cable car or brave a stairway hike. Towering above Union Sq, 'Snob Hill' has stunning views from grand hotels and Grace Cathedral. To its west is Russian Hill, with boutiques, restaurants and bars along Polk Gulch – San Francisco's historic 'gayborhood' before the Castro. Consider permission granted to follow your bliss – hop off a cable car, head to tiki bar happy hour, hear a cathedral organ recital or just watch the Bay Bridge lights twinkle. Your peak San Francisco experience awaits.

GETTING AROUND

The Powell-Hyde cable car line serves Russian and Nob Hills; Powell-Mason serves Nob Hill; and California runs from downtown through Chinatown and over Nob Hill to Van Ness Ave. Don't drive here if you can avoid it – the gradients from 24 to 31.5% are not good for your brakes or your blood pressure.

See How Cable Cars Work

Look behind the scenes at the Cable Car Museum

Hop off the Powell-Hyde or Powell-Mason cable car at Powell and Washington to see steampunk technology at work inside the **Cable Car Museum** *(cablecarmuseum.org; free)*. Check out a vintage car from inventor Andrew Hallidie's original 1873 fleet, then head downstairs to see the heart of the operation: eight giant spinning sheaves (grooved wheels) that propel the cable, guiding the cars along their routes.

TOP TIP

Find a west-facing bench at George Sterling Park to watch late-afternoon fog tumble over the Golden Gate Bridge. Alternatively, climb Filbert St to Vallejo Street Steps to see the Oakland hills glitter with sunsets.

DRINKING ON NOB HILL: CLASSIC BARS

Tonga Room: Tonight's weather forecast: foggy with 100% chance of typhoons every 20 minutes inside this 1943 tiki bar. *5-10pm Wed & Thu, to 11pm Fri & Sat*

Stookey's Club Moderne: Step up to the 1930s chrome-edged bar, where white-jacketed bartenders shake Corpse Reviver cocktails in time with jazz combos. *5pm-2am*

Top of the Mark: Toast sunsets with martinis at the sky-high 1939 piano lounge atop Mark Hopkins Hotel. *4-11 Sun-Thu, 3pm-12.30am Fri & Sat*

Summer Place: Inside windowless rock walls, happy hour unfolds nightly with seasonal cocktails and neighborly vibes. *2pm-2am Mon-Fri, from noon Sat & Sun*

BACKGROUND

The Rise, Fall, and Rise of SF Cable Cars

Carnival rides can't compare to cable cars, San Francisco's vintage 1873 public transit. The idea came to inventor Andrew Hallidie after witnessing a horse carriage struggle uphill – and come crashing downhill. Such accidents were considered inevitable, but Hallidie knew better. If hemp-and-metal cable could haul ore out of California mines, it could transport San Franciscans uphill. Skeptical city planners granted Hallidie three months to launch his 'wire-rope railway.' Four hours after the deadline, Hallidie completed a downhill test-run. His cable car was a non-runaway success: by the 1890s, 53 miles of track crisscrossed SF.

But as other cities modernized, San Francisco's wooden trolleys seemed quaint. In 1947, SF's mayor pushed to replace cable cars with buses, which he claimed were cheaper – not factoring in the costs of bus-exhaust pollution. But loyal rider Friedel Klussmann did the math: cable cars brought in more tourism dollars than they cost in upkeep. The mayor demanded a public vote – and lost to 'the Cable Car Lady' by a landslide.

Today, you can catch a cable car at Friedel Klussmann Memorial Turnaround. Novices slide into strangers' laps – no seat belts here – while regulars leap onto running boards, grab poles, and enjoy the ride. Women weren't allowed to ride running boards until 1965, when 19-year-old Mona Hutchins was arrested for breaking this bogus rule – and won her case for women to enjoy San Francisco to the fullest.

TOP EXPERIENCE

Grace Cathedral

San Francisco's Gothic hilltop cathedral took 40 years to complete, with stained glass windows celebrating science, art works honoring interfaith achievements and murals commemorating the 1906 earthquake and 1945 UN charter signing in SF. Locals light candles beneath Beniamino Bufano's smiling statue of the city's patron saint and in the Interfaith AIDS Memorial Chapel, featuring Keith Haring's bronze altarpiece.

DALTON JOHNSON/SHUTTERSTOCK

Science in Stained Glass

Among the 68 stained-glass windows lining the Cathedral are a dozen 'Human Endeavor' panes celebrating scientific achievements and social progress – look for Albert Einstein amid swirling nuclear particles, activist and Nobel Peace Prize–laureate Jane Addams and Supreme Court Justice Thurgood Marshall.

Interfaith AIDS Memorial Chapel & Keith Haring's Last Work

To the right of the entry. Grace's Interfaith AIDS Memorial Chapel features a bronze angel of compassion altarpiece by artist-activist Keith Haring – his final work before his 1990 death from AIDS. On the opposite wall hangs a section of the AIDS Memorial Quilt; beneath it is a Book of Remembrance.

Labyrinths & Events

People of all faiths wander indoor and outdoor inlaid-stone labyrinths, meant to guide restless souls through three spiritual stages: releasing, receiving and returning. Check the website for events, including spectacular choral performances (don't miss Bach's *Magnificat* at Easter) plus inclusive weekly spiritual events, such as Thursday Choral Evensong, yoga with live music ($20 to $30), sound baths and candlelit meditation services.

TOP TIPS

- There's no charge to enter if you're praying, attending services or lighting a candle.
- Sightseeing visits include a self-guided audio tour.

PRACTICALITIES

- gracecathedral.org
- Adult/senior & youth/child $12/10/free
- 10am-5pm Mon-Sat, from 1pm Sun

PEEKS FROM THE PEAKS

Climb stairways to staggering views along Vallejo steps, and wax poetic at Ina Coolbirth and George Sterling hilltop parks.

START	END	LENGTH
Vallejo Steps	Lombard Financial Center (Chase Bank)	from 2 miles; 1½ to 2½ hrs

Reach staggering heights with spectacular views along ❶ **Vallejo Street Steps** leading from North Beach toward hilltop ❷ **Ina Coolbrith Park**, named for California's first Poet Laureate. Pause to admire Bay views from the bench at Poet's Corner and you too may wax poetic.

Take the scenic route via steep stairs, past gravity-defying wooden cottages down to ❸ **Macondray Lane** – so charming, it looks like something from a novel. And it is: Armistead Maupin used this shady, hidden byway as the model for Barbary Lane in his *Tales of the City* series. Stop for an ice-cream break at ❹ **Swensen's** on Hyde and Union before you ascend Hyde toward Filbert St – San Francisco's steepest street, with a 31.5% grade and stellar views of North Beach churches and Coit Tower. One more block north on Hyde is ❺ **George Sterling Park**, where you'll find sweeping views toward the Golden Gate Bridge, overlooking the town poet George Sterling called 'the cool grey city of love.'

Finally, head downhill and west along Lombard St to mosaic-wrapped ❻ **Lombard Financial Center**, where California modernist Millard Sheets designed facade mosaics highlighting San Francisco history. During bank hours, head inside to admire floor-to-ceiling artwork by Sheets' studio.

Ina Coolbrith was a bohemian poet, editor and mentor – as well as the niece of Mormon prophet Joseph Smith.

Residents of **Macondray Lane** have green thumbs and a sense of humor. Recent garden sculptures include a family of stuffed jeans.

Japantown, Fillmore & Pacific Heights

POSTCARD-PERFECT VICTORIANS, WAVING KITTIES, MUSIC LEGENDS

The downhill sweep of Fillmore St leads from scenic hilltop parks and chic boutiques in Pacific Heights, through cultural and culinary TikTok hotspots in Japantown to buzzworthy restaurants and legendary music venues in the Fillmore – then uphill to Alamo Square's iconic Postcard Row. Don't let the quaint Victorians fool you: this neighborhood totally rocks. Japanese Americans have called this area home for over a century, and today Japantown is where J-pop stars and cosplay influencers shoot music videos in Peace Plaza. The Fillmore has been a nightlife hub since the jazzy 1930s and turned totally trippy in the psychedelic 1960s. Music legends still play live shows here. Hilltop Pacific Heights is ringed with mansions, many owned or once owned by powerful women – including nude model turned museum founder Alma Spreckels, 19th-century Black billionaire and Underground Railroad pioneer Mary Ellen Pleasant and former US House Speaker Nancy Pelosi.

TOP TIP

Every San Franciscan has a favorite Victorian. Find yours around Alamo Sq (from Golden Gate to Fell St, between Divisadero and Webster) and between Japantown's Sutter St and Jackson St in Pacific Heights. Multicolor 'Painted Lady' Victorians are irresistible photo-ops – but respect residents' privacy when taking photos.

Relax in Japantown Spas

Glow up and mellow out

Salt-scrub in the steam room, soak in the hot pool, take a cold plunge, reheat in the sauna, rinse and repeat at **Kabuki Springs & Spa** *(kabukisprings.com)*, Japantown's communal bathhouse. Men and women alternate days (cisgender and

(continued on p80)

GETTING AROUND

The 38 Geary bus will pick you up downtown and drop you right at Geary and Fillmore. Otherwise, you can hop the California cable-car line west to Van Ness Ave. From there, walk to Pacific Heights along Victorian-lined Sacramento St (one block north of California), detouring through lovely hilltop Lafayette Park. Then window-shop your way south along Fillmore St. At Post St, swing east to reach the Japan Center, or west to Pierce St, then walk south to Alamo Sq. Bus 22 helps you conquer neighborhood hills.

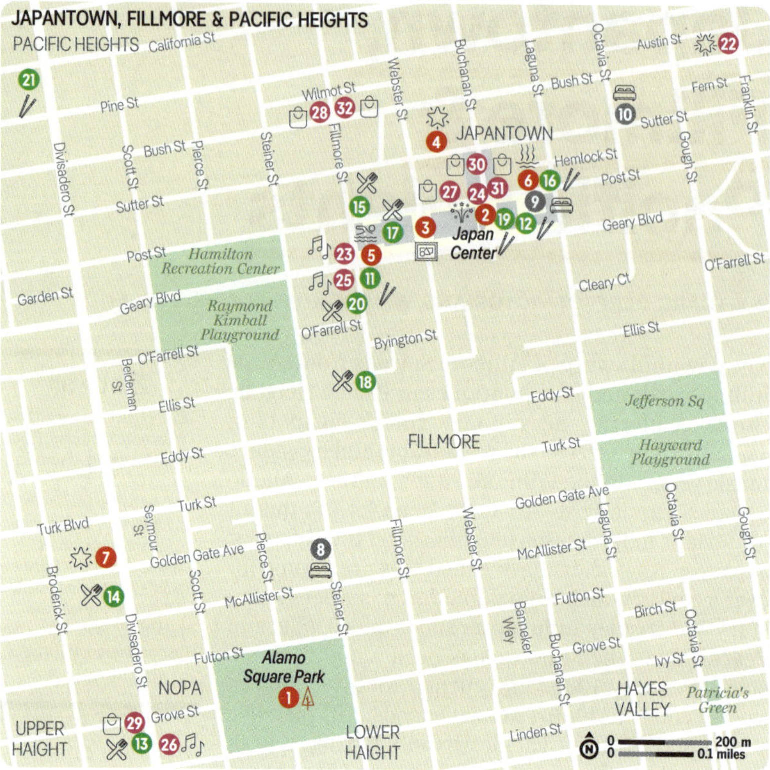

JAPANTOWN, FILLMORE & PACIFIC HEIGHTS

HIGHLIGHTS
1 Alamo Square Park
2 Japan Center

SIGHTS
3 Tokaido Arts

ACTIVITIES
4 Japanese Cultural & Community Center of Northern California (JCCCNC)
5 Kabuki Springs & Spa
6 Pearl Spa
7 Westside Cuts & Style

SLEEPING
8 Chateau Tivoli
9 Hotel Kabuki
10 Queen Anne Hotel

EATING
11 Aji Kiji
12 An Japanese Restaurant
13 Bar Crudo
14 Brenda's Meat & Three
15 Copra
16 Daeho Kalbijjim
17 Jina Bakes
see 17 Marufuku Ramen
18 Minnie Bell's Soul Movement
see 9 Nari
19 Sasa
20 State Bird Provisions
21 Tataki
see 17 Yakitori Edomasa

ENTERTAINMENT
22 Audium
23 Boom Boom Room
24 Cherry Blossom Festival
see 17 Festa
25 Fillmore Auditorium
26 Independent

SHOPPING
27 Baby the Stars Shine Bright
28 Crossroads Trading
29 Fibers of Being
see 25 In the Black
see 17 Kinokuniya Books
see 27 New People
30 Paper Tree
31 Soko Hardware
32 Zuri

EATING IN JAPANTOWN & FILLMORE: CROSS-CULTURAL FOOD

Brenda's Meat & Three: Only superheroes can finish chef/owner Brenda Buenviaje's shrimp and grits, let alone the fluffy biscuits – but it's fun trying. *8am-9pm* $

Daeho Kalbijjim: Go early or late for sizzling platters of *kalbijjim* beef topped with cheese and torched tableside. *11am-2.30pm & 4.30-9pm Mon-Fri, 10.30am-9pm Sat & Sun* $$

Minnie Bell's Soul Movement: Sip bubbly with Fernay McPherson's rosemary-infused fried chicken. *4-9pm Tue-Thu, 11am-2pm & 4-10pm Fri & Sat* $$

Yakitori Edomasa: Grilling since 1924, Edomasa makes yakitori skewers to order, from flavor-bomb chicken thighs to shitake mushrooms. *11am-2.30pm & 5-9.30pm Tue-Sun* $

TOP EXPERIENCE

Japan Center

Time travel to 1968 as you cross Japan Center's indoor wooden bridges, with *maneki-neko* (cat figurines) waving welcome from restaurant entryways. Hard to believe, but this kawaii-cute mall started with a knock-down fight. After WWII, 1500 Japantown residents returned from incarceration camps were again uprooted to build a mall. But residents and businesses rallied, converting the mall into a community hub.

KIT LEONG/SHUTTERSTOCK

East Mall, Japan Center

From Manga to Ukiyo-e

Entire afternoons disappear at **Kinokuniya Books**, between stunning art books (Daido Moriyama photography), tempting cookbooks (bento box lunches) and toys (smiling sushi plushies) – plus manga comics and Tokyo street-fashion mags. Across the hall, Kinokuniya's office and school supplies promise to make work and studying more fun – slow down with sloth-themed to-do lists and reward homework with panda-donut stickers. On Japan Center's indoor pedestrian bridge, stop at **Tokaido Arts** *(tokaidoarts.com; free)* to see a major collection of original *ukiyo-e* (Japanese woodblock prints) in mint condition – including Hokusai's sublime views of Mt Fuji, still vibrant over 200 years later.

All-Ages Entertainment

Vampire kittens and Alice in Wonderland characters occasionally roam the halls of the Japan Center, queuing politely for anime-themed photo booths and arcade games. Cosplay costumes could signal a festival, anime event or pop-up art mart – or just a typical Japan Center Saturday. Follow sounds of familiar tunes into **Festa** karaoke lounge *(festalounge.com; age 21+)*, where you too can rock the miniature stage for $2 per song plus liquid courage from yuzu shochu cocktails.

TOP TIPS

- West Mall has boutiques, arcades and sweet treats. Across Peace Plaza, the East Mall has date-night dining and cultural events.
- Top dining options include **Sasa** (p81), **Marufuku Ramen**, **Jina Bakes**, **Yakitori Edomasa** and **An Japanese Resturant** (p81).

PRACTICALITIES

- sfjapantown.org
- 8.30am-10pm
- Free

SHARP STYLES & BIG NIGHTS

Nate Thorner *(@natethebarber)* owns the barbershop **Westside Cuts & Style.**

My pops started this barbershop with a partner named Jordan. Originally they called it Hair Jordans. Pops told me don't rush – you'll find a clientele because you take your time to make it right and tight. People with notoriety come through. I accompanied my counterpart Brandon to cut hair at Chase Center for a Warriors player. People come here for consistency, a good cut and fade, and because it feels like home. Historically, this was a thriving African American neighborhood, and I'm doing my little part to keep that alive. Next door, Effin Relax makes natural products. I also like Brenda's Meat & Three (p78), Bar Crudo and Minnie Bell's (p78).

SHEILA FITZGERALD/SHUTTERSTOCK

Cherry Blossom Festival

(continued from p77)
transgender alike) and bathing suits are required on all-gender Monday and Tuesday. Bath access is $49, or $20 with shiatsu massage (from $135). Women-only, clothing-free Korean **Pearl Spa** *(pearlspasf.com)* offers access to a cedar sauna, hot tub, cool pool, warming clay-ball pit and pink salt room with treatments, including seaweed massages ($200 for 90 minutes).

Discover Hidden Talents

Learn Japanese art forms from seasoned pros

Japantown has inspiration to spare: nonprofit **Japanese Cultural & Community Center of Northern California** *(JCCCNC; jcccnc.org)* runs affordable workshops with acclaimed local artisans, chefs, artists and performers. Get hands-on experience in person and online with *kaiseki* (seasonal meal) cooking, ikebana flower-arranging, *washi ningyo* (paper dolls), *doburoku* (home-brew sake) and *magewappa* (woodcraft). Check the calendar for upcoming events, including dance and taiko drumming workshops and performances from **GenRyu Arts** *(genryuarts.org)*.

Endless possibilities unfold at **Paper Tree** *(paper-tree.com)*, the paper-craft emporium behind Ruth Asawa's bronze *Origami Fountains* on pedestrian Osaka Way. Paper Tree has inspired origami since 1968, filling display cases with astounding paper creations: cocoon dresses, minuscule frogs and vast coral reefs. Beginners can fold their own Death Star with *Star Wars* kits, while decoupage pros freestyle with *washi* (handmade paper).

EATING: DATE-WORTHY SHARED PLATES

Nari: Day-Glo flavors make Pim Techamuanvivit's Thai-California dishes as mind-blowing as Fillmore shows, including cured *kampachi* with pear and chili jam. *5.30-9pm* $$

Copra: Feast on edible art with regional Indian flavors and SF flair: Kerala shrimp mango curry and puffy passionfruit poori. *5-10pm daily, 11.30am-2pm Sat & Sun* $$

State Bird Provisions: Mini-plates pack mega-flavors, including savory ricotta-sourdough pancakes and quail nested in slow-cooked onions. *5.30-10pm* $$

Bar Crudo: Pair craft beer with local oysters and porcini-crusted black cod – plus happy-hour seafood chowder (to 6.30pm). *5-9pm Mon-Sat* $$

Japantown keeps a busy schedule of festivals and creative workshops year-round – between the **Nihonmachi Street Fair** *(nihonmachistreetfair.org)* and **Cherry Blossom Festival**, GenRyu also organizes art programs to celebrate Hina Matsuri (Girls' Day), Keiro no Hi (Respect for the Aged) and Midori no Hi (Greenery Day). Since 1925, four generations of the Ashizawa family have made it their mission to source ikebana, bonsai, tea-ceremony and Zen rock-garden supplies at **Soko Hardware** *(sokohardware.com)*, so you can take the inspiration home.

Catch Music Legends Live

Hear SF's eclectic soundtrack at its source

Music legends keep rocking neighborhood venues here – '30s blues, '50s jazz, '60s rock, '70s punk, '90s hip-hop and current headliners. **Boom Boom Room** *(boomboomroom.com)* packs its 1930s checkered-linoleum floor with R&B and funk. Lines down the block signal showtime at the legendary **Fillmore Auditorium** *(thefillmore.com)*, where Jimi Hendrix, Janis Joplin, Aretha Franklin and the Grateful Dead rocked – upstairs is lined with '60s psychedelic posters, and free posters are still distributed after sold-out shows. Bragging rights are earned at small yet mighty **Independent** *(theindependentsf.com)*, featuring indie dreamers (Magnetic Fields, Death Cab for Cutie), music legends (George Clinton, Metallica) and alterna-stars (Superchunk, Tokimonsta). Dig the vibes at **Audium** *(audium.org; tickets adult/student $30/20)*, a 1967 sound sculpture emitting meditative, 90-minute 'room compositions.'

Signature Style

Try on global trends and SF styles

Upgrade travel wardrobes with **Zuri** *(shopzuri.com)* tunics, ethically made in Kenya in joyous prints: chickens, pretzels, fireworks. **New People** *(newpeopleworld.com)* brings Tokyo style to SF, with Lolita Goth mini-pinafores at **Baby the Stars Shine Bright** *(shop.baby-aatp.com)* and mod graphic shifts at **Sou Sou** *(sousouus.com)*. **Fibers of Being** *(shopfibersofbeing.com)* offers modern styles for all genders – SF rodeo tees, nonbinary bling – and gently-worn looks sell for less at **Crossroads** *(crossroadstrading.com)*. Complete your look with sharp cuts from **Westside Cuts & Style** *(instagram.com/westsidecutsandstyle)* and accessories from **In the Black** *(intheblackshop.com)*, Fillmore's Black design showcase.

JAPANESE ARTS & CULTURE

Sensei **Melody Takata** is the founder of **GenRyu Arts** and renowned taiko drummer, shamisen player and arts educator.

I first came to San Francisco with my taiko group. Now I'm raising my two kids and teaching and performing in Japantown. The **Cherry Blossom Festival** is Japantown's biggest event, **Nihonmachi Street Fair** is going strong after 50 years and **Japan Day** *(japanweeksf.com)* is a mini-Cherry Blossom Festival. There are arts events and workshops year-round at the JCCCNC, Japan Center popups and weekly free Paper Tree origami classes. We're staging shows in the Julia Morgan-designed **Issei Women's Building**, built by and for the Japantown community, where US civil rights leaders worked. Bringing those stories forward is an honor and joy.

EATING IN JAPANTOWN & FILLMORE: SUSHI

Sasa: Enjoy *kaiseki* (a seasonally inspired menu) or order *kanpachi nigiri* and creamy scallop-salmon '49er rolls. *5.30-9pm Mon, noon-2pm & 5.30-9pm Tue-Sun* $$$

Tataki: Satiny, sustainable seafood cut with gem-like precision lures sushi savants to this cozy spot for neighborly happy hours (to 6.30pm). *4.30-8.30pm* $$

Aji Kiji: Impress picnic dates by preordering Aji's jewel-box bento – sashimi, nigiri and maki with a fish-shaped container of soy sauce. *11am-4pm Tue-Sat* $$

An Japanese Restaurant: Reserve via text for a sushi speakeasy, serving 20 lucky diners 8-course *omakase* ($135) or Pacific seafood a la carte. *5.30-9.30pm Tue-Sat* $$$

TOP EXPERIENCE

Alamo Square

These graceful 'Painted Lady' Victorian mansions have housed bordellos, jazz speakeasies and hippie communes, and survived elegantly intact – including east-end Postcard Row and the northwest-corner Westerfeld mansion, once home to SF's biggest hippie commune. Earthquakes and fire couldn't destroy these Victorians, yet redevelopment almost did, until neighbors banded together to save this historic district.

GAGLIARDIPHOTOGRAPHY/SHUTTERSTOCK

'Painted Lady' Victorian mansions

TOP TIPS

- On sunny days, claim a hilltop picnic table framed by gabled Victorian rooflines and wind-sculpted pines.
- 'Dog-o'clock' occurs around sunset, when pups frolic freely on Alamo's grassy west side.
- At the hilltop playground, kids climb up and slide down Victorian playhouses.

Meet the Painted Ladies

When prospectors struck it rich in the Gold Rush, they upgraded from downtown tenements to pastel 'Painted Lady' Victorian flats around **Alamo Square Park**, embellished to the eaves with gilded woodwork and look-at-me bay windows. Since Alamo Square's Painted Ladies were built on bedrock, many survived the 1906 earthquake – until 1950s developers began demolishing this diverse, historic neighborhood to clear the way for luxury high-rise condos. Some 38 blocks of affordable Victorian homes and small businesses were destroyed before public outcry stopped the destruction in a landmark win. Today you'll spot fresh 6-10 color schemes inspired by SF's 1970s Colorist Movement, when San Franciscans restored many Painted Ladies to their full glory.

Westerfield House

On Alamo Square's northwestern corner stands **Westerfeld House**, a gilded Stick Italianate Victorian with a spooky watchtower. This 28-room mansion was built by candy baron William Westerfeld in 1889, and survived subsequent incarnations as a jazz speakeasy and a legendary 50-person hippie commune. Filmmaker Kenneth Anger filmed satanic rituals in the tower with Church of Satan founder Anton LaVey, involving one grumpy lion coaxed up four flights of stairs.

PRACTICALITIES

- sfrecpark.org
- Free
- 5am-midnight

The Haight & Hayes Valley

SAN FRANCISCO'S HIPPIE HOTSPOT

Hippie idealism thrives in the Haight with street musicians, anarchist comic books and psychedelic murals splashed on every available surface. In the 1960s, thousands of young people from across the country flocked to the corner of Haight and Ashbury, drawn by psychedelic bands, revolutionary politics and free-love communes – a moment seen through a more critical eye in Joan Didion's 1967 essay 'Slouching Toward Bethlehem.' Counterculture kids called themselves freaks and flower children; *San Francisco Chronicle* columnist Herb Caen dubbed them 'hippies.' The Upper Haight has hung onto its roots: hippies reminisce about glory days while trailed by their embarrassed teenage relations, and new-age practitioners load up on chakra-cleansing crystals. Down in the Lower Haight there are mellower vibes on designated slow streets, where dog walkers wrangle their herds and cyclists and skaters zig-zag around steep hills. Next door in Hayes Valley, Zen monks and jazz legends drift past some of the city's best restaurants.

TOP TIP

You'll need more than fair-trade coffee or local microbrews to power through Haight St sightseeing. Veer off the main drag to Divisadero for affordable brunch and lunch spots, or head to Hayes Valley for critically acclaimed dining (reserve ahead) and shows at SFJAZZ Center.

Observe the Time at Haight & Ashbury

It's always 4:20 here

In 1967's Summer of Love, the San Francisco fog was laced with pot, incense and burning military draft cards, and at the

(continued on p86)

GETTING AROUND

Walking is the best way to explore the area's bookstores, boutiques and Victorians – start in the Upper Haight, then walk downhill to the Lower Haight and hit Hayes Valley in time for dinner. Bus lines 6 and 7 travel along Haight St, connecting downtown to Golden Gate Park. Line 22 links the Lower Haight to the Mission and the Marina, while the 43 connects the Upper Haight to the Marina. At the Van Ness Muni metro stop one block east of Hayes Valley, you can hop the N line, which stops near the Lower and Upper Haight and heads onward to Ocean Beach.

THE HAIGHT & HAYES VALLEY

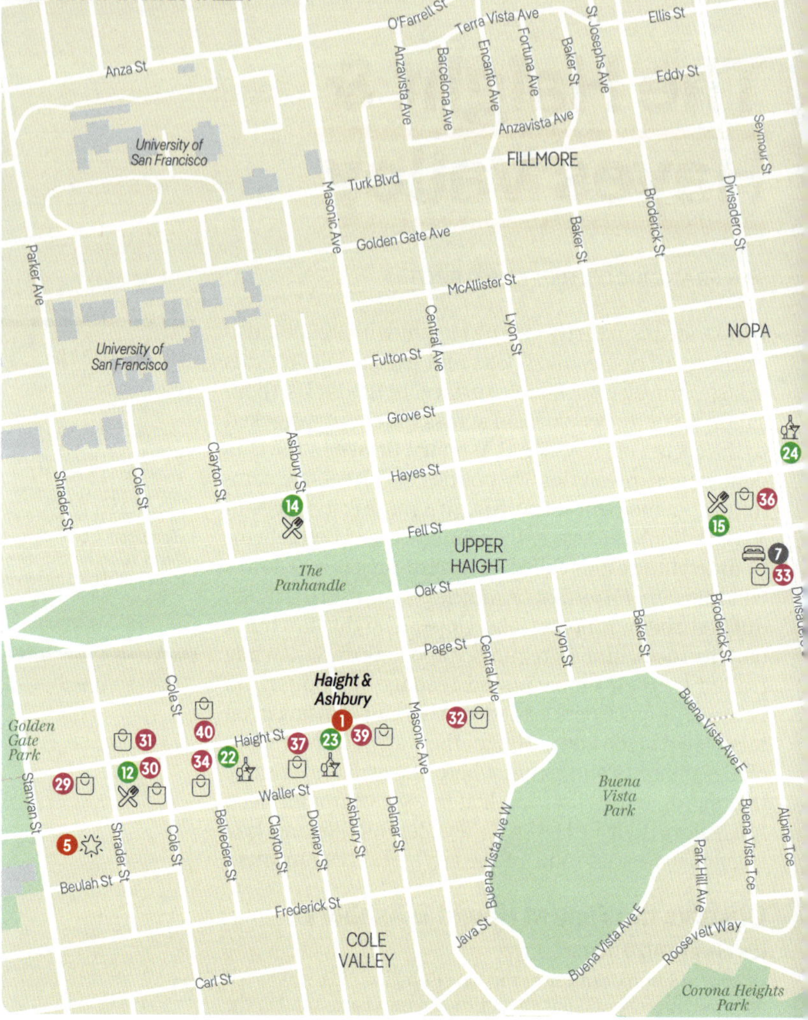

HIGHLIGHTS

1 Haight & Ashbury

2 Haight Street Art Center

SIGHTS

3 San Francisco Zen Center

ACTIVITIES

4 Church of 8 Wheels

5 Free Gold Watch

SLEEPING

6 Hayes Valley Inn

7 Metro Hotel

8 Parsonage

EATING

9 a Mano

10 Doppio Zero

11 DragonEats

12 Escape from New York Pizza

13 Gioia Pizzeria

14 Karma Cafe

15 Nopalito

16 Om Sabor

17 Otra

18 Rad Radish

19 Rich Table

20 Robin

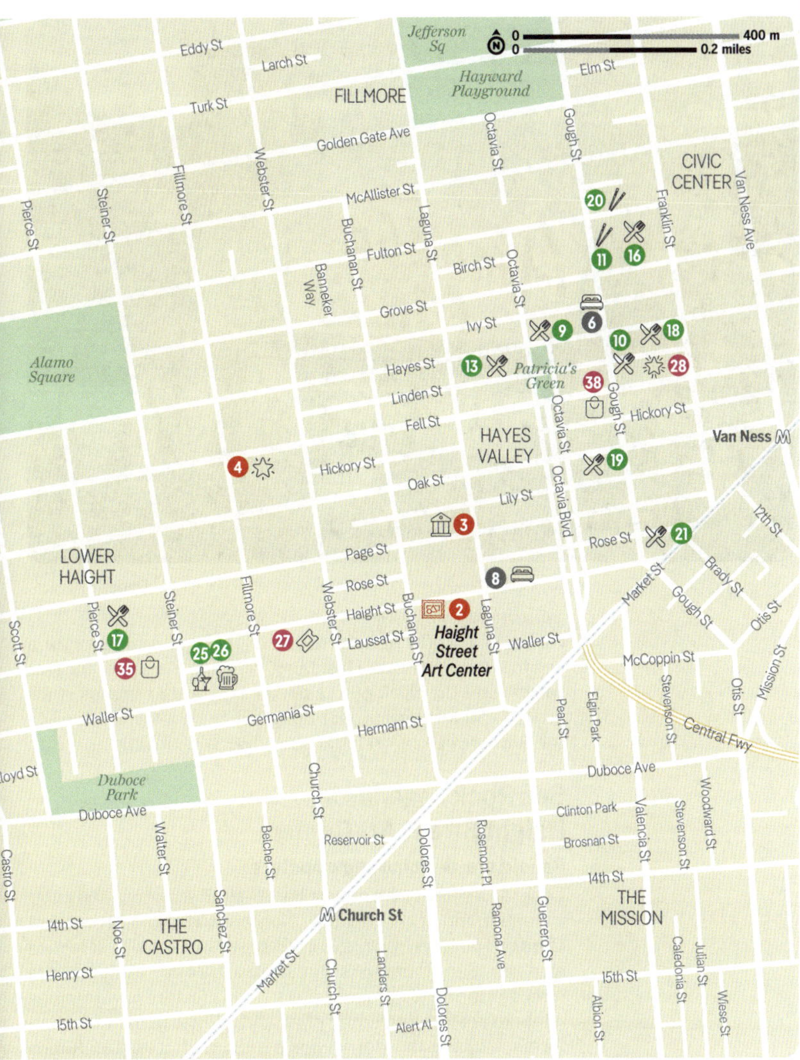

21 Zuni Cafe

DRINKING & NIGHTLIFE

see 30 Alembic
22 Aub Zam Zam
23 Club Deluxe
24 Madrone Art Bar
25 Noc Noc
26 Toronado

ENTERTAINMENT

27 Faight Collective
28 SFJAZZ

SHOPPING

29 Amoeba Music
30 Booksmith
31 Borderlands Books
32 Bound Together
33 Comix Experience
34 Decades of Fashion
35 Fuzz & Sway
36 Gamescape
37 Held Over
38 Isotope
39 Relic Vintage
40 Wasteland

GRANT HENDERSON/ALAMY

Amoeba Music

(continued from p83)
corner of **Haight & Ashbury**, a countercultural revolution began. Decades later, 'Hashbury' remains a magnet for free spirits, and the clock on the northeast corner remains stuck at 4:20 – aka International Bong Hit time, a term coined in the Bay Area circa 1971 and now observed globally.

See Rock Legends at Haight Street Art Center

Behold era-defining show posters

Look for Jeremy Fish's bronze bunny-skull sculpture and enter a wonderland of psychedelia. Nonprofit **Haight Street Art Center** *(haightstreetart.org; free)* showcases silk-screened posters – San Francisco's signature art form – at the on-site screen-printing studio and gallery. Shows feature jaw-dropping vintage posters, including glam-rock Bowie in metallic platforms. Gracing the stairwell is a hidden SF treasure: Ruben Kaddish's 1937 WPA fresco *Dissertation on Alchemy,* surely the trippiest mural ever commissioned by the US government. The center is open from noon to 6pm, Thursday through Sunday.

EATING IN HAIGHT & HAYES VALLEY: VEGAN & VEGETARIAN

Rad Radish: Plant-based menu that satisfies munchies, from Pineapple Express Impossible burgers to chili crisp cauliflower. *9am-8.30pm Sun-Fri, to 9.30pm Sat* $

Om Sabor: Creative, ecofriendly meat-free spins on nostalgic favorites inside the audiophile cocktail lounge Phonobar. *5-10pm Wed-Sat, 5-9pm Tue* $

DragonEats: Tofu banh mi will give you something to roar about at this casual, veggie-friendly Vietnamese deli. *11am-6pm Mon-Sat, to 5pm Sun* $

Otra: Start off strong with spicy salsa macha on black beans, followed by sweet potato tacos from this vegetarian-friendly menu. *5-10pm* $$

Complete Collections at Amoeba Music

Shop deep cuts and certified bops

Enticements are hardly necessary to lure fans to the West Coast's most eclectic collection of new and used music and video, but **Amoeba Music** *(amoeba.com)* offers listening stations, free zines with uncannily accurate staff reviews and runs a foundation that's saved one million acres of rainforest. This cavernous former bowling alley holds upwards of 100,000 vinyl records, CDs and cassettes covering obscure jazz to mainstream hip-hop. It also hosts Live at Amoeba free concerts.

Hit High Scores at Free Gold Watch

Retro pinball galore

You've hit the jackpot: inside a working screen-printing shop, **Free Gold Watch** *(freegoldwatch.com)* arcade is crammed with 50+ vintage pinball games. Most cost a buck or less to play, including Elvis, Godzilla and SF-favorite Dirty Harry; don't miss Secret Juju Gallery's rare 1970s games. Power up with arcade staples – pizza, hotdogs, nachos – plus craft beers and cocktails.

Go on a Vintage Shopping Spree

Wander through wardrobes of the past

Rock a new/old style from **Wasteland** *(shopwasteland.com)*, a converted-cinema vintage superstore with a wall of prized vintage concert tees. Or check out **Decades of Fashion** *(decadesoffashionsf.com)*, a wearable museum featuring Gilded Age opera gloves and *Dynasty*-era power blazers. **Relic Vintage** *(relicvintagesf.com)* is an elegant haberdashery of pinstriped suits and poodle skirts, while 1970s Western wear from **Held Over** *(@heldovervintage)* demands to go line-dancing. The vintage party keeps grooving at **Fuzz & Sway** *(@fuzznswayshop)*, a motherlode of mod dresses and funky maxi-skirts.

Get on a Roll at Church of 8 Wheels

Believe in the power of 'rolligion'

At the **Church of 8 Wheels** *(churchof8wheels.com; skate rental $5)*, worship begins with '80s music blaring from the pulpit and congregants skating backward under a disco ball. This church-turned-roller rink offers family-friendly skate sessions

HAIGHT HANGOUTS

Becka Robbins is the founder of nonprofit **Books Not Bans** *(@booksnotbans)*, sending LGBTQ+ literature to communities facing book bans. Here are her favorite reading spots in the Haight.

Aub Zam Zam
Bring a booklight and read in the bar, 'cuz books are awesome and so are Zam Zam's martinis. The jukebox provides the perfect background music.

Karma Cafe
She's giving macrame. Ditch the stressy laptop crowd and pull up with a book at this cute hippie joint. The coffee is fine, but the smoothies are where it's at.

Club Deluxe
This place is my paradise, perfect for a solitary outing with a book. Listen to the best local bands while enjoying a good read.

EATING IN THE HAIGHT & HAYES VALLEY: PIZZA

Escape from New York Pizza: Pair a slice of pesto with roasted garlic and potato with a vintage shopping spree. *10am-10pm Sun-Thu, 10am-2am Fri & Sat* $

Gioia Pizzeria: The name means joy in Italian, and that's what it delivers with seasonal toppings and housemade cannoli. *11am-10pm* $

Doppio Zero: Classic Neapolitan pizzas hot from a wood-fired oven – try the namesake. *11.30am-10pm Mon-Thu, to 11pm Fri & Sat, to 9.30pm Sun* $$

a Mano: Basic but not boring pizzas and show-stealing pastas, including handmade rigatoni. *11.30am-9.30pm Mon-Thu, to 10.30pm Fri & Sat, to 9pm Sun* $$

BEST PLACES TO GEEK OUT

Isotope: At this comic-book lounge, flip through superhero serials and eye the toilet seats signed by famous illustrators, then head upstairs to relax on comfy leather sofas with local graphic novelists, some of whom lead workshops here. Holds signings and free comic-book days. *(facebook.com/isotopecomics)*

Gamescape: Since 1985, the city's tabletop gaming headquarters has featured game supplies designed by local cooperatives. Stick around for indie board-game nights and card tournaments. *(gamescapesf.com)*

Comix Experience: Comic-book deep cuts, signed first editions and kid-friendly graphic novels all find their home in this tiny neighborhood shop. Join the club to get the best graphic novel of the month at your doorstep. *(comixexperience.com)*

at 5pm to 6.30pm on Friday, 2.30pm to 6.30pm on Saturday, and 6pm to 7.30pm Sunday and Tuesday. Afterward, anyone 18 and up can get their skate groove on at goth nights, silent discos and soul roll Sundays.

Leave Plans to Faight Collective

See what Faight has in store for you

Looking for an affordable yoga studio? Radically free craft workshop? Comedy show? Place to get a DIY thigh tat? At the crossroads of Fillmore and Haight, **Faight Collective** *(thefaight.com)* is a maker gallery upstairs and unpredictable events space downstairs, featuring yoga, open mics, live music and something called 'collective envisioning.'

Stomp for More at SFJAZZ

Find bliss at SF's premier jazz venue

Jazz legends and singular talents from Argentina to Yemen are showcased at **SFJAZZ** *(sfjazz.org)*, America's largest jazz center. Enjoy brilliant sound in Miner Auditorium, where the stage is regularly stormed by soul icon Mavis Staples, punk poet Laurie Anderson and Tony-winning dancer Savion Glover. All seats have drink holders and clear stage views. Hear fresh takes on classic jazz albums and poets riffing with combos in the downstairs Joe Henderson Lab.

Browse Book Nooks

Read, drink, repeat

Booksmith *(booksmith.com)* co-owns adjoining **Alembic** bar *(alembicsf.com)* – fair warning in case you wake up tomorrow amid piles of signed San Francisco novels. Explore literature's outer realms at **Borderlands Books** *(borderlands-books.com)*, dedicated to science fiction, fantasy, mystery and horror. Since 1976, volunteer-run anarchist book collective **Bound Together** *(boundtogether.org)* has supplied free thinkers with organic-permaculture manuals, social history and radical comics, while coordinating SF's annual Anarchist Book Fair and running the Prisoners' Literature Project – they make us tools of the state look like slackers.

DRINKING IN THE HAIGHT: EPIC NIGHTS

Noc Noc: Who's there? Trance DJs, anarchist hackers and Burning Man founders, that's who. Post-apocalyptic cave rave. *5pm-1am Sun-Thu, to 2am Fri & Sat*

Aub Zam Zam (p87): Persian arches, *1001 Nights* murals, 1930s jazz on the jukebox and top-shelf cocktails at low-shelf prices. *3pm-2am Mon-Fri, 1pm-2am Sat & Sun*

Madrone Art Bar: Bump into art installations on Motown Mondays, Saturday global disco and Prince/Michael Jackson parties. *4pm-2am Mon-Sat, 3pm-1.30am Sun*

Toronado: Glory hallelujah, beer-lovers: your prayers are answered. Genuflect before the chalkboard altar that lists 40-plus beers on tap. *11.30am-2am*

San Francisco Zen Center

Breathe in, Breathe Out

Meditate at the Zen Center

Since 1969, the Julia Morgan-designed **San Francisco Zen Center** *(sfzc.org)* has been home to one of the largest Buddhist communities outside of Asia. Watch sunlight fill the Zendo during free morning zazen *(5:25am daily)*, and check out events: half-day garden meditations, workshops blending breath work with beatboxing and Trans Sangha, meditation by and for the trans community *(7pm every other Thursday)*.

KEEPING PEACE & LOVE ALIVE IN THE HAIGHT

Ever since America's youth fled to the Upper Haight in the 1960s as a place to fit in, panhandling has been part of the scene, from buskers to teens scrounging for bus fare – no judgment, no obligation. Back in the '60s, Haight hippies and Black Panthers distributed free food around the Bay, and while you're in town, you can keep those neighborly good vibes flowing. You could pack grocery bags on Saturday at historic Haight Ashbury Food Program *(thefoodprogram.org)*, serve hot meals or make care packages at Glide's homeless service center *(glide.org)* or donate to local nonprofits – all thoughtful gestures to repay San Francisco hospitality, and ensure everyone has a chance to feel at home here.

EATING IN THE HAIGHT AND HAYES VALLEY: MEMORABLE MEALS

Rich Table: Impossible cravings begin with mind-bending dishes: porcini doughnuts, Dungeness crab latkes, sea-urchin cacio e pepe. *5-10.30pm Tue-Sat* $$$

Zuni Cafe: Turning menu staples into gourmet go-tos since 1979, like Caesar salad with house-cured anchovies. *5-9.30pm Tue-Sun, 11am-3pm Fri-Sun* $$$

Robin: Trust the chef's choice. There's no menu, but decadent ingredients like Wagyu beef and caviar are sure to please. *5-9.30pm Wed-Sun* $$$

Nopalito: Fresh, organic ingredients in colorful Mexican dishes that warm even the foggiest of days. *11.30am-9pm Sun-Tue & Thu-Sat, 4.30-9pm Wed* $$

Mission, Dogpatch & Potrero

SUNSHINE, MURALS, BOOKS & FLAVORS GALORE

GETTING AROUND

The Mission is flat and walkable, though you may want to hop a bus to Dogpatch. The 48 runs east-west from Dogpatch via the Mission to Ocean Beach, and the 22 connects Dogpatch, the Mission, Haight, Fillmore and Pacific Heights. The BART runs from downtown: hop off at 24th St or 16th St – the latter station is sketchy, but close to the bustling Valencia and 16th hub. The 14 bus connects Mission to downtown and the Embarcadero, and the 49 travels Van Ness Ave to the Wharf. Both stop near mural-lined Calle 24.

TOP TIP

You'll feel at ease walking this area by day, but keep your street smarts sharp walking alone at night – especially around the 16th St BART station and around deserted Dogpatch warehouses.

Enjoy the district's sunny microclimates with a burrito in one hand and a book in the other, surrounded by a local crowd of filmmakers, grocers, techies, skaters and novelists. Wrapped in murals and sunshine, the Mission welcomes you to hang out at bookstores, art spaces and taquerias – especially along Calle 24 (24th St), SF's designated Latino Cultural District. The Mission is also a magnet for lesbians, Asian Americans and Arab Americans – all are welcome and celebrated in multicultural Mission arts, food and festivals. There's nightlife for everyone here: lesbian bars, historic saloons, cinemas and experimental theater. Valencia St is hipster central, but don't be too quick to scoff: try their excellent coffee, baked goods, vintage shops and maker spaces. Waterfront Dogpatch is creatively repurposing rusty industrial docks into parks, arts and music venues, and Potrero throws down at punk shows and art openings.

See SF's Sunny Side at Dolores Park

Loll the day away

Welcome to San Francisco's sunny side, home to street ball and Mayan-pyramid playgrounds, taco picnics and semi-professional tanning. At **Dolores Park** *(sfrecpark.org; free)*, grassy slopes are dedicated to lolling, while lowlands host soccer, Frisbee, political protests and other local sports. Good weather brings major events, including Easter's **Hunky Jesus** drag contest *(thesisters.org; free)*, free summer movie nights and fall performances by the **San Francisco Mime Troupe** *(sfmt.org; free)*.

Join Mission Cultural Festivals

Celebrate life to the fullest

No place celebrates life quite like the Mission. SF is far from Rio, but you'd never know it during **Carnaval** *(carnaval sanfrancisco.org; free)*, when everyone shakes their tail

DAVID TRAN PHOTO/SHUTTERSTOCK

Carnaval

feathers in the Mission streets. For **Día de los Muertos** *(dayofthedeadsf.org; free)*, brass bands, lowriders and dancing skeletons honor the dead along Calle 24, community altars line **Potrero del Sol/La Raza Skate Park** *(sfrecpark.org)* and **Mission Cultural Center for Latino Arts** *(MCCLA; missionculturalcenter.org)* hosts art shows and epic mole tastings. Flor y Canto (Flower and Song) and Paseo Poetico fill Mission streets with poetry and the joy of living.

Showtime in the Mission

Hang onto the edge of your seat

Brace for impact: at Mission performance spaces like **ODC Theater** *(odc.dance)*, risky, raw dance performances leave audiences gasping. **Gray Area** *(grayarea.org; events sliding scale $0-50)* blurs boundaries between art and science, culture and technology with mind-expanding programs – immersive electronica shows, 3D art workshops, psychedelic cyberpunk festivals – in historic Grand Theater. **Chan National Queer Arts Center** *(sfgmc.org)* hosts SF's Gay Men's Chorus – as seen in the award-winning documentary *Gay Chorus Deep South* – plus boundary-pushing Q-lab theater and raucous

(continued on p94)

DRINKING IN THE MISSION: ICONIC BARS

Trick Dog: Each new menu captures an SF obsession, proof the bar often called America's best never runs out of tricks. *4pm-midnight Sun-Thu, to 2am Fri & Sat*

Royal Cuckoo Organ Lounge: DJ jams on an organ among lucha-libre-masked customers. *6pm-midnight Mon, 4pm-2am Tue-Thu, from 3pm Fri-Sun*

Pop's Bar: Approach the 1937 bar for cocktails named after lowrider cars that kick into overdrive when DJs spin. *6am-2am*

Zeitgeist: At this biker beer garden, you've got two seconds to choose a craft beer from 64 on tap – tough but fair. *2-11pm Mon-Wed, to midnight Thu, to 1am Fri & Sat, noon-9.30pm Sun*

HIGHLIGHTS
1 826 Valencia
2 Balmy Alley
3 Clarion Alley
4 Creativity Explored
5 Dolores Park
6 Mission Cultural Center for Latino Arts
7 Women's Building

SIGHTS
8 500 Capp St
9 House of Seiko
10 Incline Gallery
11 Jack Fischer Gallery
12 Southern Exposure

ACTIVITIES
13 Potrero del Sol/La Raza Skatepark
14 Precita Eyes Mission Mural Tours

EATING
15 Burma Love
16 Donaji
17 Farmhouse Kitchen Thai Cuisine
18 Flour + Water
19 Freekeh
20 Komaaj Mazze & Wine Bar
21 La Corneta Taqueria
22 La Palma Mexicatessen
23 La Taqueria
24 Old Jerusalem
25 Pancho Villa
26 Reem's
27 San Ho Won
28 Shizen
29 Taqueria El Farolito
30 Udupi Palace

DRINKING & NIGHTLIFE
31 Casements Bar
32 El Rio
33 Jolene's
34 Mother
35 Pop's Bar
36 Royal Cuckoo Organ Lounge
37 Trick Dog
38 Zeitgeist

ENTERTAINMENT
39 Alamo Drafthouse Cinema
40 Bissap Baobab
41 Brava Theater
42 Brick & Mortar

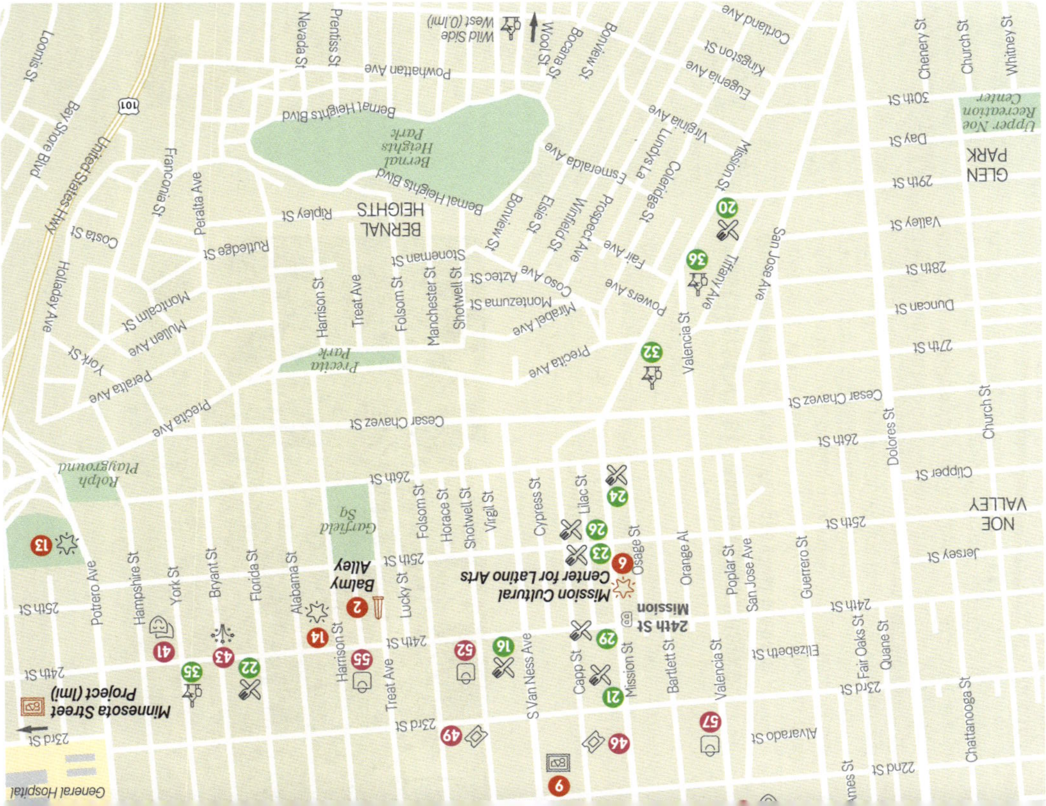

43 Carnaval
44 Chan National Queer Arts Center
45 Chapel
see 39 Foreign Cinema
46 Gray Area
47 Hunky Jesus Contest
48 ODC Theater
49 Red Poppy Art House
50 Roxie Cinema
51 Marsh

SHOPPING

52 Adobe Books & Arts Coop
53 Dog Eared Books
54 Double Down
55 Medicine for Nightmares
56 Mission Comics & Art
57 Needles & Pens
58 Sour Cherry Comics

ALEJANDRO MURGUÍA'S POETIC MISSION

Alejandro Murguía is San Francisco's Poet Laureate, American Book Award winner, MCCLA cofounder and professor of Latino Studies at San Francisco State University.

Poetry is all around us. You'll hear Mayan blessings in Balmy Alley for Flor y Canto Literary Festival, Brazilian samba songs at Carnaval and multilingual poetry in *panaderías* and at Brava Theater for Paseo Poético. Mission Cultural Center's Dia de los Muertos Aztec dances aren't performances – they're prayers. Medicine for Nightmares and Adobe Books host multilingual readings, and Precita Eyes' mural at 24th and Folsom honors Alfonso Texidor, *El Tecalote's* poetry editor. Juana Alicia's Mission library mural is a flowering cactus – a symbol of resistance on a library built by Andrew Carnegie. What could be more poetic?

(continued from p91)
drag punk Pride. **Brava Theater** *(brava.org)* has produced original works by women of color and LGBTQ+ playwrights for 40+ years, and the **Marsh** *(themarsh.org; tickets $10-50)* offers sliding-scale pricing so everyone can participate in experimental one-acts.

Toast Herstory at Lesbian Landmarks

Welcome home to Mission's legacy lesbian bars

Since 1962, **Wild Side West** *(wildsidewest.com)* has made herstory in the beer garden and made out on the pool table (Janis Joplin started it). **Mother** *(mothersf.com)* is a femme-forward, cash-only joint known for the Ex – a gingery gin cocktail that's slightly bitter – and nonalcoholic BFF – like the Ex, 'but without the drama.' Join scenes in progress for 12+ years at **Jolene's** *(jolenessf.com; free-$15)* with lesbian UHaul parties, power-suit contests and 'queer speed-friending' marathons. Swing by lesbian-owned **El Rio** *(elriosf.com)* for knockout margaritas and shameless flirting on a patio that's seen it all since 1978, including Saturday mango lesbian parties, salsa Sunday and free oyster Friday. Mission Irish pubs and lesbian bars have historically attracted different clienteles – but Irish lesbian-owned **Casements Bar** brings everyone to

EATING IN THE MISSION: CLASSIC BURRITOS

La Taqueria: Miguel Jara's burrito has hardly changed since 1972: grilled meats, slow-cooked beans, flour tortillas and housemade salsa. *11am-8:45pm Wed-Sun* $

La Corneta Taqueria: Roving mariachis serenade Mission families gathered in this mural-lined taqueria for extra-special burritos with plump prawns. *10am-9pm* $

Pancho Villa: Meal-sized 'baby burritos' are not to be confused with 'regular,' which is the size of a baby. Slather with salsas at the condiment bar. *10am-10pm* $

Taqueria El Farolito: Follow late-night lines to this no-frills, cash-only taqueria for meat-packed, forearm-sized burritos. *10am-1:45am Sun-Thu, to 2:45am Fri & Sat* $

JEJIM/GETTY IMAGES

Dolores Park (p90)

the mural-lined patio for Guinness, 50+ Irish whiskeys and California-fresh pub grub.

See Something New in Old Mission Cinemas

Catch eye-opening Mission movies

The Mission's 1909 **Roxie Cinema** *(roxie.com)* is a neighborhood nonprofit with an international reputation for year-round film festivals, including Center for Asian American Media's **CAAMFest** *(caamfest.com; May)*, LGBTQ+ **Frameline Film Fest** *(frameline.org; June)*, **Jewish Film Festival** *(jfi.org; July)* and **Arab Film Festival** *(arabfilminstitute.org; November)*. **Alamo Drafthouse Cinema** *(drafthouse.com)* screens blockbusters and cult revivals in a 1932 movie palace, while serving movie-themed cocktails, mocktails, beer, burgers and all-day brunch. At **Foreign Cinema** *(foreigncinema.com)*, timeless films accompany chef Gayle Pirie's seasonal, sustainable California cuisine.

Load Up on Comics & Zines

Spend action-packed afternoons in the Mission

Heads will roll and fists will fly inside **Mission:Comics & Art** *(missioncomicsandart.com)*, featuring indie comics *(Snotgirl,*

BRAVA FOR NEW MURALS

Under Brava Theater's towering vintage marquee, a glorious new mural features two women breathing life into this historic 1926 deco theater. Brava has been staging new works by women and queer playwrights here for more than 40 years – from V-day monologist Eve Ensler to Culture Clash comedy – and now hosts more than 200 events annually. The colorful wraparound mural by Agana and her crew covers the entire three-story Brava building, with larger-than-life female figures invoking creative spirits, plus a gentle reminder to 'smash the patriarchy' over the ticket booth.

EATING IN THE MISSION: SPECIAL OCCASIONS

San Ho Won: Minimalist bistro serving maximalist Korean flavors – *jebi churi* filet packs more flavor than an entire steakhouse. *5-9.30pm Thu-Sun, to 10pm Fri & Sat* $$$

Flour + Water: Rustic yet elegant Italian dishes, from classic mortadella-stuffed tortellini to creative duck and butternut garganelli. *5-9.30pm* $$

Farmhouse Kitchen: Farm-to-table Thai, with turmeric-laced Sonoma fried chicken and Make a Wish cocktails in genie's lamps. *11.30am-2pm & 5-8.30pm Sun-Thu, 4.30-9.30pm Fri & Sat* $$

Donaji: Celebrate with deep Oaxacan flavors and organic Californian ingredients in red mole–braised short ribs and churro s'mores. *5-10pm Wed & Thu, to 10.30pm Fri & Sat* $

MISSION SCHOOL COOL

In the '90s, skate culture, underground comics and graffiti met in Mission alleys – and the art world hasn't been the same since. Art critic Glen Helfand dubbed the movement 'Mission School,' including artists who drew outside the lines of fine arts' programs like SF graffiti/mural/zine/skate artists Margaret Kilgallen, Barry McGee, Ruby Neri and Chris Johanson. SF's indie art spaces invited Mission School artists indoors, launching the 'Beautiful Losers' group show – outsider slang from Leonard Cohen's 1966 counterculture novel – with a 2008 documentary that made Mission School artists mainstays at museum shows and art fairs. What's next? Find out in Mission alleys.

SABRINA DALBESIO/LONELY PLANET

Red Poppy Art House

Head Lopper) alongside marquee titles *(Walking Dead, Star Wars).* **Sour Cherry Comics** *(sourcherrycomics.com)* earns fan followings for its vast queer comics selections, community fundraisers and DIY zines. Entertain new ideas at zine newsstand **Needles & Pens** *(needles-pens.com)*, from *Crap Hound* collages to Finn Cunningham's *Mental Health Cookbook*. **Dog Eared Books** *(dogearedbooks.com)* picks include graphic novels and zines, including Jordan Karnes' *It Hasn't Stopped Being California Here*. **Double Down** zine emerged from SF's women and nonbinary street-skater scene, and its HQ stocks back issues and inspiration galore.

Dream on in Mission Bookstores

Get lit in the Mission

Stranger-than-fiction events unfold during October's **Litquake** *(litquake.org)*, America's biggest, most outlandish literary festival, with authors spilling secrets over drinks at the legendary **Lit Crawl**. **Adobe Books & Arts Coop** *(adobebooks.com)* delivers wall-to-wall inspiration – limited-edition art books, rare cookbooks, well-thumbed poetry – plus zine launch parties and art openings. **Medicine for Nightmares** *(medicine fornightmares.com)* showcases bilingual books in front, art shows and community events in back. When you're running

EATING IN THE MISSION: VEGETARIAN & VEGAN

Shizen: No boring cucumber rolls here. Enjoy eggplant nigiri and mushroom and tempura asparagus rolls with gochujang aioli. *5-9pm Sun-Thu, 4-9.30pm Fri & Sat* $$

La Palma Mexicatessen: Handmade tamales, *huaraches* (stuffed masa) and pupusas (tortilla pockets) with vegan, vegetarian or meat fillings. *8am-5pm Wed-Mon* $

Udupi Palace: Hot dates call for a 2ft-long paper *dosa* (lentil-flour pancake) and satisfying *idli* (fluffy lentil-rice cake) with coconut chutney. *noon-8.30pm* $

Burma Love: Flavors here hug your tongue, then deliver a swift kick – get fermented tea-leaf salad, caramelized eggplant and top-notch cocktails. *11.30am-3pm & 5-10pm* $$

low on pirate supplies and fresh ideas, nonprofit **826 Valencia** *(826valencia.org)* stocks spyglasses and McSweeney's publications to support youth writing workshops.

Explore the Mission's Alternative Art Spaces

See breakthrough art in unusual spaces

Be the first to glimpse artworks destined for museum retrospectives, international art fairs and Marc Jacobs handbags, all by local artists with developmental disabilities at nonprofit **Creativity Explored** *(creativityexplored.org)*, and join the creative fray at **Imaginate Saturdays** *(noon-3pm; free; all ages welcome)*. Lose track of time in the repurposed watch-repair shop that's now **House of Seiko** gallery *(houseofseiko.info; free)*, and ramp up your art collection at **Incline Gallery** *(inclinegallerysf.com; free)*, an ex-mortuary ramp where bodies were once transported. Art ties the room together at nonprofit **Southern Exposure** *(soex.org; donations welcome)*, from fundraising drawing rallies to Resist and Rejoice art parties. At nonprofit **500 Capp St** *(500cappstreet.org; free Sat visits)*, the Mission home of late sculptor David Ireland overflows with experimental installations.

Look Ahead at Minnesota Street Projects

See gallery shows that launch art movements

An old factory showcases new talents at nonprofit **Minnesota Street Project** *(minnesotastreetproject.com)*. Shows here are free and fearless, from meticulously crafted dreamscapes at **Eleanor Harwood Gallery** *(eleanorharwood.com)* to **Jack Fischer Gallery**'s multimedia think-pieces *(jackfischer gallery.com)*. **Casemore Gallery** *(casemoregallery.com)* features renowned photographers – Jim Jocoy's club-kid portraits, Todd Hido's eerie suburban subdivisions – and **Anglim/Trimble** *(anglimtrimble.com)* launches Bay Area art movements, from Beat assemblage to Bay Area conceptualists. Galleries stay open until 8pm for First Saturday artist talks and workshops.

Cheer on the Warriors

Catch a game at the Chase Center

The Bay Area's frequent NBA champions (four times since 2014) play basketball to win at San Francisco's new **Chase Center** *(chasecenter.com)*. Between seasons, the Chase Center hosts marquee pop and comedy headliners.

BEST MISSION MUSIC VENUES

Chapel: Musical prayers are answered in a 1914 California arts-and-crafts landmark with heavenly acoustics for folkYEAH! indie artists and performance -art mayhem.

Brick & Mortar: Break out of radio ruts and playlist loops with outlandish bands rocking the mortar loose, from breakthrough Popscene shows to NPR Tiny Desk artist showcases.

Bissap Baobab: Come for shareable Senegalese food, stick around for live acts and DJs after 9pm – bachata, Cuban jazz, Afrobeats, flamenco and jam sessions.

Red Poppy Art House: A snug Mission storefront doubles as a concert hall for international artists-in-residence, from Armenian duduk virtuosos to Argentine tango quartets.

EATING IN THE MISSION: BEST MEZZE

Komaaj Mazze & Wine Bar: Brilliant flavors rarely found outside northern Iran like pomegranate-glazed smoked trout. *5.30-9pm Tue-Thu, noon-3pm & 5.30-10pm Fri-Sun* $$

Reem's: Acclaimed chef Reem Assil serves sensational, sustainable Palestinian Californian comfort food. *11am-3pm & 5-9pm Tue-Sat* $

Freekeh: Share classic dips and tangy *musakhan* (chicken or mushrooms rolled into lavash) with arak limonada. *5.30-9pm Tue-Sun, 10am-2.30pm Sat & Sun* $

Old Jerusalem: Bond over generous portions of Palestinian and Syrian classics, including shawarma and *mansaf* (lamb pilaf)). *11am-10pm Wed-Mon* $

TOP EXPERIENCE

Mission Murals

Frida Kahlo and Diego Rivera have no idea what they started. Since the Mexican power couple came to SF for a working honeymoon in the 1930s, they've inspired generations of muralists to create 500-plus Mission murals — a splendid show of political dissent, community pride and street-art bravado. Today, multistory murals cover Calle 24, SF's Latino Cultural District.

JOHN LANDER/ALAMY

Clarion Alley

TOP TIPS

- Outdoor murals are free for all to enjoy – but if you're posting a pic on social media, kindly credit the muralist.
- Muralists lead weekend **Precita Eyes walking tours** that last just under two hours. Proceeds fund mural upkeep and new commissions.

PRACTICALITIES

- Buses 12, 14, 48 and 49 stop at Calle 24
- BART 24th St Mission stop is blocks from Balmy Alley.

Balmy Alley

Inspired by Mexican artists Frida Kahlo and Diego Rivera, Mujeres Muralistas (Women Muralists) began painting garage doors here in 1973, turning a neglected backstreet into a neighborhood landmark. Today **Balmy Alley** murals are maintained by nonprofit **Precita Eyes** *(precitaeyes.org; mural tours adult/youth $25/10)*, including early Frida Kahlo homages, a 1985 memorial for El Salvador activist Archbishop Óscar Romero and Lucía González Ippolito's homage to 'Women of the Resistance.'

Clarion Alley

Most graffiti artists shun broad daylight – but not in **Clarion Alley,** SF's street-art showcase maintained by neighbors and Clarion Alley Collective. Over 900 murals have been created by Clarion artists since 1992, but few survive the tests of time and tagging – survivors include Megan Wilson's daisy-covered *Tax the Rich* and Jet Martinez' glimpse of Clarion Alley inside a forest spirit.

Women's Building

America's first women-owned-and-operated community center has housed 150 women's organizations since 1979 – and the 1994 *Maestrapeace* mural celebrates the **Women's Building** as a herstory landmark. Mission muralistas worked with 100 volunteers to cover the building with goddesses and women trailblazers.

The Castro

WELCOME TO THE GAYBORHOOD!

Rainbow flags gaily wave hello at the world's premier LGBTQ+ culture destination, spiritual home to club kids, career activists, leather daddies and drag stars alike. San Francisco's Castro district became a global queer hub in the 1970s, when Castro businessman Harvey Milk became California's first openly gay elected official. Along Market and Castro Sts, Rainbow Honor Walk sidewalk plaques honor Milk and 67 other LGBTQ+ heroes – including civil rights leader James Baldwin, Nobel Laureate Jane Addams and local icons including trans activist Lou Sullivan and SF's Absolute Empress José Sarria. Castro nightlife is legendary, but when the sun comes out, the neighborhood really shines – being out in broad daylight is a freedom this community fought for and thoroughly enjoys, especially on weekends when everyone's out and about at Castro cafes, stores and community venues. The little neighborhood under the giant rainbow flag remains a global symbol of freedom.

TOP TIP

The F streetcar stops at Jane Warner Plaza, named for the pioneering lesbian officer who patrolled the Castro. On sunny days, rainbow-themed seating and bizarre public art make for prime people-watching, – including glimpses of Castro nudists, legally obliged to cover up with strategically placed socks.

Showtime at Castro Theatre

Organ overtures at a deco-fabulous theater

The towering neon marquee blinks welcome to the C-A-S-T-R-O at the **Castro Theatre** *(castrotheatre.com),* architect Timothy Pflueger's 1922 Spanish-Moorish-Asian fantasy cinema. Showtime starts when the mighty organ rises – and no, that's not a euphemism. The 'Mighty Wurlitzer' pipe organ emerges

GETTING AROUND

Strutting is the preferred method of travel in the Castro. Historic F line streetcars run to the Castro from Fisherman's Wharf, covering Market St through downtown. Trouble is, they sometimes get stuck in traffic and you can wait for what feels like forever. If the service is slow, take underground-metro K, L or M trains, which move (much) faster beneath Market St – same ticket, same price. J trains travel from downtown along Church St to 18th St and beyond. The 24 connects the Castro to bustling Divisadero St, and the 33 goes to the Haight and the Mission.

THE CASTRO

HIGHLIGHTS
1 GLBT Historical Society Museum

SIGHTS
2 Photo Booth Museum by Photomatica

ACTIVITIES
3 Eureka Valley Library

SLEEPING
4 Beck's Motor Lodge
5 Hotel Castro
6 Parker Guest House

EATING
7 Anchor Oyster Bar
8 Beit Rima
9 Blind Butcher
10 Cafe de Casa
11 Dinosaurs Sandwiches
12 Fable
13 Fisch & Flore
14 Frances
15 Gai Chicken Rice
16 Poesia Cafe
17 Spike's Coffees and Teas
18 Thoroughbread & Pastry

DRINKING & NIGHTLIFE
19 440 Castro
20 Beaux
21 Midnight Sun
22 Moby Dick
23 QBar
24 The Cafe
25 Twin Peaks Tavern

ENTERTAINMENT
26 Castro Theatre

SHOPPING
27 Apothecarium
28 Cliff's Variety
29 Fabulosa Books
30 Local Take
31 Stag & Manor

INFORMATION
32 Strut

EATING IN THE CASTRO: BUDGET PICKS

Dinosaurs Sandwiches: Monster banh mi sandwiches stomp hunger with Vietnamese fixings, topped with jalapeños, mayo and pickled carrots. *10am-7pm* $

Gai Chicken Rice: The solution to cold snaps and tentative tummies is Hainan-style poached chicken with rice, soup and cucumber salad. *11am-9pm* $

Beit Rima: Palestinian comfort food: braised lamb, *shakshuka* and lemony hummus that makes you pucker up. *11am-9pm Sun & Tue-Thu, to 9.30pm Fri & Sat* $

Fisch & Flore: Enjoy fresh seafood and watch the entire gay world go by from the sun-drenched corner patio. *2-9pm Wed & Thu, 11am-10pm Fri-Sun* $$

from the orchestra pit to play show tunes, leading crowd sing-alongs to Judy Garland's anthem 'San Francisco' before all-star drag revues, A-list queer comedy and premieres for LGBTQ+ Frameline Film Festival.

Pay Respects at GLBT Historical Society Museum

Know your queer history

America's first queer history museum showcases a century of San Francisco LGBTQ+ ephemera – including Harvey Milk's campaign literature and Keith Haring's posters urging SF to 'Act Up Fight AIDS' – alongside exhibits highlighting queer culture throughout history. **GLBT Historical Society Museum** *(glbthistory.org; entry $10)* has collected community history since 1985, capturing deep struggles and sheer queer joy that make visits bonding experiences for the LGBTQ+ community and allies alike. The shop features books researched here, historic posters – yes, SF's 1970 Gay-In was an actual event – and fridge magnets quoting Harvey Milk: 'You gotta give 'em hope.' Indeed.

Read the Rainbow at Fabulosa Books

Oh so Fabulosa!

Fabulosa means 'fabulous' in Polari, 19th-century gay theater slang – and the selection at **Fabulosa Books** *(fabulosabooks.com)* is as fabulously colorful as the Castro's rainbow crosswalks, with categories ranging from Lesbians!! to Gender-Funky Sci-Fi. Dig through bins of vintage ephemera, browse forgotten literary masterpieces and don't miss author readings packed with local characters. Nonprofit Books Not Bans operates out of the (literal) closet in the back, sending LGBTQ+ books to communities where access is restricted.

Strut Your Stuff

Life-saving care and life-affirming art

In the 1980s and '90s, the AIDS epidemic devastated the Castro – but amid incalculable loss, the community founded life-saving San Francisco AIDS Foundation, the nonprofit behind **Strut** *(sfaf.org)*. This landmark community center offers free and low-cost health services, including PrEP and PEP, health screenings, walk-in counseling, substance-abuse treatment and support groups. ID required; privacy assured. Strut's event calendar includes gallery shows, open mics and Beyond Binary art afternoons.

PANORAMAS & POSES IN THE CASTRO

Panda Dulce is a founding queen of Drag Story Hour. Here are her recs for family-friendly afternoons in the Castro.

Walk up Kite Hill: At this rocky **overlook**, you can follow Market St to where the wharf kisses the Bay.

Strike a pose: I love to take visitors of all ages to the **Photo Booth Museum**. Snap some old school, four-shot strips in retro photo booths.

Be regaled with a drag story hour: Join us at the **Eureka Valley Library**, where drag artists perform fun read-alouds for kids. Remember to ask permission to take a photo or selfie. Cash tips are customary and appreciated.

EATING IN THE CASTRO: COZY CAFES

Poesia Cafe: Traditional focaccia and espresso drinks in a snug indoor-outdoor space. *8am-6pm Sun, to 5pm Mon, 7.30am-5pm Tue-Thu, to 6pm Fri & Sat*

Cafe de Casa: Dark roast coffee and colorful Brazilian fare to match the Castro's rainbow spirit. *8am-6pm Mon-Sat, to 5pm Sun*

Thoroughbread & Pastry: Chocolate bread, olive *fougasse* and sourdough sandwiches from SF Baking Institute founder Michel Suas. *8am-4pm Wed-Fri, to 5pm Sat & Sun*

Spike's Coffees and Teas: Cute bulldogs scowl from to-go cups at this fiercely independent coffee spot. *7am-5pm Mon-Fri, from 7.30am Sat & Sun*

BEST SHOPPING FOR HIM & HOME

Apothecarium: Consult experts at America's best-designed marijuana dispensary, according to *Architectural Digest,* then appreciate the local art and designer couches. *(apothecarium.com)*

Cliff's Variety: DIY maestros at the 1936 general store with gasp-worthy window displays won't raise an eyebrow at your need for silver body paint and a jar of rubber nuns.

Local Take: Take in the local scenery with Castro Theatre marquee prints, F streetcar T-shirts or belt buckles featuring vintage Muni maps. *(localtakesf.com)*

Stag & Manor: Dashing decor lets you take the Castro home: brass lanterns wink welcome at guests, and fair-trade throw pillows show dates how thoughtful yet laid-back you are. *(stagandmanor.com)*

GIMAS/SHUTTERSTOCK

Castro Theatre (p99)

Toast Freedom in Historic Gay Bars

Brace for stiff drinks and drag numbers

The vintage rainbow neon arrow points the way to a local landmark: originally opened in 1935, **Twin Peaks Tavern** became the world's first gay bar with windows open to the street in 1971. You can call anyone Ishmael at **Moby Dick** so long as you're buying. Its sign has been a Castro photo-op since 1977, and the commemorative mural outside is fab. The most happening bar on Castro St is **440 Castro** *(the440.com)* – a magnet for bearded dudes, especially on 2-for-1 Wednesday and Friday. 'Servicing the Castro for over 50 years' is no small claim to fame – and **Midnight Sun** *(midnightsunsf.com)* lives up to its motto daily with good vibes and strong drinks (2-for-1 until 9pm daily).

Dance the Night Away

Hit the rainbow dance floor

With a Harvey Milk mural and rainbow light-up dance floor, **The Cafe** *(cafesf.com)* is the obvious place to throw your own coming-out party, with the likes of Latinx Picante Thursday and lesbian Sugar Saturday; check the calendar. Club kids shimmy and shout over remixes on the dance floor at **QBar** *(qbar-sf.com),* while smokers flirt on the patio. The candy store of Castro clubs, **Beaux** *(beauxsf.com)* serves every flavor: Pan Dulce Wednesday, go-go Manimal Friday, Big Top Sunday featuring *Rupaul's Drag Race* stars and monthly sapphic dance party LesBeaux.

EATING IN THE CASTRO: HOT DINNER DATES

Frances: Menus showcase handmade pastas, juicy steaks, local wines and lumberjack date cake to satisfy your discerning lumberjack date. *5:15-9:15pm Tue-Sat* **$$$**

Anchor Oyster Bar: Since 1977, Castro's port of call for sustainably sourced local oysters and cioppino (seafood stew). *2-8pm Thu-Mon* **$$$**

Blind Butcher: Intimate seating, moody lighting, standout steaks and decadent vegetarian dishes make this a date-night go-to. *5-10pm daily, 11am-3pm Sat & Sun* **$$**

Fable: Snag a garden table and sip on California wines paired with local halibut or bougie burgers. *11am-9pm Mon-Fri, 10am-10pm Sat, 10am-9pm Sun* **$$**

Golden Gate Park & the Avenues

SF'S WILD STRETCH OF IMAGINATION

Bison roam, penguins waddle, hippies drum and surfers rip along San Francisco's most outlandish stretch of scenery. Paved paths and off-road trails criss-cross the 50-block-long Golden Gate Park, good for both mellow strolls and epic hikes. Along the residential avenues that cover 50-odd (occasionally very odd) blocks from Stanyan St to Ocean Beach, you'll find Korean BBQ, Gaelic jam sessions, French pastries and Hong Kong movie matinees. This is one chill global village, where hard-core surfers and gourmet adventurers hang out and chow down together. South of Golden Gate Park are candy-colored Sunset District homes, mom-and-pop restaurants on Irving St and surf hangouts around Judah and 45th. North of the park are indie boutiques and cinemas, plus some of SF's best bakeries, bars and affordable dining.

GETTING AROUND

The N line streetcar runs from downtown through the Sunset to Ocean Beach. Buses 1, 31 and 38 run from downtown through the Richmond, while 7 and 6 head from downtown through the Haight to the Sunset. Buses 5 and 21 skirt the northern edge of Golden Gate Park, while north–south buses 28, 29 and 44 cut across the park. Bus 2 covers Clement St, 33 connects to the Haight, Castro and Mission.

Catch the Stern Grove Festival

See headliners for free in SF's urban dell

America's oldest free music festival has rocked the Sunset's shaggy redwood and eucalyptus grove every summer since 1938 – recent headliners include Sleater-Kinney, Diana Ross, Tegan & Sara, Janelle Monáe, X and SF's own Michael Franti. **Stern Grove Festival** *(sterngrove.org)* tickets are available by online lottery: they're released six weeks before shows, and winners have 72 hours to claim them before they're given away to other lucky fans.

TOP TIP

Opera divas, indie acts, bluegrass greats and hip-hop heavies take turns rocking SF gratis, from the often wintry days of June through golden October afternoons. Most concerts are held in Sharon Meadow or at the Polo Fields on weekends; for upcoming events, consult *golden-gate-park.com*.

Explore the Sunset Surf Scene

Stay dry or get wet with Sunset surfers

Dip your toes into SF surf culture at **Mollusk** *(mollusksurfshop.com)*, where legendary shapers (surfboard makers) create limited-edition boards, and surfer-artists show in the back gallery. Surfers browse wetsuits, *Surfer's Journal* back issues

(continued on p108)

★ **HIGHLIGHTS**

1. California Academy of Sciences
2. de Young Museum
3. Golden Gate Park
4. Lands End
5. Legion of Honor
6. Ocean Beach

● **SIGHTS**

7. Breast Cancer Memorial Garden
8. Buffalo Paddock
9. Conservatory of Flowers
10. Japanese Tea Garden
11. Lands End Lookout
12. Lincoln Park
13. National AIDS Memorial Grove

see 1 Osher Rainforest Dome

14. San Francisco Botanical Garden
15. Sunset Dunes
16. Sutro Baths
17. Sutro Heights Park

● **ACTIVITIES**

18. Aqua Surf Shop
19. Coastal Trail
20. Lincoln Park Golf Course
21. Out There Watercolors
22. Sharon Art Studio

see 1 Steinhart Aquarium

● **EATING**

23 Aziza
24 Bettola
25 Chapeau
26 Dragon Beaux
27 Han Il Kwan
28 Hook Fish Co
29 Mamahuhu
30 Manna
31 Mini Potstickers
see 24 Taqueria Los Mayas
32 Thanh Long
33 The Laundromat

● **DRINKING & NIGHTLIFE**

34 Beach Chalet

● **ENTERTAINMENT**

35 Hardly Strictly Bluegrass
36 Outside Lands

● **SHOPPING**

37 Case for Making
38 Mollusk

PUNG/SHUTTERSTOCK

Conservatory of Flowers

TOP EXPERIENCE

Golden Gate Park

When San Franciscans refer to 'the park,' there's only one that gets the definite article: Golden Gate Park. Everything SF holds dear is here: free spirits and free music, butterfly domes and underground art, tiny penguins and hushed redwood groves, tenacious bonsai and massive bison. Landmark venues celebrating nature, music, art and science are dotted across the park's 1017 acres.

DON'T MISS

- de Young Museum
- San Francisco Botanical Garden
- California Academy of Sciences
- Conservatory of Flowers
- National AIDS Memorial Grove
- Hardly Strictly Bluegrass Festival

Natural Wonders

SF's mile-wide and 3-mile-long wild streak starts with the **Conservatory of Flowers** *(gggp.org;,adult/youth & senior/child $17/7/3)*, a restored 1878 greenhouse full of orchids, lilies and carnivorous plants – check the online schedule for holiday light shows and art events. Combined tickets *(adult/youth & senior/child $33/21/9)* offer same-day admission to the Japanese Tea Garden and 55-acre **San Francisco Botanical Garden**, which covers a world of vegetation from South African savanna to New Zealand cloud forest. Plants here are serenaded by professional musicians at **Flower Piano** *(gggp.org/flowerpiano)*.

PRACTICALITIES

● sfrecpark.org ● 24hr ● free

At the park's wild western edge, bison have roamed the **Buffalo Paddock** since 1889. Blue butterflies alight on your shoulders in the **Osher Rainforest Dome**, starfish wave hello in **Steinhart Aquarium** and penguins waddle their way through the **California Academy of Sciences** *(calacademy.org; adult/child from $49/45)*, championing weird, wild science since 1853. Night owls party at **NightLife events** *($25; 6-10pm Thu; ages 21+)*, featuring themed cocktails and Planetarium shows. Kids may not technically sleep during Academy Sleepovers, but they might jump-start science careers.

Art in the Park

The park's all-star art attraction is the **de Young Museum** *(famsf.org; adult/youth $20/free)*. Main-floor exhibits range from Inuit carvings to California prison photography; upstairs features Oceanic carvings and the textile collection; and blockbuster basement retrospectives range from surrealist Frida Kahlo to photographer Ansel Adams. For park panoramas, take the elevator up to the top of the 144ft **observation tower** – or cloudwatch in James Turrell's Skyspace installation, hidden under the Osher Sculpture Garden. Access is free to the tower and store; ticket includes free same-day entry to the Legion of Honor (p108). City-supported nonprofit **Sharon Art Studio** offers workshops to create your own masterpieces *(1-3 day workshops $150-350; ages 18+)*, and **Out There Watercolors** runs outdoor painting expeditions *(outtherewatercolors.com; $120 per hour, up to 4 people, ages 12+)*.

Park Music Events

Golden Gate Park has hosted epic festivals ever since the 1967 Human Be-In urged free spirits to 'tune in, turn on, drop out.' Dig the vibes year-round at free **Music Concourse** shows, weekend **Hippie Hill** drum circles and the free annual **420 Festival** *(420hippiehill.com)*, named after International Bong Hit Time (4:20pm). Mega-festivals are held around the **Polo Fields** – notably **Hardly Strictly Bluegrass** *(hardlystrictly bluegrass.com; free)*, held the first weekend in October, and alt-Coachella fest **Outside Lands** *(sfoutsidelands.com)*, held the first weekend in August.

Meditative Moments

Since 1894, the 5-acre **Japanese Tea Garden** *(gggp.org; adult/youth & senior/child $15/7/3; first hour free)* has blushed pink with cherry blossoms in spring and turned flaming red with maple leaves in fall. Don't miss the meditative Zen Garden and Tea House fortune cookies (introduced right here). For peaceful reflection ringed by redwoods and paving-stone tributes, step into the **National AIDS Memorial Grove** – founded in 1991 to commemorate millions of lives lost to the AIDS epidemic. At **Breast Cancer Memorial Garden** *(sfrecpark.org)* off Conservatory Dr, the secluded hilltop is ringed with benches and flowers.

PARK ORIGINS

Golden Gate Park was considered impossible when first backed by San Franciscan voters in 1866. New York's Central Park architect Frederick Law Olmsted balked at transforming 1017 acres of dunes into parkland, so plans fell to civil engineer William Hammond Hall. He insisted that instead of planned casinos, racetracks and a plaster igloo village, Golden Gate Park should showcase – here's a radical idea – nature.

TOP TIPS

- John F Kennedy Dr is pedestrian-only starting at 9th Ave – a weekend hotspot with roller disco and free Lindy Hop dance lessons.
- Pick up bicycle rentals inside the park at Parkwide Bike and Surrey (*parkwide.com; rentals from $22.50/2hrs*).
- When the weather's behaving, pedal boats and rowboats are available daily at the restored 1946 Stow Lake Boathouse *(row/pedal boats $26/32.50)*.
- Kids flock to the park's historic children's playground to ride the vintage 1912 carousel *(adult/child $2.50/1)*, scoot down 1970s concrete slides and scale the new climbing wall.

WHAT HAPPENED TO SUTRO BATHS?

It's hard to imagine from these ruins, but Victorian dandies and working stiffs once converged here for bracing baths in woolen rental swimsuits. Millionaire Adolph Sutro built hot and cold indoor pools in 1896 to accommodate 10,000 bathers – but in 1897, bath bouncers denied Black San Franciscan John Harris access. He promptly sued Sutro and won a landmark case for desegregating community facilities. The baths went bust in 1952, and in 1964 developers began razing them to build high-rise condos amid a public outcry. An arsonist burned what was left of the bath buildings in 1966, possibly for the insurance money. But even in ruins, the baths remain iconic, providing a fitting backdrop for 1971's comedy classic *Harold & Maude*.

(continued from p103)
and *Surfing Guide to California*, while kooks (newbies) try on Mollusk's 'kelp bed cruiser, wave peruser' T-shirts. Ready to hit the waves? Most SF surfers get their start in protected coves, like East Beach at Crissy Field (p51). Check out rental surf gear and surf lessons offered at **Aqua Surf Shop** *(aquasurfshop.com; lessons $120 to $150; rental per day bodyboard/wetsuit $10/15, surfboard $25-35).*

Mingle with Masterpieces at the Legion of Honor

Look inside the city's monumental treasure box

A museum as eccentric and illuminating as San Francisco itself, the **Legion of Honor** *(famsf.org; adult/child $20/free)* showcases eclectic art treasures: Monet water lilies and John Cage soundscapes upstairs, ancient cuneiform tablets and Enrique Chagoya's border-crossing Mayan codex downstairs. Each year, the Legion invites provocative contemporary artists to engage

EATING IN THE SUNSET: MEGA-FLAVOR MEALS

Thanh Long: Classic crab – roasted, tamarind or 'drunken' – with garlic noodles and warm An family welcomes. *4.30-8pm Sun, Wed & Thu, to 9pm Fri & Sat* $$

Hook Fish Co: Join surfers at weathered wooden tables for fresh, sustainable Pacific seafood in tacos or burritos, atop salads, or in fish and chips. *11.30am-9pm* $

Mini Potstickers: Dumpling experts pack mini-dumplings with Wagyu beef and flavor-bomb veggies. *10.30am-3pm & 5-8.30pm Mon-Fri, 10.30am-8.30pm Sat & Sun* $

Manna: Home-style Korean cooking, including *kalbi* (BBQ short ribs) and *dol-sot bibimbap* (sizzling stone pot rice); parties of four max. *11am-9.30pm Tue-Sun* $

VENTU PHOTO/SHUTTERSTOCK

Golden Gate Bridge viewed from Lands End

with the priceless permanent collection – Wangetchi Mutu positioned her bronze *Shavasana* sculptures of two Black women in the long shadow of Rodin's *The Thinker*. Blockbuster shows range from Guo Pei's fantasy couture to Picasso's sketchbooks, alongside selections from the **Achenbach Collection's** 90,000 works on paper. Entry to the downstairs **museum cafe** and store is free, and museum entry is free after 4.30pm. Tickets cover free same-day entry to the de Young Museum (p107).

Hike to Lands End

Wander along the edge of the continent

Looking out from **Lands End** *(nps.gov/goga)* at the wild, endless Pacific, you'll realize that ancient mapmakers had a point – if ever there were a place for mermaids, monsters and magic, this is it. Trails through this rugged landscape reward you with glimpses of shipwrecks, sea lions and the Golden Gate Bridge. At low tide, follow the steep path past the ruins of **Sutro Baths** and through the sea-cave tunnel to sublime Pacific panoramas.

THANKS, BIG ALMA

Legions of art fans owe thanks to 'Big Alma' de Bretteville Spreckels, the SF sculptor's model who changed the art world. In 1902, she publicly sued the gold miner 'personal defloweration' and 'breach of promise' – and won. Then Big Alma volunteered to model for Union Sq's Goddess of Victory monument, towering triumphantly with a cast-in-bronze wardrobe malfunction. The statue-selection-committee chair was sugar baron Adolph Spreckels, who became Big Alma's 'sugar daddy' and left her his fortune. Big Alma raised funds to rebuild post-earthquake SF, investigated working conditions for women for the US Department of Labor and donated the Legion and Maritime Museum to her beloved San Francisco.

EATING IN THE RICHMOND: DELIGHTFUL DINNERS

Aziza: Cal-Moroccan plates arrive with fragrant fanfare: wild salmon tagine, lamb *shakshuka* and chicken confit bastilla. *5-9.30pm Wed-Sun, 10.30am-2pm Sat & Sun* $$$

Mamahuhu: Fresh takes on nostalgic Chinese American classics: sustainable beef and broccoli, sweet-and-sour cauliflower, shiitake-mushroom mapo tofu. *11.30am-9pm* $

Chapeau: Head to this family-owned French bistro for well-priced tasting menus ($50-92) that feature classics like onion soup and duck cassoulet. *5-9pm Wed-Sun* $$$

The Laundromat: The only thing you'll clean at Laundromat is your plate – memorable square pizzas come loaded with tasty toppings. *8am-2pm & 5-9pm Wed-Sun* $

MELANIE HOBSON/SHUTTERSTOCK

Sutro Baths (p109)

Above the baths, you'll find the **Lands End Lookout** visitor center and **Sutro Heights Park** public gardens, built in 1885 and splendidly restored with native plants. From the Lookout, the **Coastal Trail** winds along Lands End bluffs, offering end-of-the-world views and low-tide sightings of coastal shipwrecks along the way to **Lincoln Park** *(sfrecpark.org)*. America's legendary coast-to-coast Lincoln Hwy officially ends at this 100-acre park, which served as San Francisco's cemetery until 1909. At Lincoln Park, you can duck into the Legion of Honor (p108) or descend the gloriously tiled Lincoln Park Steps (near 32nd Ave). If you've got energy to burn, push onward through the Presidio to reach the Golden Gate Bridge – or book in advance for a round at scenic **Lincoln Park Golf Course** *(lincolnparkgolfcourse.com; weekday/weekend $54/61)*.

EATING IN THE RICHMOND: LUNCH

Taqueria Los Mayas: *Panuchos* (bean-filled tortillas) come piled with Yucatecan *cochinita pibil* (tangy barbecued pork) and housemade salsas. *11am-9pm* $

Dragon Beaux: Hong Kong meets Vegas at Geary Blvd's decadent Cantonese dim sum restaurant. *11am-3pm & 5-9pm Mon-Fri, from 10am Sat & Sun* $$

Bettola: Your friendly neighborhood *tavola calda* (hot table) dishes lasagna, prosciutto-loaded white pizza and brined rotisserie chicken. *11am-9pm* $

Han Il Kwan: Join surfers and grandmas for epic lunches: sizzling meats and stone bowls brimming with bibimbap. *11am-8pm Sun & Mon, to 9pm Thu-Sat* $

TOP EXPERIENCE

Ocean Beach & Sunset Dunes

At this blustery, atmospheric city beach, the sun sets over the Pacific – though fog banks may swallow it first. Standing on this serene stretch of golden sand with your back to the city, you can watch the Pacific ebb and flow as it always does, with only a few brave surfers to remind you what century you're in.

MARLEYPUG/SHUTTERSTOCK

Ocean Beach

San Francisco's 3.5-mile **beach** is not like most California scenes in Hollywood movies – this moody, misty setting is better suited to meditative solo walks or bonding with friends. This was the original site of Burning Man; bonfires are allowed in artist-designed fire pits from March to October until 9.30pm. Swimmers, beware riptides; beachcombers, mind sneaker waves. Face the Pacific and spot brave surfers, passing ships and sea lions bobbing in the waves.

Sunset Dunes

At the southern end of Ocean Beach is a new 50-acre waterfront park called **Sunset Dunes**. By popular vote in 2024, San Francisco converted a section of highway to park trails for joggers, cyclists, skaters and walkers to enjoy. Stick to paths in areas undergoing habitat restoration and keep dogs on leash to protect wildlife. The dunes offer shelter for birdwatching – including skittish snowy plover shorebirds in winter – plus picnics and outdoor painting expeditions with **Out There Watercolors** (p107). To paint the sunset, pick up art supplies at nearby **Case for Making** *(caseformaking.com)*, where artisans make pigments specifically to capture subtle Pacific hues.

TOP TIPS

- Take a break at the **Beach Chalet** *(beachchalet.com)*, with splendid 1930s frescoes.
- Break out your favorite costume for **Bay to Breakers** *(baytobreakers.com)*, a truly fun 7.5-mile run from the Embarcadero to Ocean Beach. Joggers dressed as salmon run upstream.

PRACTICALITIES

- parksconservancy.org
- 24hr; parking lot closes at 10pm
- Free

Places We Love to Stay

$** Budget **$$** Midrange **$$$ Top End

Presidio, Marina & Fisherman's Wharf

MAP P48

HI San Francisco Fisherman's Wharf $ Get million-dollar waterfront views in an ex-army barracks that's now SF's top hostel. Choose private rooms or dorms (some co-ed), all with shared bathrooms and a communal kitchen offering free breakfasts.

Marina Motel $ Stay at a sitcom-set vintage 1939 motel with kitschy-cute rooms with kitchenettes – scuffed but well-maintained, with murals and free parking off busy Lombard St.

Hotel del Sol $$ With splashy beach-ball color schemes, palm-lined courtyard and heated outdoor pool, the Marina's mid-century motor lodge is SF's top choice for families.

Lodge at the Presidio $$ The officers' post turned ecolodge has dashingly handsome guestrooms with pillowtop beds, historic photos and commanding views – request a room overlooking the Golden Gate Bridge.

Infinity Hotel $$ Smartly contemporary yet snugly comfortable, the Infinity on Lombard St offers unexpected perks: bonus bidets, steam showers and roof-deck views from here to infinity.

Argonaut Hotel $$$ Built as a cannery in 1908, Fisherman's Wharf's top hotel remains a waterfront character, with exposed-brick walls, century-old beams and nautical decor in snug guest rooms.

Inn at the Presidio $$$ The Presidio's former officers' quarters now welcome civilians as a national-park lodge, with oversize rooms featuring pillowtop beds, suites with gas fireplaces and hiking trailheads out back.

Kimpton Alton $$$ The Wharf's hip hangout has sleek modern guestrooms big enough to use in-room yoga mats, record players and workstations so you can pretend to work remotely.

Union Street Inn $$$ Live like a Victorian socialite at this grand B&B with six antique-filled guestrooms, afternoon tea in lush gardens and generous breakfasts in the parlor.

Downtown, Civic Center & SoMa

MAP P58

citizenM San Francisco Union Square $ An elevator operator guides you to the colorful modern lobby at this Dutch boutique chain; rooms are small, iPad-controlled, clean, hip and affordable – plus there's a rooftop deck.

HI San Francisco Downtown $ In a restored historic building near the Tenderloin, hostel rooms are safe and clean, nonsqueaky bunks have personal power points and the shared lounge and kitchen are sociable.

Orchard Garden Hotel $$ SF's first LEED-certified green hotel is surprisingly affordable and conveniently located just outside Chinatown, with a gym, a rooftop deck and optional breakfast at the sustainable Roots restaurant.

Hotel Nikko $$ Convenient Union Sq hotel with friendly staff and quiet, decent-sized rooms with luxurious high thread-count linens. On-site restaurant Anzu offers a Japanese breakfast included in room rate.

Palace Hotel $$$ The 1906 landmark Palace remains a monument to turn-of-the-century grandeur, with Maxfield Parrish paintings in the bar, teatime in the marble Garden Court and a vast pool.

Beacon Grand $$$ Right off Union Sq, the Beacon offers magnificent welcomes in its Spanish-Moroccan lobby and smallish rooms with business-class amenities and proper beds – plus dynamite cocktails at Starlite rooftop bar.

Chinatown & North Beach

MAP P66

San Remo Hotel $ Built in 1906, this North Beach boarding house offers cheerful Italian grandma-styled rooms with eclectic antique furnishings and shared bathrooms. Remodeled rooms have private baths, but lack space and character. No elevator.

Pacific Tradewinds Hostel $ San Francisco's smartest all-dorm hostel has a fully equipped kitchen (free coffee, tea and PB&J sandwiches), spotless showers, sturdy bunk beds, laundry (free sock wash), luggage storage, no lockout time and, best of all, fun staff. No elevator.

Green Tortoise Hostel $ North Beach's hostel encourages bonding with pool, ping-pong, games, co-working stations and weekly live music shows in the sunny ballroom. Perks include a sauna, free breakfast, good wi-fi, on-site laundry and communal kitchen. Dorm rooms have generous lockers.

Hotel Bohème $$ The quintessential North Beach inn has smallish rooms named after Beat writers with wrought-iron beds, original artwork and small bathrooms. Some rooms face noisy Columbus Ave and there's no elevator – but novels practically write themselves here.

Washington Square Inn $$ Facing sunny Washington Sq, this 1910 inn offers snug retro-mod guestrooms, some with a bathroom across the hall. But this is a charming location, with a sociable front room for coffee. No elevator or on-site staff; entry via digital key system.

Nob Hill & Russian Hill MAP P74

Music City Hotel & Hostel $ This Lower Nob Hill (aka 'Tendernob') music-themed hostel has decor dedicated to Green Day and the Beatles. It's committed to the cause with a live music venue attached to the lobby.

Fairmont San Francisco $$$ Magnificent marble lobby, opulent mosaic penthouse suite – plus San Francisco eccentricity, including the tiki Tonga Room and the circus-mural Cirque Bar. Guest rooms have business-class comfort. For historic appeal, reserve in the original 1906 building; for jaw-dropping views, go for the tower.

Japantown, Fillmore & Pacific Heights MAP P78

Queen Anne Hotel $$ Once a girls' boarding school, this grand 1890 pink Victorian mansion is period-perfect: carved wood beds, antique vanities, tasseled curtains. Rooms are comfy, though the wallpaper is too close for comfort in some. Includes continental breakfast, afternoon tea and sherry.

Chateau Tivoli $$ The source of neighborhood gossip since 1892, this gorgeous Painted Lady mansion hosted Isadora Duncan, Mark Twain and (rumor has it) the ghost of a Victorian opera diva. Antique-filled rooms, most with ensuite baths and no TV; 3-course breakfast included.

Hotel Kabuki $$$ Japanese mid-century modern meets 1960s SF in cleverly updated decor: Noguchi tables flank shibori tie-dyed bedheads, trippy collages adorn slate-gray walls. Helpful concierges, meditation garden, well-equipped fitness center and best of all: dinner on-site at Nari.

The Haight & Hayes Valley MAP P84

Hayes Valley Inn $ Like a European pension, this reasonable find has simple rooms: two with bunks, two with singles and the turret rooms fit three. All share bathrooms, a napping dog in the parlor and welcoming staff. No elevator.

Metro Hotel $$ Hip Divisadero St is lined with boutiques and restaurants, and Metro Hotel is in a prime position. Rooms are cheerful and clean, and quirky art enlivens newly refreshed rooms. No elevator.

Parsonage $$$ At this 1883 Italianate Victorian, with original Carrara-marble fireplaces, rose-brass chandeliers and period furnishings, antique-adorned rooms are named after San Francisco's grand dames. Architect Julia Morgan gets the best views. Two-night minimum.

The Castro MAP P92

Beck's Motor Lodge $$ This mid-century motel is looking sharp, young for its age and even a tad upscale. A gay go-to, rooms here book out early for Pride and Folsom Street Fair.

Hotel Castro $$ Stay out late and wake up inspired in the Castro, amid stunning photo-mosaics of Harvey Milk and Sylvia Rivera at this smart boutique hotel. Enjoy signature cocktails in the downstairs lounge and sunsets on the rooftop terrace.

Parker Guest House $$ Make your gay getaway in grand style at this Edwardian estate. Guestrooms feature stately beds and generous closets for coming out of, and continental breakfasts, wine and sherry are included.

JAMES KIRKIKIS/SHUTTERSTOCK

Fairmont San Francisco

Researched by
Ryan Ver Berkmoes

Marin County & Bay Area

WHERE THE COAST MEETS THE BAY

From wild walks by the Pacific to the magnificence of Hwy 1, from redwood splendor to bounteous tables, the greater Bay Area endlessly beguiles.

The San Francisco Bay Area encompasses a bonanza of natural vistas and wildlife. Cross the Golden Gate Bridge into Marin County and visit wizened ancient redwoods body-blocking the sun, and herds of elephant seals chilling on the sands of Point Reyes. Gray whales blow spray off the filigreed coast, while hawks prowl the skies over the wild sands and shaggy hills of the Marin Headlands.

In the East Bay, Oakland is the diverse, radically proud place San Francisco once was. Berkeley sparked the locavore food movement that spread worldwide and, together with its long-standing university, continues to be at the forefront of environmental and left-leaning political causes. North, you'll find gritty bayside towns and national park sites recalling nearly forgotten chapters of history.

Academic and urbane Stanford University is the soul of Palo Alto, which in turn is the heart of Silicon Valley, the land of start-up legends and louche billionaires. Travel the world without leaving San Jose, the low-key powerhouse anchor to the valley's fortunes.

Meandering along endlessly beautiful coast south of San Francisco, Hwy 1 traces 70 miles of undeveloped coastline south to Santa Cruz. Spot whales offshore, and seals and sea otters close in. Lose count of the sandy cove beaches and ribbons of dunes amid wetlands and redwoods. Pause for an hour or a day in Half Moon Bay, Pescadero or a bend in the road.

ANATOLIY LUKICH/SHUTTERSTOCK

THE MAIN AREAS

For places to stay in Marin County & Bay Area, see p160

JASON TODD/GETTY IMAGES

Left: Elk, Point Reyes National Seashore (p126); Above: Muir Woods (p124)

PALO ALTO
Silicon Valley's well-heeled center.
p146

SAN JOSE
Vibrant and multicultural.
p151

HALF MOON BAY
Top stop on Hwy 1.
p154

Find Your Way

The Bay Area surrounds the San Francisco Bay, which breaks up this large region into individual areas. The coasts are more unified in their raw beauty and intrigue.

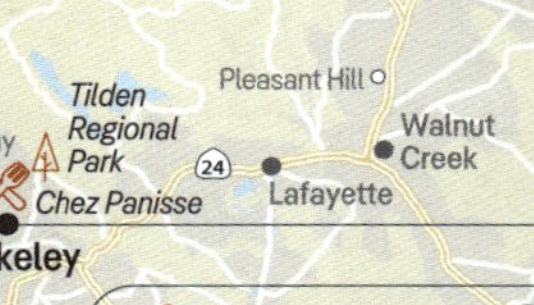

Sausalito, p120

Reachable by ferry, a town right on the bay with bohemian roots, and gateway to the Marin Headlands and Muir Woods and beyond.

Berkeley, p138

The famous university town is a delight to explore on foot, from the campus to the surrounding neighborhoods. Head north for intriguing national park sites.

Point Reyes, p126

A beautiful national seashore with miles of wave-tossed beaches, some teeming with enormous elephant seals. A must stop before continuing on Hwy 1.

Oakland, p130

The big city across the bay from San Francisco offers intriguing, walkable and contrasting neighborhoods, with some of the region's best eating.

Colma
San Bruno
San Francisco International Airport
Hayward
Pleasanton
Livermore
Pacifica
San Mateo
Sunol
Fremont
Montara
Moss Beach
Princeton
Redwood City
East Palo Alto
Sunol Regional Wilderness
Half Moon Bay
Palo Alto
Milpitas
Mountain View
Santa Clara
San Jose
San Gregorio
La Honda
Cupertino
Pacific Ocean
Pescadero
Saratoga
Los Gatos
0 — 50 km
0 — 25 miles

Half Moon Bay, p154

The anchor of the sensational segment of Hwy 1 between San Francisco and Santa Cruz. Be overawed by myriad wonders north and south.

Palo Alto, p146

The heart of Silicon Valley has an enticing downtown and the genteel charms of Stanford University. Further afield are beautiful open spaces.

San Jose, p151

The state's third-largest city is a web of international neighborhoods with Mexican, Vietnamese, Japanese and other cultures. It's near top Silicon Valley sights.

CAR

The ideal way to explore the Bay Area. Hwy 1 north and south of the Golden Gate is best experienced with the freedom of your own wheels. A car is less necessary in the main cities of the East Bay and Peninsula.

TRAIN

The Bay Area is well-connected by train. BART has fast services from San Mateo via San Francisco to all the major points in the East Bay. Caltrain is another winner, knitting together the Peninsula from SF to San Jose, via Palo Alto.

FERRY

An expanding network of ferries connects the cities around the bay in fast and scenic style. It's *the* way to visit Sausalito and a fine way to reach Larkspur and the Smart train north. Oakland and Alameda are also easily reached.

Plan Your Time

Marin County and the Bay Area is a region where you can spend your time savoring just one place, or you can indulge your every peripatetic urge.

LUUUSI/SHUTTERSTOCK

Tennessee Beach (p124)

If You Only Do One Thing

- Head to Marin County. If coming from San Francisco, you can take the ferry to **Sausalito** (p120) and have lunch. Afterward, walk back to SF via **Fort Baker** (p121) and across the Golden Gate Bridge, with its incredible views of the Bay Area and massive ships passing below. Or, go deeper into the county and take the shuttle bus to **Muir Woods National Monument** (p124) to feel the otherworldly presence of the magnificent stand of old-growth redwoods.

- If in a car, stop at the **Marin Headlands** (p122) for the superb views, then follow Hwy 1 north through beach towns like **Stinson Beach** (p124). Finish at **Point Reyes National Seashore** (p126), which combines beaches with raw nature, including massive elephant seals in season.

Seasonal Highlights

Winter may bring rain, but Bay Area temperatures inspire envy. Spring and fall are beautiful, while summer ranges from chilly on the coast to blazing inland.

JANUARY

Winter storms (in non-drought years) mean driftwood on the beaches, pounding surf and salmon running in some redwood-forest streams. Pack your rain gear.

MARCH

With spring, hillsides trade tawny brown for impossibly bright green speckled with orange California poppies. Driving two-lane backroads amongst the rolling hills, you'll swear the vivid virescence makes your eyes hurt.

MAY

One of the best months to visit the Bay Area. The weather is warm and the inland areas have not yet reached temperatures that suck in the fog. Visitor numbers are manageable.

Three Days to Travel Around

● After don't-miss Marin County, add in the essential East Bay. **Oakland** (p130) and **Berkeley** (p138) abut and, with their utterly different personalities, will give you days and days of diverse activities and eating.

● In Oakland, stop by the **Oakland Museum of California** (p132) for an enlightened look at the state. Walk around **Lake Merritt** (p134), and stop by **Jack London Sq** (p133) for a drink where the man himself once did homework and later drank.

● In Berkeley, walk the **Cal campus** (p138), soaking up the atmosphere, and enjoy some superb meals. Then pop north to Richmond for the eye-opening exhibits of societal change at the **Rosie the Riveter WWII Home Front National Historic Park** (p144).

If You Have More Time

● Get your vehicle and cruise Hwy 1, south from **Pacifica** (p157). In fact, you may wish to do this if you only have one day. The 70 miles to Santa Cruz along this fabled road make up one of the world's most beautiful drives. Stop off at any beach that catches your eye, but know that to see them all would require a month or more. There are coves like **Gray Whale Cove State Beach** (p157) and wide-open expanses like **Gazos Creek State Beach** (p159). See the tiny tidepool creatures that live in the rocks at **Fitzgerald Marine Reserve** (p157).

● Stop for lunch at **Half Moon Bay** (p154) or **Pescadero** (p158) and circle back to SF, or continue to Santa Cruz and beyond.

JUNE

Watch for **county fairs** to start being held around the region with their bodacious foods, cheesy thrill rides, barnyard animals, familiar stage acts and fireworks.

AUGUST

If visiting from afar, pack warm clothes! The sight of visitors in shorts and t-shirts shivering while trying to enjoy the splendors of Hwy 1 on a foggy day has entertained residents for decades.

OCTOBER

How big is your pumpkin? The famous **Half Moon Bay Art & Pumpkin Festival** (p156) celebrates the Halloween icon while neighboring fields are dotted with enormous numbers of the seasonal orange icons.

DECEMBER

Colder temps bring crisply clear skies so you can appreciate the mountains surrounding Silicon Valley and along the coast. If you're lucky, the tops of Mt Tamalpais and Mt Diablo will get dusted with snow.

Sausalito

VIEWS | VILLAGE | FERRY RIDES

GETTING AROUND

Golden Gate Ferry *(goldengate.org; adult/child $14/7)* links regularly with San Francisco's Ferry Building. Blue & Gold Fleet ferries sail from Pier 41 in the Fisherman's Wharf area for a similar price. These 30-minute rides afford fabulous bay views. Golden Gate Transit buses frequently cross the Golden Gate Bridge to/from San Francisco and also further north to San Rafael and Sonoma County. Marin Transit offers public bus service as far as Bolinas and Point Reyes.

TOP TIP

Parking can be a pain – if you're just visiting town and/or hiking locally, take the ferry from San Francisco. If you're combining a visit to Sausalito with the nearby Marin Headlands and Point Reyes, a car is essential – prepare for parking challenges.

Perfectly arranged on a sheltered harbor on the bay, Sausalito is undeniably lovely. Named for the tiny willows that once populated the banks of its creeks, it's famous for its colorful houseboats bobbing in the bay. Much of the well-heeled downtown has uninterrupted views of San Francisco and Angel Island.

A major tourist hub, Sausalito is jam-packed with souvenir shops and fair-to-middling boutiques. It's the first town you'll encounter after crossing the Golden Gate Bridge from San Francisco.

Sausalito began as a busy lumber port with a racy waterfront. Dramatic changes came in WWII when Sausalito became the site of Marinship, a vast shipbuilding yard just north of the center. After the war a new Bohemian period began, with hundreds of residents living on houseboats. Today the town defines genteel.

Interactive Bay Exhibit

The whole bay in miniature

One of the coolest things in this beautiful town, fascinating to both kids and adults, is the Army Corps of Engineers' **Bay Model Visitor Center** *(spn.usace.army.mil/Missions/Recreation/Bay-Model-Visitor-Center; free)*. Housed in one of the old Marinship warehouses, it's a 1.5-acre hydraulic model of San Francisco Bay and the delta region that shows how the whole bay works.

Walking Sausalito & the Golden Gate Bridge

San Francisco's best day-trip walk

One of the Bay Area's best walks begins and ends in San Francisco (p41) and features some of the region's best scenery.

Catch a mid-morning ferry to Sausalito, enjoying the views of Alcatraz and Angel Island. Stroll the town and get refreshments and a picnic. Follow East Rd south along the beautiful shoreline until you reach Fort Baker. Walk under the **Golden Gate Bridge** and curve up the access road until you reach the popular viewpoint.

Cross the bridge on the eastern walkway (the west side is for cyclists). Dress warmly! It's 1.7 miles across. It's 5 miles from

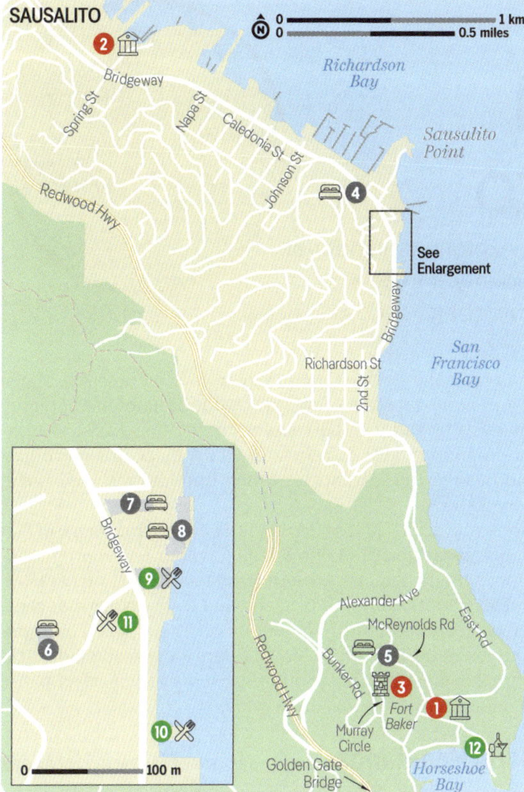

SIGHTS
1 Bay Area Discovery Museum
2 Bay Model Visitor Center
3 Fort Baker

SLEEPING
4 Casa Madrona Hotel & Spa
5 Cavallo Point
6 Gables Inn Sausalito
7 Hotel Sausalito & Suites
8 Inn Above Tide

EATING
9 Barrel House Tavern
10 Scoma's
11 Venice Gourmet Delicatessen & Pizzeria

DRINKING & NIGHTLIFE
12 Travis Marina

Sausalito to the San Francisco side of the bridge, where you can stroll onwards to the Presidio and the Marina.

Enticing Fort, Seafront & Museum

Explore Fort Baker

Below the north tower of the Golden Gate Bridge, surprisingly uncrowded **Fort Baker** *(nps.gov/goga; free)* hides in plain sight. Stroll Horseshoe Bay, watch the winter-time crab fishers, and get a snack or lunch from one of several good outlets.

A highlight is the **Bay Area Discovery Museum** *(bayareadiscoverymuseum.org; $20)*, a child-centric, indoor-outdoor facility.

HISTORIC FORT BAKER

Fort Baker helped guard the entrance to the San Francisco Bay. The army tried to stem its perennial problem of desertion by making the facilities here better than average with porches, large windows and even indoor toilets!

Today trails extend along the coast and you can even spend the night in former officers' quarters at the luxe **Cavallo Point Lodge** (p160).

EATING & DRINKING IN SAUSALITO: OUR PICKS

Scoma's: Old-school classics such as cioppino (a piquant seafood stew) and Crab Louie salads served on a pier. Fresh seafood line-up changes daily. *11.30am-9.30pm* $$$

Venice Gourmet Delicatessen & Pizzeria: In the center, build a picnic with Italian sandwiches, prepared foods and baked goods or a crispy pizza. *9am-5pm* $

Barrel House Tavern: Waterfront tavern serves California cuisine like local cheeses and charcuterie fare. Good list of regional beer, wine and spirits. Book. *11am-9pm* $$

Travis Marina: Fort Baker's near-secret bar welcomes everyone with incredible bay and bridge views. Regular live music. *4-8pm Fri, noon-8pm Sat, noon-6pm Sun*

Beyond Sausalito

Spend a day or a week exploring the natural wonderland of Marin County. It's like a concentrate of fresh outdoor goodness.

Places

GETTING AROUND

Ferries from San Francisco serve Tiburon and Larkspur. The latter connects with the Smart train, which runs north to San Rafael and on to Santa Rosa via Petaluma.

Golden Gate Transit and Marin Transit operate local bus services along the Hwy 101 corridor. Marin Transit also serves Stinson Beach, Bolinas and Point Reyes via connections from Sausalito.

Just across the Golden Gate Bridge from San Francisco, Marin County is a collection of wealthy, wooded hamlets that hang tenuously by haute hippie roots as an ever-more-affluent tech-era population gets comfortable. It's a place of superb natural beauty and adventure, which unfolds west and north of Sausalito.

Geographically, Marin County is a near mirror image of San Francisco, although Marin is much wilder and more mountainous. Redwoods grow on the coast-side hills, surf crashes against remote cliffs and beaches, and trails crisscross scenic Marin Headlands, Muir Woods and Mt Tamalpais. These glorious surroundings make Marin County an excellent day trip or weekend escape from San Francisco, or the perfect pause on a longer coastal California journey.

Marin Headlands

TIME FROM SAUSALITO: **10 MINS**

Awesome views, hikes & animal sanctuary

The cliffs and hillsides of the **Marin Headlands**, a mere 15 minutes by car from Sausalito, rise majestically at the north end of the Golden Gate Bridge, their rugged beauty all the more striking given the fact that they're only a few miles from San Francisco's urban core. A smattering of forts and bunkers are left over from a century of US military occupation. It's no mystery why this is one of the Bay Area's most popular hiking and cycling destinations: as the trails wind through the near-pristine headlands, they afford stunning views of the sea, the bridge and San Francisco, and lead to isolated beaches and secluded picnic spots.

The historical **Point Bonita Lighthouse** *(nps.gov/goga/pobo; free)* is a breathtaking half-mile walk from Field Rd parking area. Harbor seals haul out seasonally on nearby rocks.

At the western end of Bunker Rd sits spectacular **Rodeo Beach** *(parksconservancy.org/parks/rodeo-beach)*, partly protected from wind by high cliffs. All along the coastline you'll find cool old battery sites – abandoned concrete bunkers dug into the ground with fabulous views. Start at **Battery Townsley** *(free)*, a half-mile walk or bike ride up from the Fort Cronkhite parking lot. The **Coastal Trail** leads to **Muir Beach**. The headlands are also laced with superb mountain-biking trails. The **Julian Trail** is a rewarding 12-mile dirt loop.

MICHAEL VI/SHUTTERSTOCK

Memorial plaque, Angel Island Immigration Station

Above Rodeo Beach, the **Marine Mammal Center** *(marine mammalcenter.org; free)* rehabilitates injured, sick and orphaned sea mammals before returning them to the wild. Reserve a slot in advance and you can see adult seals and pups being cared for from an observation deck.

Angel Island

TIME FROM SAUSALITO: **15MIN**

Once notorious oasis in the bay

In the middle of San Francisco Bay, **Angel Island** was a hunting and fishing ground for the Miwok people. In the early 20th century, it was nicknamed the 'Ellis Island of the West' as it had a US Immigration Station that was used to screen and detain Chinese immigrants as part of the racist Chinese Exclusion Act. Later, the island served as a military base, a WWII Japanese internment camp and an anti-aircraft missile site. Besides the **Immigration Station** *(aiisf.org; adult/child $5/3)*, there are forts and bunkers with thought-provoking displays amid the natural beauty.

History aside, Angel Island is a natural wonderland. You can hike the 5-mile perimeter trail with its all-star views of the Bay Area, or to the summit of 788ft Mt Livermore. Alternatively, enjoy a picnic in a protected cove or beach, looking out at the seemingly close yet distant urban grid. On most days crowds are few, even though access is easy by ferry from San Francisco, Sausalito and Tiburon. Bikes can be rented near the daytime cafe by the ferry dock.

BEST STATE PARKS IN MARIN COUNTY

China Camp State Park: Just northeast of San Rafael, this park preserves a Chinese shrimp-fishing village from the beginning of the 19th century. Fishers and their families were able to live here away from the rampant racism found across California. *friends ofchinacamp.org; parking $5*

Olompali State Historic Park: Marin County was once among the homes of the Coastal Miwok people. The park preserves the site of a village that was inhabited from about 6000 BCE until 1850. Reach it from Hwy 101 in Novato. *olompali.org; parking $8*

Samuel P Taylor State Park: In the coastal hills along Sir Francis Drake Blvd, this large preserve has groves of redwoods and streams that fill with spawning salmon in winter. *parks.ca.gov*

EATING BEYOND SAUSALITO: OUR PICKS

Village Sake: World-class Japanese food in Fairfax; the *izakaya* (pub-style fare and tapas-like small dishes) are paired with craft beers and sake. *5-8pm Wed-Sun* $$$

Madcap: West of San Rafael in San Anselmo is this outpost for beautifully crafted Californian fare. Ever-changing Asian-accented menu. *5-8.30pm Tue-Sat* $$$

Parkside Cafe: On Stinson Beach, the snack bar serves soft-serve ice cream, the restaurant aims higher with seafood platters garnished with caviar. *7.30am-9pm* $$

Pelican Inn: Oh-so-quaint pub takes you from Muir Beach to the Cornish Coast. Trad high-end pub fare. Beef Wellington is ideal on a foggy day. *11am-10pm* $$

BEST BEACHES

Tennessee Beach: Many say the 1.8-mile hike to this secluded cove is their favorite ever, given the stark Pacific scenery of jagged rocks, sheer hills and raw, natural scenery.

Muir Beach: A quiet hamlet with a pretty gray-sand beach. Hike here from the headlands or Muir Woods.

Stinson Beach: The wide, blond sand buzzes on warm, sunny weekends. The town has a handful of eateries and lots of vacation rentals.

Bolinas: This surfer's hangout got on the map for being off the map: road signs to the town often vanish in the night.

Steep Ravine Beach: The name says it: park along Hwy 1 and hike down a challenging trail for nearly a mile to an often deserted, rocky beach.

BRET J UNGER/SHUTTERSTOCK

Cathedral Grove, Muir Woods

Camping on Angel Island mixes serene isolation with an evening light show around the bay.

Golden Gate Ferry operates up to four ferries daily to Angel Island from San Francisco's Ferry Building from April to October *(goldengate.org; round-trip adult/child $31/16; 30 minutes)*. There's a reduced schedule November to March. Buy tickets before boarding.

Angel Island–Tiburon Ferry operates ferry service to the island from downtown Tiburon from May to September *(angelislandferry.com; round-trip adult/child $18/15; 15 minutes)*. Schedules vary by the day; book online in advance.

Muir Woods

TIME FROM SAUSALITO: **30 MINS**

Small hikes to big trees

Wander among an ancient stand of the world's tallest trees in 550-plus-acre **Muir Woods National Monument** *(nps.gov/muwo; adult/child $15/free)*, a 30-minute drive from Sausalito. Only by luck did this stand of old-growth coast redwoods *(Sequoia sempervirens)* survive the massive clear-cutting of the 19th and 20th centuries.

The shortest hiking option is the 1-mile **Main Trail Loop**, a gentle walk alongside Redwood Creek to the 1000-year-old trees at **Cathedral Grove**; it returns via **Bohemian Grove**, where the tallest tree in the park stands more than 258ft high and where you can see how coast redwoods have evolved to

EATING BEYOND SAUSALITO: BEST CASUAL DINING

Pupuseria Blankita: El Salvadorean restaurant serves sublime handmade *pupusas* (corn cakes) with fillings from cheese to veggie to grilled steak. *10am-8pm* $

Sam's Anchor Cafe: Decades-old waterfront cafe in Tiburon known for vintage cocktails and excellent brunch and lunch fare. *noon-10pm* $$

Kitchen Sunnyside: New-age socialists mix with tech billionaires for elevated comfort food in Mill Valley. Best seats are on the sidewalk. *8.30am-2.30pm* $$

Sunday Marin Farmers Market: In a region of excellent farmers markets, one of the best. Vast array of produce and prepared foods; dozens of food trucks. *8am-1pm Sun* $

survive regular forest fires. More bracing is the 2-mile hike up to the top of the aptly named Cardiac Hill to reach the **Dipsea Trail**, which climbs over the coastal range and down to Stinson Beach.

You can also walk down into Muir Woods by taking trails from the Panoramic Hwy, such as the **Bootjack Trail** from the Bootjack picnic area, or from Mt Tamalpais' Pantoll Station campground, along the **Ben Johnson Trail**.

Note that visitors to Muir Woods must reserve and pay in advance for parking at the park, or weekend shuttle transportation from the Larkspur Landing Ferry Terminal. Check online *(gomuirwoods.com)* for details and current conditions.

Try to come midweek, early in the morning or late in the afternoon, when tour buses are less common. Even at busy times, a short hike will get you out of the densest crowds and onto trails with huge trees and stunning vistas. A woodsy cafe serves local and organic food and hot drinks. Note: in 2025, the Trump Administration ordered the removal of signage highlighting the important roles played by Indigenous people and women in saving Muir Woods.

Mt Tamalpais

TIME FROM SAUSALITO: **45 MINS**

Hike Marin's peak

Looming over Marin County and a 45-minute drive from Sausalito, majestic **Mt Tamalpais** (Mt Tam; 2572ft) holds more than 60 miles of hiking and biking trails, lakes, streams, waterfalls and an impressive array of wildlife – from plentiful newts and hawks to rare foxes and mountain lions. Wind your way through meadows, oaks and madrone trees to breathtaking vistas over the San Francisco Bay, Pacific Ocean, towns, cities and forested hills rolling into the distance.

Mt Tamalpais State Park *(parks.ca.gov; free)* encompasses about 10 sq miles of parklands and more than 60 miles of trails. Don't miss the summit of **East Peak**. Panoramic Hwy climbs from Hwy 1 through the park, then winds downhill to Stinson Beach.

San Rafael

TIME FROM SAUSALITO: **15 MINS**

Frank Lloyd Wright's architectural masterpiece

The oldest and largest town in Marin, **San Rafael**, a quick 15-minute drive north of Sausalito, is slightly less upscale than most of its neighbors but doesn't lack atmosphere in its strollable downtown.

Just north, the region's premier architectural sight is the eye-catching **Marin County Civic Center** *(marincounty.gov; free)*, the flamboyant masterpiece by Frank Lloyd Wright (1867–1959), who didn't live to see its 1962 completion. Wright designed the horizontal hillside buildings to flow with the natural beauty of the county's landscape, with sky-blue roofs, sand-colored walls and a gold tower pointing to the heavens. Self-guided tours are fascinating, but check for the regular free guided tours.

In utter contrast to the south, **San Quentin State Prison** is the notorious hulking mass best viewed from the Larkspur ferry.

BEST SHOPS

Bolinas People's Store: Small co-op grocery store near the beach. Serves fair-trade coffee and sells organic foods, camping supplies and other goods.

Nicasio Valley Cheese Company: Sample the soft cheeses at one of Marin County's most renowned cheesemaking shops in rural Nicasio.

Book Passage: One of the Bay Area's best bookstores in Corte Madera. Hosts big-name author appearances.

Depot Bookstore & Cafe: Bohemian Mill Valley has its own great bookstore in an old train station that was once served by a logging railroad.

Sustainable Exchange: Get locally made, fair-trade products from cosmetics to housewares in San Rafael. Ten minutes browsing can easily turn into an hour.

Point Reyes

RUGGED NATURE | WILDLIFE | OUTDOOR ADVENTURE

GETTING AROUND

Barring bad traffic, you can reach the entrance to the national seashore in about 1½ hours from San Francisco. From here to the furthest reaches of the park can take another 45 minutes of driving. Marin Transit runs public buses as far as Inverness via Olema, the park's Bear Valley Visitor Center and Point Reyes Station from San Rafael. Roads are narrow, so cycling can be challenging on the main roads.

TOP TIP

A mile west of Olema, the **Bear Valley Visitor Center** *(nps.gov/pore; 9.30am-5pm)* has maps, information and worthwhile exhibits. It's a vital first stop to find out about wildlife-spotting conditions, including beach closures and mandatory shuttle buses to busy areas. The Earthquake Trail details the San Andreas Fault, which runs close by.

Windswept Point Reyes peninsula is a rough-hewn beauty that has always lured marine mammals and migratory birds; it's also the site of scores of shipwrecks. In 1579, Sir Francis Drake landed here to repair his ship, the *Golden Hind*. During his five-week stay, he mounted a brass plaque near the shore claiming this land for England. In 1595, the first of many ships lost in these waters went down. Despite modern navigation, the dangerous waters here continue to claim boats and bits of cargo from catastrophes over the decades still wash up on shore.

Point Reyes National Seashore protects 100 sq miles of pristine ocean beaches and coastal wilderness. It has phenomenal outdoor opportunities. Hikes take you to remote corners where you can spot huge animals, from elks to elephant seals, and walk wave-tossed beaches where your footprints will be the only human evidence amid driftwood, seashells and shorebird scratchings.

Hit the Beaches

Point Reyes' world-class coast

Virtually every strip of sand is a long drive from anywhere at Point Reyes, but every one is worth the effort. **Limantour Beach** is a great all-around beach with an array of wilderness hikes and stunning sunsets. **Drakes Beach** is backed by white sandstone cliffs and is arguably the most gorgeous of the main beaches. There's also the seasonal **Kenneth C Patrick Visitor Center**, which offers information, especially in elephant-seal mating season. West-facing **Point Reyes Beach** offers 11 miles of solitude. On many days the sky turns an iridescent vermilion at sunset. Bring a blanket and enjoy the show.

Trails, Seabirds & Elk Reserve

Hike the Point Reyes wilderness

Alluring trails crisscross Point Reyes over hillsides and along the shoreline. For views, the **Inverness Ridge Trail** heads for around 3 miles up to **Point Reyes Hill** (1339ft), affording

spectacular vistas of the entire national seashore. Savor the raw beauty of the beaches extending off to the horizon.

For wildlife, **Pierce Point Rd** continues to the huge windswept sand dunes at **Abbotts Lagoon**, full of peeping killdeer and other shorebirds. At the end of the road is historical **Pierce Point Ranch**, the trailhead for the 9.4-mile round-trip **Tomales Point Trail** through the **Tule Elk Reserve**. The many elk are an amazing sight, standing with their big horns against the backdrop of **Tomales Point**. The herd is one of the last in the lower 48 states of the US. You may or may not see herds of dairy cows, depending on the results of a controversial 2025 agreement to remove them to allow the elk more freedom.

HIGHLIGHTS
1 Point Reyes National Seashore

SIGHTS
2 Abbotts Lagoon
3 Alan Sieroty Beach
4 Drakes Beach
5 Limantour Beach
6 Pierce Point Ranch
7 Pierce Point Rd
8 Point Reyes Beach
9 Point Reyes Hill
10 Tomales Point
11 Tule Elk Reserve

ACTIVITIES
12 Blue Waters Kayaking
13 Bolinas Ridge Trail
14 Inverness Ridge Trail
15 Tomales Bay Trail
16 Tomales Point Trail

SLEEPING
17 Cottages at Point Reyes Seashore
18 Dancing Coyote Beach Cottages
19 Motel Inverness
20 Nick's Cove
21 Tomales Bay Resort & Marina
22 Tomales Hotel

EATING
23 Bovine Bakery
24 Cafe Reyes
25 Saltwater Oyster Depot
26 Tap Room
27 Toby's Coffee Bar

SHOPPING
28 Point Reyes Books

INFORMATION
29 Bear Valley Visitor Center
see 4 Kenneth Patrick Center

EATING NEAR POINT REYES: OUR PICKS

Saltwater Oyster Depot: Chef-run bistro in Inverness with a sophisticated local seafood menu. Seasonal offerings feature the famous oysters. *5-8pm Fri-Mon* $$

Tap Room: Inverness spot for sandwiches, burgers and noodle bowls alongside microbrews and top regional wines. A convivial mix of residents and visitors. *4-9pm Mon-Sat* $$

Bovine Bakery: The place to get breakfast and/or a picnic near the entrance to the peninsula. Organic treats, sandwiches, breads and good coffee. *7am-4pm* $

Cafe Reyes: Enjoy wood-fired pizza inside, on the patio or to go at this Point Reyes Station favorite. Great range of toppings. *noon-8pm* $$

Beyond Point Reyes

The beauty and bounty of nature extend beyond Point Reyes to the little towns situated on Hwy 1 wending north along the coast.

Places

GETTING AROUND

You'll need your own wheels to get around the region beyond Point Reyes. This stretch of Hwy 1 is among the most popular, so expect to travel slowly.

Your best views will be on the left heading north. Do everyone a favor, especially long-suffering locals, and use the many pullouts to let speedier drivers pass. It's easy to get caught up in the incredible scenery and have cars pile up behind you, but having more than five cars stacked up behind you is a moving violation in California traffic law.

If you have a timetable for your journey along Hwy 1 continuing on from Point Reyes, toss it out the window. There are many alluring little villages where you can sample the products of the bay, plus the dairies and ranches that thrive in the rolling green hills. Plan on stopping often.

Point Reyes Station is the gateway to the north. Pause at Point Reyes Books, where the staff curate regional titles, many written by local authors. From here, Hwy 1 hugs Tomales Bay, where you can see the famous oyster farms. Cafes and restaurants serving the same dot the road which continues inland to the village of Tomales, from where you can detour to hidden Dillon Beach.

Marshall

TIME FROM POINT REYES: **15 MINS**

Oh, shucks!

Fresh oysters from **Tomales Bay** are a much-loved local specialty. From south to north, the following three waterfront restaurants are all right on Hwy 1 in and around barely there Marshall, 15 to 20 minutes' drive north of Point Reyes Station. On weekends, they get crowded and you might find a band playing. Sitting on an open deck with a local microbrew (there are many, although Stumptown is always great) and some tasty freshly shucked oysters is sublime.

The relaxed **Marshall Store** *(11am-3pm)* has a fine deck perfect for slurping down BBQ or raw local oysters, sourced from the restaurant's own farm. Smoked-seafood plates are also good, as is anything made with crab in season (winter, if available).

Hog Island Oyster Company is a minor oyster empire in Marshall. It has several outlets, including a **retail shack** *(9am-5pm)* selling fresh local shellfish and seafood plus picnic supplies, a much-loved reservation-only outdoor **oyster bar** *(11am-4pm Fri-Mon)* and a full-service restaurant to the south, **Tony's Seafood** *(11.30am-4pm Tue-Thu, to 7.30pm Fri & Sun)*.

Dive deep – not literally! – into the oyster experience on a Hog Island Oyster Company **Farm Tour** *(hogislandoysters.com; $48-180)* where you'll see how they're farmed, harvested and shucked. Book tours (75 minutes to three hours) in advance.

ANDREW MONTGOMERY/LONELY PLANET

Oysters, Marshall Store

At vintage 1930s **Nick's Cove** *(11am-7pm)*, perched over Tomales Bay, trophy heads are mounted on knotty-pine walls and there's a roaring fireplace. The seafood dishes – including the local oysters – are impeccable. It's a sprawling place, with a pier out into the bay and **rooms** (p160).

Dillon Beach

TIME FROM POINT REYES: **45 MINS**

Surf, sand & views

Dillon Beach is one of the most worthwhile detours you'll make off Hwy 1 in Marin County. The 19th-century village of Tomales, where the Dillon Beach road begins, offers plenty of reasons to stop for its excellent cafes.

Once you're fueled up on good eats and coffee, make the 4-mile jaunt west to the sand. The drive passes outcrops of weirdly sinuous boulders as you get ever-greater glimpses of the Pacific. In peak summer season, you might notice that flocks of rental cars in your rearview mirror have thinned.

Once down at the sand, you will find plenty of parking and a relaxed, welcoming attitude. Firewood is sold at the park entrance so you can have a bonfire on the wide, flat beach. An immediate highlight is the view of Tomales Point at Point Reyes National Seashore directly across the water. Walk south for empty stretches and dunes.

BEST OUTDOOR ADVENTURES AROUND POINT REYES

Bolinas Ridge Trail: An undulating 10.5-mile route for hikers or cyclists, has great views, and starts about 1 mile east of Olema.

Alan Sieroty Beach: On a tiny peninsula on Tomales Bay, this beach is sheltered and faces south. Families like the calm waters.

Blue Waters Kayaking: Offers various guided tours of Tomales Bay; otherwise, you can rent kayaks to explore the bay on your own. *bluewaterskayaking.com; tours from $115*

Tomales Bay Trail: A great all-around loop trail that takes in the best of local scenery (in spring, the viridian grasses hurt your eyes).

Food & Farm Tours: Explore the bounty of West Marin County, from organic dairies to produce farms to cheese producers. *foodandfarmtours.com; tours from $250*

EATING AROUND POINT REYES: QUICK EATS

Toby's Coffee Bar: Snack bar in a Point Reyes Station feed store perfectly captures the local vibe. Excellent coffee drinks and snacks. *6.30am-5pm* $

Route One Bakery & Kitchen: Superb flat-pan pizza by the slice draws residents from afar to Tomales. Bakery items, sandwiches and coffee also reward. *7.30am-2pm* $$

Out the Door: The fresh fish tacos will have you lining up for more at this takeout spot in Tomales. Options change daily. *noon-6pm Fri-Mon* $

Coastal Kitchen: On a bluff above Dillon Beach, casual eats served on a deck with brilliant sunset views. Longer summer hours. *noon-7pm* $$

Oakland

STATE MUSEUM | WORLD FOOD | WORLD-CLASS ARCHITECTURE

GETTING AROUND

Oakland is well-connected. Amtrak serves Sacramento, the Central Valley and San Jose. BART serves the East Bay, Oakland's airport, San Francisco and SFO. AC Transit runs a dense network of bus routes, and San Francisco Bay Ferry links Jack London Sq to San Francisco's Ferry Building *(25 minutes)*.

Oakland is where the Bay Area's diverse, artsy and radical folks have enshrined a free-thinking way of life. Oaklanders are fiercely proud that their home retains the mixed ethnic tableau and unapologetic left-wing politics San Francisco once enshrined, and they know this backdrop is threatened by million-dollar residential homes, already present even in formerly middle-class neighborhoods.

Oakland is full of historical buildings and colorful businesses. With such easy access from San Francisco via BART or ferry, it's worth spending part of a day exploring here on foot or by bike.

Oakland's eateries are among the Bay Area's best, most innovative and most affordable, due to the cultural diversity and the fact that up-and-coming chefs can more readily start a business here. The city abounds with favorites in walkable neighborhoods. Uptown, Temescal and Rockridge attract culinary trendspotters. Oakland's busiest and hippest bars are in the Uptown district, often just a short stumble from BART.

TOP TIP

Broadway is the backbone of downtown Oakland, running north from touristy Jack London Sq. The genteel Rockridge neighborhood lies west of Broadway along College Ave, near the Berkeley border. Downtown, Telegraph Ave branches off Broadway and heads north to Berkeley via the vibrant Temescal neighborhood (between 40th and 51st Sts).

The City's Heart

Downtown Oakland & Chinatown

Pedestrianized **City Center**, between Broadway and Clay St, 12th and 14th Sts, forms the heart of downtown Oakland. Enjoy a free noontime concert. Nearby **Oakland City Hall** is a beautifully refurbished 1914 beaux-arts masterpiece. Walking the streets, look for old gems such as the 1914 **Cathedral Building**, a Gothic Revival wonder on a triangular plot. It was a setting for Boots Riley's 2018 sublime dark comedy *Sorry to Bother You.*

Old Oakland, west of Broadway between 8th and 10th Sts, is lined with restored historical buildings dating from the late 19th century. The area has a lively restaurant and after-work scene. Stop in at happening **Oeste** *(5-10pm)* for a

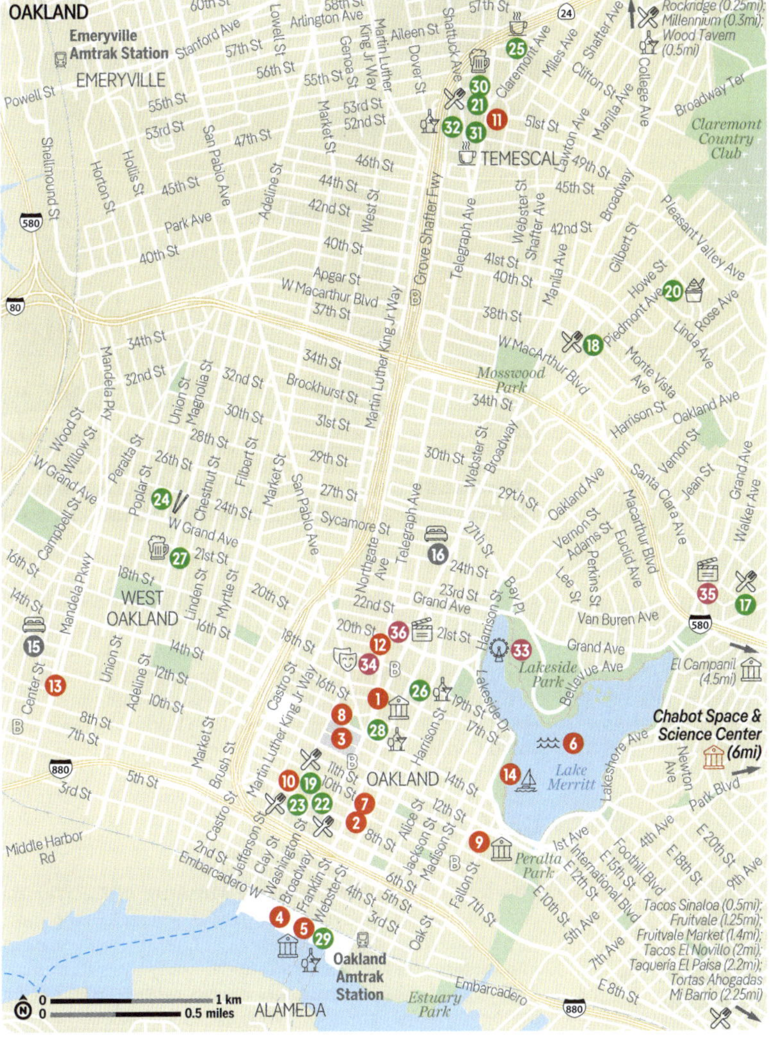

SIGHTS

1 Cathedral Building
2 Chinatown
3 City Center
4 Jack London Square
5 Jack London's Cabin
6 Lake Merritt
7 Oakland Asian Cultural Center
8 Oakland City Hall
9 Oakland Museum of California
10 Old Oakland
11 Temescal
12 Uptown
13 West Oakland

ACTIVITIES

see 4 California Canoe & Kayak
14 Dolce Vita Gondola

SLEEPING

15 B-Love's Guest House
16 Kissel Uptown Oakland

EATING

17 Arizmendi Bakery
18 Commis
19 Cook and Her Farmer
20 Fentons Creamery
21 FOB Kitchen
22 Horn Barbecue
see 4 Jack London Square Farmers Market
23 Oeste
24 Soba Ichi

DRINKING & NIGHTLIFE

25 Alem's Coffee
26 Bar 355
27 Ghost Town Brewing
28 Golden Bull Bar
29 Heinold's First & Last Chance Saloon
30 Kingfish Pub & Cafe
31 North Light
32 Snail Bar

ENTERTAINMENT

33 Children's Fairyland
34 Fox Theater
35 Grand Lake Theatre
36 Paramount Theatre

NOTABLE NEIGHBORHOODS

North of downtown, **Uptown** is home to the art-deco **Fox Theater** and **Paramount Theatre**, and a lively arts, restaurant and nightlife scene. The area stretches roughly between Telegraph and Broadway.

Continuing north, Telegraph Ave runs into the **Temescal** neighborhood, which is one of Oakland's best for walking, browsing and being surprised.

North yet again, genteel **Rockridge** merges seamlessly into Berkeley.

College Ave is another fine strip for eating, drinking and shopping.

East of downtown, sprawling **Fruitvale** is the center of Oakland's Hispanic culture. Besides tremendous food, there is top shopping. Grab an ice cream at the **Fruitvale Public Market** *(unitycouncil.org/property/public-market; 10am-7pm)*.

NICOLASMCCOMBER/GETTY IMAGES

Oakland Museum of California

great music-and-drinks scene coupled with a wide-ranging menu, plus a hopping rooftop bar.

East of Broadway and bustling with commerce, Oakland's workaday **Chinatown** centers on 8th and Webster Sts, as it has since the 1850s. Wholesale markets spill into the streets; check out the changing exhibits at the **Oakland Asian Cultural Center** *(oacc.cc; free)*. Grab a quick lunch at one of the many storefront cafes.

California's Museum

Right In Oakland

The top draw is the **Oakland Museum of California** *(museumca.org; adult/child $19/free)*. Dedicated to the state, its permanent galleries range from California's diverse ecology and history to art – from traditional landscapes to reimagined cartography. It's the museum celebrating the state – for better and worse – that should be in the capital, Sacramento, but isn't. Watch for blockbuster temporary exhibitions. It's open 11am to 5pm Wednesday to Sunday.

EATING IN OAKLAND: CASUAL DINING

Horn Barbecue: Oakland's own celebrity chef, Matt Horn, serves the masses his renowned brisket, pulled pork and sausage. Finish with banana pudding. *noon-9pm* $$

Fentons Creamery: Everyone wants a scoop of luscious ice cream at this old-school Piedmont Ave parlor. Also has old-fashioned lunches and snacks. *11am-10pm* $

Arizmendi Bakery: Great for breakfast or lunch near Lake Merritt. Bakery co-op not for the weak-willed: vegetarian pizza, chewy breads and gigantic scones. *8am-8pm* $

Cook and Her Farmer: Grab a stool or a table at this oyster joint and wine bar inside Swan's Market in Old Oakland. *11am-8pm* $$

A Square with a Past & a View

Waterfront Jack London Sq

The waterfront where writer and adventurer Jack London caroused in the 1890s now bears his name. **Jack London Sq** offers great opportunities for kayaking around the harbor or strolling the docks, especially when the **Farmers Market** *(11am-4pm Sun)* takes over. Contemporary redevelopment has added generic urban condos, plus popular restaurants and bars. **California Canoe & Kayak** *(calkayak.com)* rents kayaks and stand-up paddleboards (SUP). Book ahead for a tour ($59) along the waterfront.

On the edge of the square, **Jack London's Cabin** is reconstructed in part using the logs from his original 1898 cabin in the Yukon territory of Canada, and the historical wooden hovel allows visitors a peek inside life during the gold-rush era. Seemingly more popular is a statue of a wolf (or maybe a sled dog, or is it *The Call of the Wild's* Buck?), which kids love to pose with.

Stop by nearby **Heinold's First & Last Chance Saloon** *(11am-8pm)*, an 1883 bar constructed from wood scavenged from an old whaling ship and, yes, a favorite of London's. (There's a photo of him as a student 'studying' there at age 10 in 1886.) Keeled to a severe slant during the 1906 earthquake, the building's tilt might make you feel self-conscious about stumbling before you even order (avoid the tilt by drinking at the inviting outdoor tables).

The International Blvd Taco Hunt

Sublime Mexican food

Running southwest from Oakland's center, International Blvd lives up to its name. It's the crucible for a world of Bay Area cultures. One of the most famous is its extraordinary Mexican and Central American fare, which you can enjoy at restaurants, sidewalk and alley tents and busy taco trucks.

When Michelin called the exquisite little **Taquería El Paisa** *(9am-9pm)* a 'temple of tacos,' International Blvd had reached a superlative level of recognition. And the hype is not unjustified, the tacos are excellent: simple, fresh and garnished with *nopales* (cactus).

Given that new choices open regularly, your best option is to make your own discoveries on the stretch roughly between 20th and 50th Aves. Here are a couple of options to start.

Tortas Ahogadas Mi Barrio *(9am-6pm)* celebrates Jalisco-style food, which includes tacos dorados. Savor the fiery salsa.

OAKLAND'S HIDDEN LANDMARK

Somewhat hidden away near the hills of East Oakland is a landmark structure that is rarely visited, yet has proved to be one of the most influential buildings of the 20th century.

The initially unremarkable, 72-ft **El Campanil** was built as the bell tower for the former Mills College. Designed by the incomparable Julia Morgan (p142), it was constructed with reinforced concrete, a then-radical choice by the groundbreaking architect.

Two years after completion, the devastating 1906 earthquake destroyed thousands of Bay Area buildings, including many by Morgan's critics. However, the El Campanil was untouched. In the decades since, it's been a model for the use of reinforced concrete in buildings worldwide and continues to bring Morgan acclaim as one of the great structural engineers.

EATING IN OAKLAND: OUR PICKS

Millennium: Beloved for vegan surprises like pumpkin tamales and parsnip *okonomiyaki* (Japanese savory pancakes). Opt for the tasting menu. *5-9pm* $$

Commis: Chef James Syhabout's paean to innovative dining, on Piedmont Ave. Reserve a counter seat for the kitchen show. Menus are fixed-price. *5-10pm Tue-Sat* $$$

FOB Kitchen: Janice Dulce's Filipino restaurant in Temescal. Order anything with pork plus the garlic rice. Cocktails and a popular weekend brunch. *11am-9pm* $$

Soba Ichi: Long waits for a table are spent in a West Oakland garden – if the handmade soba noodles don't sell out first. *5-9pm Wed-Sun* $$

WEST OAKLAND

Battered by the 1989 earthquake, bedeviled by homeless encampments, surrounded by freeways, suburbanites and a busy container port, **West Oakland** embodies every non-gentrified aspect of the city's history. It's here that the Black Panther Party began its uncompromising campaign for African American rights. Its free lunch programs for school kids are still revered today. A few decades earlier, CL Dellums led the railway porters union as it fought both for better wages and also for the civil rights of people across the US. Throughout West Oakland vibrant murals celebrate the area's heritage and culture. Experience the past and present on the **Black Liberation Walking Tour** *(blwt.org)*, an occasional event that tells the neighborhood's stories.

The **Tacos El Novillo** food truck *(8am-11.30pm)* is first among many and gives you too many choices: taco or burrito? Which of the many meats? (The carnitas – seasoned pulled pork – gets raves...)

Another winning truck, **Tacos Sinaloa** *(9am-1am)*, assembles plates of tacos with artistic care, right down to the slices of radish. Seafood options are popular and the burritos will see you through a long journey.

Lovely Lake Merritt

Find fun day and night

Follow Grand Ave east of Broadway from the center and you'll run into the serene shores of **Lake Merritt**, one of Oakland's treasures. An urban respite, the lake is a popular place to stroll or go running (a 3.2-mile paved path circles the water), with bonsai and botanical gardens, a bird sanctuary, green spaces, a boathouse and gondola rides with **Dolce Vita Gondola** *(dolcevitagondola.com; $135)*.

Grand Ave (north of the water) and Lakeshore Ave (east of the lake) are pedestrian-friendly streets with intriguing shops, restaurants, cafes and bars. Look for the landmark 1926 **Grand Lake Theatre** *(renaissancerialto.com)* on the lake's northern edge. It's home to the wildly popular annual

DRINKING IN OAKLAND: OUR PICKS

Ghost Town Brewing: Goth meets industrial-cool at a West Oakland brewery known for its IPAs. Lots of seating indoors, plenty outside for when the fog clears. *3-10pm*

Wood Tavern: Top California wines in Rockridge, plus locally sourced, casual food. Grab a stool at the bar or a table with friends. *11.30am-9pm Tue-Sun*

Bar 355: Classy cocktail bar near Lake Merritt. Order an old-fashioned or a sidecar; alternatively, the bartenders know how to make anything classic. *4pm-2am Mon-Sat*

Golden Bull Bar: Beloved smallish venue downtown that packs in 150 people for wide-ranging local bands, from techno to punk and beyond. *4pm-midnight Wed-Sun*

THOMAS WINZ/GETTY IMAGES

Gondolas, Lake Merritt

Noir City Film Festival *(noircity.com)*, hosted by TCM's Eddie Muller, celebrating film noir movies.

A Playground of Fantasies

Everyone loves children's fairyland

Kids of all ages love Lake Merritt's **Children's Fairyland** *(fairyland.org; adult/child $19/17)*, a 10-acre attraction that dates from 1950 and hasn't changed much since – we say that with love! With its little Aesop theater and Peter Rabbit's garden, it ticks all the nostalgia boxes for a sweeter, simpler time that probably didn't exist. The park's oldest ride is a beautifully restored, *Alice in Wonderland*-themed carousel dubbed the **Wonder-Go-Round**.

Explore the Cosmos

To infinity and beyond

Stargazers go gaga over the **Chabot Space & Science Center** *(10am-5pm Fri-Sun; adult/child $24/19)*, a kid-oriented science and technology center in the Oakland Hills with loads of exhibits on subjects from space travel to galactic phenomena, as well as cool planetarium shows. It's the official visitor center for the South Bay's NASA Ames Research Center. Check out gear that will be used on future space missions.

TEAM BETRAYAL

As recently as 2019, Oakland had three major league sports teams playing at its aging multipurpose sports complex, the **Oakland Coliseum**. Today, it has none.

First to go was the NFL's Oakland Raiders, which decamped to Las Vegas in 2019. Despite having rabid fans, no agreement on building the team a new stadium could be reached.

The NBA's Golden State Warriors were next, although they didn't go far. A grand new sports palace, the Chase Center, lured them across the bay to San Francisco.

Finally, baseball's Oakland A's left in 2024 for Las Vegas via Sacramento. Fans and the city felt betrayed by a team that had demanded a new stadium and then when the conditions were met, left anyway.

DRINKING IN TEMESCAL: OUR PICKS

Alem's Coffee: East African cafe on Temescal's edge; the outdoor patio is a popular community gathering place in the morning. Good hot chocolate. *7am-7pm*

Snail Bar: Natural and organic wines are just some of the uncommon treats; small-plate pairings change weekly. *5-10pm Wed-Sun*

North Light: Cocktail bar with a bookstore; albums – many for sale – provide tunes. Creative booze mix, vegan treats and patio tables. *4pm-midnight*

Kingfish Pub & Cafe: Beloved dive bar with cheap beer in what was once a bait shop. Play shuffleboard on the back patio. *3pm-midnight*

Beyond Oakland

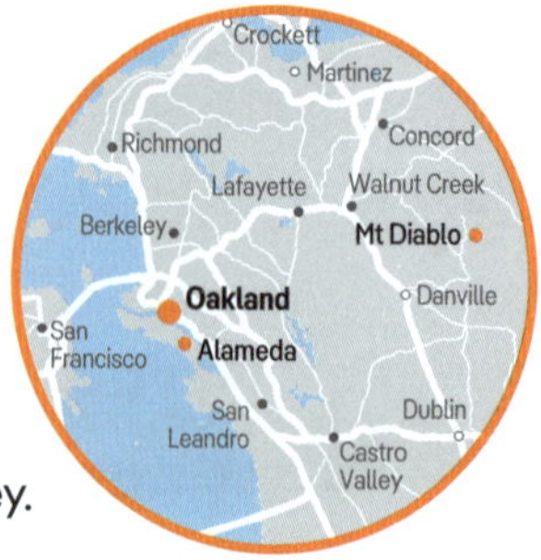

The East Bay is not all Oakland and Berkeley. Natural and cultural attractions range from the bay to the peaks.

Places

GETTING AROUND

Alameda is reached by buses from Oakland and two ferry lines from San Francisco. BART heads south down the East Bay as does Amtrak and AC Transit buses. Emeryville is the end point for Amtrak's long-distance *California Zephyr* train.

Mostly, however, for experiences further afield such as Mt Diablo, having your own wheels will be a great help.

A lower cost of living (compared to SF), a creative arts scene, offbeat shopping, woodsy parks and better weather are just some of the attractions that lure people to the East Bay.

Alameda is an actual island, thanks to a narrow channel separating it from Oakland. Its surrounding waterfront has sensational bay views and attractions to fill an afternoon. Elsewhere, the string of towns heading south to Fremont and its vast Tesla factory defines no-nonsense.

Near the base of the soaring alabaster Bay Bridge, Emeryville was once the home of thriving Ohlone villages, which featured towering shell mounds built from bay oyster and clam shells. Today it's mostly known for Pixar Animation Studios (not open for visitors).

Alameda

TIME FROM OAKLAND: **10 MINS**

Base Spirits

The west end of Alameda, only 10 minutes by car from Oakland, was once a major naval air station. Long closed, the former base is slowly being transformed into a new neighborhood. Most significantly, several vast old hangars near the USS *Hornet* have been repurposed as Spirits Alley, prosaically known as Monarch St.

Top draws include **St George Spirits** *(stgeorgespirits.com; tastings from $19)*, the alley's anchor, which makes gin, vodka and whiskey. **Gold Bar Distillery** *(goldbarwhiskey.com; classes from $49)* offers classes in making cocktails from its high-end whiskeys.

Floating veteran of war & space

When they splashed down after their lunar landing, the Apollo 11 astronauts were lifted aboard the **USS Hornet Sea, Air & Space Museum** *(uss-hornet.org; adult/child $25/10)*, a Cold War–era aircraft carrier that began life in WWII. It's now docked amidst the old naval base. On a self-guided tour of this immense warship, you'll see an array of historic aircraft on display in the hangar deck and up top on the wind-blown flight deck. The Hornet's role in the Apollo moon-landing missions is fully covered.

JCHANGCC/SHUTTERSTOCK

USS *Hornet*

Mt Diablo

TIME FROM OAKLAND: 1 HR

The East Bay's tallest point

Collecting a light dusting of snowflakes on the coldest days of winter, **Mt Diablo** (3849ft) is more than 1200ft higher than Mt Tamalpais in Marin County. On a clear day (early on a winter morning is a good bet) the views from Diablo's summit are vast and sweeping. To the west you can see over the bay and out to the Farallon Islands; to the east you can look out over the Central Valley to the Sierra Nevada.

The peak is contained within **Mt Diablo State Park** *(parks.ca.gov; vehicle entrance $10)*, which offers rock climbing, stargazing, wildflowers in springtime and the tarantula mating season in the fall. It's threaded by more than 170 miles of hiking trails good for every taste and ability. Birdwatchers may spot hundreds of species, including peregrine falcons and other raptors.

The park's highlight is literally at the top of the peak, where the beautiful and historic **Summit Museum Visitor Center** *(free)* dates from 1942. It features a lookout tower and displays about the park's natural and cultural history. There's even an aviation beacon dating to WWII. Easily reached by car – and by numerous hiking trails – the summit gets crowded on weekends. Find some peace on the Mary Bowerman Loop, an easy 0.8-mi loop trail around the summit that mixes natural beauty with sweeping views.

The park is in Contra Costa County, 14 miles east of Oakland. It's most easily accessed off I-680 at Danville or Walnut Creek.

EAST BAY RAP & HIP HOP

Since the 1980s, West Coast rap and hip-hop have spoken truth. LA has often been in the forefront, but Oakland and the East Bay have been right there too. The son of a Black Panther leader, Tupac Shakur combined party songs and hard truths learned on Oakland's streets until his death in 1996.

The breakout artist in the 1990's was Oakland native MC Hammer, with his landmark album *Please Hammer Don't Hurt 'Em*. Reacting against the increasing commercialization of hip-hop, the Bay Area scene produced underground 'hyphy' (short for hyperactive) artists such as E-40 and Mistah F.A.B. More recently, East Bay groups like Blackalicious, The Coup, Michael Franti & Spearhead, and Kamaiyah are known for their political commentary.

EATING & DRINKING IN THE EAST BAY AREA: OUR PICKS

Los Carnalitos Restaurant: Buried in a Hayward strip mall with uncommon choices such as *cochinita* (slow-roasted pork). *9am-9pm Mon-Sat* $

Domenico's Italian Deli: We dare you to navigate the myriad sandwich options at this Alameda fave toppings, cheeses, breads, spreads... they're all superb. *11am-5pm Mon-Sat* $

Spinning Bones: Creative bistro with Pacific flavors. Roasted meats, seasonal vegetables and offbeat sandwiches. Special bento menu for kids. *11.30am-8pm* $$

Forbidden Island Tiki Lounge: In Alameda, one of the Bay Area's most infamous tiki bars serves every rum-soaked cliché imaginable. Potent mai tais. *4pm-midnight*

Berkeley

CULTURED & LEARNED | GARDENS | ARCHITECTURE

GETTING AROUND

Berkeley is well served with three BART stations; the Downtown Berkeley stop is convenient to most sights and campus. AC Transit buses cover the main roads and provide links across the East Bay. There's limited ferry service to San Francisco.

TOP TIP

Telegraph and Shattuck Aves are packed with cafes, cheap restaurants and bookstores. Berkeley's Little India runs along University Ave. College Ave in Elmwood near Rockridge is lined with shops and bakeries. The popular Gourmet Ghetto stretches along Shattuck Ave north of University Ave. Further northwest, Solano Ave boasts offbeat shops.

Berkeley is synonymous with protest, activism and left-wing politics. Here, 'woke' is an essential attribute, not an aspersion.

But beyond those tropes is a busy, attractive city, a blend of yuppie and hippie and student, all existing side by side with great regional restaurants, twee toy stores, Latin American groceries, high-end organic food halls and the misty green campus of the University of California, Berkeley (aka 'Cal'). It's easy to stereotype 'Bezerkeley' for some of its recycle-or-else PC crankiness and occasional overbearing self-righteousness. But some of that attitude is justified: at the end of the day Berkeley has, more often than not, been on the right side of environmental and political issues that have defined the rest of the nation.

Green spaces in the hills and on the flats of the bay, plus enticing neighborhoods, make Berkeley a good day trip or stop from anywhere in the Bay Area.

UC Berkeley Campus

Go Bears!

The Berkeley campus of the **University of California** (called 'Cal' by both students and locals; *berkeley.edu*) is the oldest university in the state. Founded in 1866, the first students arrived in 1873. Today, Cal has more than 40,000 students, over 1500 professors and more Nobel laureates than you could point a particle accelerator at.

From groovy **Telegraph Ave**, enter the campus via **Sproul Plaza** and **Sather Gate**, a center for people-watching, soapbox oration and pseudotribal drumming. Just wandering the campus is a delight – on a sunny afternoon, you may be tempted to join in some Frisbee throwing.

Stop by the **Koret Visitor Center**, off Piedmont Ave in Memorial Stadium where Cal's Golden Bears play football, for information or to join a guided tour. The website has an array of downloadable self-guided tours and maps.

HIGHLIGHTS
1 Chez Panisse

SIGHTS
2 BAMPFA
3 Bancroft Library
4 Campanile
5 Gilman Hall
6 Sather Gate
7 Telegraph Avenue
8 University of California – Berkeley

SLEEPING
9 Berkeley City Club
10 Downtown Berkeley Inn
11 Graduate Berkeley
12 Hotel Shattuck Plaza

EATING
13 Berkeley Bowl Marketplace
14 La Note

DRINKING & NIGHTLIFE
15 Cornerstone

ENTERTAINMENT
16 Aurora Theatre Company
17 Berkeley Playhouse
18 Berkeley Repertory Theatre
19 Freight & Salvage Coffeehouse

SHOPPING
20 Book Society
21 Dark Carnival Imaginative Fiction Bookstore
22 Moe's Books
23 Pegasus Books
24 Sleepy Cat Books

INFORMATION
25 Koret Visitor Center

NO BERKELEY, NO BOMB?

The University of California, Berkeley, gave the world the core ingredient of the atomic bomb and the man who led its invention.

J Robert Oppenheimer became a physics professor at Cal in 1927 and became best friends with Ernest Lawrence, the legendary Cal experimental physicist. As brilliantly chronicled in the movie *Oppenheimer* (2023), he was recruited in 1942 for the Manhattan Project to develop the first atomic bomb. A year later, at age 39, he was put in charge.

In 1941, Cal discovered plutonium, the core element of the first atomic bombs. The movie shows **Gilman Hall** on campus, where today an array of memorial plaques on the wall outside of **Room 3407** mark the chemistry lab where this occurred.

Officially called Sather Tower, the **Campanile** *(10am-4pm)* – as it is widely known – was modeled on St Mark's Basilica in Venice. The 307ft spire offers fine views of the Bay Area, and at the top you can stare up into the carillon of 61 bells. Concerts at 7:50am, noon and 6pm are a treat.

Inside a stainless-steel exterior, **BAMPFA** *(Berkeley Art Museum and Pacific Film Archive; bampfa.org; adult/child $18/free)* holds galleries showcasing artworks, from ancient Chinese to cutting-edge contemporary. Its film series are top-notch.

The **Bancroft Library** houses, among other gems, the papers of Mark Twain, a copy of Shakespeare's folios and a diary from the Donner Party. Its public exhibits include the surprisingly small gold nugget that sparked the 1849 gold rush.

Berkeley's World-Famous Restaurant

Chez Panisse changed dining globally

California cuisine, farm-to-table, seasonal fare, sustainably sourced. These are just some of the food trends that **Chez Panisse** *(5.30-8:45pm Mon-Sat)* and its superstar proprietor Alice Waters can take at least some credit for. The ubiquitous Waters can be found on TV shows, and in books, articles and more.

Pull out all the stops with a prix-fixe meal at the restaurant downstairs, which first opened in 1971. As always, the menu changes daily and is as good and popular as ever. Despite its fame, the place has retained a welcoming atmosphere. The menu showcases the bounty of California in ways both creative and delicious. Alternatively, the upstairs a la carte **cafe** *(11.30am-2.30pm Tue-Sat, 5-10pm Mon-Sat)* is less expensive and a tad less formal. Reservations at both venues are accepted one month ahead.

Entertaining Downtown

Head out of town

Berkeley's downtown, centered on Shattuck Ave between University Ave and Dwight Way, abounds with shops, restaurants and restored public buildings. The nearby Arts District on Addison St stars the acclaimed thespian stomping grounds of the **Berkeley Repertory Theatre** *(berkeleyrep.org)* and **Aurora Theatre Company** *(auroratheatre.org)*. Hear live folk music from around the globe at the historic **Freight & Salvage Coffeehouse** *(thefreight.org)*.

Beauty in Berkeley's Hills

Revel in Cal's Botanical Garden

Nature begins in the hills right at the east end of campus. With 34 acres and more than 10,000 types of plants, the **UC Botanical Garden at Berkeley** *(botanicalgarden.berkeley.edu; adult/child $18/8)* has one of the most varied collections in the country. Flora from every continent except Antarctica is lovingly tended here, with special emphasis on Mediterranean species that grow in California. You'll also find areas devoted to the Americas, the Mediterranean and southern Africa.

GADO IMAGES/GETTY IMAGES

Chez Panisse

Stretch your legs on the nearby fire trail that loops around surrounding Strawberry Canyon, offering great views of town and the off-limits Lawrence Berkeley National Laboratory. Find the trailhead on the east side of Centennial Dr just southwest of the botanical garden.

The Smartest Posie Patch

Wander Tilden Park Botanical Garden

Further up from Cal's garden, 2079-acre **Tilden Regional Park** *(ebparks.org/parks/tilden; free)* is Berkeley's best park and has its own notable garden.

The wonderfully wild-looking **Botanical Garden** celebrates native California plants and has an excellent visitor center. Here, you'll find volunteers eager to explain the myriad species being grown. Many of these knowledgeable people are retirees from Cal with a lifetime of experience both teaching and

EATING & DRINKING IN BERKELEY: CASUAL DINING

Berkeley Bowl Marketplace: Vast indie supermarket with foods from the Bay Area and the world; huge produce department with rare varieties. *9am-8pm* $

Acme Bread: One of the region's best bakeries, beloved for its take on classic sourdough bread. Memorable snacks like the ham and cheese croissant. *8am-4pm* $

La Note: Casual cafe with a strong French accent. Popular at breakfast (goat cheese is an option), lunch brings salads and sandwiches. Sunny garden. *8am-2pm* $$

Cornerstone: Welcoming bar with regular live music. Seating inside and outside, 50 tap beers (many unusual) and tasty comfort food. *11.30am-midnight*

BERKELEY'S BEST BOOKSTORES

Moe's Books: New and used books in a vast store south of campus. Renowned for its knowledgeable staff, enjoy browsing across four floors.

Dark Carnival Imaginative Fiction Bookstore: One of the oldest science-fiction, fantasy and horror bookstores west of the Mississippi. It's all controlled chaos; lose yourself in the stacks.

Pegasus Books: Right on the Shattuck Ave commercial strip, Pegasus has great staff recommendations and daily specials on new and used titles.

Book Society: Browsing for books in this cozy, comfy space is all the better given the machines in back that dispense wine by the glass.

Sleepy Cat Books: You'll find the namesake felines dozing away as you browse the carefully curated selection of offbeat fiction and hard-to-find nonfiction.

PAUL CHINN/THE SAN FRANCISCO CHRONICLE VIA GETTY IMAGES

Swimming pool, Berkeley City Club

researching horticulture, so you can expect any question you conjure up to result in detailed and well-informed answers!

Whiteboards list daily events, which can include tours, lectures and other informative activities.

Elsewhere, Tilden Park has nearly 40 miles of hiking and multiuse trails of varying difficulty, from paved paths to hilly scrambles, including part of the magnificent Bay Area Ridge Trail.

Berkeley's Landmark Architect

See Julia Morgan's creations

Julia Morgan's ties with Cal began when she became the first woman to graduate from the civil engineering program. She is best known as William Randolph Hearst's favorite architect and the designer of Hearst Castle, but over her prolific career she designed more than 700 buildings, including some noteworthy Berkeley creations. (One of her Oakland buildings changed engineering practices worldwide, p133.)

Julia Morgan Hall (1911) was originally a meeting place for female students (who, like Morgan, a Cal alum, were a small minority over 100 years ago). Now relocated to the UC Botanical Garden, it exemplifies her low-slung designs clad in redwood. At the southwest corner of campus, the **Berkeley City Club** (1929) picks up many of Hearst Castle's Moorish and Romanesque design elements. It's now a hotel (p160).

The **Berkeley Playhouse** (1910) on College Ave is typically understated and makes beautiful use of redwood. It was built as the St John's Presbyterian Church and is on the National Register of Historic Places.

Beyond Berkeley

Follow the bay to visit sights, far from the tourist glitz of San Francisco, Marin and Napa, which are nonetheless uniquely compelling.

Many of the most interesting sights and activities beyond Berkeley as you head north and east around the bay toward the Sacramento Delta are close to the water. This includes three national parks that each cover a significant aspect of American life: the wholesale societal changes brought by WWII, the emergence of an appreciation for America's natural splendor and a little-visited memorial to an avoidable and shocking wartime tragedy.

Along the bay, trails, parks and open places provide diverse ways to get outside in the fresh breezes off the water. You can walk, hike, fly a kite, paddle a kayak, sail a boat, learn to ride an SUP or revel in the funkiest of al fresco art.

Places

GETTING AROUND

Richmond is well served by BART and Amtrak. AC Transit buses provide local coverage in Alameda County. Further east, services become more sparse and having your own wheels is the most practical way to tour around.

When driving East Bay freeways such as the I-80, be aware that they become heavily congested during morning and evening rush hours.

East Bay Waterfront

TIME FROM BERKELEY: **10-20 MINS**

Action & art at the shore

Looking west from the East Bay Shore, the San Francisco Bay makes a beautiful backdrop for a photo – even when it's not sunset – what with Alcatraz, the city skyline and the distant Golden Gate Bridge.

A string of parks and public spaces from Emeryville through Albany offers plenty of options for enjoying the view, playing in the bay breezes and getting out on the water.

Berkeley Recreation & Wellbeing Adventures *(recwell.berkeley.edu/wellness-offerings/adventures)* is run by UC Berkeley at the **Berkeley Marina**. Open to non-students, it organizes sailing, windsurfing, SUP and kayaking classes and gear rental. Reservations are a must through the website.

Go fly a kite at **Cesar Chavez Park** at the north end of the Berkeley Marina. With nearly 20 acres of flat, unobstructed waterfront and near-constant breezes, this is an ideal venue for sending your own creation aloft. Finding the right kite is easy, thanks to **Highline Kites** *(highlinekites.com)*, which sets up shop in a truck at the north end of the park every weekend *(1.30-6.30pm)*. Prices start at under $15 and the colorful choices are vast.

Discover community-made outdoor art, nearly 200 species of birds and wild, windy walks at the **Albany Bulb**, a legacy landfill that juts out into the bay and dates back over 100 years to a time when communities (and a dynamite factory!)

CYCLING THE MISSING LINK

Cruising on two wheels across the Golden Gate Bridge is one of the Bay Area's iconic cycling experiences. But there's another, longer, bridge that you can ride across. No, sadly, it's not the Bay Bridge, but rather, the unheralded, unloved **Richmond–San Rafael Bridge** in the North Bay. One entire lane on the upper deck of the span has been walled off for bikes, which has been a real boon for exploring the region.

Using combinations of BART and the San Francisco–Larkspur Golden Gate ferry, you can create huge circle rides of various lengths from the East Bay and San Francisco. The 5.5-mile bridge affords grand views of Marin, Alameda and Contra Costa Counties and the bay while you ride.

dumped their garbage in the water. Today it offers one of the region's most offbeat walks, a 1.8mi looping stroll past castles, soaring figures, abstract shapes and more, all made from found junk and flotsam.

Richmond

TIME FROM BERKELEY: **20 MINS**

Rosie the Riveter's home

The struggle for civil rights and women's equality is the focus of one of the East Bay's most significant historical sites, the **Rosie the Riveter WWII Home Front National Historic Park** *(nps.gov/rori; free)*. Located on the bay in Richmond, this illuminating museum is part of what remains of four adjoining Kaiser shipyards built during WWII.

Thousands of workers toiled here in shifts around the clock. To meet the insatiable need for labor, scores of women were brought into the workforce, along with a huge number of African Americans, who had faced discrimination in California. They achieved the remarkable feat of building nearly 750 freighters and warships during WWII using mass-production techniques.

Displays cover the huge societal changes spawned by the shipyards and the challenges the workers faced in finding housing and basic life balance. Then, when the war ended, the shipyards closed and jobs disappeared, other than a few at the pollution-belching refineries on the bay – which remain in operation. Richmond is still depressed decades later.

Look for the large freighter, the **SS Red Oak Victory** *(redoakvictory.us; $15-25)*, docked across from the visitor center. It's one of the last surviving ships to be built here and is open 10am to 3pm Sunday.

Martinez

TIME FROM BERKELEY: **30-45 MINS**

John Muir's home

Naturalist John Muir's former residence is part of the **John Muir National Historic Site** *(nps.gov/jomu; free)*. It sits in a pastoral patch of farmland in bustling, modern Martinez, far up the bay, near the beginning of the Sacrament--San Joaquin Delta.

Though Muir wrote of sauntering the Sierra Nevada with a sack of tea and bread, it may be a shock for those familiar with the iconic Sierra Club founder's ascetic weather-beaten appearance that this house (built by his father-in-law in 1883) is a model of Victorian Italianate refinement, with a tower cupola and a daintily upholstered parlor.

EATNG & DRINKING BEYOND BERKELEY: OUR PICKS

Seabreeze: Casual choice near the Berkeley Marina with a few terrace tables. Fish sandwiches, fries and clam chowder are all made to go. *9am-6pm* **$$**

Kaleidoscope Coffee: In compact Point Richmond, the charming neighborhood west of the national historic site, serves great coffee and snacks. *7am-7pm* **$**

Bull Valley Roadhouse: Port Costa roadhouse dating to 1897, with classic American fare and potent cocktails. Ambitious menu with casual options. *noon-9pm Wed-Sun* **$$**

States Coffee: House-roasted coffee served in the heart of Martinez; good snacks and baked goods. Plot out your day on the lovely patio. *7am-4pm* **$**

EWY MEDIA/SHUTTERSTOCK

Rosie the Riveter WWII Home Front National Historic Park

Muir's 'scribble den' has been left as it was during his life, with crumpled papers overflowing from wire wastebaskets and dried-bread balls – his preferred snack – resting on the mantelpiece.

Acres of the family's fruit orchards still stand, and visitors can enjoy seasonal samples. The grounds include the 1849 **Martinez Adobe**, part of the ranch on which the house was built, and oak-speckled hiking trails on nearby **Mt Wanda** (660ft), named for one of Muir's daughters.

A little-known & moving memorial

On July 17, 1944, 320 sailors and civilians were killed when ammunition being loaded onto a freighter exploded at the Port Chicago military base, east of Martinez.

The disaster was heard and felt in Oakland, 30 miles away and beyond. The ship being loaded vanished. Despite the disaster's scope, it's little known today. Most of those killed were African American sailors, working under horrific conditions. During WWII the US military was still segregated and African Americans were given the worst jobs.

Today, the **Port Chicago Naval Magazine National Memorial** *(nps.gov/poch; free)* is a simple and poignant monument at the blast site. It receives few visitors as the location is an active military base, and visits require advance reservations.

THE EAST BAY'S LESSER-KNOWN SIGHTS

Crockett: One of the historic towns dotting the bayshore has an appealing dash of vintage charm.

Benecia: Across the narrow Carquinez Strait, this city was once the state's capital (1853–54) as recalled at the **Benicia Capitol State Historic Park** *(adult/child $3/2).*

Port Costa: Hidden by barren hills, this 19th-century waterfront hamlet has popular weekend roadhouses next to train tracks.

Eugene O'Neill National Historic Site: Hidden in the San Ramon Valley, the Nobel-winning playwright of *The Iceman Cometh* lived here from 1937. *nps.gov/euon; free*

Niles Canyon Railway: Old steam and diesel trains follow a scenic route between Niles and Sunol. *ncry.org; adult/child from $25/15*

Palo Alto

AFFLUENT NEIGHBORHOODS | UNIVERSITY TOURS | HIKING

GETTING AROUND

Speedy and newly electrified Caltrain commuter trains serve San Francisco (50 minutes) and San Jose (25 minutes). VTA buses connect Palo Alto with the rest of Silicon Valley, including San Jose. Stanford University has a free public shuttle service for the campus and the immediate area.

TOP TIP

Stanford University presents a self-consciously rural appearance and adjoins a namesake luxury shopping center. Both are west of the busy Caltrain tracks. Downtown is a walkable delight. Past pricey neighborhoods and Hwy 101, East Palo Alto is a separate city, which enjoys little affluence.

Palo Alto is Silicon Valley's ritziest city. Even a modest bungalow here may cost over $2 million, while upscale boutiques, bistros and spas crowd downtown streets.

It's also the mythical heart of Silicon Valley. Bill Hewlett and David Packard got their start here in their legendary garage (you can see it at 367 Addison Ave). Steve Jobs lived and died here. Larry Page and Sergey Brin were students at Stanford University when they started Google. The list goes on. But it's not all lightness and joy. Palo Alto was the home of convicted fraudsters Elizabeth Holmes and Sam Bankman-Fried, while the ethics of the billionaire venture capitalists on Sand Hill Rd and tech oligarchs are ever more questioned.

Sprawled across nearly 13 sq miles just west of downtown, Stanford University lays claim to the city's soul. Built by Leland Stanford, one of the original 'robber barons,' it grew to become a prestigious, wealthy and conservative institution.

Exploring Stanford

Touring art and architecture

Stanford University *(stanford.edu)* is one of America's top universities academically and among the most expensive. The faux California Mission Revival–style campus is a genteel place to stroll, with public artwork and murals. (Note: the rivalry with publicly funded UC Berkeley is intense.) Having been built on the site of the Stanford family's horse farm, the university maintains the humble-brag nickname The Farm.

Stop by the **Stanford Visitor Center** *(visit.stanford.edu)* off Galvez St for self-guided tour info and maps. Many cover the multitudes of public art around campus. Download the Stanford Mobile app which has walking tours.

Auguste Rodin's *Burghers of Calais* bronze sculpture marks the entrance to the **Main Quad** (begun 1887), an open plaza where the original 12 campus buildings – a mix of Romanesque

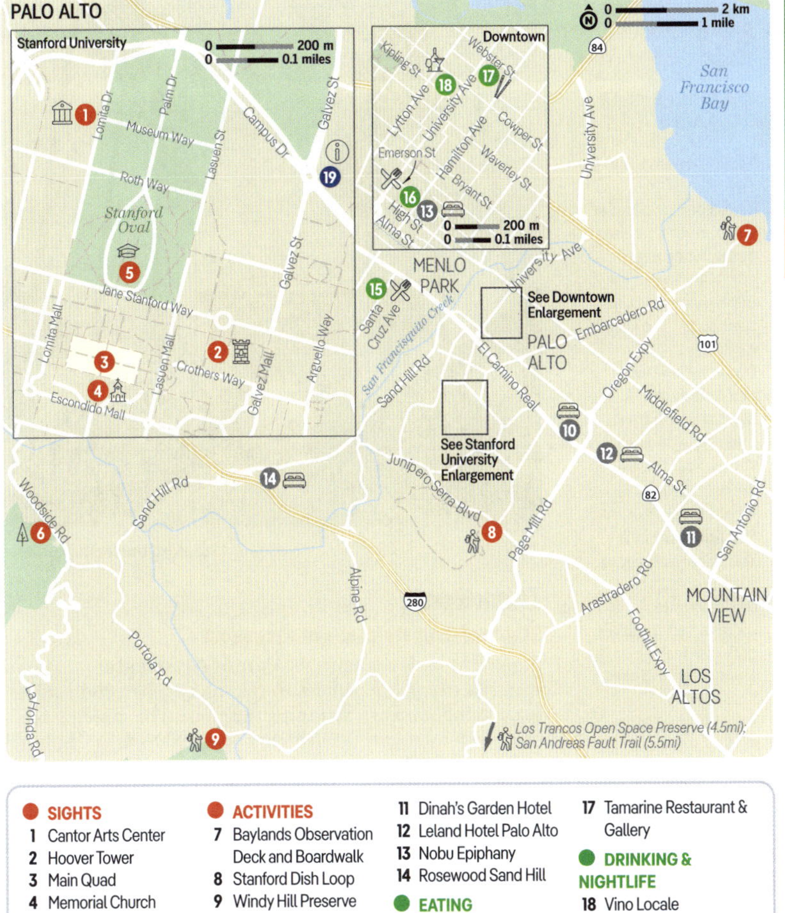

SIGHTS
1 Cantor Arts Center
2 Hoover Tower
3 Main Quad
4 Memorial Church
5 Stanford University
6 Wunderlich County Park

ACTIVITIES
7 Baylands Observation Deck and Boardwalk
8 Stanford Dish Loop
9 Windy Hill Preserve

SLEEPING
10 Coronet Motel
11 Dinah's Garden Hotel
12 Leland Hotel Palo Alto
13 Nobu Epiphany
14 Rosewood Sand Hill

EATING
15 Camper
16 Palo Alto Creamery
17 Tamarine Restaurant & Gallery

DRINKING & NIGHTLIFE
18 Vino Locale

INFORMATION
19 Stanford Visitor Center

and Mission Revival styles – are joined by the **Memorial Church** (1903). The church is noted for its beautiful mosaic-tiled frontage, stained-glass windows and five organs with more than 8000 pipes.

A campus landmark to the east of the Main Quad, the 285ft-high **Hoover Tower** *(hoover.org/library-archives/visit/hoover-tower; $8)* is part of the conservative Hoover Institution, a Stanford-affiliated public policy research center. An elevator-accessed observation platform on the 14th floor offers sweeping Bay Area views.

BEST HIKES NEAR PALO ALTO

Stanford Dish Loop: The hilly 3.7-mile paved path is popular with runners, walkers and science nerds who want to see the 150ft-diameter radio telescope ('the Dish').

Baylands Observation Deck and Boardwalk: A hub for hiking trails that follow the bay shoreline through parks and wildlife-filled estuaries.

San Andreas Fault Trail: Learn all about earthquake geology on this gentle 1.5-mile self-guided path inside the **Los Trancos Open Space Preserve**.

Wunderlich County Park: Untouched peninsula nature: trails follow hillsides, gulches and streams under shady redwoods and oaks.

Windy Hill Preserve: For more outdoor options, head west into the Santa Cruz Mountains. Start at this grass-covered hilltop where trails radiate into the redwoods.

PANDORA PICTURES/SHUTTERSTOCK

Stanford University (p146)

Think Rodin

Stanford's masterpiece of a museum

Fronted by Ionic columns, the **Cantor Arts Center** *(museum.stanford.edu; free)* includes works from ancient civilizations to contemporary art, spanning the globe. The museum is renowned for its Rodin collection of over 200 works displayed both inside and out in a garden. Of course there's a de rigueur *The Thinker*. Rotating shows are eclectic in scope and include well-curated photography exhibitions.

EATING & DRINKING IN PALO ALTO: OUR PICKS

Camper: In Palo Alto's symbiotic twin Menlo Park, classic NorCal seasonal menu of locally sourced food prepared creatively. *10am-1pm Sat & Sun, 5-8:45pm Mon-Sat* $$$

Tamarine Restaurant & Gallery: Exquisite Vietnamese food served in artful surrounds. Cocktails pair with small and large plates. *11.30am-2.30pm & 5-9pm* $$$

Palo Alto Creamery: A downtown institution, sparkling chrome-and-red-booths and a look from 1923; famous for breakfasts, milkshakes and pies. *8am-9pm* $$

Vino Locale: Wine bar in a Victorian house with an inviting terrace. Unpretentious by local standards, the focus is on regional foods and tasty bites. *3-9pm*

Beyond Palo Alto

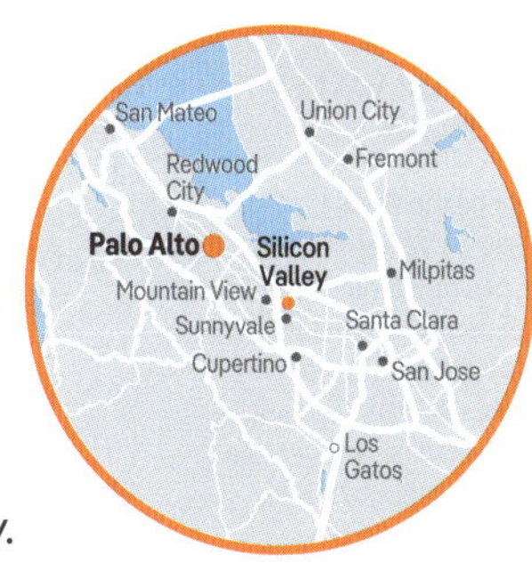

Roam the land where billionaires are spawned and enjoy your own tech fantasy. Divert to bay and mountain pleasures.

South of San Francisco, squeezed tightly between the bay and the coastal foothills, a long swath of cities, towns and suburbia runs down to San Jose. Dotted inside this area are famous names such as Silicon Valley, Menlo Park and Mountain View.

You won't find Silicon Valley on any map: it's a nickname coined in the 1970s. As silicon chips form the basis of modern computers, and the Santa Clara Valley – stretching from Palo Alto through Sunnyvale and Cupertino to San Jose – is thought of as the birthplace of the tech revolution, the region is dubbed 'Silicon Valley.' It's hard to imagine that through the 1960s it was still a region of apricot, Bing cherry and walnut orchards.

GETTING AROUND

Silicon Valley's streets and freeways are often traffic-clogged with frustrated Lamborghini drivers (and others). Caltrain efficiently links city and town centers between San Francisco and San Jose. VTA provides fill-in bus and light-rail services. However, your own wheels are best for visiting this sprawling area. Choose your freeway: Hwy 101 is the spine of Silicon Valley, while the I-280 is the less congested, scenic alternative.

Silicon Valley

TIME FROM PALO ALTO: **20-45 MINS**

Tech's got a history

The vast and well-funded **Computer History Museum** *(computerhistory.org; adult/child $20/free)* in Mountain View has themed exhibits drawn from its 100,000-item collection. Displays cover the range of technology and, depending on your interest, can easily absorb half a day. Artifacts range from the abacus to iPhone prototypes. Docents are often industry luminaries who've got time to kill now that their IPOs have vested.

The storied chipmaker Intel – one of the reasons Silicon Valley got its name – runs the reinvigorated **Intel Museum** *(intel.com; 9am-5pm)* in Santa Clara, which covers the use of silicon in producing microchips, several decades of nearly unbelievable innovation in chip production and – not surprisingly – Intel's involvement, plus you can see how chips are made.

Visiting tech icons

Apple occupies a chunk of its longtime corporate home of Cupertino. Its **Visitor Center** *(apple.com/retail/appleparkvisitorcenter; 10am-7pm)* has an Apple Store, a sleek cafe and a rooftop deck that allows a glimpse of the company's infamous 'flying saucer' headquarters. The basement bathroom corridors are eerily reminiscent of the Apple TV+ series *Severance*, about an evil corporation dedicated to mind control.

SILICON VALLEY TIMELINE

Since the 1950s Silicon Valley has spawned thousands of companies thanks to its ecosystem of talented people, many universities, and venture capitalists and others ready with funding.

1950s: Major corporations like Hewlett-Packard, Lockheed and Xerox set up in the Santa Clara Valley. Tech companies form to serve them, making early semiconductors.

1957: The birth of Fairchild Semiconductor is a foundational moment, spawning legends like Intel.

1960: Researchers discover the remarkable properties of silicon in chips.

1969: The earliest form of the internet includes Stanford.

1970s: Apple, Atari and Oracle are founded.

1980s: Adobe, Cisco and Sun Microsystems are founded.

1990s: Google, Netflix, Netscape, PayPal and Yahoo are founded.

2000s: Facebook, Twitter and Uber are founded.

Google, in Mountain View, finally has a public facility called the **Google Visitor Experience** *(visit.withgoogle.com; 9am-7pm)* and, like Google, it's huge. There's a store, but there's also bayside trails, public art, games, displays, cafes and much more. You can easily spend a couple of hours here.

Meta's headquarters is an agglomeration of office buildings surrounded by parking lots near the Dumbarton Bridge across from East Palo Alto. Nothing is open to the public. The one visitor-friendly location is the **Meta Store** *(meta.com; 11am-6pm Mon-Sat)*, hidden away in Burlingame. Here you can try out the company's latest virtual-reality gizmos and, yes, buy a T-shirt.

Valley towns worth a look

Cities and towns line the peninsula south from San Francisco, flowing seamlessly from one to the next. The more notable names include the following:

San Mateo has good bayshore parks, such as the **Coyote Point Recreation Area** *(parks.smcgov.org/coyote-point-recreation-area)*.

Atherton is the wealthiest zip code in the USA, with old-money families that predate Silicon Valley. Vast mansions are cloistered between high hedges and fences.

Woodside has good casual-chic roadside cafes on Hwy 84 and is the gateway to the magnificent open lands of the Santa Cruz Mountains along Skyline Blvd.

Saratoga and **Los Gatos** are rarified neighbors. Each has an atmospheric town center ready-made for strolling – a local rarity.

EATING & DRINKING IN SILICON VALLEY: OUR PICKS

Buck's Restaurant of Woodside: Legendary meeting place for tech entrepreneurs and VCs, who discuss funding over upscale diner fare at picnic tables. *8am-9pm* $$

DH Noodles: Lanzhou-style Chinese specialities (hand-pulled noodles and rich beef broth), reflecting the region's Muslim influence. Near Cupertino. *11am-9pm* $$

Dolce Spazio Dessert Cafe: House-made gelato in sexy flavors like 'Oreogasmic.' Not the place for fruity sorbets; also cakes and shakes. In Los Gatos. *noon-10pm* $

Das Bierhauz: Tech-fave in Mountain View; a beer garden serving German classics and over a dozen Old World beers on tap in big steins. *11am-10pm* $$

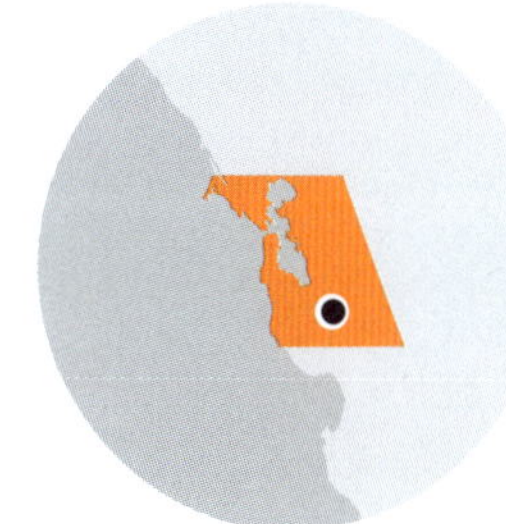

San Jose

HISTORY PARK | MUSEUMS | DIVERSE CUISINES

Though culturally diverse and rich in history, San Jose – carpeted with Silicon Valley's suburbia – has always been in San Francisco's shadow. Founded in 1777 as El Pueblo de San José de Guadalupe, San Jose is California's oldest Spanish civilian settlement. Its downtown is fairly modest for a city that's California's third-most populated (after LA and San Diego). It does bustle with 20-something partiers on weekends, in part thanks to its large namesake state university.

Industrial parks, high-tech computer firms, surprisingly leafy neighborhoods and strip malls are sprawled across the city's landscape. Underneath all this is fertile land where some of the world's most bounteous orchards grew as recently as the 1960s.

This West Coast multiethnic melting pot has excellent restaurants scattered throughout. While specific sights are few, the city is a good pit stop on the way to Santa Cruz, Monterey or north to San Francisco.

GETTING AROUND

San Jose is a transportation hub. Its busy airport has international and domestic flights and is a good alternative to San Francisco's. Caltrain offers excellent service up the peninsula to San Francisco. Amtrak regional trains serve Oakland, Sacramento and the Central Valley. Amtrak's wonderful long-distance *Coast Starlight* runs north to Seattle and south to LA. VTA runs bus and light-rail service across the South Bay.

Oddball Sight

Touring one lady's obsession

San Jose's top attraction is also the strangest: **Winchester Mystery House** *(winchestermysteryhouse.com; adult/child from $46/23)* is a ridiculous yet fascinating and elaborate Victorian mansion filled with 160 mostly non-utilitarian rooms with dead-end hallways and a staircase that runs up to a ceiling. It was the obsession of Sarah Winchester, who seemingly couldn't live without constant hammering. Guided tours cover the basics and previously little-seen corners.

TOP TIP

Drive 9 miles northwest of downtown San Jose to the tiny old village of **Alviso** in the estuary at the south end of the bay. This is big-sky country and there are hikes galore on the trails of the **Don Edwards San Francisco Bay National Wildlife Refuge** *(fws.gov/refuge/don-edwards-san-francisco-bay)*.

Architecture Tour

Walk into the past

Historical buildings from all over San Jose have been brought together in **History Park** *(historysanjose.org; free)*, an

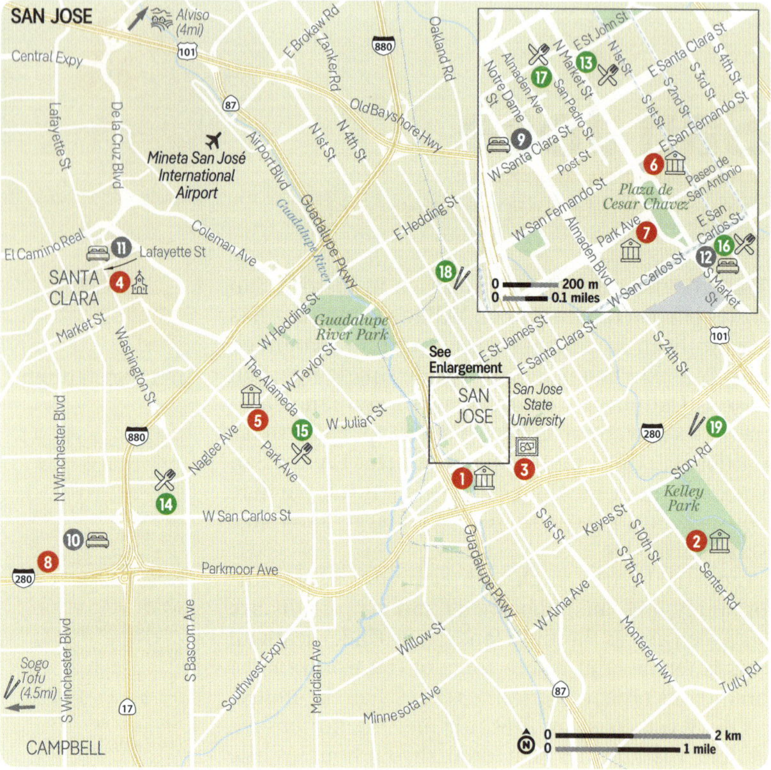

SAN JOSE

SIGHTS

1 Children's Discovery Museum
2 History Park
3 MACLA
4 Mission Santa Clara de Asís
5 Rosicrucian Egyptian Museum
6 San Jose Museum of Art
7 Tech Interactive
8 Winchester Mystery House

SLEEPING

9 Hotel De Anza
10 Hotel Valencia
11 Kasa University-Airport Santa Clara
12 Westin San Jose

EATING

13 Back A Yard Caribbean Grill
14 Falafel's Drive In
15 Luna Mexican Kitchen
16 Original Joe's
17 San Pedro Square Market
18 Shuei-Do Manju Shop
19 Vịt Đông Quê

EATING IN SAN JOSE: OUR PICKS

Original Joe's: Downtown institution serving casual meals including sublime burgers. Comfy booths and a full bar. *4-10pm* **$$**

Back A Yard Caribbean Grill: The sauces and marinades are all made in-house. Fab jerk chicken and curried goat. *11am-8pm Tue-Sun* **$$**

San Pedro Square Market: Travel the world at this vibrant food hall. Choices include Italian, Peruvian, Korean and, yes, American. *11am-10pm* **$$**

Falafel's Drive In: A beloved San Jose institution for nearly 60 years; pitas brim with crunchy, herby falafel and creamy tahini. *10am-8pm* **$**

Winchester Mystery House (p151)

CREATISTA/SHUTTERSTOCK

immersive open-air museum that recreates the 19th century in the valley. The centerpiece is a scaled-down replica of the 1881 **Electric Light Tower**. Other buildings include the 1880 **Pacific Hotel**, which houses an old-timey ice-cream parlor and rotating art exhibits, and **migrant houses**, which show the spartan living conditions of farmworkers. Park exhibits highlight Chinese, Portuguese and other early communities. Galleries in various buildings have worthwhile special exhibitions.

Santa Clara has tech companies surrounding its namesake university, which is home to the 1777 **Mission Santa Clara de Asís** *(scu.edu/missionchurch; free)*.

SAN JOSE'S BEST MUSEUMS

Tech Interactive: An excellent technology museum that examines subjects from robotics to biofeedback, genetics to virtual reality. *thetech.org; adult/child $36/28*

San Jose Museum of Art: Permanent collection of 20th-century works plus imaginative changing exhibits. *sjmusart.org; adult/child $20/free*

MACLA: Gallery highlights Latino artists; one of the Bay Area's best community arts spaces, with live music, theater and thought-provoking visual-arts exhibits. *maclaarte.org; free*

Rosicrucian Egyptian Museum: Extensive collection includes statues, household items and mummies. *egyptianmuseum.org; adult/child $15/10*

Children's Discovery Museum: Yet another science museum, this one with hands-on displays for kids. *cdm.org; $18*

EATING IN SAN JOSE: OUR PICKS

Shuei-Do Manju Shop: Japanese pastries, candy and shaved ice; beloved for its house-made mochi (rice-based pastries). *10am-4pm Thu-Sun* $

Luna Mexican Kitchen: Brings a farm-to-table ethos to sophisticated Mexican fare. The bar goes beyond the margarita cliches. *9am-9pm* $$

Vịt Đông Quê: Simple storefront stars in the Little Saigon neighborhood with its duck dishes and piquant accompaniments. *10am-7pm Wed-Mon* $$

Sogo Tofu: Long-running strip-mall stalwart offers picnic-worthy meals made with its own organic tofu. *8am-5pm* $

Half Moon Bay

SURFING | COASTAL WALKS | PUMPKINS

GETTING AROUND

SamTrans provides useful local bus services. Route 294 runs on the frequently traffic-clogged Hwy 92 over to the peninsula and the Hillsdale Caltrain station. Route 117 runs north along Hwy 1 to Pacifica. On weekends, especially in summer, Hwy 1 through Half Moon Bay gets jammed with traffic.

Home to a long coastline, mild albeit foggy weather (bring layers!) and Mavericks, one of the biggest and gnarliest surf breaks on the planet, Half Moon Bay and neighboring Miramar and El Granada are prime real estate.

The Ohlone people lived here for thousands of years before Spanish missionaries colonized the land in the late 1700s; it was developed as a beach resort in the early 1900s and was a destination for smuggled booze from Canadian ships offshore during Prohibition. Today, it's the main coastal town between San Francisco (29 miles north) and Santa Cruz (49 miles south) and makes an ideal Hwy 1 pit stop.

Although the shallowness of the bay means it should be called Quarter Moon Bay, the long stretches of sandy beach and coastal bluffs attract surfers, hikers and active-minded weekenders. The small downtown is architecturally historic and good for a stroll.

TOP TIP

Mavericks is the intense surf break that became world famous thanks to videos beginning in the 1990s – waves here can top 60ft after storms. A surf competition was held here sporadically until 2016. To glimpse the distant action, take binoculars and hike around **Pillar Point** west of the namesake harbor.

Fun on the Coast

Lazing, hiking and kayaking

Crescent-shaped and over 4 miles long, **Half Moon Bay State Beach** *(parks.ca.gov)* is a beautiful ribbon of sand along the Pacific. Much of it is nearly untrodden and it's easy to leave other visitors behind as you walk along the sandstone cliffs and dunes.

The 7.2-mi **Coastside Trail** runs the length of Half Moon Bay from the bluff above Manhattan Beach north to Pillar Point Harbor. Look for driftwood after storms and watch for whales offshore.

When the bay is calm, get out and cruise on the water with **Half Moon Bay Kayak Co** *(hmbkayak.com; from $30hr)*, which rents kayaks and SUP sets.

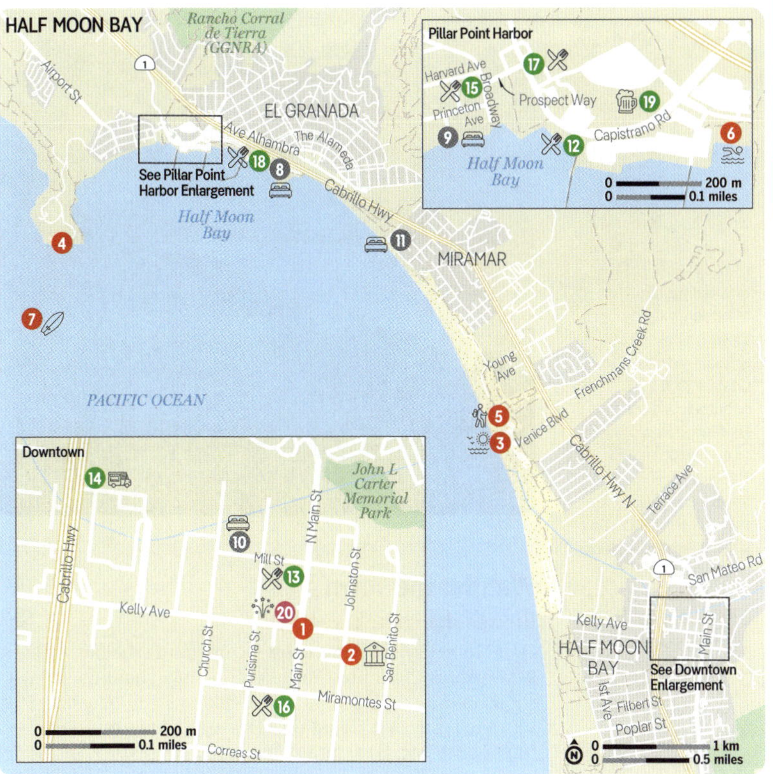

SIGHTS
1 Downtown Half Moon Bay
2 Half Moon Bay Coastside History Museum
3 Half Moon Bay State Beach
4 Pillar Point

ACTIVITIES
5 Coastside Trail
6 Half Moon Bay Kayak Co
7 Mavericks

SLEEPING
8 Beach House Half Moon Bay
9 Inn at Mavericks
10 Mill Rose Inn
11 Oceanfront Beach Villa

EATING
12 Barbara's Fishtrap
13 Ciya Mediterranean Cuisine
14 Dad's Luncheonette
15 Jettywave Distillery
16 Moonside Bakery & Cafe
17 Old Princeton Landing Public House & Grill
18 Sam's Chowder House

DRINKING & NIGHTLIFE
19 Hop Dogma Brewing Co

ENTERTAINMENT
20 Half Moon Bay Art & Pumpkin Festival

GREAT PUMPKINS

Starting early in the fall, fields are dotted with bright, nearly radiant pumpkins. The spectacle of rolling fields tightly speckled with orange stretching into the distance provides some of the only competition for attention with the views on the ocean side of the road. The best fields for the spectacle are south of Half Moon Bay.

Leading up to Halloween, pumpkin vendors line Hwy 1. The two-day **Half Moon Bay Art & Pumpkin Festival** *(hmbpumpkinfest.com)* in mid-October is famous for its pumpkin weigh-off, where beasts grown by fanatical cultivators (who zealously guard their secrets) can weigh more than 2500lb.

OXANA MILITSINA/SHUTTERSTOCK

Half Moon Bay

Wander the Town

Browse shops and have lunch

Half Moon Bay's old **downtown** comprises six blocks of early 20th-century buildings dotted with cafes, boutiques, bookshops and more. It's good for an hour's stroll or more. Stop into the renovated **Coastside History Museum** *(halfmoonbayhistory.org; free)* for exhibits on local history, including surfing, and for a look inside the restored 1919 town jail.

EATING & DRINKING IN HALF MOON BAY: OUR PICKS

Jettywave Distillery: One of many fine choices near Pillar Point Harbor, serves locally caught seafood with Med and Thai accents. *noon-8pm Fri-Sun* $$

Barbara's Fishtrap: At Pillar Point Harbor serving clam chowder and Bay Area standards. *11am-8.30pm* $$

Sam's Chowder House: Causes Hwy 1 traffic backups on weekends. Famous for its namesake clam concoction. *11am-8.30pm* $$

Hop Dogma Brewing Co: Top NorCal brewery serves hop-forward beers like Nintai, a Japanese-style rice lager, and West Coast IPAs. *2-8pm*

Old Princeton Landing Public House & Grill: Half Moon Bay's top venue for live music; all-day bar with elevated bar chow. *9am-11pm* $$

Ciya Mediterranean Cuisine: Uses local ingredients and produce for dishes that capture flavors from around the Eastern Med. *11am-9pm* $$

Moonside Bakery & Cafe: Makes a fine croissant; top-end diner for breakfast and lunch; baked treats stretch around the storefront. *7.30am-3.30pm* $

Dad's Luncheonette: Old caboose on Hwy 1 near downtown; serves creative hamburgers. Red wine by the can. *11am-4pm Thu-Sun* $

Beyond Half Moon Bay

One of California's highlights, the famous drive on Hwy 1 south from San Francisco is one of the state's unmissable pleasures.

The 70-mile stretch of the Pacific Coast Hwy (Hwy 1) from San Francisco to Santa Cruz is one of California's most bewitching oceanside jaunts. Outside of Half Moon Bay, it's a sinuous ribbon of road, passing beach after beach. From Pacifica to the end of San Mateo County is 41 miles; just enjoying this stretch can easily fill an entire day, even before you reach Davenport and the splendors of Santa Cruz County. Besides the easily accessed beaches alongside Hwy 1, there are countless others hidden from view. If you see a string of vehicles with surfboard racks parked roadside, you'll find a trail across the fields leading to some impossibly lovely cove reached by an often perilous cliffside trail.

Pacifica

TIME FROM HALF MOON BAY: **30 MINS**

Wild pleasures & promises

The lazy beach town of Pacifica, just 15 miles south of downtown San Francisco and 20 minutes by car north of Half Moon Bay, signals the end of the city's urban sprawl and the start of the wild Pacific coastline. Pacifica's real appeal is as the gateway to the spectacular run south on Hwy 1.

Pacifica State Beach *(parks.ca.gov; free)* is long, scenic and gets pounded by surfable waves. Gear rental is available nearby at **Nor-Cal Surf Shop** *(norcalsurfshop.com)*.

Immediately south of Pacifica is the **Devil's Slide**, a gorgeous coastal cliff area now bypassed by a tunnel. Hikers and cyclists cruise along the **Devil's Slide Trail**, a 1.3-mile section of the old road. Parking areas perch above the sheer, filigreed cliffs, with waves crashing below and pelicans flying overhead.

Montara & Moss Beach

TIME FROM HALF MOON BAY: **15 MINS**

Life in the tidepools

The villages of **Montara** and **Moss Beach** punctuate a stretch of coast interwoven by cliffs and sand. Just north, **Gray Whale Cove State Beach** is one of the coast's many popular clothing-optional beaches. At Moss Beach, the fabulous **Fitzgerald Marine Reserve** *(fitzgeraldreserve.org; free)* protects tide pools teeming with sea life such as colorful starfish, crabs and urchins. A small visitor center provides an introduction to the wealth of

Places

GETTING AROUND

SamTrans bus route 117 runs from Half Moon Bay to Pacifica. From there, buses connect to BART stations. Route 294 runs on the frequently traffic-clogged Hwy 92 to the peninsula and the Hillsdale Caltrain station.

On weekends, especially in summer, Hwy 1 through Half Moon Bay gets thick with tourist traffic. Further south, you'll need your own vehicle to follow the coast to Santa Cruz County. Experienced cyclists brave the narrow shoulders of Hwy 1 from Pacifica to Santa Cruz.

BEST SIGHTS INLAND FROM HWY 1

Skyline Blvd (AKA Hwy 35): Follows the ridge of the Santa Cruz Mountains, for vistas from the ocean to the San Francisco Bay. Passes many parks and trailheads.

Hwy 84: Runs for 20 curvaceous miles between Hwy 1 and Woodside, through open spaces, redwoods and the tiny one-bar hamlet of La Honda.

Sky Londa: Big-tree-shaded crossroads of Hwys 35 and 84; buzzes with hikers and outdoor enthusiasts comparing notes at the cafe.

Butano State Park: Witness nature's recovery from the 2020 wildfires in a serene park webbed with hiking trails. *parks.ca.gov; free*

Portola Redwoods State Park: Some 2800 acres of redwood-carpeted clefts and hillsides, riven by creeks and waterfalls along mossy banks. *parks.ca.gov; per vehicle $10*

life along the coast. The best time to visit the tidepools is near low tide, the website gives the daily tide schedule. And don't overlook the harbor seals and the trail leading into the old cypress forest.

Pescadero

TIME FROM HALF MOON BAY: **25 MINS**

Rural charm, toats & good food

A foggy speck of coastal crossroads between Half Moon Bay and Santa Cruz, 19th-century Pescadero is 2 miles inland from Hwy 1 and the coast with its orgy of scenery. It's a place of old buildings and old-fashioned farms that seems far removed from Silicon Valley, just over the hills that are emerald-green in spring and parched to burlap-brown the rest of the year.

On weekends the tiny downtown strains its seams with long-distance cyclists panting for carbs and day-trippers dive-bombing in for lunch at favored stops like **Duarte's Tavern**.

Year-round attractions include **Harley Farms Goat Dairy** *(harleyfarms.com; tours from $60)*, where you can get close to the cloven-hoofed sources of the delicious soft cheese that's for sale along with other deli items. Farm tours include kids (the goat kind) which kids (the human kind) love – as do older human kids. You can also taste wines from the local **Sante Arcangeli Family Wines** *(santewinery.com)*, known for its pinot noirs and chardonnays.

Out at the sea-breeze-scented coast, the wild Pacific beaches are populated by seals and pelicans. The state parks offer a cornucopia of tide-pool rocks, coves and inland forests of redwood canopies interspersed with fields of bushy artichokes.

Beaches, tidepools & wetlands

Pescadero State Beach *(parks.ca.gov; parking $8)* features a long strand (keep an eye out for seals) backed by dunes and interrupted by rocky tide pools. Stop to explore the marine-life-rich coastal tide pools on rocky outcroppings. On stormy days, the parking area facing the turbulent Pacific is a fine place for a picnic.

Pescadero Marsh Natural Preserve is on the inland side of Hwy 1, at the turn for Pescadero. The main **Pescadero Marsh Trail** winds through these verdant wetlands. Look for blue herons, deer, raccoons, foxes and, sniff, skunks.

Bean Hollow State Beach *(parks.ca.gov; free)* is another beguiling mix of sand and rocks. The eroded sandstone cliffs here have shapes that Antoni Gaudí would've been envious of, pockmarked by groovy honeycombed formations called tafoni. The park's highlight is **Pebble Beach**, where the shore is awash with bite-sized eye candy of agate, jade and carnelian.

WHERE TO EAT IN PESCADERO

Duarte's Tavern: Always thronged by happy masses feasting on crab cioppino, cream of artichoke soup and olallieberry pie. Reserve. *11am-3pm Wed-Mon* $$

Arcangeli Grocery Co: Prime purveyor of picnics, famed for hot-from-the-oven stuffed artichoke-herb bread, which some enjoy more than others. *11am-5pm Wed-Mon* $

Downtown Local: Spot that Tonka truck you forgot at the beach in this cafe jammed with memorabilia while you wait for your coffee. *8am-5pm* $

Mercado & Taqueria De Amigos: Classic line-up of well-made Mexican food served from an old corner gas station. Enjoy at the picnic tables or on a picnic. *9am-8pm* $

Pigeon Point

TIME FROM HALF MOON BAY: **30 MINS**

Unmissable beacon

Occupying a small outcrop, the 115ft-high **Pigeon Point Light Station** (1872) is one of the West Coast's tallest lighthouses. It's part of the **Pigeon Point Light Station State Historic Park** *(parks.ca.gov; free)*, which includes one of this coast's rare places to stay, the **HI Pigeon Point Lighthouse** (p161) hostel.

After years of work, the lighthouse once again stands proud with a nearly new exterior. Besides the fresh paint, it has new stainless-steel details. Visits to the interior should be allowed again sometime after 2026. In the meantime, the lighthouse remains active with an automated LED beacon. Walk the trails along the bluff and look out for gray whales in winter.

Stroll your own ribbon of sand

South of the lighthouse, **Gazos Creek State Beach** is nearly 1.5 miles-long. Untrodden sand, blustery wind and ceaseless waves are the norm. Note how the devastating 2020 fires in the Santa Cruz Mountains came right down to Hwy 1 and crossed over to the ocean's edge. Across Hwy 1, get a snack, lunch, a fresh beer and a tank of gas at **Highway 1 Brewing Co** *(noon-5pm Fri-Sun)*, one of the few oases on this stretch of the Pacific Coast Hwy.

Año Nuevo State Park

TIME FROM HALF MOON BAY: **35 MINS**

Witness elephant seals on the beach

Año Nuevo State Park *(parks.ca.gov; parking $10)* is home base for one of the world's largest mainland breeding colonies of northern elephant seals. More raucous than a full-moon beach rave, up to 10,000 boisterous elephant seals party down year-round on the dunes of **Año Nuevo Point**, their squeals and barks reaching fever pitch during the winter pupping season.

During the mating and birthing time from December to the end of March (peak season), visitors are only permitted access to the reserve on heavily booked guided tours. Tour bookings can be made 56 days in advance *(reservecalifornia.com; $11)*.

The rest of the year, free visitor permits from the entrance station are required; arrive before 3.30pm April to November. From the ranger station, it's a 3- to 4-mile round-trip hike on sand to whichever beach the seals are on that day; allow two to three hours. Dogs are not allowed. Amidst all the focus on the elephant seals, it's easy to forget that Año Nuevo itself is a beautiful and untouched coastal area with scores of birds.

WHY IS IT SO FOGGY?

When the summer sun's rays warm the air over the chilly Pacific, fog forms and hovers offshore, where prevailing winds drive it onshore, where it often burns off within a mile or two. Meanwhile, the state's interior, the Central Valley, which is ringed by mountains like a giant bathtub, gets scorching. The main break in the mountains is at the bay; as the inland warm air rises, it sucks in foggy air that flows around the Bay Area.

In July, it's not uncommon for noncoastal areas to top 100°F (38°C), while the coast barely reaches 70°F (21°C). It's why you see so many shivering tourists on Hwy 1, who thought it was 'summer.'

EATING & DRINKING ALONG HWY 1: OUR PICKS

Sage Bakehouse: Cool roadside bakery with a large deck offering ocean glimpses in Montara. Savory pies in the Brit tradition. Many teas plus coffee. *7am-6pm* $

El Gran Amigo: This Montara outfit has been slinging prized 'supershrimp' burritos, carne-asada tacos, and combo plates for decades. Good salsa. *10.30am-9pm* $

Moss Beach Distillery: Overlooking the cove where bootleggers used to unload Prohibition liquor; heated ocean-view deck. Steaks, seafood, cocktails. *noon-7.30pm* $$

Pie Ranch: Near the Santa Cruz County line, a wooden-barn wonderland of prepared foods made with house-grown produce and berries. Don't miss. *11am-5pm* $

Places We Love to Stay

$ Budget $$ Midrange $$$ Top End

Sausalito

MAP P121

Gables Inn Sausalito $$ Tranquil, stylish and peaceful. The inn includes a historical 1869 home and has 13 rooms, four cottages and three apartments, some with grand views.

Hotel Sausalito & Suites $$ Near the ferry dock, this stolid 1915 hotel has loads of period charm. Rooms enjoy partial bay views.

Inn Above Tide $$$ Posh and spacious rooms and suites – most with private deck and fireplace – that levitate over the water near the ferry terminal. Huge views.

Casa Madrona Hotel & Spa $$$ Classic Sausalito hotel with modern amenities. The property is divided into a 12-room, 'hillside' mansion and a collection of 'harborside' cottages, all with bay views.

Cavallo Point $$$ Spread over 45 scenic acres of landmark Fort Baker, luxe rooms in officers' quarters or contemporary, stylish 'green' accommodations with exquisite bay views.

Marin County Beaches

Pelican Inn $$ Twee English cottage in Muir Beach with cozy rooms and a popular pub. Close to the beach and Muir Woods.

Sandpiper Lodging at the Beach $$ A quick stroll to Stinson Beach; rooms and cabins are comfy and cute, all with a gas fireplace and kitchenette; in a lush garden.

Smiley's $$ Seven rooms in separate buildings behind this Bolinas bar (with good, casual food) that dates to 1851. Rooms are modern, with bright, contemporary decor.

Waters Edge Hotel $$$ A large deck extends over the bay in Tiburon; tasteful rooms have an elegant minimalism, with romantic water views.

Inverness

MAP P127

Cottages at Point Reyes Seashore $$ Tucked into the woods, family-friendly with kitchenette rooms. Activities include tennis, hot tub, croquet, and horseshoes. Also, a saltwater pool and private nature trail.

Motel Inverness $$ Appealing motel with fine service. Not many rooms with views, but the property is on gorgeous wetlands. Common area has seasonal roaring fire.

Tomales Bay Resort & Marina $$ Basic bayside marina motel with 36 great-value rooms and an unheated pool. Chat with fishers on the docks and see how they're bitin'.

Dancing Coyote Beach Cottages $$$ Serene modern cottages on Tomales Bay with skylights and decks with views in all directions. Full kitchens and fireplaces.

Marshall

MAP P127

Tomales Hotel $$ In the heart of town, vintage wooden hotel reopened in 2022 with nine modern rooms. Wide porches run around two floors.

Nick's Cove $$$ Fronting a peaceful cove at Marshall, waterfront vacation cottages variously feature wood-burning fireplaces, deep soaking tubs and private decks.

Oakland

MAP P131

B-Love's Guest House $ Artist Traci 'B-Love' Bartlow rents out rooms in her West Oakland house which includes a garden. Shared bathroom with Bartlow's photography on the walls.

Kissel Uptown Oakland $$$ A hip boutique hotel in Uptown. Large, comfortable and modern rooms across six floors. Close to nightlife.

Berkeley

MAP P139

Downtown Berkeley Inn $ Near downtown, budget motel has good-sized rooms with minimal frills offering a balance of budget and proximity to Berkeley's main drag.

Graduate Berkeley $$ Only a block from campus, seven-story 1928 hotel plays up its ties to the university. Collegiate-inspired details throughout.

Hotel Shattuck Plaza $$ A 100-year-old downtown jewel with red Italian glass lighting, flocked Victorian-style wallpaper – and a peace sign tiled into the floor.

Signature Inn Berkeley $$ Reimagined motel-style inn a few blocks south of Berkeley's main drag and university. Good-sized rooms with a dash of style; plenty of parking.

Berkeley City Club $$$ Designed by Julia Morgan (p133), refurbished 1929 historical landmark building has lush and serene Italianate courtyards. Some rooms have great Bay views.

Claremont Resort & Club $$$ The East Bay's glamorous white 1915 landmark with elegant restaurants, a fitness center, swimming pools, tennis courts and a full-service spa.

Richmond

Hotel Mac & Suites $$ In the appealing enclave of Point Richmond, a vintage three-story brick hotel combined with a modern wing. Comfortable rooms with relaxed style.

East Brother Light Station Bed & Breakfast $$$ One of many tiny islands dotting the bay, this one is unique for having an 1873 lighthouse and a B&B. Incredible views; access by boat from Richmond.

Palo Alto

MAP P147

Coronet Motel $ Tidy, family-owned, two-story motel in an incredible location near Stanford. Contemporary rooms, kitchenette suites and a small outdoor pool.

Dinah's Garden Hotel $ South of the university campus and downtown, has great rates, oversized rooms, balconies, garden-filled grounds and an outdoor pool.

Leland Hotel Palo Alto $$ Upscale motel-style inn that keeps prices low by limiting staff. Rooms have many extras like cookies; the location is near nightlife.

Nobu Epiphany $$$ In an elegant highrise, sleek downtown boutique hotel has its own tech concierge. Light, airy rooms have myriad luxuries.

Rosewood Sand Hill $$$ Storied low-rise hotel sprawls over a hillside. Massive designer-style rooms with distant views. Off famous Sand Hill Rd. Thursday is billionaires' singles night in the bar.

San Jose

MAP P152

Hotel De Anza $$ Opened during the Jazz Age, this downtown high-rise is an art deco beauty that pays homage to the property's history.

Kasa University-Airport Santa Clara $$ Close to Santa Clara University, contemporary hotel with a huge roof deck that includes a pool, sweeping Silicon Valley views and more.

Hotel Valencia $$$ Boutique hotel in the Santana Row shopping complex near Winchester Mystery House. Outdoor pool and hot tub create a stylish oasis of contemporary design.

Westin San Jose $$$ Better known by its old name, the Sainte Claire, this atmospheric 1926 landmark has a drop-dead gorgeous lobby with stretched-leather ceilings.

Inn Above Tide

AURORA ANGELES/SHUTTERSTOCK

Montara & Around

HI Point Montara Lighthouse Hostel $ On a site dating to 1875, the current lighthouse was moved here in 1928. Fab views, kitchen and firepit plus private rooms and dorms.

Ocean View Inn $$ Modest-sized, modern inn across from cliffs overlooking the ocean. Rooms have contemporary decor and there are big views from the deck.

Half Moon Bay

MAP P155

Oceanfront Beach Villa $$ Modern complex on Miramar Beach away from Hwy 1. Most rooms have ocean views; sleep to the sounds of surf.

Mill Rose Inn $$ Right near the center of Half Moon Bay on a large plot with private gardens filled with flowers.

Inn at Mavericks $$$ Oceanfront luxury, spacious rooms with gas fireplaces and private decks or patios. Close to Pillar Point Harbor.

Beach House Half Moon Bay $$$ Overlooking the bay from the bluffs near Pillar Point Harbor, loft-style suites with wood-burning fireplaces; outdoor heated pool.

Pescadero & Around

HI Pigeon Point Lighthouse $ One of the few places to stay on this stretch of coast is also the most coveted. Book well ahead; don't miss the hot tub.

Costanoa $$ Coastal resort with tent bungalows, rooms in woodsy lodges and cabins with porches. Many activities.

Pescadero Creek Inn $$ Private two-room cottage and spotless Victorian rooms in a restored century-old farmhouse with a tranquil creekside garden.

For places to stay in Napa & Sonoma Wine Country, see p224

LATYPOVA/GETTY IMAGES

Above: Hot-air balloons over the Napa Valley (p168); Right: Bodega Head Trail (p210)

THE MAIN AREAS

NAPA
Wine epicenter.
p168

ST HELENA
Quaint northern Napa Valley hub.
p180

SONOMA
History-rich wine-valley town.
p188

PETALUMA
Retro downtown with gastronomic flair.
p197

Researched by
Alexis Averbuck

Napa & Sonoma Wine Country

WHERE VINEYARDS, REDWOODS AND OCEAN MEET

California's premier wine valleys celebrate its vineyards, rolling hills, redwoods and unspoiled coast with fantastic food, wine and cool communities.

In a single day in Napa Valley, you can wallow in volcanic mud in Calistoga, learn how to make roux in St Helena and spend a wild night among giraffes on a Wine Country safari. That's after tasting some of the world's best vintages. Here, organic family wineries dare to make wines besides classic cabernets, while bicyclists commuting between former stagecoach stops wave hello to sous-chefs weeding organic kitchen gardens.

Head west to Sonoma County to wander thousand-year-old redwoods, pop a bottle of bubbly in Healdsburg and meet the talent behind farm-to-spliff dispensaries in Sebastopol. The region remains a magnet for free spirits. Adventure author Jack London attracted like-minded bohemians to Sonoma Valley while romantics and rebels roamed the Russian River Valley, establishing Guerneville as a pioneering LGBTQ+ resort.

Emerging at the coast, fishing towns like Bodega Bay bring in the Pacific's bounty, and trails wind across windswept bluffs. Your heart will soar with untrammeled views of waves crashing along the shore – most of the land out here is protected.

Good living seems to come naturally here, but people work hard to make that possible. Napa and Sonoma have faced fire, earthquakes, droughts and floods. But after each disaster, the people in America's fanciest farmland rebound. Raise a toast to Napa and Sonoma: living proof that with exceptional dedication and a splash of liquid courage, California dreams really do come true.

VENTU PHOTO/SHUTTERSTOCK

SEBASTOPOL
Artsy bohemian hangout.
p201

RUSSIAN RIVER VALLEY
Wine, redwood and river playground.
p213

HEALDSBURG
Laid-back chic, wine, art and food.
p218

Find Your Way

Napa and Sonoma counties and their myriad smaller valleys are surprisingly vast. They're easiest seen with your own wheels, but transit.511.org is a helpful resource to see the interlocking transit networks, mostly geared toward residents.

Russian River Valley, p213

Glide in a canoe, kayak or inner tube down the lazy summer river, or cruise valley wineries to the fantastic Sonoma Coast.

Sebastopol, p201

Get to know local wine-makers, bakers, distillers, musicians, gardeners and budtenders in California's most prolifically creative farm town.

Petaluma, p197

Vibe on classic Americana along an exquisitely preserved riverfront downtown loaded with breweries and dining options.

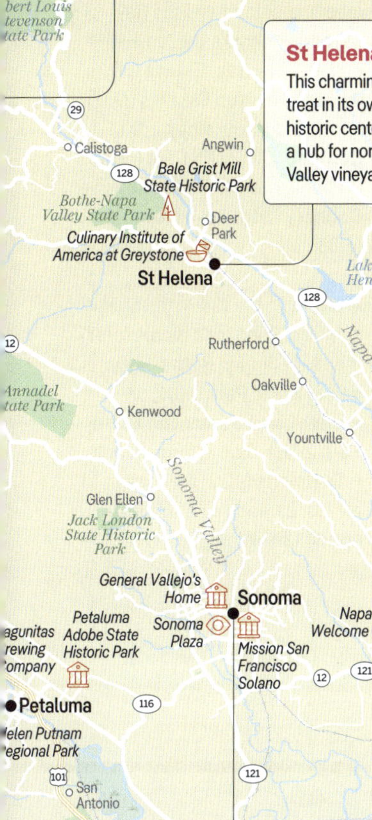

Healdsburg, p218

Wine-taste and boutique-browse your way around the plaza before cycling to nearby vineyards or debating the merits of all the dinner restaurants.

St Helena, p180

This charming town is a treat in its own right, with a historic center, but it's also a hub for northern Napa Valley vineyards.

Napa, p168

Wine and dine like a rock star, with California's most prized reds, world-acclaimed chefs' tasting menus, and restorative brunches at five-star resorts.

Sonoma, p188

Stroll beneath palm trees along the adobe-lined plaza into California's past. Then seek sustenance at myriad restaurants and tasting rooms.

CAR

Hitting the road is the best way to explore sprawling Wine Country. This way you can discover its secluded valleys and cool-cat towns, and tour the wineries scattered across the countryside. Don't drive buzzed, though – book a tour or a rideshare instead.

TRAIN

Sonoma-Marin Area Rail Transit (SMART) offers rail services in Sonoma and Marin counties from the Sonoma County Airport to downtown San Rafael. The Napa Valley Wine Train takes you from downtown Napa to St Helena and back in tourist coaches.

BICYCLE

Wine Country is a dream for cyclists. For many, the highlight of a California trip is the sun-dappled, winery-lined roads and trails linking valley wineries. They're scenic, mostly flat, and easy for beginners. Some of the regional parks also offer adrenaline-pumping mountain biking.

Plan Your Time

Go with the flow in Wine Country: stroll small towns or cycle to sun-drenched vineyards before a siesta and a meal that defines 'farm-to-table.' Or venture towards the coast for riverfront redwoods and rugged ocean-scapes.

PEREZOO/SHUTTERSTOCK

Table Rock, Robert Louis Stevenson State Park (p187)

Short on Time

- If you're an oenophile new to the region, head to **Napa** (p168). Start at town tasting rooms like **Gamling & McDuck** (p170) before roaming out to vineyards in **Carneros** (p176), where vines meet marshland and the Bay beyond. Pick your poison: high-end art at **Donum Estate** (p178) or **Hess Persson Estates** (p177) or relaxed family vineyards at **Robledo** (p193) and **Ceja** (p176). Prebook a cooking class at **Culinary Institute of America** (p183).

- North up the valley, the tastings continue. Shop for a **picnic** (p182) then walk it off in **Bothe-Napa Valley State Park** (p186) or **Robert Louis Stevenson State Park** (p187). Dine extremely well in **St Helena** (p183) then wash all your cares away with a **hot-springs soak** (p186).

Seasonal Highlights

Make summer reservations in Napa and Sonoma Valleys and on the coast. Hotel rates also jump during September and October's grape-crushing.

MARCH

Cinephiles delight in the **Sonoma Valley Film Festival** (p193), running for over 20 years. Vineyards are sprouting after their winter pruning and temperatures are mild during **Wine Road Barrel Tasting** (p207) in Sonoma County.

MAY

Napa's three-day **BottleRock** (p173) festival of music, food and wine is followed by **La Onda** (p173) music festival. **Women's Weekend** (p214) rolls into Guerneville and **Healdsburg Wine & Food Experience** (p221) celebrates local makers.

JUNE

Healdsburg Jazz Festival (p221) kicks off at venues across town, while **Art at the Source** (p191) open-studio visits allow you to visit artists' ateliers throughout Sonoma County.

Three Days to Explore

● Continue your Wine Country adventure with a look inside the adobe mission on **Sonoma's plaza** (p188). Then meander along the valley's vine-lined roads, stopping frequently for tastings at spots like **Gundlach-Bundschu Winery** (p192). Explore **Bartholomew Estate** (p193), an oak-dotted winery and preserve, then channel *The Call of the Wild* at **Jack London State Historic Park** (p194).

● Get a teeny taste of western Sonoma County, which makes Napa and Sonoma look uptight by comparison. Grab lunch in Santa Rosa at **Mitote Food Park** (p207) before making a beeline for **Sebastopol** (p201). Tour **organic farms** (p203) or take a walk from beach to bluff in **Sonoma Coast State Park** (p210) before kicking back with oysters and chilled wine at **Rocker Oysterfeller's** (p211) or **Fishetarian** (p210) in **Bodega Bay**.

If You Have More Time

● Raft up in the **Russian River Valley** (p213) where you can combine **a float on the river** (p215) with mescal cocktails at **El Barrio** (p216) in Guerneville or seafood on the coast at **Café Aquatica** (p217) or **River's End** (p217) in Jenner. Time your trip for Occidental's **Thursday Farmers Market** (p209) and dance outside at dusk or hit up the **great local breweries** (p208).

● Wine-taste your way up **Westside Rd** (p217) to **Healdsburg** (p218). If it's a Tuesday or Saturday morning, its abundant **farmers market** (p221) is a must for wares well beyond food, or on Tuesday afternoon, plan to picnic at a **free summer concert** (p221) on the plaza. If you love to cycle, peddle the wine roads of the **Dry Creek Valley** (p221) or along **West County trails** (p205).

JULY

Fourth of July celebrations light up across Napa and Sonoma counties, and peak season for floating the Russian River brings the **Monte Rio Variety Show** (p217), with unannounced celebrity guests, such as Conan O'Brien.

AUGUST

High summer brings the booming **Sonoma County Fair** (p207) to Santa Rosa. Guerneville's **Lazy Bear Week** (p214) and Sebastopol's **Gravenstein Apple Fair** (p203) light up western Sonoma County.

OCTOBER

During the grape harvest (or 'crush'), America's biggest wine competition, **Sonoma Harvest Fair** (p207), pairs well with the **Sonoma County Art Trails** (p191) open-studio tours across the county.

NOVEMBER

During **Wine & Food Affair** (p221) let your taste buds be your guide to 100 Sonoma County wineries offering a featured dish and wine pairing. **Napa Valley Film Festival** (p173) kicks off in Napa.

Napa

WORLD-FAMOUS WINES | ART COLLECTIONS | TOP CUISINE

TOP TIP

Wine tasting in Napa Valley is a pricey undertaking. Some tasting fees are waived with a set bottle purchase. To save, consider more reasonably priced Russian River, Healdsburg and Alexander Valley wineries (p223); they also sometimes accept walk-ins. Many wineries will ship for you, or get Bodega Shipping Co *(bodegashippingco.com)* to do it.

Your first stop in Napa may be the only one you need for a dream Wine Country getaway. With laid-back downtown tasting rooms, historic music halls featuring major musicians and Oxbow Public Market offering affordable gourmet fare, downtown Napa is where Napans come to relax.

Napa's riverbank parks are part of the town's sustainable 'living river' design to manage seasonal floods. And its lush hillsides kick off the steady carpet of wineries running straight up the valley.

It's hard to believe that in 2014 this was the epicenter of an earthquake that registered 6.0 on the Richter scale, causing $1 billion in damage. While Napa was rebuilding, the 2017, 2019 and 2020 fires hit – and when winter rains finally came, so did Napa River floods. Yet, through it all, Napa kept rebuilding – steadily and thoughtfully – and the city remains the sweet spot where wine flows and conversation meanders, just like the Napa River.

Historic Streets & Tasting Rooms

Sample wines in the central city

Napa's buzzy **1st St** is lined with indie wine-tasting rooms in historic storefronts and casual bistros packing California-grown flavor into globe-trotting menus.

GETTING AROUND

Downtown Napa is centrally located in Napa Valley, between scenic Silverado Trail to the east and busy St Helena Hwy/Hwy 29 to the west. The multiuse **Napa Valley Vine Trail** *(vinetrail.org)* connects downtown Napa to Yountville, St Helena to Calistoga and American Canyon to Vallejo. **Vine** *(vinetransit.com)* bus C gets you around downtown Napa; bus 10 gets you from downtown Napa to St Helena and Calistoga. Bus 11 links downtown Napa to the Vallejo Ferry Terminal, where ferries run to San Francisco. Express bus 29 connects Napa to El Cerrito del Norte BART station. You can pay *(adult/child $2/1.25)* with cash (no change given) or with a Bay Area transit Clipper card.

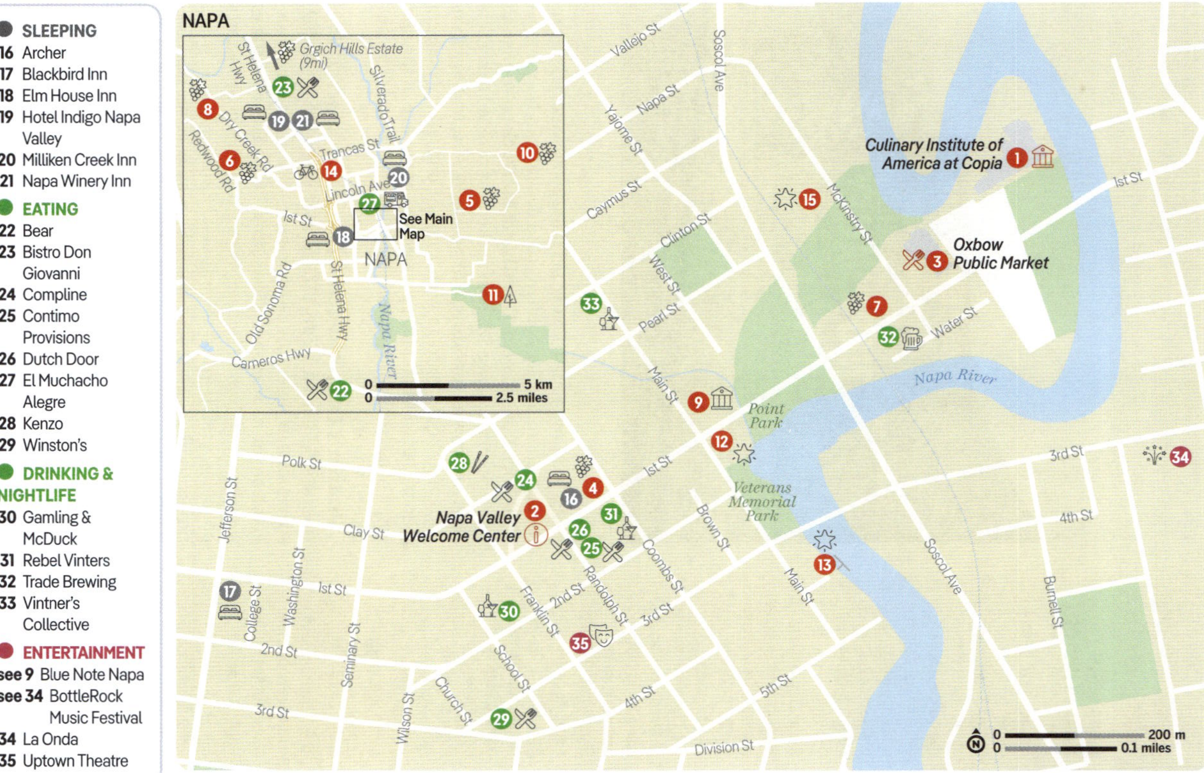

HIGHLIGHTS

1 Culinary Institute of America at Copia
2 Napa Valley Welcome Center
3 Oxbow Public Market

SIGHTS

4 Brown Downtown
5 Covert Estate
6 Hendry
7 Krupp Brothers Downtown Tasting Room
8 Matthiasson Winery
9 Napa Valley Opera House
10 Palmaz
11 Skyline Wilderness Park

ACTIVITIES

12 Napa Valley Balloons
13 Napa Valley Gondola
14 Napa Valley Vine Trail
15 Napa Valley Wine Train

SLEEPING

16 Archer
17 Blackbird Inn
18 Elm House Inn
19 Hotel Indigo Napa Valley
20 Milliken Creek Inn
21 Napa Winery Inn

EATING

22 Bear
23 Bistro Don Giovanni
24 Compline
25 Contimo Provisions
26 Dutch Door
27 El Muchacho Alegre
28 Kenzo
29 Winston's

DRINKING & NIGHTLIFE

30 Gamling & McDuck
31 Rebel Vinters
32 Trade Brewing
33 Vintner's Collective

ENTERTAINMENT

see 9 Blue Note Napa
see 34 BottleRock Music Festival
34 La Onda
35 Uptown Theatre

NAPA WINE-MAKING HISTORY

Grapes have been grown on this 5-by-35-mile strip of farmland since the gold rush. But earthquakes and juice-sucking phylloxera bugs struck, followed by Prohibition and the Great Depression. Napa had 140 wineries in the 1890s, but by the 1960s only around 25 remained.

In 1976 winemakers entered a few bottles into a blind tasting competition in Paris – and to much surprise, Napa wines took top honors. As Napa's reputation grew, global wine conglomerates moved in. With land now priced at up to $1 million an acre, independent, family-owned wineries work hard to stand their ground.

Today, Napa wine tasting is not just famous, it allows you to get hold of many vintages only available on-site.

Get to know your friendly neighborhood winemaker/cartoonist Adam McClary and his cat Theodosia in Napa's most punk-rock tasting room, **Gamling & McDuck** *(gamlingandmcduck.com; tasting $35)*. No neckties or rarefied cabernets here. At **Brown Downtown** *(brownestate.com; tastings from $50)*, find liquid courage with Duppy Conqueror, Jamaican folklore hero of Bob Marley songs and namesake of the epic white wine from Brown Estate, Napa's first African American–owned winery.

Vintner's Collective *(vintnerscollective.com; tastings from $50)*, housed in an 1875 former saloon and brothel, specializes in super small-batch wines. You don't need a reservation for its standard $50 tasting. Or hit **Rebel Vinters** *(rebelvintners.com; tastings from $30)*, with board games on tables, graffiti art on the walls and California indie wines lining the bar. Then join the golden-hour stroll past lovingly restored Victorian houses and take a breather along grassy riverbanks.

EATING IN NAPA: EASY BITES

Winston's: Start the day with amazing baked goods and stick-to-your-ribs breakfast sandwiches with a happy brunching crowd. *7am-2pm* $

Contimo Provisions: Midday is prime for outstanding sandwiches... but it also makes killer biscuit sandwiches for breakfast. *8am-3pm Tue-Sat* $

Dutch Door: Beloved casual takeout joint featuring all-organic food, from fried chicken to kale bowls. *11.30am-3pm Wed & Thu, to 6pm Fri & Sat* $

El Muchacho Alegre: If tacos are your jam, head for this taco truck parked at 751 Jackson St in an out-of-the-way residential neighborhood. *10am-8pm Mon-Sat* $

PGIAM/GETTY IMAGES

Napa Valley Wine Train

Napa by Train or Gondola

Kick back, take it all in

Chug along in the **Napa Valley Wine Train** *(winetrain.com; ticket incl dining from $223)* from downtown Napa to St Helena and back in a plush vintage dining car, with meal service included and optional winery stops...if you choose one, make it historic **Grgich Hills Estate** *(p185; grgich.com)*, which aims to produce wines sustainably through regenerative farming practices. Trains depart from Napa Valley Wine Train Depot on McKinstry St near 1st St.

If floating is more your speed, glide downstream with **Napa Valley Gondola** *(napavalleygondola.com; from $175)* on a private gondola, watching the sun set over the city. Your gondolier can serenade you in Italian, but the scenery and wine on offer are totally California, dude. On this single-oared boat you and up to five friends can hang out with ducks, spot herons and otters, and see how ecologists are restoring Napa River.

WINE-TASTE LIKE A PRO

Swirl, sniff and swish. Swirl your wine in the glass to release aromas, then have a good sniff to excite your salivary glands. Take a small sip and swish it around your mouth so all your taste buds get in on the action.

Sip and spit. If you love what you're tasting, you'll want to try plenty – and that means pacing yourself. It's fair game to spit out your last sip, or even pour leftovers into the spittoon (aka 'chuck bucket').

Remember to eat. Some wineries serve bites; otherwise snack in between.

Consider joining wine clubs carefully. Your pourer may suggest joining their wine club (to buy discounted bottles annually). Don't feel pressured, especially if you're tipsy and fuzzy on the details.

EATING IN NAPA: FINE DINING

Kenzo: Napa Michelin-starred Japanese magic paired with top wine and sake in chic minimalist harmony. Book ahead. *5.30-8.30pm Wed-Sun* $$$

Compline: This cozy, unpretentious bistro/wine bar offers a short, seasonal menu of hearty dishes. *5-11pm Wed & Thu, 11.30am-11pm Fri-Sun* $$$

Bistro Don Giovanni: With copper pans, garden fountains and black-vested waiters, the Don ladles on Italian charm. Weekends get packed and loud. *11.30am-9pm* $$$

Bear: Stanly Ranch's creative Californian fare spans Asian-dressed oysters to delicate handmade pastas. *7am-10pm* $$$

TIPS FOR NAPA ON A BUDGET

Free wine-tasting passes: Once you reserve your accommodations, call the concierge to ask what wine-tasting passes they have available.

Wining & dining downtown: Downtown Napa has the broadest, best selection of affordable dining options in Napa Valley, or head to **Oxbow** to see what's cooking. Downtown Napa tasting rooms offer a choice of wine by the glass or reasonably priced tasting flights. Restaurants will let you bring your own wine with minimal/no corkage.

Free sights & entertainment: CIA at Copia offers free museum shows, demos, tastings and other events daily. You might luck into free music at Oxbow – especially on Locals' Night *(Tuesday 5–8pm)*.

BRUCE YUANYUE BI/GETTY IMAGES

Oxbow Public Market

Food Markets & Cooking Classes

Daytime grazing in gourmet style

Deliciousness abounds in Napa. But why commit to just one dining establishment when you could graze at a dozen of Napa's finest? At **Oxbow Public Market** *(oxbowpublicmarket.com)*, assemble the meal of your California dreams with all-star dishes – perhaps Hog Island Oyster Co oysters mignonette and Eiko's *hamachi* sushi bonbons with Fieldwork Brewing Company farmhouse ale, followed by Ritual Coffee espresso. Or if it's breakfast time, don't miss Model Bakery's treats.

Also in the Oxbow area, downtown Napa's **Culinary Institute of America at Copia** *(ciaatcopia.com; classes from $85)* offers drop-in cooking or wine classes, demos, documentaries and star-chef panels too spicy for TV. Hit the free Chuck Williams Culinary Arts Museum upstairs, buy Marketplace gadgets and signed cookbooks downstairs, or have a meal at the Grove.

If you'd like to throw in a little wine and beer tasting while you're in the Oxbow area, **Krupp Brothers Downtown Tasting Room** *(kruppbrothers.com; tastings from $45)* and **Trade Brewing** *(tradebrewing.com)* are just across the street from each other.

DRINKING IN NAPA: WINERIES NEAR DOWNTOWN

Palmaz: Julio and Amalia Palmaz produce Napa's most buzzworthy wines on its 600-acre hillside estate. *by appointment*

Matthiasson Winery: This sustainable winery, a short drive on Napa's western low slopes, makes a citrusy rosé of syrah and robust Napa white blend. *by appointment*

Hendry: Joyful wine aficionados make this low-key winery a fave. Fees waived with equivalent purchase. Four estate hiking tours per year. *by appointment*

Covert Estate: Part of the Coombsville appellation using sustainable methods to make Bordeaux-style cabernet franc, cabernet sauvignon, syrahs. *by appointment*

Live Local Music & Festivals

Grooving and movies

Hitting high notes since 1880, the opulent **Napa Valley Opera House** has survived earthquakes and fires to find its second wind, and is making a late-breaking career shift into jazz. The **Blue Note Napa** *(bluenotenapa.com)* calendar features weekend global jazz talent and midweek locals' nights – and the drinks menu here puts other clubs to shame, with cult wines and house-brewed craft beer. With restored 1937 art deco swagger and excellent sound, tiny **Uptown Theatre** *(uptowntheatrenapa.com)* hosts big names in music and comedy.

FOR GASTRONOMES

You really can't beat California for food and wine. To learn more about the state's **food scene**, see p30.

Plan to be in Napa in May for breakout-hit three-day music, food and wine festival **BottleRock** *(bottlerocknapavalley.com)*, where huge lineups include marquee names such as Janelle Monáe, Green Day and Ice Cube. The same group also puts on the festival **La Onda** *(laondafest.com)* for two days at the end of May, featuring primarily Spanish-language musical genres.

Or celebrate the silver screen at November's **Napa Valley Film Festival** *(napavalleyfilmfest.org)*, where movies about food and wine are obvious crowd-pleasers, but the roster includes documentaries and narrative films as well.

Fresh Air in a Wild Park

Hiking Skyline Wilderness Park

Feeling like stretching your legs and getting a good look at the Napa views? Head to **Skyline Wilderness Park** *(skylinepark.org)*. The park blooms with springtime wildflowers and California perennials in its Martha Walker Native Plant Habitat. Check it out then hit over 25 miles of hiking and mountain-biking trails, an archery range or disc-golf course. You're allowed to picnic with wine – so pick up supplies in town before you come. You can also camp with either tents or RVs. Be sure to reserve ahead during events like the BottleRock festival.

Napa & Sonoma Valley Wineries

California wine country is famous. But with 1000 wineries to choose from across Napa and Sonoma counties, where do you even begin? To make your next favorite wine easier to find, we're giving you a few places to start. Sustainably produced wines are a hallmark of the region. Learn more on p171.

Where to sip if you love...

Vineyard Walks & Inspiring Views

Many wineries set in the vineyards (as opposed to city-based tasting rooms) offer vineyard tours and walks for an increased price. Some of our favorite views and walks in the Napa Valley are at **Chappellet Winery** (p184), **Cuvaison Winery** (p176) and **Pride Mountain Vineyards** (p185). And don't forget art-forward **Hess Persson Estates** (p177) and **Donum Estate** (p178).

Food Pairings

Food and wine pairings are a common part of high-end tastings. Servings are usually super small, and range from simple charcuterie to gourmet.

Napa Valley's **Brasswood** *(brasswood.com; tastings from $20)* is beloved for its excellent on-site **restaurant** (p182). At **VJB Cellars** *(vjbcellars.com; tastings from $30)* in Sonoma Valley, taste prized Italian wines like robust white friulano and aleatico rosé while lunching in its **gourmet deli** (p196).

Other foodie moments include Windsor's **Bricoleur Vineyards** *(bricoleurvineyards.com; tastings from $40)* where you can splash out on a multicourse extravaganza of pairings. **Mayo Family Winery Reserve Room** (p196) also offers small plates; and food and wine pairings feature at **Flowers** (p217), **Idlewild** (p220) and **Davis Estates** *(davisestates.com; tastings from $100)*, to name but a few.

Tasting on a Budget

In the **Napa Valley** we like **Bennett Lane Winery** (p185) *(tastings from $35)*, **Nichelini Family Winery** (p184) *(tastings $30, occasional flashback Friday with $15 tastings)* and Brasswood *(tastings from $20)*. In **Sonoma Valley** try **Kunde** (p196) *(tastings from $25)* and **Gundlach-Bundschu** (p192) *(tastings from $25)*. Around **Sebastopol** visit **Balletto** (p204) *(tastings from $20)*, **Freeman** (p204) *(tastings from $35)*, **Iron Horse** (p204) *(tastings from $35)*, **Martinelli** (p205) *(tastings from $25)* and **Hanna** (p223) *(Russian River location tastings $30)*. **Russian River Valley** includes **Porter Creek** (p217) *(tastings $30)*, **Porter-Bass** (p217) *(tastings $25, waived with purchase)* and **Korbel** *(tastings from $15)*. **Dry Creek Valley's Unti Vineyards** (p222) *(tastings $25, waived with bottle purchase)* and **Emmitt-Scorsone Wines** (p222) *(tastings $25)* pair well with **Alexander Valley's Soda Rock Winery** (p223) *(tastings from $25)*. Remember: tasting rooms often have lower rates than wineries.

Sparkling Wines

If you're looking for a bit of bubbly, hone right in on Carneros' **Domaine Carneros** and **Artesa** or Napa's excellent **Schramsberg** (p187). Further west in Russian River, **Iron Horse Vineyards** (p204) and **Equality Vines** (p215) are tops, while **Korbel** is a widely distributed mega-producer.

HOW TO...

Book Ahead Almost all of the wineries in Napa and Sonoma are reservation-based, so book ahead.

Walk-Ins Some accept walk-ins when they have an open spot. Check first online on **Tock** *(exploretock.com)*.

Napa Valley Welcome Center *(visitnapavalley.com)* occasionally have wine-tasting passes (ask at your hotel, too).

Telephoning The old-fashioned method still works and is worth trying at the last minute – you might get lucky!

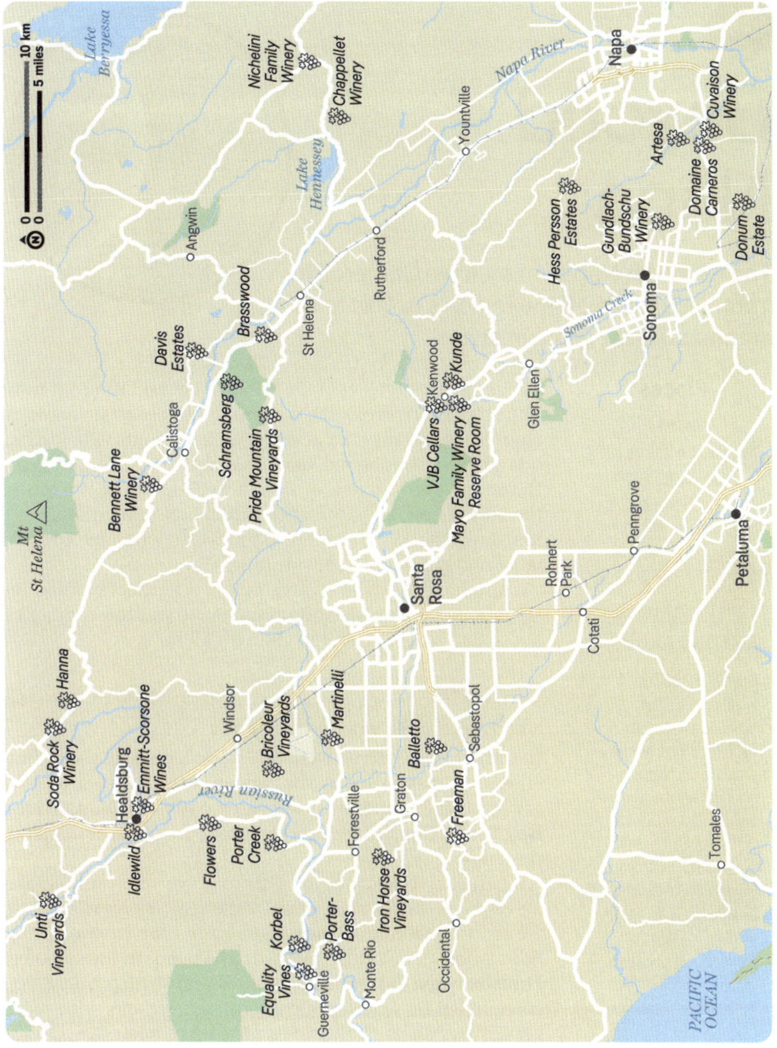

DIY or guided tour?

If you don't have a designated driver, book a ride with Designated Drivers Napa Sonoma. Guided tours can make everything friction-free, but add to the cost. Often you pay for the tour itself, as well as all the tasting fees, food, a fuel fee and a tip for the driver/guide.

Platypus Wine Tours *(platypustours.com)* specializes in backroad vineyards, historic wineries and family-owned operations.

Active Wine Adventures *(activewine adventures.com)*, covering Napa and Sonoma, works up your appetite for gourmet food, wine and craft beer, with your choice of adventures.

Laces and Limos *(lacesandlimos.com)* offer slow, scenic routes around Napa Valley in chauffeured tuk-tuk (auto-rickshaw).

You can also go vineyard-hopping by bicycle...try Getaway Adventures/Wine Country Bikes *(getawayadventures.com)*, Sonoma Adventures *(sonoma-adventures.com)* and Backroads *(backroads.com)* for Napa and Sonoma bike tours.

Beyond Napa

The southern Napa Valley, from Carneros to Yountville, kicks off the region's exquisite wine, art and culinary game in style.

Places

GETTING AROUND

Summer and fall weekend traffic crawls, especially on Hwy 29 between downtown Napa and St Helena at around 5pm, when wineries close. For scenic drives from Yountville, follow Silverado Trail north, or take Mt Veeder Rd through pristine countryside west of Yountville. The Vine *(vinetransit.com)* bus 10 doesn't stop in Yountville proper, but across Hwy 29 at the Veterans' Home.

The southern stretches of the Napa Valley, radiating out from Napa town, range from the moist pinot-noir coastal vineyards rimmed by marshes in Carneros, to fancy Yountville further inland. Wineries abound, more than we can list here. Whether you're in for the day, or have a week to roam, you'll find the best the region has to offer – from excellent vintages, astonishing vistas and world-class meals to lonesome country lanes and old-school roadside diners.

It also happens to be an area rich in art collections and installations, so plan ahead to reserve entry at these wineries and spend some extra time taking it all in.

Carneros

TIME FROM NAPA: **15 MINS**

Moody wetlands, vaunted vineyards

In Carneros, preserved wetlands stand alongside the rolling vineyards, making a drive or cycle through this zone an otherworldly jaunt off the Napa beaten path. The **Napa River Bay Trail** *(napaoutdoors.org)* loops south of Carneros along the shore.

Whether by **bike** (p178) or with your own car, you can take an exquisite break with some of the region's most majestic views at **Cuvaison Winery** *(cuvaison.com; tastings from $60)*, where undulating vineyards join ponds in the distance. **Hudson Napa Valley** *(hudsonranch.com; tastings from $100)*, surrounded by vast succulent gardens, beckons with more great views and a tasting of its olive oil to boot.

Low-key **McKenzie-Mueller Winery** *(mckenziemueller.com; tastings $35)* is tucked into the heart of Carneros' vineyards. The romance started in the vineyards at **Ceja** *(cejavineyards.com; tastings from $40)*...Amelia Morán met Pedro Ceja in 1967, when they were both picking grapes for Mondavi in Napa. Marriage, kids and decades of trailblazing later, Amelia is the first Mexican-American woman winery president – and that vineyard romance is captured in Ceja's signature pinot noir, aged chardonnay and Vino de Casa, a satiny blend of Italian arneis and chardonnay. You can taste their wines at their tasting room on the outskirts of Sonoma.

LEONARD ZHUKOVSKY/SHUTTERSTOCK

Cellar, Hess Persson Estates

Across the Valley

TIME FROM NAPA: **15 MINS**

Art collections paired with wine

Climb a winding country road 20 minutes' drive west of Napa up beyond vineyards through oak forests to an ivy-covered hill-top stone winery at **Hess Persson Estates** *(hesspenssonestates.com; tastings from $85 incl museum, museum walk with director $110)*. Here, wine tastings can be paired with California's finest private contemporary-art collection. Thought-provoking installation art starts with Leopoldo Maler's 1974 burning typewriter – an homage to his uncle, a newspaper editor killed by Argentina's junta. Other highlights include Anselm Kiefer's sculpture of lead shingles from Cologne Cathedral, and Andy Goldsworthy's giant ball of manzanita branches.

Scrap-metal sheep dotting the hillside hint that something unusual is afoot on 217 acres of Carneros countryside at **di Rosa Center for Contemporary Art** *(dirosaart.org; adult/child $25/5)*. This groundbreaking collection was the personal passion of free-spirited reporter-turned-grape-farmer Rene di Rosa, who hung hyperrealist Robert Bechtle paintings on the ceiling and installed spooky Tony Oursler videos in his cellar. Today the gatehouse gallery showcases Viola Frey's monumental 1970s ceramic sculpture, David Best's art cars and visiting California artists, while inspiration overflows into the Sculpture Meadow.

NAPA CREATIVITY

Carolyn Ellis, a Napa artist, calls out her favorite places to experience art. *carolynellis.com*

Hess Art Collection: World-class modern art, with an amazing drive up Mt Veeder Rd through vineyards with views.

Di Rosa Center for Contemporary Art: Sculpture garden, galleries and picnic grounds with 1600 artworks.

R+D Kitchen, Yountville: Best burger, chocolate sundae and cocktails.

Napa Lighted Art Festival: Transforms Napa into a mini Burning Man, with large-scale light projections and sculptures. *donapa.com; late Jan to late Feb*

Donum Estate Art Collection (p178): Hands-down best sculpture garden in the valley.

EATING & DRINKING IN CARNEROS: OUR PICKS

Angelo's Wine Country Deli: Look for the cow on the roof roadside for fat sandwiches with smoked meats. *9.30am-4.30pm Wed-Mon* **$**

Boon Fly Café: Leisurely weekend brunches with killer eggs Benedict with jalapeño hollandaise, handmade doughnuts and excellent burgers. *7am-9pm* **$$**

Lou's Luncheonette: Fried chicken, and po'boys, hush puppies, burgers and milkshakes. At a simple whitewashed diner with a patio. *8am-3pm Wed-Sun* **$**

Kivelstadt Cellars & WineGarten: Wrap up with live music at this easygoing wine garden. There's a playground for kids, too. *11am-5pm Thu-Mon* **$$**

HOW DO I BECOME A CALIFORNIA WINE AFICIONADO?

Pour yourself a nice glass and settle in with one of these top wine books: Jon Bonné's *The New California Wine: A Guide to the Producers and Wines Behind a Revolution in Taste* (2013), Jane Lopes' *Vignette: Stories of Life and Wine in 100 Bottles* (2019), Julia Harding and Jancis Robinson's *The Oxford Companion to Wine* (2015), and Eric Asimov's *How to Love Wine: A Memoir and Manifesto* (2012).

Also, during crush (autumn harvest), when vine leaves turn brilliant colors and you can smell fermenting fruit on the breeze, farmers throw big parties with vineyard workers. To score party invitations, join your favorite winery's wine club. No one wants to miss the good times – reserve ahead and budget accordingly.

Craving some Ai Weiwei with your chardonnay or pinot? The extraordinary contemporary-art collection at nearby **Donum Estate** *(thedonumestate.com; tastings from $75)* is surrounded by lavender fields, vineyards and an organic farm. Take the tour, glass of chardonnay in hand, roaming Yayoi Kusama's polka-dotted pumpkin, Gao Weigang's brass-tube maze and Keith Haring's embracing figures.

If you're an architecture buff, head north to **Quixote Winery** *(quixotewinery.com; tastings from $50)* – that gold-leafed onion dome sprouting from the grassy knoll is the work of Austrian eco-architect Friedensreich Hundertwasser, whose signature crayon-colored ceramic pillars frame broken-tile mosaic walls.

Cycling Napa Valley

What better way to cruise the vineyards than by bike? The **Napa Valley Wine Trail** *(vinetrail.org)* connects vineyards, wineries, downtown Napa and Yountville via 12.5 miles of walking and cycling paths. The trail is just a piece of an ambitious 47-mile stretch that will eventually connect the Vallejo Ferry Terminal to Calistoga. For now, to bike onward to Calistoga, take tree-lined Silverado Trail instead of hot, traffic-heavy Hwy 29.

You can rent a bike or book a tour at **Napa Valley Bike Tours** *(napavalleybiketours.com; bicycle/e-bike rental per day $54/94, tours from $150)* or **Calistoga Bikeshop** *(calistogabikeshop.com; bicycle/e-bike rental per day from $50/93, tours from $170)*. Other biking guides cover parts of the Napa Valley, too, and give a range of tours. We like Getaway Adventures/Wine Country Bikes (p175), based in Calistoga and Healdsburg.

Lovely picnic spots

While a picnic in the vineyards is bucket-list material, strict zoning laws make it tricky to find places to picnic legally in Napa.

JAMIE PHAM/ALAMY

Cuvaison Winery (p176)

If you're heading to a winery, call ahead to see if picnicking is allowed (it's customary to buy a bottle of your host's wine if it is). If you don't finish your wine, stash it in the trunk – California law forbids driving with an uncorked bottle in the car.

Here's a short list of prime picnic spots, in south–north order across Napa Valley: Skyline Wilderness Park (p173), Gundlach-Bundschu Winery (p192) or Bartholomew Estate Winery (p193), Pride Mountain Vineyards (p185), Bothe-Napa Valley State Park (p186) and Old Faithful Geyser (p186).

Yountville

TIME FROM NAPA: **25 MINS**

Play with the culinary all-stars

Planets and Michelin stars are mysteriously aligned over **Yountville**, a tiny Western stagecoach stop 25 minutes' drive north of Napa that's been transformed into a global dining destination. It sounds like an urban legend – until you take a stroll down Yountville's quiet, tree-lined Washington St.

Say hey to interns weeding **French Laundry herb gardens** and trainee sommeliers grabbing lunch at the **Tacos Garcia** truck. You've just met the talents behind a thousand meals of a lifetime each week – and you can probably buy them a beer later. **French Laundry** *(thomaskeller.com)* itself dazzles through nine opulent courses (if you can get a reservation), but you can also grab takeout at **Bouchon Bakery** *(bouchonbakery.com)* – just wait in the hefty line.

For a bit of wine tasting, head across the valley floor to a batch of excellent wineries: **Antinori Napa Valley** *(antinorinapavalley.com)*, **Shafer Vineyards** *(shafervineyards.com)* and **Regusci Winery** *(regusciwinery.com)*.

CARNEROS, WHAT'S IN A NAME?

This stretch of bayfront lowlands spanning both Napa and Sonoma counties is 15 minutes' drive south of Napa. Historically it was shared by Patwin people to the east and Coastal Miwok to the west. Mexican shepherds named it Los Carneros ('The Rams') back in the 1830s – and until recently, sheep had the run of the place. In the 1960s, savvy farmers reckoned that thin-skinned pinot-noir grapes might actually prefer the foggy, damp microclimates that made woolly sheep feel right at home.

Carneros is an American Viticultural Area (AVA) spanning Napa and Sonoma counties. Though online addresses indicate one county or another, the sights are all in the same vicinity.

FOR WINE LOVERS

California's broad array of wine regions mean you find top tipples all across the state. Check out **Paso Robles' wineries** for more top cabs or **Santa Ynez Valley** near Santa Barbara, and pretend you're in the movie *Sideways*.

St Helena

WINE AND CUISINE | EXHILARATING WALKS | RICH HISTORY

GETTING AROUND

Parking in downtown St Helena is next to impossible on summer weekends. Tip: look behind the visitor center. Napa Vine *(vinetransit.com)* connects St Helena to downtown Napa and Calistoga on bus 10, and provides transit around town on the St Helena Shuttle for $1. To schedule a pickup, call 707-963-3007 or access its website or Ride the Vine app during operating hours.

TOP TIP

St Helena is loaded with fabulous restaurants and nearby wineries where you'll need reservations. If you haven't booked, you can shop for a picnic (p182). **St Helena Welcome Center** *(sthelena.com)* has information and lodging assistance, and can help with winery booking.

Even people with places to go and wine to drink can't resist a closer look at St Helena (pronounced ha-LEE-na). One or two blocks down Main St, cars suddenly swerve to the curb so that passengers can photograph this road that looks exactly like a Western movie set. But this scene is the real deal: three blocks of Main St are a designated National Historic District, covering 160 years of California history – including the 1913 Cameo Cinema, one of the oldest movie theaters still in operation in America.

Today Main St is lined with restaurants, gourmet shops and tasting rooms. Further up the street, the 1889 Greystone Cellars château is home to the Culinary Institute of America. If you're thirsty, you're in luck: there's more than an acre of wine grapes per resident in St Helena.

Stroll Through Wine-Making History

Visit a mill and winery from St Helena's past

Stroll the historic downtown of St Helena and you may wonder, what's the story behind this pretty little town? Well, this area was Native Wappo land until it was taken by Spain, and became a territory of Mexico – more specifically, the property of Maria Ygnacia Soberanes, the niece of Mexican commander General Vallejo. The matriarch of a family of savvy businesswomen.

Doña Maria sold off parcels of land that had potential as vineyards, but saved the best for her daughters, giving Isadora the Bale grist mill – still grinding flour today – and prime vineyards to Caroline. See history in action at the mill, now in **Bale Grist Mill State Historic Park** *(parks.ca.gov)*, where you can watch the original French buhr millstones grind flour on the weekends, and take home bags of just-ground cornmeal for a donation. In October, join the **Old Mill Days** *(napavalleystateparks.org; admission $5)* living-history festival.

Romance and business converged again when Caroline married German winemaker Charles Krug. Together they were pioneers in planting vineyards and they founded Napa's first

HIGHLIGHTS

1 Culinary Institute of America at Greystone

SIGHTS

2 Charles Krug

SLEEPING

3 El Bonita Motel
4 Harvest Inn
5 Wydown Hotel

EATING

6 Charter Oak
7 Cook St Helena
see 1 Gatehouse Restaurant
8 Goose & Gander
9 Gott's Roadside
10 Model Bakery
11 Napa Valley Olive Oil Company
12 Roman Holiday
13 Sunshine Foods
14 WF Giugni & Son

DRINKING & NIGHTLIFE

15 Erosion Tap House

SHOPPING

16 Farmers Market
17 Lolo's Consignment
18 New West KnifeWorks
19 Pearl Wonderful Clothing
20 Wild Plum Books
21 Woodhouse Chocolates

INFORMATION

22 St Helena Welcome Center

BEST SHOPPING IN ST HELENA

Woodhouse Chocolates: Graze delectable chocolates handmade by a Culinary Institute of America–trained mother-and-daughter team. *woodhousechocolate.com*

New West KnifeWorks: Gleaming, high-performance artisanal knives, hand-carved cutting boards and colorful blown-glass olive-oil decanters. *newwestknifeworks.com*

Lolo's Consignmen: Forgot a sweater for wine-cellar tastings, or are stilettos slowing your roll through vineyards? Hit Lolo's. *lolosconsignment.com*

Wild Plum Books: Take a digital detox with a good used book. *wildplumbooks.com*

Pearl Wonderful Clothing: One of several chichi-meets-casual clothing boutiques along Main St. *pearlwonderfulclothing.com*

ROSANGELA PERRY/SHUTTERSTOCK

Culinary Institute of America at Greystone

commercial winery in 1861. **Charles Krug** *(charleskrug.com; tastings from $50)* vineyards are still producing (though they were bought by Mondavi in 1943, the start of their empire). You can stop here, too, on the Napa Valley Wine Train (p171). Don't confuse this winery with Krug, the famous champagne house from Reims, France – they are unrelated.

Shop for a Picnic

Graze from delis to markets

Whether it's wine or romance that leads you to St Helena, you're in the right place, but what if you need a picnic to eat in the valley? Stop by century-old businesses still open today, including jam-packed **Napa Valley Olive Oil Company** *(nvoliveoilmfg.com)*, where salami swings from the rafters and wooden crates brim with picnic possibilities – crusty bread, nutty cheeses, meaty olives – plus Napa olive oil.

At excellent **WF Giugni & Son** *(giugnis.com)* pile meats onto bread until your sandwich looks like it belongs in a comic strip, then drizzle with 'Giugni juice' (red-wine-vinegar dressing).

EATING IN NORTHERN NAPA VALLEY: LUXURY LIVING

Auro: Exquisite 7-course tastings menus in pure California elegance, paired with wine to match. A meal of a lifetime. *5-9pm Wed-Sat* $$$

Brasswood Bar + Kitchen: Fresh mozzarella, handmade pastas and pizzas paired with the winery's cab sauvignons and malbecs. *11.30am-9pm* $$$

Charter Oak: Enjoy a romantic dinner in an 1878 sherry distillery. Each dish showcases signature seasonal ingredients, often from this farm. *11.30am-8.30pm* $$$

Goose & Gander: Step inside this arts-and-crafts cottage to discover a swanky clubhouse bistro. Slip downstairs to the basement speakeasy. *4.30-10pm* $$$

You can also hit **Sunshine Foods**, the town's best grocery store, which has a delicious deli. Grab a pint of top gelato at **Roman Holiday** *(romanholidaygelato.com)*.

If you're in town on a Friday morning, fill your bag at St Helena's **Farmers Market** *(sthelenafarmersmkt.org)* at Crane Park, half a mile south of downtown. Since 1986, farmers and friends have converged around pristine local produce, ready-to-eat homemade treats, flowers, crafts and live music. Look for demos with star chefs in the tent and kids' programs under the redwood trees.

Cooking & Wine-Tasting Classes

Celebrate food and wine at the CIA

Final exams never tasted as good as the ones served at the renowned **Culinary Institute of America at Greystone** *(CIA; ciachef.edu/california)* inside an 1889 stone château. Taste A-students' work at the **Gatehouse Restaurant** and bakery–cafe, and educate your palate at weekend wine-tasting classes and cooking demonstrations. Get in on the action with hands-on one-day classes and load up on gourmet-school supplies in the gadget- and cookbook-filled shop. For more classes and demos, visit the **CIA at Copia in downtown Napa** (p172).

Float over Napa Valley

Ballooning and flying in Wine Country

If you think Wine Country scenery is breathtaking, wait until you see it from 3000ft up in the air. The biplane and balloon rides here have limited capacity, so book ahead and prepare yourself for a once-in-a-lifetime, adrenaline-rush experience.

Napa Valley's signature hot-air-balloon flights leave early, at around 6am or 7am, when the air is coolest and mists are rising from the vineyards. Many offer a champagne toast or brunch on landing. Call **Balloons Above the Valley** *(balloonrides.com)*, **Napa Valley Balloons** *(napavalleyballoons.com)* or **Aloft** *(nvaloft.com)*, Napa's most established ballooning outfit.

Vintage Aircraft Co *(vintageaircraft.com)* flies over Sonoma in old-school biplanes with an expert pilot who'll do loop the loops on request.

DOÑA MARIA'S LOVE STORY

When Maria Ygnacia Soberanes fell for English Protestant Dr Edward Turner Bale, it caused an uproar. Dr Bale became a Mexican citizen and converted to Catholicism, winning over the Vallejo family – and co-ownership of Maria's 28 sq miles of land.

The couple had six children together by 1849, when the news arrived: gold had been discovered in California. Dr Bale headed for the hills during the gold rush, but this time he was out of luck. He died within months, leaving Doña Maria with kids, mining debts and a legal fight to own her own land as a woman – back then this wasn't allowed under US law.

EATING & DRINKING IN ST HELENA: OUR PICKS

Model Bakery: Get renowned fluffy cornmeal-dusted English muffins, breads and baked goods, but be prepared for long lines on weekends. *6am-4pm* $

Gott's Roadside: Hit this retro burger joint, and sprawl on the lawn and feast on grass-fed beef burgers oozing with Point Reyes blue cheese. *11am-9pm* $

Cook St Helena: Small space, small menu and big flavors are signatures of this local-favorite bistro for earthy Cal-Italian cooking. *11.30am-8.30pm Mon-Fri* $$

Erosion Tap House: Beer on tap and wine, but save room for the ice-cream flight. *3-8pm Mon & Wed, from noon Thu-Sun* $

Beyond St Helena

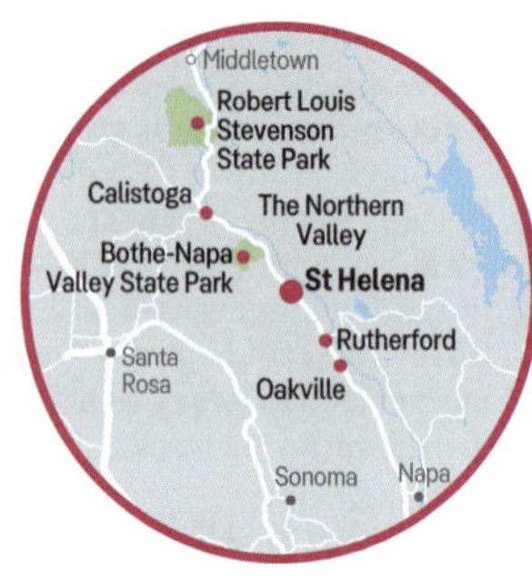

Vaunted vineyards and spritzing hot springs carpet the northern end of the Napa Valley, radiating out from St Helena.

Places

Today when wine aficionados look at this green valley around Oakville and Rutherford, they see red – thanks in no small part to Robert Mondavi, the visionary vintner who knew back in the 1960s that Napa was capable of more than jug wine. His marketing savvy launched Napa's premium reds to cult status. Meanwhile up the road, trailblazing winemaker Mike Grgich made history in 1976 with the first Napa chardonnay to win over French judges in international wine competitions. Further north, Calistoga bubbles with mineral hot springs, and the hills around this part of Napa Valley are studded with excellent wineries – more than you can explore on one trip.

GETTING AROUND

Downtown Calistoga is flat, easy and charming to walk/bike around. Napa Vine bus 10 gets you from Calistoga to St Helena and downtown Napa. Vine operates a Calistoga Shuttle, providing door-to-door service within city limits. To schedule a pickup, call 707-963-4229 or access its app or website during operating hours.

Find biking information and rentals at **Calistoga Bikeshop** (p178) *(calistogabikeshop.com).*

The Northern Valley

TIME FROM ST HELENA: **20 MINS**

Wonderful wineries & lone lakes

Pick your geographical zone around St Helena and wineries abound. Here's our quick-and-dirty guide to the regions.

Cruise 10 minutes from St Helena to the eastern hills for a spectacular drive along Sage Canyon Rd by **Lake Hennessey** (where you can stop and fish for a bit) to reach oak-topped Pritchard Hill and the thrilling **Chappellet Winery** *(chappellet.com; tastings from $125).* Magnificent views vie for your attention as you taste in the barrel-filled vaulted redwood winery itself. Pair it with the much humbler **Nichelini Family Winery** *(nicheliniwinery.com; tastings $30)*, perched on a dramatic ravine. It was founded in 1890 and has been in the same family ever since. Some summers it runs a flashback Friday with $15 tastings, and it accepts walk-ins any day. You can continue along to **Lake Berryessa** for more water sports and picnic spots.

On the other side of Lake Hennessy, and also family-owned, **Amizetta Vineyards** *(amizetta.com; tastings $100)* has sweeping views back toward the lake and books up – plan ahead to survey the panorama during a personalized wine-tasting experience.

On the valley floor, pop into 100%-organically-farmed **Ghost Block Estates** *(ghostblockwine.com; tastings from $55)* or nearby **Frog's Leap** *(frogsleap.com; tastings from $45)*, where you can follow vineyard cats through enchanted gardens, and drink in the views from the loft of an 1884 barn. Across the

JOHN S LANDER/LIGHTROCKET VIA GETTY IMAGES

Indian Springs (p186)

way, **Round Pond** *(roundpond.com; tastings from $40)* also offers fantastic food upgrades on a vineyard-view stone patio and its olive-oil tastings, too.

Go west, high into the Spring Mountain District (AVA; American Viticultural Area) and smack on the county boundary, to reach family-owned **Pride Mountain Vineyards** *(pridewines.com; tastings from $50)*. Winemaker Matt Ward's sustainable-farming vineyard team shares credit for its cult-status cabernet and merlot. Along a valley just north, in the misty pine trees near Bothe-Napa Valley State Park (p186) **Stony Hill** *(stonyhillvineyard.com; tastings from $85)*, is one of the oldest wineries in the region, and one of the first producers of chardonnay in the US.

North of Calistoga, seek out **Bennett Lane Winery** *(bennettlane.com; tastings from $35)* for its sustainable farming practices and fab cabernets.

Oakville & Rutherford

TIME FROM ST HELENA: **10 MINS**

Laid-back life in the valley

Sprawling winery complexes along Hwy 29 dominate the landscape with gilded signs and gated entrances – including **Robert Mondavi** *(robertmondaviwinery.com; tastings from $60)* and **Grgich Hills Estate** *(grgich.com; tastings from $60)*, a stop on the **Napa Valley Wine Train** (p171). Grgich Hills won the Great Wine Capitals Sustainable Wine Tourism Practices award in 2024.

You'll recognize the hamlets of **Oakville** and **Rutherford** when you hit the historic 1881 **Oakville Grocery** *(oakvillegrocery.com)*, 10 minutes' drive south of St Helena. Turn off Hwy 29 onto cross-valley roads, and you'll find the excellent **La Luna Taqueria & Market** *(lalunamarket.com)*, where the wine-fridge sign says 'Tacos y vinos' – accept the invitation.

BEST WINERIES TO WALK OR BIKE TO FROM ST HELENA

Cliff Family Winery *(cliffamily.com)*: Sustainably produced wines, food truck and community spirit.

Spring Mountain Vineyard *(springmountainvineyard.com)*: A good winery to pair with **Fantesca Estate & Winery**, just up the road.

Sinegal Estate *(sinegalestate.com)*: Dating to 1879, with lush gardens and a pond, featuring cabernet sauvignon and franc, pinot noir and sauvignon blanc.

Tres Sabores *(tressabores.com)*: Sauvignon blanc named a *New York Times* top 10 pick and a collectors' favorite rare rosé.

Joseph Phelps *(josephphelps.com)*: Here's the secret to Phelps' iconic red-blend Insignia, made with each season's best grapes since 1974: there are no rules.

ROBERT LOUIS STEVENSON IN THE NAPA VALLEY

Honeymoons in Napa Valley are often epic – but the 1880 honeymoon of Robert Louis Stevenson and Fanny Osbourne was epically awful. Robert was sick and they were broke, so they wound up squatting in an abandoned bunkhouse at extinct volcanic cone Mt St Helena's Silverado Mine, now part of Robert Louis Stevenson State Park.

There are details at St Helena's **Robert Louis Stevenson Museum** *(stevensonmuseum.org; donations welcome)* of how this honeymoon trip inspired Stevenson's travel memoir *The Silverado Squatters*, making his reputation for harrowing adventure stories that eventually included *Treasure Island* and *Strange Case of Dr Jekyll and Mr Hyde*.

Offbeat organic wineries abut low-key high-end hotels hidden in the heart of Napa Valley, such as **Rancho Caymus** *(ranchocaymusinn.com)*, built by pioneering vintner Mary Tilden Morton; and **Auberge du Soleil** *(aubergedusoleil.com)* with its vaunted restaurant, a prime spot for champagne-soaked proposals.

Bothe-Napa Valley State Park

TIME FROM ST HELENA: **5 MINS**

Hike, swim & camp

If you're looking for a fine place for a picnic, look no further – with redwoods for shade in summer, wild orchids in spring, bright leaves in fall and soft moss carpets in winter, **Bothe-Napa Valley State Park** *(napaoutdoors.org/parks; per car $10)* is fantastic year-round.

About 8000 years ago, Native Koliholmanok people inhabited this area, and past the park entrance you'll find a Native American plant garden, as well as trailheads for the Redwood Trail (1.5 miles one-way) and Ritchey Trail (4 miles one-way), passing the ruined 1880s homestead of firefighting philanthropist Lillie Hancock Coit, benefactor of Coit Tower (p70) in San Francisco.

Cool off in summer at the outdoor **swimming pool** near the Ritchey Creek campground (p224) and day-use picnic area. You can also stay over in cool yurts and cabins.

Calistoga

TIME FROM ST HELENA: **15–25 MINS**

Hot springs & champagne

With soothing natural hot springs, bubbling volcanic mud pools and a dramatically spurting geyser, Nilektsonoma (Calistoga), 15 minutes' drive north of St Helena, was renowned across Talahalusi (Napa Valley) by the Indigenous Wappo (Brave) people for some 8000 years. Then in 1859 a braggart named Samuel Brannan came along and claimed to have discovered the place. The town's odd name comes from Brannan, believing it would develop like the New York spa town, Saratoga. Apparently Sam liked his drink, and at the founding ceremony tripped on his tongue, proclaiming it the 'Cali-stoga' of 'Sara-fornia.' The name stuck.

By 1873 Brannan had lost a fortune promoting **Calistoga** as California's signature spa resort. But look around Calistoga today and you might think he'd pulled it off.

At **Indian Springs** *(indianspringscalistoga.com)* guests can glide from mud baths to an Olympic-sized outdoor spring-fed pool then move on to **Sam's Social Club** *(samssocialclub.com)* for bubbly bathrobed happy hours. Across the street, the 1952 spa-motel **Dr Wilkinson's** *(drwilkinson.com)* offers de-stress sessions in mineral-water pools, extra-squishy mud baths and 'beer brew' (hops-infused mineral baths).

Most spa treatments are adults-only, but **Old Faithful Geyser** *(oldfaithfulgeyser.com; adult/child $15/9)* keeps tykes entertained, as do mineral hot-springs pools at 1947 **Calistoga Motor Lodge & Spa** *(calistogamotorlodge.com)* and best-value **Roman Spa Hot Springs** *(romanspahotsprings.com)*.

For more adult bubbly, explore the historic sparkling-wine caves at Green Certified **Schramsberg** *(schramsberg.com; tastings from $65)* and glimpse the traditional French champagne riddling and racking methods before sampling the *tête de cuvées* (best of the vintage). Don't-miss wineries include **Vincent Arroyo** *(vincentarroyo.com; tastings $30)* and **Olabisi** *(olabisiwines.com; tastings $40)* for exclusive small-batch wines.

Wildlife safaris & petrified trees

Kids ready for some extra thrills? Really splash out and spice it up over the hill at **Safari West** *(safariwest.com; from adult/child $110/45)*. They'll be ecstatic on a jeep trip among giraffes, zebras and flamingos, plus overnight glamping. For the general safaris you must be four years old, but some of the private ones don't have age limitations.

En route, swing into the **Petrified Forest** *(petrifiedforest.org; adult/child $14/6)*, where three million years ago a volcanic eruption at Mt St Helena blew down the stand of redwoods, now petrified.

THE DIRTY LOWDOWN

Calistoga mud isn't just wet dirt: it's a blend of volcanic ash, peat and hot mineral spring water. If you're wondering why some baths cost more, it might be the silkier mud with higher volcanic ash content... or maybe it's the marketing.

Mud-bath packages take one to 1½ hours, combining semi-submergence in warm mud, hot mineral-water soaking and a steam bath or blanket-wrap. Variations include thin, painted-on clay-mud wraps (called 'fango' baths, good for those uncomfortable sitting in mud), herbal wraps and seaweed baths. Check for midweek deals from lodging sites and the **Calistoga Visitors Center** *(visitcalistoga.com)*. Reservations are essential, so book ahead, especially for summer weekends.

Robert Louis Stevenson State Park

TIME FROM ST HELENA: **1 HR**

Hike & bike tough ascents

The extinct volcanic cone of **Mt St Helena** marks a dramatic end to Napa Valley, and you can explore it at **Robert Louis Stevenson State Park** *(napaoutdoors.org; free)*. It's a strenuous 5-mile climb to the peak's 4343ft summit, but what a view – 200 miles on a clear day.

For a shorter hike with views over valley vineyards, take **Table Rock Trail** (2.2 miles one-way) from the parking-area trailhead.

Super-fit hikers can also tackle the nearby **Oat Hill Mine Trail**. It's one of Northern California's most technically challenging trails – 8.3 miles (one-way) with an elevation change of 1500ft along an 1893 stagecoach route – and draws hardcore mountain bikers and hikers. For shorter but still challenging day hikes, turn back midway at Holm homestead's stone ruins. This trailhead's at the intersection of Hwy 29 and Silverado Trail.

Check conditions and seasonal closures before setting out, as the park gets snow in winter. There's no water (so bring your own), restrooms, trash collection (pack yours out) or camping.

EATING & DRINKING IN CALISTOGA: OUR PICKS

Bella Bakery: Your friendly neighborhood top-notch bakery and coffee bar, with perfect quiche and chocolate-layer cake. *6am-2pm Mon-Sat, from 7am Sun* $

Lovina: Garden lunches here are a dream – and inspiration for chef Leticia Martinez, who composes produce into California sensations. *5-9pm nightly, 10am-2pm Sat & Sun* $$

Buster's Southern BBQ: Napa Valley's favorite back-to-basics barbecue stop, with sunny outdoor tables. *10am-8pm, to 7pm Sun* $

Solbar: Chill out at luxe Solage resort with creative cocktails in the lounge or on the patio. *7am-9pm Sun-Thu, to 9.30pm Fri & Sat* $$$

Sonoma

MISSION HISTORY | ART AND SHOPS | DELICIOUS WINES

TOP TIP
There are lots of historic inns and romantic cottages suitable for a midrange budget, but those counting pennies will have better luck in Santa Rosa or Petaluma. Off-season rates plummet. Reserve ahead and ask about parking, as some inns don't have lots. **Sonoma Valley Visitors Bureau** *(sonomavalley.com)* offers loads of local information.

Enchanting downtown Sonoma seems a world apart from mundane everyday life. Stroll streets lined with long-standing trees and Victorian houses, and you'll find heritage inns, indie boutiques and some 30 tasting rooms. A bicycle ride away are more parks, historic sites, sensational family-owned restaurants and (how did you guess?) wineries.

Native Americans originally converged here at the village of Huichi to trade goods and songs. Many died in outbreaks of measles and smallpox that arrived with the friars of Mission Solano. When Mexico secularized California's missions and the lands were officially returned to Native Americans, those land deeds were not honored. Instead, Sonoma's mission vineyards were claimed by settlers.

On one particularly drunken night in 1846, a band of settlers took over the Sonoma barracks and proclaimed a breakaway Bear Flag Republic. Not a shot was fired, and after a confusing month US forces claimed Sonoma as US territory.

Plaza Ringed by Monuments

Amble through California history

The city of Sonoma's pride and joy is the **plaza** – the largest town square in all of California, it's surrounded by local

GETTING AROUND

Sonoma Hwy (Hwy 12) is lined with wineries and runs up the valley from Sonoma town, past Glen Ellen, through Kenwood to Santa Rosa, then on to western Sonoma County. From Napa you can get a rideshare to downtown Sonoma, where many sights, wine-tasting rooms and restaurants are within walking or cycling distance (there is no bus service between the two towns). Public transportation is not convenient, so it's best to have your own wheels to explore the valley and its wineries. In a pinch, Sonoma County *(sctransit.com)* bus 32 is the local free shuttle, and infrequent buses 30 and 34 (also serving Petaluma) go up the valley to Santa Rosa. Bus 40 goes southwest to Petaluma on weekdays only.

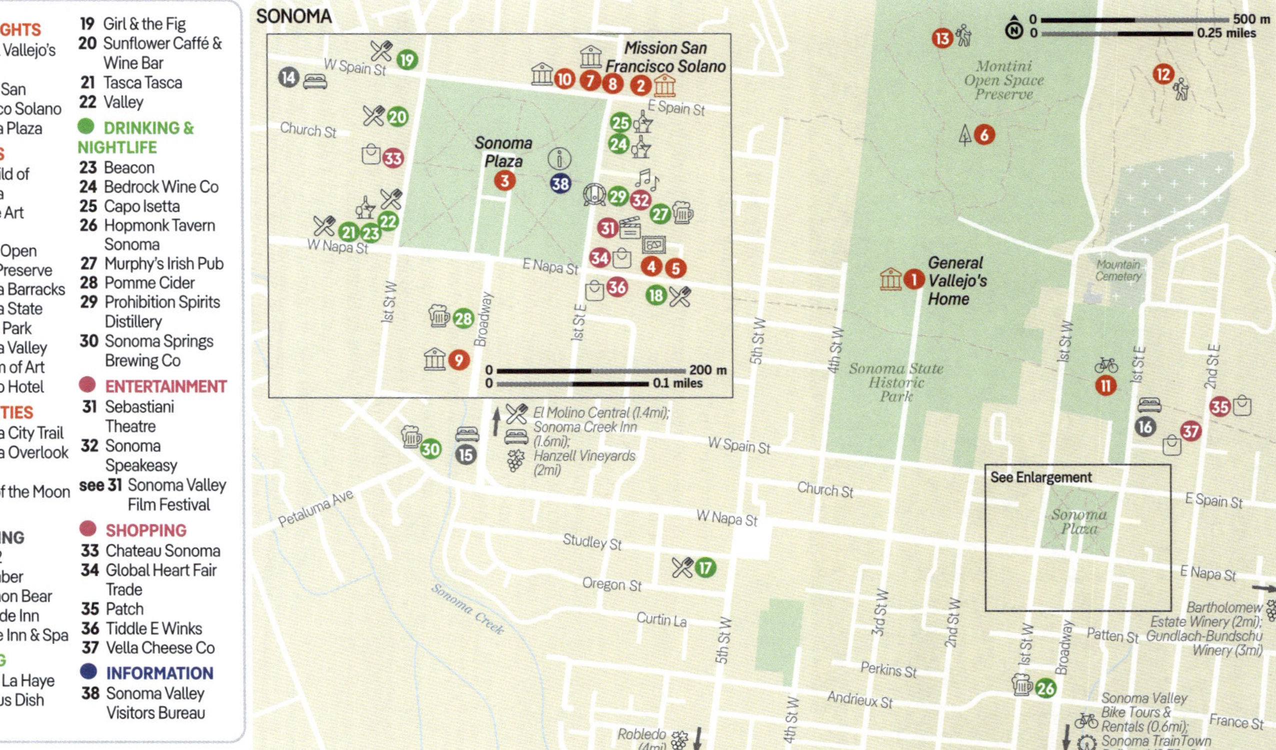

HIGHLIGHTS
1 General Vallejo's Home
2 Mission San Francisco Solano
3 Sonoma Plaza

SIGHTS
4 Arts Guild of Sonoma
5 La Haye Art Center
6 Montini Open Space Preserve
7 Sonoma Barracks
8 Sonoma State Historic Park
9 Sonoma Valley Museum of Art
10 Toscano Hotel

ACTIVITIES
11 Sonoma City Trail
12 Sonoma Overlook Trail
13 Valley of the Moon Trail

SLEEPING
14 An Inn 2 Remember
15 Cinnamon Bear Creekside Inn
16 Cottage Inn & Spa

EATING
see 5 Cafe La Haye
17 Delicious Dish
18 Enclos
19 Girl & the Fig
20 Sunflower Caffé & Wine Bar
21 Tasca Tasca
22 Valley

DRINKING & NIGHTLIFE
23 Beacon
24 Bedrock Wine Co
25 Capo Isetta
26 Hopmonk Tavern Sonoma
27 Murphy's Irish Pub
28 Pomme Cider
29 Prohibition Spirits Distillery
30 Sonoma Springs Brewing Co

ENTERTAINMENT
31 Sebastiani Theatre
32 Sonoma Speakeasy
see 31 Sonoma Valley Film Festival

SHOPPING
33 Chateau Sonoma
34 Global Heart Fair Trade
35 Patch
36 Tiddle E Winks
37 Vella Cheese Co

INFORMATION
38 Sonoma Valley Visitors Bureau

KIT LEONG/SHUTTERSTOCK

Sonoma City Hall

history, a venerable old theater, **city hall**, food and – oh, yes – drinking options. The **Tuesday night markets** are a tradition, May to November, with live music, food, produce and artisan's wares. Arrive early and bring a picnic for the **free jazz concerts** *(sonomavalleyjazzsociety.org)* from 6pm to 8.30pm every second Tuesday of the month from June to September.

Anchored by adobe **Mission San Francisco Solano** *(sonomaparks.org)*, the plaza's sights allow you to time-travel across 200 years of California history. The 21st and final California mission was built in 1823 by Native American conscripts and lasted just 11 years. Mexico's Comandante of Northern California, General Vallejo, commissioned the other big adobe, **Sonoma Barracks**, to house his troops in 1834. Displays capture 19th-century life and describe how Sonoma's Bear Flag Republic started. The lobby of the 1886 **Toscano Hotel** is beautifully preserved – have a peek inside.

The stately 1852 **home of General Vallejo** is a half-mile northwest. When Mexico lost California to the US, Vallejo lost his official position, but the master strategist quickly became a US citizen, a California senator and spring-water supplier to the city of Sonoma.

One **Sonoma State Historic Park** joint ticket *(adult/child $3/2)* gives same-day admission to them all, plus the **Petaluma Adobe** (p199) at General Vallejo's former ranch, 15 miles away.

EATING IN SONOMA TOWN: THE HIGH LIFE

Enclos: This 30-seat temple of California cuisine sources produce from organic Stone Edge Farm & Winery. Global flavors. *5-9pm Wed-Sat* $$$

Cafe La Haye: Warm feelings are mutual between farmers, chefs and visitors at cozy La Haye. Produce is sourced within 60 miles. *5.30-9pm Tue-Sat* $$$

Girl & the Fig: Celebrated bistro with hearty feasts of rustic French fare and large space for eating alfresco. *11.30am-9pm Mon-Thu, from 10am Sat & Sun* $$$

Tasca Tasca: Sea, garden, land: choose your next culinary adventure and this inspired tapas bar will take you there. *11.30am-9pm* $$

Pair Local Art & Libations

Creativity for all the senses

Sonoma remains staunchly independent-minded and proud of its creativity, which is on display at **Sonoma Valley Museum of Art** *(svma.org; adult/child/family $10/free/15)* and the **Arts Guild of Sonoma** *(artsguildofsonoma.org; admission free)*. Make an appointment to visit collective **La Haye Art Center** *(lahayeartcenter.com; admission free)* in a converted foundry where you can tour its gallery and meet the artists – sculptor, potter and painters – in their studios.

In June join **Art at the Source** *(artatthesource.org; free)* and in October **Sonoma County Art Trails** *(sonomacountyarttrails.org; free)*, each are two-week events that give you a chance to travel from studio to studio, learning about local artists. The maps of the ateliers are available year-round and are a good resource for art lovers.

Book ahead at **Bedrock Wine Co** *(bedrockwineco.com; tastings from $45)* to pair your art with wines in a historic saltbox cottage hung with tintype portraits and antique Sonoma maps. Morgan Twain-Peterson and Chris Cottrell are reviving California's old vine-field blends with grapes sourced from tiny NorCal ('Northern California') blocks, including classic zinfandels and obscure varietals like Alicante Bouschet.

Or, compare quaffs at **Pomme Cider** *(pommecidershop.com; flight of ciders $21)*, with its convivial cascades of cider on tap.

Shopping in Sonoma Town

Unusual souvenirs and tasty treats

Sonoma is lavish in its boutiques and eclectic shops. Step back in time at **Tiddle E Winks** *(tiddleewinks.com)*, a retro 1950s variety store packed with nostalgic fun for all ages: windup toys, classic board games and penny candy.

French whimsy meets California quirk at **Chateau Sonoma** *(chateausonoma.com)*, Sarah Anderson's curiosity cabinet of a shop. Visit **Global Heart Fair Trade** *(globalheartfairtrade.com)* for unique handmade gifts, festive clothing and jewelry, recyclable decorations and artisan chocolates in support of a worthwhile cause: all sales ensure living wages for makers.

Right in downtown Sonoma, pick up heirloom tomatoes and more, from May to November, at the **Patch**, California's oldest community-run urban farm, beloved by neighbors and protected from developers for at least 150 years. Across the street, **Vella Cheese Co** *(vellacheese.com)* has been making

TOUGH HISTORY

Miwok, Pomo, Wintun and Wappo people thrived in this fertile region for about 10,000 years before they began trading with Russian trappers and Spanish ranchers some 300 years ago, and were subsequently wiped out by disease and genocide.

Over the centuries, Sonoma County's rich agricultural lands (from dairies to apple orchards), terraced vineyards and pristine forests have been hit with earthquakes, wildfires, floods and droughts.

Nonetheless, modern and pioneering conservation initiatives have successfully protected west Sonoma County's ancient redwoods, which were once heavily logged to build San Francisco, and the California Coastal Commission preserves its raw, rocky coastline.

EATING IN SONOMA TOWN: RELAXED & DELICIOUS

Valley: This welcoming wine bar dishes up creative, seasonal offerings...California comfort food at its best. *9am-3pm & 5-9pm Thu-Mon* $$

El Molino Central: Sustainably homegrown ingredients and Sonoma's Mexican culinary traditions at this 1930s roadside mainstay. *11am-8pm Mon-Thu, from 9am Fri-Sun* $

Delicious Dish: Succulent burgers, fresh-catch fish sandwiches and salads with fries at a field-side diner with a patio. *10.30am-6.30pm Mon-Thu, to 2.30pm Fri* $

Sunflower Caffé & Wine Bar: The big back garden at this local hangout is a great spot for breakfast, a no-fuss lunch or afternoon wine. *8am-3pm* $$

BEST HIKES & BIKES NEAR SONOMA

Montini Open Space Preserve: Trails wind above Sonoma, with their rolling grassland and oak woodlands. Trailheads at 1st St W and 4th St W in Sonoma lead to two overlooks, and the trail from 4th St is ADA-accessible. *overlookmontini.org*

Valley of the Moon Trail: This Montini trail connects to beautiful, volunteer-maintained **Sonoma Overlook Trail**: It's 3 miles of spectacular hiking through oaks, bay trees and native wildflowers.

Sonoma City Trail: Downtown Sonoma is small, flat and perfect for biking with this 1.5-mile trail. *sonomacity.org*

Sonoma Valley Bike Tours & Rentals: Rents bikes, e-bikes and tandem bikes. Rentals include helmets and – crucially – a winery map. Also guided rides. *sonomavalleybike tours.com*

spaghetti Western for almost 100 years – its two-year-aged dry jack is meant for shaving atop rustic dishes.

Kids Cut Loose on Trains & Rides

Live it up at the Sonoma TrainTown Railroad

All aboard! At **Sonoma TrainTown Railroad** *(traintown.com)* kids ride the rails *($9.75)* in miniature boxcars, while adults squeeze in and try not to bang into anything on the 1.25-mile, 20-minute loop through narrow tunnels and shrunken towns. Toddlers pose in engineer caps on the carousel, and older kids squeal on vintage 1968 rides, including the Mine Train coaster and Ferris wheel *($4.25 per ride).*

Vineyards near Sonoma Town

Family-friendly wineries

Several Sonoma wineries were damaged by fires in 2017 and 2019. They've regrouped and replanted with more climate-resilient grape varietals and new fire-preventing measures. The inspired vintages they're producing are proudly featured on Sonoma menus.

California's oldest family-run winery, **Gundlach-Bundschu** *(gunbun.com; tastings from $25, incl tour from $80)*, looks like a castle, and everyone gets a royal welcome at the bar. Six generations of Bundschus have kept the delightful dry gewürztraminer flowing since 1858. Bike down a country lane past farmstead donkeys for a tour of the 1800-barrel cave and a picnic by the pond. Concerts regularly rock Gun-Bun's redwood barn and outdoor amphitheater.

Sonoma's most idyllic winery, **Hanzell Vineyards** *(hanzell.com; tasting & tour $90)*, has views to die for over Sonoma all

KENT SORENSEN/SHUTTERSTOCK

Gundlach-Bundschu winery

the way to San Francisco Bay. Take your seat in the historic stone barn for exceptional organically produced chardonnays and pinot noirs.

Sprawling **Bartholomew Estate Winery** *(bartholomewestate.com; tastings from $45)* was established in 1857 at the birth of California's wine industry under Hungarian count Ágoston Haraszthy, and now its certified-organic vineyards produce sauvignon blanc, cabernet sauvignon and zinfandel. Picnics are allowed in the estate's sun-dappled private park (free and open to visitors); there's a 3-mile trail through vineyards, oaks, madrones and redwoods. Pass the pond to reach an overlook with sweeping vistas. You can also go riding on horseback with **Sonoma Valley Trail Rides** *(sonomavalleytrailrides.com; ride & tasting $160)*.

Robledo *(robledofamilywinery.com; tastings from $40)* winery was built from the ground up by Reynoldo Robledo, who started in the industry as a farm worker in 1968 and became Sonoma's go-to vineyard expert. His kids run the winery now, and welcome you to estate tastings at the hand-carved bar.

For wineries, restaurants and lodging in Carneros further south, see p176.

BEST LIVE MUSIC & ENTERTAINMENT

Hopmonk Tavern Sonoma: An 1888 farmhouse comes roaring back to life as a booming tavern and year-round beer garden, serving a dozen Hopmonk microbrews plus guest beers. Stick around for live music Friday through Sunday, and brace for the unexpected at Wednesday open mics. *hopmonk.com*

Sonoma Speakeasy: Live music, karaoke, mixologists and good vibes. *sonomaspeakeasy.com*

Murphy's Irish Pub: Both a pub and a music venue. *sonomapub.com*

Sebastiani Theatre: Sonoma plaza's community-run, 1934 Mission Revival cinema hosts global indie art-house films, director-led screenings, and in March the **Sonoma Valley Film Festival** *(sonomafilmfest.org)*. *sebastianitheatre.com*

DRINKING IN SONOMA: FROM COCKTAILS TO WINE BARS

Prohibition Spirits Distillery: Versions of Italian aperitifs, elderflower gins, brandy distilled from prickly pear. *11am-6pm Sun-Thu, to 7pm Fri, 10am-7pm Sat*

Capo Isetta: Smack on the plaza, this welcoming wine bar spreads the good life with mellow tunes, excellent wines and friendly staff. *noon-9pm*

Beacon: Loud, busy speakeasy vibes rise on crowded weekends. Classic cocktails and inventive mixology are the orders of the day. *5-11pm*

Sonoma Springs Brewing Co: One of two brewpubs to the west of the plaza. Makes a range of IPAs and German-style beers. *3-9pm Mon-Fri, from 1pm Sat & Sun*

Beyond Sonoma

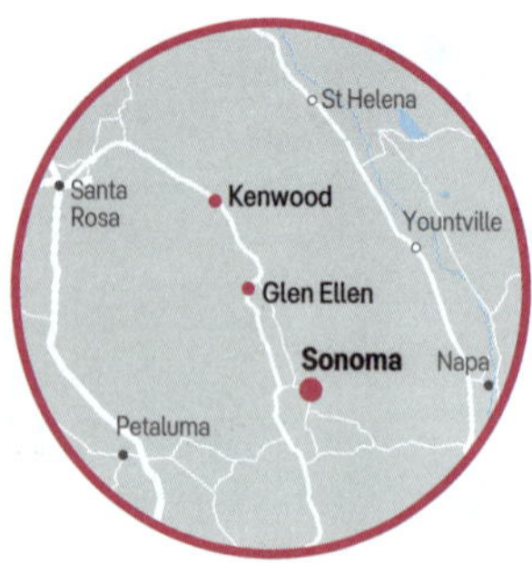

Century-old vines and charming settlements that are both fun-loving and down-to-earth fill the Sonoma Valley.

Places

GETTING AROUND

Sonoma Valley has around 40 wineries. To go vineyard hopping, you'll realistically want a car or bicycle. Glen Ellen is a nice bike ride from Sonoma – 7 miles on quiet country roads. Kenwood is another 5 miles north. Or book Designated Drivers Napa Sonoma *(ddnapasonoma.com)*. Infrequent Sonoma County Transit *(sctransit.com)* bus 34 goes north from Sonoma to Santa Rosa and 30 goes to Santa Rosa (also looping in Petaluma)

The rhythm of Sonoma Valley is an easy groove to fall into, following tracks worn over thousands of years. Here you're tracing the steps of Miwok, Pomo and Wintun people who converged in this lush valley to feast, relax and swap stories. They called this place the Valley of the Moon, and the mystical name has stuck locally. Heading up the valley from Sonoma, the tiny, quaint 19th-century resort town of Glen Ellen is full of surprises: acclaimed restaurants, recycled art masterpieces, rare Japanese maples, wilderness horseback rides, stiff martinis and luxury cottage hideaways. Further north, the batch of vineyards known as Kenwood lures you with wine-pairing feasts and hikes up Sugarloaf to appreciate where you've been.

Glen Ellen

TIME FROM SONOMA: **15–25 MINS**

Creative haunts

A 20-minute drive north of the town of Sonoma, tiny **Glen Ellen** (population 1200) is a jumble of little cottages behind white picket fences along a poplar-lined creek. Back in 1905 it was a swinging resort town with natural hot springs that lured California's rich and renowned, including the world's most famous author at the time, Jack London.

The town has remained a magnet for trailblazing writers and artists, including gonzo journalist Hunter S Thompson and food writer MFK Fisher – you can tour her **Last House** on the wildflower-laden **Bouverie Preserve** *(egret.org; suggested $20 donation)*. You must reserve.

Get the call of the wild at Jack London's ranch

Even a novelist can farm land as fertile as Sonoma's, as you'll see 25 minutes' drive north of Sonoma town at **Jack London State Historic Park** *(jacklondonpark.com; per car $10)*, where the adventure author of *The Call of the Wild* and his wife, editor and fellow writer Charmian Kittredge London built Beauty Ranch as their writing retreat and pioneering organic farm. At the **museum,** insightful displays cover Jack's death-defying travels and his controversial ideas, including socialism and Darwinism. Don't miss Jack's rejection letters in the downstairs bookstore. From the museum, it's a hilly half-mile walk to the ruins of their Wolf House, passing **Jack's grave site** along the way.

Jack London State Historic Park

Wineries and farms

You're in the heart of Sonoma, one of the world's most prestigious pinot-noir regions, and **Talisman Wines** *(talismanwine.com; tastings from $45)* has award-winning vintages to prove it. Founder/winemaker team Scott and Marta Rich collaborate with legendary pinot growers from Carneros to the Sonoma coast. Pixar animator John Lasseter's **Lasseter Family Winery** *(lasseterfamilywinery.com; tastings from $60)* specializes in organic wines in the Rhône and Bordeaux traditions.

At the southern end of Glen Ellen, **Oak Hill Farm** covers 25 acres with organic flowers and produce, framed by lovely oaks and manzanita trees. Buy from the farm's **Red Barn Store** on Saturdays, April to December.

Soak in hot springs

Jump into Sonoma tradition at **Morton's Warm Springs** *(mortonswarmsprings.com; admission $23)*, 3.5 miles north of Glen Ellen. Geothermal springs have attracted families here for 10,000 years, and today, 108°F (42°C) mineral springwater fills two pools at this local-favorite, vintage-1950s day resort. Come for the afternoon – there's an organic cafe, BBQ, lawns and volleyball. To keep water pristine, wait 15 minutes after applying sunscreen, and shower before entering the pools. Reserve – it usually books out on weekends.

BEST WILDERNESS PARKS & GARDENS IN SONOMA VALLEY

Sugarloaf Ridge State Park: Explore around 25 miles of fantastic hiking and biking trails. There's **camping** (p224). *sugarloafpark.org*

Sonoma Valley Regional Park: Oak woodlands with trails, includes ADA-accessible 1.2-mile Valley of the Moon trail. Picnic areas and dog park. *parks.sonomacounty.ca.gov*

Sonoma Botanical Garden: World-renowned 25-acre botanical garden specializing in flora of Asia. *sonomabg.org*

Hood Mountain Regional Park: Wilderness trails for hiking, biking, horseback riding crisscross 3600 acres, including **Mt Hood**. Hike-in camping 2 miles into the park. *parks.sonomacounty.ca.gov*

EATING IN GLEN ELLEN: OUR PICKS

Les Pascals Patisserie: Flaky, butter-glossed croissants, baguettes, savory quiches, tarts. *6am-4.30pm Mon, Tue, Thu & Fri; from 7am Sat & Sun* $

Mill at Glen Ellen: South of town, this beloved venue crafts casual fare that can be adapted to vegans and vegetarians. *11.30am-7.30pm Wed-Sun* $$

Glen Ellen Star: *Food & Wine* star chef Ari Weiswasser and Erinn Benziger-Weiswasser (from Benziger Winery) keep food excellent and mood relaxed. *5-9pm* $$$

Wine Country Chocolates: When chocolate, wine and ice cream are all you need... be an aficionado of daily ganache selections. *11am-4pm Thu-Sat* $

BEST WINE COUNTRY COOKING CLASSES

Culinary Institute of America at St Helena and Napa: Wine and food classes.

Epicurean Connection, Sonoma: Cheese- and butter-making with pros. *theepicurean connection.com*

Sonoma Food Tour, Sonoma: Culinary and wine tours. *sonomafoodtour.com*

Parker Hill Provisions, Healdsburg: Lisal Moran teaches baking, pasta and art. *parkerhillprovisions.com*

Central Milling, Petaluma: Bread, baby, bread. Galettes, croissants, baguettes, oh my! *centralmilling.com*

Sonoma Family Meal, Petaluma: This nonprofit's programs combat food insecurity and offering job training for residents. *sonomafamilymeal.org*

STEVE PROEHL/GETTY IMAGES

Kunde winery

If you're looking for a swishier spring, glide 5.5 miles south of Glen Ellen to the area called **Boyes Hot Springs**. There, you'll indulge yourself at **Fairmont Spa at Sonoma Mission Inn** *(fairmont.com; day use from $99)* a classic Spanish Mission-style resort updated with elemental modern twists: flower-shaped pools, stone firepits, heated terra-cotta floors.

Kenwood

TIME FROM SONOMA: **25 MINS**

Northern Sonoma Valley wineries

Rolling grass- and vine-covered hills rise from Sonoma Valley. Its 40-odd wineries get less attention than Napa's, but many are equally good. If you love zinfandel, syrah and pinot noir, you're in for a treat. A few **Kenwood area** landmarks (there is no town per se, rather a collection of vineyards 25 minutes' drive north of Sonoma town) have stood the test of time – including the little 1860s red schoolhouse, now **Muscardini Cellars** *(muscardinicellars.com; tastings from $35)* tasting room. It's also home to **B Wise** tasting room *(bwisevineyards.com; tastings $30, cave tastings $100)*, which welcomes walk-ins; or book ahead to taste in its Moon Mountain cave.

Friendly **Kunde** winery *(kunde.com; tastings from $25)*, on a historic ranch of vast vineyards, offers mountaintop tastings with impressive valley views and guided hikes (reserve). Or just stop by for a tasting (a rarity, in reservation-required Wine Country). Also visit VJB Cellars (p174) for Italian varietals and food.

EATING IN KENWOOD: OUR PICKS

Mayo Family Winery & Reserve Room: Wining and dining: tasting paired with seven small plates. *by appointment 10.30am-6.30pm Thu-Mon* **$$$**

Salt & Stone: French food craving from Sonoma's Bordeaux-style wines? Stop for a bistro meal on a sunny patio. *11am-9pm Thu-Tue, 2.30-9pm Wed* **$$**

Golden Bear Station: High concept, beautifully presented comfort food, from homemade pastas and pizzas to pork chops in a Cali-mod room. *5-9pm Wed-Sun* **$$$**

La Cucina at VJB: For authentic Italian sandwiches and salads, order at the counter of VJB's Italian-varietal winery. Homemade sauce, pesto, mozzarella. *10am-4pm* **$**

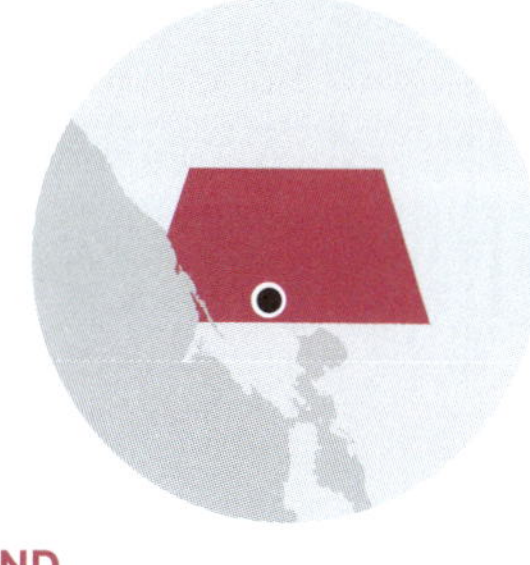

Petaluma

VINTAGE VIBE | FOODIE ENCLAVE | FRESH FARMLAND

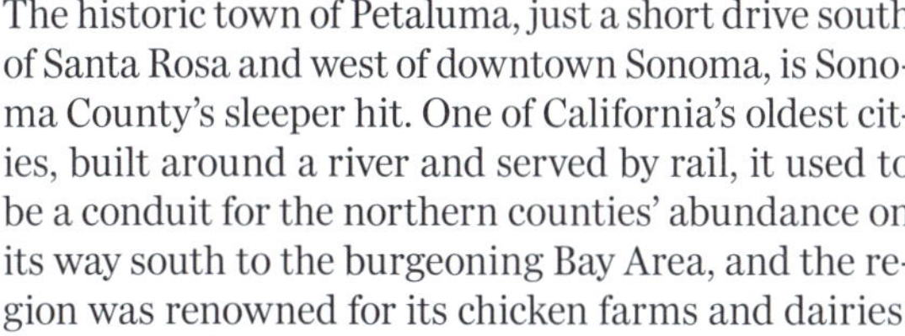

The historic town of Petaluma, just a short drive south of Santa Rosa and west of downtown Sonoma, is Sonoma County's sleeper hit. One of California's oldest cities, built around a river and served by rail, it used to be a conduit for the northern counties' abundance on its way south to the burgeoning Bay Area, and the region was renowned for its chicken farms and dairies.

Now Petaluma grabs attention for its walkable, quaint downtown, packed with dining venues, taprooms and wine bars, and its foggy and wind-whipped wine appellation, dubbed 'the Petaluma Gap.' The region's chardonnays, pinot noirs and syrahs have earned a reputation for their elegance and complexity. It's also home to two of the Bay Area's premier breweries.

Petaluma is a fine place to while away the day, exploring the food-and-drink havens of the city's old brick-building downtown center, then party into the night.

TOP TIP

The word Sonoma describes a town, a valley and a much bigger county, so always check *where*, when someone says 'we're in Sonoma.'

Get to Know a Bay Area Boomtown

Cruising the Petaluma strip

Petaluma was established in 1858 and its charming downtown area (packed with unique iron-front architecture that survived the 1906 earthquake) and lovingly preserved Victorian houses are on the National Register of Historic Places. Learn more at the free **Petaluma Historical Library &**

GETTING AROUND

Reach Petaluma from San Francisco via Golden Gate Transit *(goldengate.org)* bus or from the Larkspur Ferry on SMART rail *(sonomamarintrain.org)*, which continues north to Santa Rosa and its airport. Groome Transportation *(groometransportation.com)* buses serve Oakland Airport and SFO.

Getting around by car is easiest, and parking spots abound outside of the walkable town center. Within town, you can also ride Petaluma Transit *(transit.cityofpetaluma.net)* buses. Infrequent Sonoma County Transit *(sctransit.com)* bus 30 and 49 link to Sonoma. Buses 44 and 48 head north to Santa Rosa.

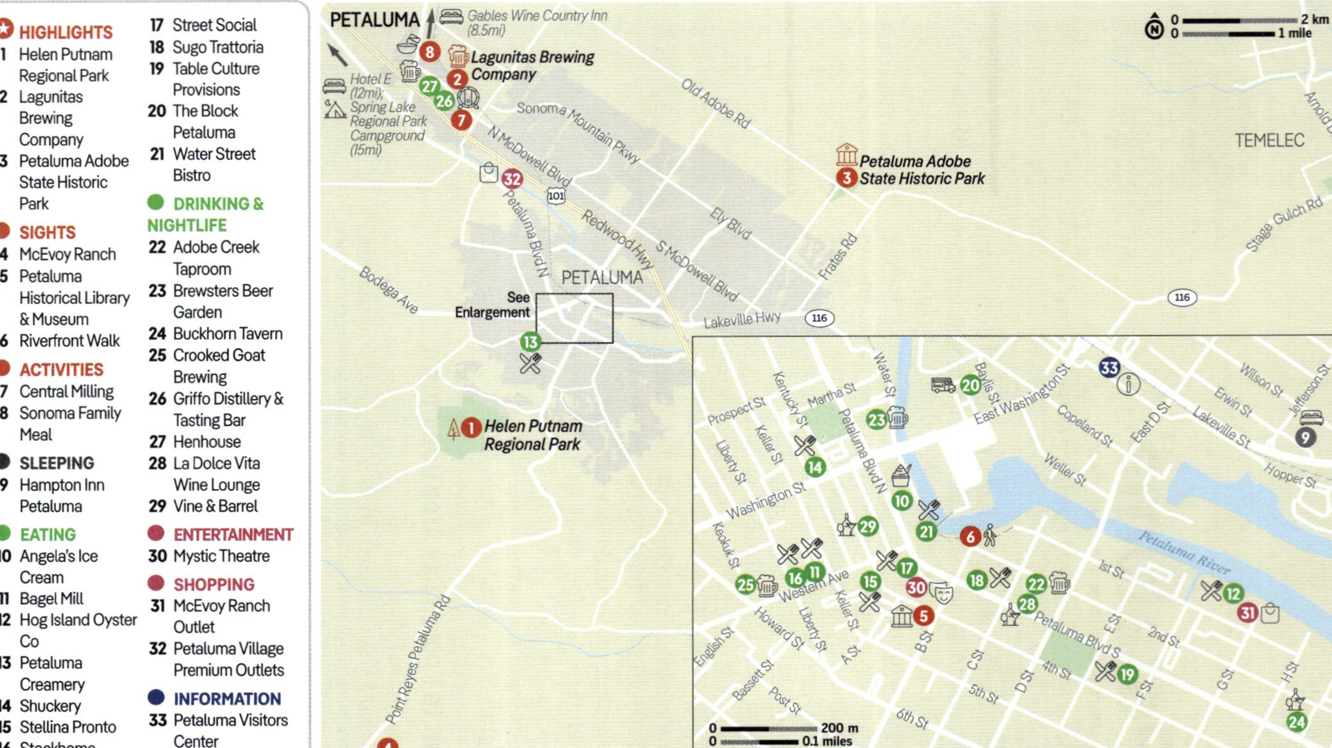

HIGHLIGHTS
1 Helen Putnam Regional Park
2 Lagunitas Brewing Company
3 Petaluma Adobe State Historic Park

SIGHTS
4 McEvoy Ranch
5 Petaluma Historical Library & Museum
6 Riverfront Walk

ACTIVITIES
7 Central Milling
8 Sonoma Family Meal

SLEEPING
9 Hampton Inn Petaluma

EATING
10 Angela's Ice Cream
11 Bagel Mill
12 Hog Island Oyster Co
13 Petaluma Creamery
14 Shuckery
15 Stellina Pronto
16 Stockhome
17 Street Social
18 Sugo Trattoria
19 Table Culture Provisions
20 The Block Petaluma
21 Water Street Bistro

DRINKING & NIGHTLIFE
22 Adobe Creek Taproom
23 Brewsters Beer Garden
24 Buckhorn Tavern
25 Crooked Goat Brewing
26 Griffo Distillery & Tasting Bar
27 Henhouse
28 La Dolce Vita Wine Lounge
29 Vine & Barrel

ENTERTAINMENT
30 Mystic Theatre

SHOPPING
31 McEvoy Ranch Outlet
32 Petaluma Village Premium Outlets

INFORMATION
33 Petaluma Visitors Center

Museum *(petalumamuseum.com)*, housed in a spectacular neoclassical building and providing a bounty of local information and weekly walking tours between May and October.

Strolling the **riverfront walk** is a treat, though kayaks have replaced the paddleboats and steamers of yore. George Lucas' seminal, Academy Award–nominated film *American Graffiti* (1973) was primarily filmed here. The annual May festival **Salute to American Graffiti** *(americangraffiti.net)* sees 400 classic cars cruising the strip and you can watch the movie on a big screen.

Go further back in the past just 4 miles northeast of town at the historic Rancho de Petaluma, where General Vallejo planted the area's first grapevines. The 1830s residence stands today as the **Petaluma Adobe State Historic Park** *(petalumaadobe.com; adult/child $3/2 ticket includes* Sonoma State Historic Park; p190).

Sample Farm-Fresh Goodies

Petaluma's olive oil, cheese and ice cream

All the abundant farms, rolling hills and grazing cows you see in the distance produce top food and dairy. Taste olive oil southwest of town at **McEvoy Ranch** *(mcevoyranch.com; tastings from $35)*. You can also have lunch or take a ranch tour *(from $55)*. It has an **outlet** downtown with up to 40% savings on olive oils and its line of lotions and soaps.

Pop into **Petaluma Creamery** *(springhillcheese.com)* for organic local cheeses and ice cream. There's also great ice cream at **Angela's Ice Cream** *(angelasicecream.com)*, which also has other branches around the region. If you'd like to get out onto a dairy farm, check with **Petaluma Visitors Center** *(visitpetaluma.com)* to find out which rural dairies and creameries are open to the public. Shoppers looking beyond food, will also love the **Petaluma Village Premium Outlets** *(premiumoutlets.com)* north of town, and myriad art and antique shops in town.

Eating Your Way Through Petaluma

California cornucopia

Start out at one of the town's many bakeries or cafes, like **Stellina Pronto** *(stellinapronto.com)* for Italian sweet or savory pastries, or learn why sourdough is queen at The **Bagel Mill** *(thebagelmill.com)*.

Lunch at **Water Street Bistro** *(waterstreetbistropetaluma.com)*, where excellent French fare meets riverfront views. The crab chowder is to die for. Keep the seafood theme going at the

BEST PETALUMA SPOTS FOR MICROBREWS

Lagunitas Brewing Company *(lagunitas.com)*: One of the US' top breweries, a pioneer of microbrewing beloved for its IPAs and imperial stout.

Henhouse *(henhousebrewing.com)*: Palace of Brewing with a Santa Rosa location, too. Focuses on fresh brews and community experience.

Crooked Goat Brewing *(crookedgoatbrewing.com)*: Taproom for Sebastopol brewery: great line of sours, lagers, West Coast IPAs.

Adobe Creek Taproom *(adobecreekbrewing.com)*: Outpost of Novato brewery, with IPAs, lagers and stouts.

Brewsters Beer Garden *(brewsters-beergarden.com)*: Listen to live music, drink beer and eat snacks at picnic tables.

DRINKING IN PETALUMA: TOP WATERING HOLES

La Dolce Vita Wine Lounge: Settle into the golden, romantic light for myriad wines with small plates and pizzas. *3-9pm Tue-Thu, to 10pm Fri & Sat*

Vine & Barrel: Talkative owner serves wines and tapas at a wooden bar in this wine shop. *noon-5pm Sun & Wed, to 9pm Thu, to 11pm Fri & Sat*

Griffo Distillery & Tasting Bar: Stock up on spirits and quaff cocktails, sometimes with live music. *9am-5pm Mon-Wed, to 9pm Thu, 2-7pm Fri-Sun*

Buckhorn Tavern: Sidle up to the bar at Petaluma's old-school landmark bar, complete with a pool table and occasional karaoke. *10am-1am*

WELCOME TO FLATBACK

The word Petaluma comes from the Miwok words *pe'ta* (flat) and *lu'ma* (back), referring to the gentle openness of the valley behind the hill. Mexico's Comandante of Northern California, Mariano Guadalupe Vallejo, then used it for his giant Rancho Petaluma, granted to him in 1834.

In the 1830s, Mexico had won a war against Spain, and got stuck with an unwanted prize: Spain's missions in California. Mexico decreed that the land should revert to native control – but the memo was somehow mislaid by Comandante Vallejo. Settlers, including Vallejo, snapped up extensive mission lands, including ranches and vineyards. The nearby town of Vallejo, 27 miles southeast of Petaluma, retains the Comandante's name.

DENISTANGNEYJR/GETTY IMAGES

Petaluma waterfront

Shuckery *(theshuckeryca.com)*...oysters of course, paired with wine or sangria. Compare and contrast the bivalves at **Hog Island Oyster Co**'s *(hogislandoysters.com)* cool hole-in-the wall on the riverfront.

You can really mix it up at **Stockhome** *(stockhomerestaurant.com)* for Swedish-Mediterranean delights. In the evening, go classic at **Sugo Trattoria** *(sugotrattoria.com)*, or embrace a real date-night treat with the always inventive tasting menus at **Table Culture Provisions** *(tcprovision.com)*. Nip into the 100-year-old Lan Mart Building to discover what's on the menu at **Street Social** *(streetsocial.social)*, where wildly creative dishes change constantly.

For a more casual night, slide into **The Block** *(theblockpetaluma.com)*, for a rotating lineup of food trucks, including a permanent pizzeria. Gather around one of the firepits and grab a local microbrew, too.

Want to dig deeper? Take one of the cooking classes (p196) in the area.

Walk for Photo Ops of Rolling Hills

Sweeping views form Helen Putnam Regional Park

Roam the hills just outside of Petaluma at **Helen Putnam Regional Park** *(parks.sonomacounty.ca.gov; parking per car $7)* to get fantastic views of the town and the rolling hills, emerald in winter and spring, and sere beige in summer – a great spot for pics. The park is dog friendly, too.

Catch a Play or Movie

Be a culture vulture

Petaluma has a top North Bay venue: the 1911 **Mystic Theatre** *(mystictheatre.com)*, originally built for vaudeville but now hosting live music and occasional film screenings. For theatre-lovers the **Cinnabar Theater** *(cinnabartheater.org)* company stages plays in two different venues.

Sebastopol

WEST COUNTY HUB | ART | ECLECTIC CUISINE

No amount of fermented fruit can explain free-spirited Sebastopol. In the 19th century, independent Pomo villagers and immigrant apple farmers formed a US township in the Pomo homeland of Bitakomtara. According to legend, an epic 1850s bar brawl here was jokingly compared to the famous Crimean War battlefront, underway at the time, and the nickname Sebastopol stuck.

While the rest of Wine Country started growing grapes, Sebastopol kept growing heirloom apples, vegetables and wildflowers developed by local horticulture hero Luther Burbank. Back-to-the-land hippies brought fresh ideas to western Sonoma County, including organic farming, home beekeeping and marijuana cultivation. Now even the traffic medians are pesticide free, and the entire town is a nuclear-free zone. Anywhere you go, you can't miss the local characters, some more famous than others. Tom Waits lives on the outskirts, and Grateful Dead drummer Mickey Hart occasionally jams. Sebastopol just keeps bringing legends to life.

GETTING AROUND

Central Sebastopol is best walked or biked, and trails radiate through the countryside. Cyclists can take the paved Joe Rodota Trail to Santa Rosa and then the SMART train south (Petaluma or Larkspur Landing's Bay Ferry to San Francisco). Sonoma County Transit *(sctransit.com)* buses include a free local shuttle (Route 24). Central Sebastopol is a great walking town.

TOP TIP

Sebastopol Area Chamber of Commerce & Visitors Center *(sebastopol.org)* has maps and information. Buy *Sebastopol Walks* by Richard Nichols for town walks and country rides and rambles on the Joe Rodota Trail, through bird-watchers' paradise wetland **Laguna de Santa Rosa** – its learning center *(lagunafoundation.org)* hosts exhibits and activities – and beyond.

Fantastical Sculptures, Local Creativity & Vintage Wares

Art for art's sake

A cow rides a tractor, a rocket blasts off the lawn and a dinosaur grabs a red convertible for lunch: it's all happening on **Florence Ave**, in dozens of sculptures by **Patrick Amiot** *(patrickamiot.com)* which are painted by Brigitte Laurent and made for neighbors' yards from recycled junk. You'll spot plenty more throughout the county, and you can order pieces at their **Big Times Art Studio**.

Skip the airport souvenirs and opt for art instead...around the corner at **Sebastopol Center for the Arts** *(sebarts.org; admission free)*, see the world from the perspective of Sonoma County's boundary-pushing artists, working in media from

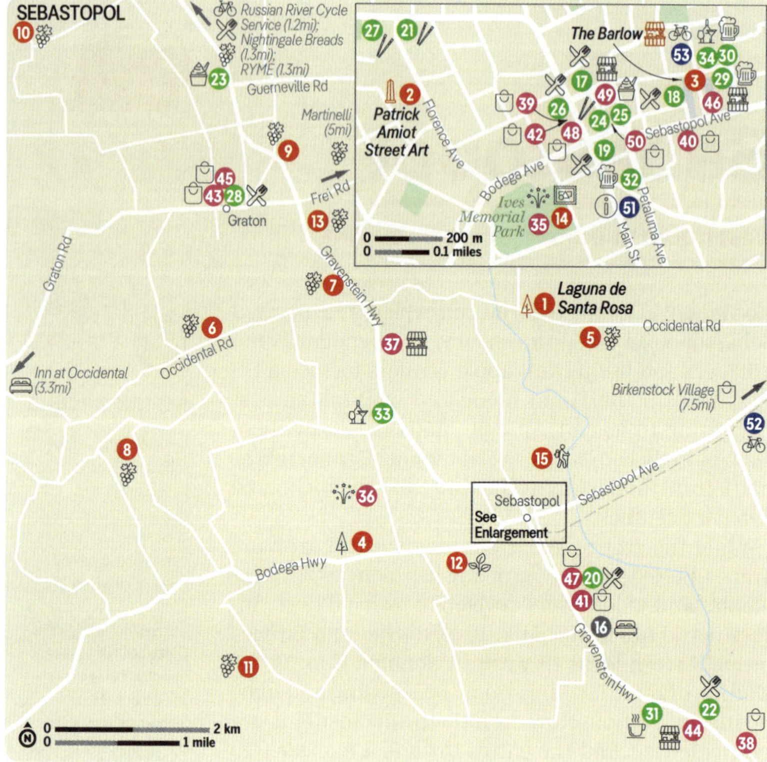

HIGHLIGHTS
1 Laguna de Santa Rosa
2 Patrick Amiot Street Art
3 The Barlow

SIGHTS
4 Atascadero Creek Ecological Reserve
5 Balletto
6 Char Vale
7 Emeritus
8 Freeman
9 Furthermore Wines
10 Iron Horse Vineyards
11 Littorai
12 Luther Burbank's Gold Ridge Experiment Farm
13 Merry Edwards
14 Sebastopol Center for the Arts

ACTIVITIES
15 West County Regional Trail

SLEEPING
16 Fairfield Inn & Suites

EATING
17 Cozy Plum
18 Fern Bar
19 Goldfinch
20 Incas Peruvian Cuisine
21 Khom Loi
22 La Bodega Kitchen
23 Mom's Apple Pie
24 Ramen Gaijin
25 Screamin' Mimi's
26 Sebastopol Cookie Co
27 Sushi Tozai
28 Willow Wood Market Cafe

DRINKING & NIGHTLIFE
29 Crooked Goat Brewing
30 Golden State Cider Taproom
31 Hardcore Espresso
32 Hopmonk Tavern
33 Horse & Plow
34 Region

ENTERTAINMENT
35 Apple Blossom Festival
36 Gravenstein Apple Fair

SHOPPING
37 Andy's Produce
38 Antique Society
39 Artisana
40 Attico
41 Beekind
42 Copperfield's Books
43 Graton Gallery
44 Midgley's Country Flea Market
45 Mr Ryder & Co Art & Antiques
46 Sebastopol Community Market
47 Solful
48 Sumbody
49 Sunday Organic Farmers Market
50 Toyworks

INFORMATION
51 Sebastopol Area Chamber of Commerce & Visitors Center

TRANSPORTATION
52 Joe Rodota Trail
53 Revel Cycles

fiber arts to glass and plain ol' paint (used to glorious effect). It organizes excellent open-studio weekends countywide, with **Sonoma County Art Trails** *(sonomacountyarttrails.org)*, in October, and **Art at the Source** *(artatthesource.org)*, in June.

Charming central Sebastopol is also dotted with creative shops, from **Artisana** *(artisanafunctionalart.com)* with hand-hewn housewares and jewelry; **BeeKind** *(beekind.com)* for all things bee-based; and **Toyworks** *(sonomatoyworks.com)*, any tot's dreamscape. At **Sumbody** *(sumbody.com)*, mushrooms, goats' milk and chocolate are ingredients in ecofriendly, small-batch bath products. Feed your head at independent **Copperfield's Books** *(copperfieldsbooks.com)*.

Browse antique and vintage stores like **Attico** *(atticostore.com)* and macro-collective **Antique Society** *(instagram.com/antiquesociety.sebastopol)*, and on Sundays search for treasures at sprawling **Midgley's Country Flea Market** *(mfleamarket.com)*.

In the hamlet of **Graton**, 4 miles to the north, swing by **Graton Gallery** *(gratongallery.net)* and **Mr Ryder & Co Art & Antiques** *(facebook.com/MrRyderAntiques)* next door to round it all out.

Apples, Daisies & Good Times

Hearty horticulture and hard cider

Sebastopol had a reputation for boozy shenanigans long before Sonoma County's wine industry took off, because the heirloom-apple orchards that thrived here weren't originally intended for roadside bakery **Mom's Apple Pie** *(momsapplepieusa.com)*. They were used to make hard cider – a tradition upheld today at **Hopmonk Tavern** *(hopmonk.com)* and **Horse & Plow** *(horseandplow.com)* tasting room, and celebrated twice annually at the **Apple Blossom Festival** *(appleblossomfest.com)* in April and **Gravenstein Apple Fair** *(gravensteinapplefair.com)* in August.

The old apple cannery on the edge of Sebastopol was repurposed into **The Barlow** *(thebarlow.net)*, home to Sebastopol's upstart makers, including **Golden State Cider Taproom** *(drinkgoldenstate.com)*, celebrated **Crooked Goat Brewing** *(crookedgoatbrewing.com)*, **Region** *(drinkregion.com)* tasting room, as well as several wineries.

About 150 years ago, horticulturalist Luther Burbank cultivated fruit trees and daisies (like popular Shasta daisies, the 1901 hybrid of flowers from three continents) at **Luther Burbank's Gold Ridge Experiment Farm** *(wschs.org/farm; admission free)*, which is open to the public. You can also reserve to taste namesake Gold Ridge Farms' organic apple and olive-oil products.

Get to Know West County Winemakers

Pinots, chardonnays and more

In the 1970s, while chef Alice Waters established California cuisine, **Merry Edwards** *(merryedwards.com; tastings from $45)* was championing California wine from her vineyard – becoming the first woman in Napa's Winemakers' Hall of Fame while

BEST WAYS TO GO LOCAL

Sonoma County Farm Trails: Family-friendly farms, pick-your-own orchards, some of the best organic plant nurseries. *farmtrails.org*

Sunday Organic Farmers Market: Live music in town square with vats of organic kombucha, small-batch elderberry syrup and dried maitake-mushroom jerky. *sebastopolfarmersmarket.org*

Sebastopol Community Market & Andy's Produce: Admire the fruits of West County's labor at these food markets. *cmnaturalfoods.com; andysproduce.com*

Solful *(solful.com)*: Meet Your Pot Farmer events at Sebastopol's cannabis dispensary.

Birkenstock Village: Santa Rosa's family-owned shoe store. *birkenstockvillage.com*

HOMEGROWN BOUNTY

Nicholas Izzarelli, Sebastopol native and owner-operator of **Goldfinch** tells us his favorite ways to eat local. *goldfinch sebastopol.com*

Check out a farmers market or winery (**Iron Horse** is my go-to), and meet incredibly talented and hardworking people showcasing what this county has to offer. As for restaurants, I LOVE **Terrapin Creek** (p210) in Bodega Bay. Every dish is thoughtful, delicious and perfectly executed. **Khom Loi** offers locally sourced dishes with amazing Thai street-food flavors. On the coast, stop by **Hog Island Oyster Co** or **The Marshall Store** for the freshest seafood, beautiful scenery and chill Sonoma County vibes.

putting California pinots on the map. Just north on Hwy 116 at **Furthermore Wines** *(furthermorewines.com; tastings from $35)*, start with pinot, break for *bocce* and live music, then return to the urgent matter of pinot, or better yet, its mysterious rosé of pinot noir.

Redwoods encircle **Freeman** vineyards *(freemanwinery.com; tastings $40)*, trapping mists that winemaker/founder Akiko Freeman captures in cool-climate pinots and chardonnays. Vineyards are actually a minority crop on **Littorai** *(littorai.com; tastings from $70)*, a 30-acre biodynamic estate, where bees, birds and beneficial insects create an integrated ecosystem.

Roll along pastoral Green Valley Rd – surrounded by rolling farmland, apple orchards and vineyards, plus the occasional Shetland pony – to raise a toast at **Iron Horse Vineyards** *(ironhorsevineyards.com; tastings from $35)* with sparkling wines that have been served at White House inaugurations.

Sebastopol is ringed by vineyards, so you can just keep going, with **Emeritus** *(emeritusvineyards.com; tastings from $40)*, **Balletto** *(ballettovineyards.com; tastings from $20)* and **Char Vale** *(charvalewinery.com; tastings from $28)* and if space is available, walk-ins are welcome.

EATING IN SEBASTOPOL: OUR PICKS

Goldfinch: Delectable locally sourced fare with killer cocktails and golden atmosphere. *11.30am-8.30pm Wed-Sun, from 5pm Mon & Tue* **$$$**

Ramen Gaijin: Upbeat mood fueled by (spicy!) pork-belly ramen, (tasty!) short ribs and cocktails (fun!). Book ahead. *noon-9pm Tue-Sat* **$$**

Fern Bar: Come for '70s atmosphere, with stained-glass and amber lighting – stay for shared plates. *4-9pm Mon-Thu, 11am-10pm Fri-Sun* **$$**

La Bodega Kitchen: Inspired vegan and vegetarian food paired with wine from the adjoining wine store. *4-9pm Thu-Mon* **$$**

Incas Peruvian Cuisine: Savory dishes, from chicken stew to braised lamb shank. *11.30am-9pm Mon-Sat, noon-8pm Sun* **$$**

Sushi Tozai: Enjoy the catch off the Pacific coast with delicious sushi. Cheerful family-run spot. *5-9pm Tue-Sun* **$$**

Cozy Plum: Delicious vegan wraps, bowls, burgers, sandwiches and tacos. Large portions and quick service. *11am-8pm* **$$**

Willow Wood Market Cafe: In Graton: comfort food, champagne cocktails. *9am-8pm Mon-Sat, to 3pm Sun* **$$**

DIANE N ENNIS/SHUTTERSTOCK

Sebastopol vineyard

Cycle West County Trails

Peddle through orchards and vineyards

What better way to experience the scenery than to peddle the region's bike trails through vineyards, orchards and wetlands? The mostly paved 5.5-mile **West County Regional Trail** *(parks.sonomacounty.ca.gov)* is protected from cars most of the way, and links Sebastopol, Graton and Forestville with farm and pasture views, and a nice elevated boardwalk north of Graton that passes through the **Atascadero Creek Ecological Reserve** *(wildlife.ca.gov; free)*. Look online for multiple access points. This track connects to rails-to-trails greenway **Joe Rodota Trail** *(parks.sonomacounty.ca.gov)* to Santa Rosa.

Rent bikes and e-bikes in Sebastopol at **Revel Cycles** *(revelcycles.com; 2 hours bike/e-bike $40/60)* or in Forestville at **Russian River Cycle Service** *(russianrivercycles.com; half-/full-day rental from $35/45)*, at the head of the trail.

FORESTVILLE'S BEST STOPS

The main drag of little **Forestville**, between Sebastopol and the Russian River, is lined with old-timey storefronts.

Nightingale Breads: The aroma of Jessie Frost's organic breads changes traffic patterns. Stop for a bite. *nightingale breads.com*

RYME: Beloved tasting room *(tastings $35)*: a low-key, more affordable way to sample local wines. *rymecellars.com*

Martinelli: Quaint red barn on River Rd where the family-owned winery *(tastings from $25)* has been bucking convention since 1887, when a young Tuscan winemaker eloped to California to grow grapes on notoriously steep, rocky Jackass Hill. Award-winning zinfandels, pinots and muscat. *martinelli winery.com*

EATING & DRINKING IN SEBASTOPOL: INDIE FOODS & SWEET TREATS

The Barlow (p203)**:** Two-acre village of indie food producers, ice creamers, artists, winemakers, coffee roasters and distillers. *hours and prices vary*

Screamin' Mimi's: Luscious homemade ice cream served by the ounce. Choose from a seasonal lineup of flavors. *11am-9.30pm Sun-Thu, to 10pm Fri & Sat* $

Sebastopol Cookie Co: Indie bakery making restorative triple-chocolate cookies, snickerdoodles and more. *8.30am-5pm Tue-Sat, 9am-3pm Sun* $

Hardcore Espresso: Shambolic spot with quirky art around gardens and patios and crammed inside, plus top coffee and baked goods. *5.30am-5.30pm* $

Beyond Sebastopol

Trace valleys through forested mountains out to the Pacific Coast, reveling in homegrown fare and easygoing settlements.

Hills undulate from Sebastopol and Graton to the Pacific in the west and up to the Russian River in the north, the valleys golden in summer. In winter and spring, rain-greened pastures rise to the redwood- and oak-topped hills. Vineyards carve up the acreage, as do historic communes and quintessential Northern California hamlets.

World-class wineries, a nationally famous day spa, and excellent creameries, bakeries and restaurants spice up the mix. So too do heartfelt gatherings like Occidental's farmers market, where live music fills the night sky as folks from the hills around come down and say hi.

This is a region in which to kick back, drop out and see what happens.

Santa Rosa

TIME FROM SEBASTOPOL: **20 MINS**

Get to know the downtown

Wine Country's biggest city, **Santa Rosa** *(visitsantarosa.com)* is modern-day Americana, with cottage rose gardens, hikers trekking **Trione-Annadel State Park** *(parks.ca.gov; admission free)* and life booming in the culturally Latinx **Roseland** neighborhood.

GETTING AROUND

A vehicle is the easiest way to get around outside of Sebastopol and Santa Rosa – buses, while they do run in the countryside, are infrequent. Seasoned cyclists ply country lanes – be alert whether you're on two wheels or four. Sonoma County Transit *(sctransit.com)* buses radiate out from Santa Rosa. Santa Rosa City Bus *(srcitybus.org)* runs an extensive network of local buses in that city (using a Bay Area–wide Clipper Card). **Santa Rosa Transit Mall** is a regional hub. Golden Gate Transit *(goldengate.org)* buses run between San Francisco and Santa Rosa. Mendocino Transit *(mendocinotransit.org)* bus 95 goes from Santa Rosa to Bodega Bay and up the coast to Pt Arena. Bus 65 goes north to Windsor and beyond. SMART train *(sonomamarintrain.org)* goes between Sonoma County Airport in the north, via Santa Rosa and Petaluma, south to Larkspur and the SF Ferry system.

Groome Transportation *(groometransportation.com)* buses shuttle between Sonoma County Airport, Santa Rosa, and San Francisco and Oakland airports.

JANE TYSKA/MEDIANEWS GROUP/THE MERCURY NEWS VIA GETTY IMAGES

Russian River Brewing Co

The main heart and shopping stretch is **4th St** along central **Old Courthouse Sq**. The city makes international news each year when **Russian River Brewing Co** *(russianriverbrewing.com)* releases its brilliantly bitter double IPA Pliny the Elder, which prompts campouts at the door, and remains a place of pilgrimage for craft-beer lovers year-round.

Walk 4th St to reemerge across the freeway at historic **Railroad Sq** and take in the tree-shaded, mural-lined streets of the **South A Street Art District**, stopping and smelling the flowers – many are fragrant varietals; like the Santa Rosa, plum developed for delight, utility and sustainability just up the street at **Luther Burbank Home & Gardens** *(lutherburbank.org; grounds free, tour adult/child $12/free)*. This is where pioneering horticulturist Luther Burbank (1849–1926) cultivated 800 hybrid plant species over 50 years.

To learn more, take a trip through Sonoma County's past, present and future in the **Museum of Sonoma County** *(museumsc.org; 11am-5pm Wed-Sun)* in side-by-side history and art museums.

Take an international food tour

Santa Rosa is a world tour in excellent eats – from homemade dim sum at **Hang Ah** *(hangahdimsum.com)* to Ethiopian at **Abyssinia** *(my-abyssinia.com)*, French pâtisserie and bread at **Goguette** *(goguettebread.com)* and **Pascaline** *(pascalinebistro.com)*, a favorite local hangout for delicate pastries and bistro-style brunch.

Santa Rosa is awash with good Mexican restaurants, especially around the Roseland area on Sebastopol Rd. Sample widely at **Mitote Food Park** *(mitotefoodpark.com)*, where taco trucks actually make specialties from all over Mexico alongside a bar. Markets like **Lola's** *(lolasmarkets.com)* also have great taqueria counters.

Across the street, **O Sushi** *(santarosaosushi.com)* is one of our favorites for Japanese. Or try **Sushi Rosa** *(sushirosa.com)* by Old Courthouse Sq.

SONOMA COUNTY'S FAIRS

Sonoma County Fair: Monster truck rallies, the NorCal BrewFest, Elvis Impersonation Contest, World Championship Grape Stomp, a Hall of Flowers, a petting zoo: this is a 10-day festival of Americana. Concerts are free with admission. In August. *sonomacountyfair.com*

Sonoma Harvest Fair: America's biggest and arguably toughest wine competition – 1000 wines judged blind, by winemakers, sommeliers and critics – see if you agree with Double Gold winners, feast on award-winning food. In October. *harvestfair.org*

Wine Road Barrel Tasting: In March, wineries from Alexander Valley to Russian River throw open wine-cave doors to sample from the barrel. *wineroad.com*

BEST SANTA ROSA BREWERIES

Russian River Brewing Co: World-famous releases of IPA Pliny the Elder. Sip triple-IPA Pliny the Younger with pizza. *russianriverbrewing.com*

Cooperage Brewing Company: Barrel-aged sours, stouts and more. *cooperagebrewing.com*

Iron Ox Brewing Company: IPAs, spiked seltzers and sodas and hop water, beer cocktails, food truck. *ironoxbeer.com*

Shady Oak Brewing: Family-owned, making sour ales and IPAs, often with wild yeast and regional ingredients. *shadyoakbrewing.com*

Henhouse Brewing: Tap-masters explain the brews; another location in Petaluma. *henhousebrewing.com*

Barley & Bine Beer Cafe: Windsor's brewpub has 38 taps of Cali goodness. *barleybinebeercafe.com*

DAVIDGREITZER/GETTY IMAGES

Wild Flour Bread bakery

'Good grief, Charlie Brown!'

Beloved worldwide, the *Peanuts* comic strip was drawn in Santa Rosa by cartoonist Charles M Schulz. If you fly into **Charles M Schulz Sonoma County Airport**, you can take your pic with Snoopy in the terminal. Keep an eye out for giant fiberglass statues all over the city, part of the **Peanuts on Parade** celebration of the characters.

The wonderful-for-all-ages **Charles M Schulz Museum** *(schulzmuseum.org; adult/child $12/5)* follows the journey of Snoopy, Charlie Brown, Lucy and the gang from their 1950 introduction to last laughs in 2000. Downstairs are original Schulz drawings. Upstairs are artists' tributes to *Peanuts*, plus an exacting recreation of Schulz' art studio: markers on a reclaimed-wood desk and a video of Schulz drawing – a fluid poem in ink. Schulz was originally from Minnesota, and so built an **ice rink** *(snoopyshomeice.com)* on-site, too. Check the website for public skating hours and prices.

Freestone

TIME FROM SEBASTOPOL: **15 MINS**

Escape to a unique day spa

From the instant you turn onto **Bohemian Hwy** at Freestone, you're in for a wild ride. Freestone is a former stagecoach stop with a current population of 32, yet the road is

EATING & DRINKING IN SANTA ROSA: SNACKS, CAFES & BARS

Bird & the Bottle: When you're not sure what you're craving, try a little bit of everything... from grilled lamb meatballs to duck confit tacos. *11.30am-9pm* $$$

Criminal Baking Co: Join the line for triple-cheese knishes, deep-dish quiches, quinoa salad bowls, and toasted-rye chocolate-chip cookies. *7.30am-3pm* $

Espressioso's Coffee: Conveniently located on 4th St with ethically sourced coffee roasted by the owners and spot-on coffee drinks. *6am-6pm Tue-Sun* $

Willi's Wine Bar: Grab a spot on the heated patio or sociable bar for wine-tasting, comparing Sonoma and international wines, and pair with tapas. *11.30am-9pm* $$$

lined with cars. People arrive from far and wide to nibble on planet-sized sticky buns at **Wild Flour Bread** *(wildflourbread.com)* and get buried up to their necks in cedar chips – a Japanese tradition – at **Osmosis Day Spa** *(osmosis.com)*. The spa ritual here begins with organic tea in the bonsai garden, then proceeds to a redwood tub full of soft, fermenting cedar and rice bran – the woodsy aroma and dry-enzyme action will warm you to the bone. Up until recently, it's been the only cedar bath in North America (the other is in Lake Tahoe), and attracts celebs and hippies alike.

FOR ART LOVERS

In addition to reveling in the *Peanuts* museum or local winery Paradise Ridge, where outdoor sculptures thrill on a gorgeous hillside, experience more art at **San Francisco's downtown museums** (p57 and p61).

Occidental TIME FROM SEBASTOPOL: **20–30 MINS**

Farmers market party and offbeat treats

Occidental (population 1126) is the surprising mountaintop lumber town that time forgot and trees reconquered – with help from visionary ecologists and back-to-the-land hippies. The power of countercultural thinking is celebrated when partying breaks out mid-May to October at the Thursday **Occidental Community Farmers Market** *(occidentalcommunityfarmersmarket.com)*. Crafts, flowers, cheese, organic produce, mushrooms and giant pans of Pacific seafood paella fill the street, and musicians light up the evening as friends and family mingle. Grab great draft brews at **Altamont General Store** *(altamontgeneralstore.com)* and sit curbside and watch the world go by, or combine family-style epic ravioli with local vintages at the **Union Hotel** *(unionhoteloccidental.com)*.

Drop by **Bohème Wines Cellar Door** *(bohemewines.com)* for wine tasting. At **Hinterland & Neon Raspberry** *(neonraspberry.com)* everything is recycled, organic and/or women-made with punk attitude.

Check the schedule at **Occidental Center For the Arts** *(occidentalcenterforthearts.org)* to keep it all going.

Soar through the trees

North of Occidental, get your adrenaline going on a zipline through the redwoods at **Sonoma Zipline Adventures** *(sonomacanopytours.com; zipline from $109)*. Afterwards you can wind down the hill to reach the Russian River at Monte Rio.

Cruise from redwoods to the wide-open ocean

Sonoma County's most memorable drive may not be through the grapes (though Westside Rd is a contender; see p217), but along these 10 miles of winding byway from Occidental to the ocean. It's best in the late morning, when fog lifts and sun filters through the trees.

First, reach the ridgeline on **Coleman Valley Rd**, head left onto Joy Rd and right onto Fitzpatrick Lane to find a hidden glory: the **Grove of the Old Trees** *(landpaths.org)*. Picnic or stroll the easy 1-mile loop trail.

Back on Coleman Valley Rd, pass gnarled oaks and craggy rocks to ascend 1000ft, until the vast blue Pacific unfurls

BEST SONOMA COAST STATE PARK WALKS

Bodega Head: This 265ft promontory is great for whale-watching (sometimes docents dot the trail for explanations).

Pomo Canyon Red Hill Trail: One of Greater Bay Area's premier trails from Pomo Canyon up over coastal hills to Shell Beach (6.5 miles walked as a loop).

Shell Beach: Boardwalk and trail lead to a stretch perfect for tide-pooling and beachcombing.

Kortum Trail: This 3.75-mile trail connects **Wright's Beach** to **Blind Beach** just south of Goat Rock Beach.

Goat Rock Beach: Walk to the harbor seals lazing at mouth of the Russian River. Rock archway offshore.

Salmon Creek Beach: Situated around a lagoon; 2 miles of hiking, good waves for surfing.

at your feet. The road ends at coastal Hwy 1, where you can explore Sonoma Coast State Park and eat oysters in serene **Valley Ford**.

Bodega Bay

TIME FROM SEBASTOPOL: **30 MINS**

Sonoma Coast State Park

Stretching 16 miles north from **Bodega Head** to **Vista Trail**, four miles north of Jenner, the glorious **Sonoma Coast State Park** *(parks.ca.gov)* is actually a series of beaches separated by beautiful rocky headlands. Some are tiny, hidden in little coves, while others stretch wide. Most are connected by hiking trails winding along the bluffs. Bring your camera – the views are stunning, with rock outcrops, mini islands, inlets and crashing waves.

During summer, morning fog generally burns off by midday. Exploring this area makes an excellent daylong adventure, but facilities are minimal, so bring water, food and sun protection, as well as a charged cell phone (though signal is spotty), in case of emergency. Surf is often too treacherous to wade through, so keep a close eye on children.

EATING IN BODEGA BAY: SEAFOOD FORWARD

Spud Point Crab Company: Crab shack serving salty-sweet crab sandwiches and real clam chowder (which wins local culinary prizes). *hours vary* $$

Terrapin Creek Cafe & Restaurant: Elegant restaurant repping the slow-food movement. Locally sourced dishes lean seafood. *4.30-8.30pm Thu-Mon* $$$

Fishetarian: This always-reliable fish market and deli features a deck near the water and a seafood menu (from oysters and ceviche to fish sandwiches). *11am-8pm* $$

Gourmet Au Bay: Head to the spacious deck to enjoy a salty breeze with your snacks at this sophisticated wine bar. *noon-6pm Thu-Sun, to 3pm Mon* $$

VENTU PHOTO/SHUTTERSTOCK

Bodega Bay

Fishing, whale-watching & marine life

Bodega Bay's downtown, houses, restaurants, hotels and shops, along busy Hwy 1, is not made for strolling. But on the west side, a peninsula resembling a crooked finger juts out to sea at Bodega Head, forming the entrance to **Bodega Harbor**, one of the North Bay's premier fishing and crabbing spots. This is your chance to get out and try your hand at catching ling cod, rock cod, king salmon and Dungeness crab. We like **Reel Magic Sport Fishing Charters** *(reelmagicsportfishing charters.net)* and **Bodega Bay Sportfishing Center** *(bodegabaysportfishing.com)*. You can also go whale-watching from here with **Bodega Bay Whale Charters** *(bodegabay whalecharters.com)*.

Celebrate it all at **Bodega Bay Fishermen's Festival** *(bbfishfest.org)* in May.

If you want to get into the water, easygoing one-stop-shop **Bodega Bay Surf Shack** *(bodegabaysurf.com)* has all kinds of equipment rentals, including SUPs and kayaks, lessons and good local information. It also rents bikes for landlubbers.

Also on the peninsula, **Bodega Marine Laboratory & Reserve** *(marinescience.ucdavis.edu)*, run by UC Davis, has docent-led tours on Friday afternoons (reserve).

THE BIRDS

Bodega Bay is a pearl in a string of sleepy fishing towns that line the North Coast and was the setting of Alfred Hitchcock's terrifying 1963 avian horror flick *The Birds*. Although special effects radically altered the actual layout of the town, you still get a good feel for the supposed site of the farm owned by Mitch Brenner (played by Rod Taylor). The once-cozy **Tides Wharf & Restaurant**, where much havoc occurs, is still there but is now a restaurant complex. Venture 5 miles inland to the tiny town of **Bodega** and you'll find two icons from the film: **Potter Schoolhouse** and **St Teresa of Avila Church**. Both stand just as they did in the movie – a crow overhead may make the hair rise on your neck.

EATING AROUND OCCIDENTAL: OUR PICKS

Hazel (Occidental)**:** Join a fabulous dinner party – wine flows and *oohs!* erupt as dishes arrive bubbling from wood-fired ovens. *5-9pm Tue-Sun* **$$$**

Howard Station Cafe (Occidental)**:** Since the 1870s, Howard's has restored travelers and ranchers with reliable, generous, comforting brunches. *7.30am-2pm* **$**

Rocker's Roadhouse (Valley Ford)**:** Oyster and New Orleans-style cooking. Also has a spot in Bodega Bay (Rocker Oysterfeller's). *11am-8pm, from 10am Sun* **$$**

Farmhouse Inn (Forestville)**:** The region's Michelin-starred River Rd gourmet landmark, with refined, locally raised organics. *5.30-8.30pm Thu-Mon* **$$$**

CRUISING THE SONOMA COUNTY COAST TO MENDOCINO

Celebrate an uninterrupted stretch of coastal highway that skirts rocky shores, secluded coves and wind-sculpted beaches.

START	END	LENGTH
Bodega Bay	Mendocino	110 miles; 5 hrs

Start alongside the fishing fleets of ❶ **Bodega Bay**, cruising through the wild Pacific coast scenery of Sonoma County State Park (p210) until you reach the seal colony at the mouth of the Russian River at Goat Rock in ❷ **Jenner**. Continuing north, stretch your legs again at **Jenner Headlands Preserve** or continue straight to ❸ **Fort Ross State Historic Park**, a reconstruction of a 19th-century Russian fur-trading fort.

From there, the road twists past the free ❹ **Kruse Rhododendron State Natural Reserve** rhododendron groves. One of the best reasons to spend the night around these parts is ❺ **Salt Point State Park**, a 6000-acre stunner with sandstone cliffs dropping into a kelp-strewn sea and hiking trails crisscrossing windswept prairies and wooded hills.

Weather-beaten but ritzy private community ❻ **Sea Ranch** lines an ocean bluff with five beaches open to the public. Next up, ❼ **Gualala** is a hub for weekend getaways, with its **arts center**. Another half-hour up the coast, climb ❽ **Point Arena Lighthouse**, which has guarded the windy point since 1908. Slip a little further north to ❾ **Elk**, a hamlet famous for clifftop views of towering rock formations. Overnight in ❿ **Mendocino**.

END ❿ Mendocino
0 20 km
0 10 miles
Mendocino National Forest
Albion
Navarro
Anderson Valley
101
Ukiah
Elk
❾
1
Philo
128
Boonville
Russian River
Clear Lake
Lakeport
Anderson River
❽
Flumeville
Yorkville
Cloverdale
Gualala ❼
Lake Sonoma
Asti
❻
Sea Ranch
Lake Sonoma Recreation Area
Geyserville
101
Dry Creek
Stewarts Point
❹
❺
Healdsburg
Austin Creek State Recreation Area
Windsor
❸
1
Guerneville
PACIFIC OCEAN
❷
Bridgehaven
Jenner
Sebastopol
Occidental
Bodega
START ❶
Bodega Bay

Look for the unique, redwood swirl of **Sea Ranch Chapel**. You can pop in from dawn to dusk.

At Sea Ranch, **Stengel Beach** has a large, free parking lot and a short cypress-lined trail to a wooden staircase to the beach.

The road plunges down a canyon to **Russian Gulch State Beach**, a windswept arc of creamy sand, then switchbacks up to the bluff-top.

Russian River Valley

RIVER FLOATS | MISTY WINES | REDWOOD FORESTS

The Russian River has long been a good-time summer-weekend destination for Northern Californians who come to canoe, hike redwood forests, BBQ, taste wine and live life at a lazy pace.

Though the source of the Russian River is north in Ukiah, and the valley begins outside of Healdsburg, when locals talk about hitting 'The River,' they mean the wide stretch starting around lively Guerneville, winding past mellow Monte Rio and Duncans Mills, and flowing into the Pacific at Jenner. For thousands of years, Indigenous Pomo people called this river on the east side of their homelands the Ashokawna ('eastern water'). But once Russians established Fort Ross as a trading post for bear pelts, it became known as the Russian River.

Lately, Russian River Valley vineyards have taken their place among California's important wine appellations, especially for cold-weather grapes like pinot noir. Easy days floating on the river call for toasts, ably supplied by local wineries and Sonoma County microbreweries.

TOP TIP

Get top-tier year-round guided birding tours throughout the region with Teresa and Miles Tuffli whose website *(imbirdingrightnow.com)* is a font of info on the abundant birds of the river. For fishing info and supplies, visit **King's Sport & Tackle** *(kingsrussianriver.com)*. The **Russian River Visitor Center** *(russianriver.com)* provides additional insights in Guerneville.

Happening Town with LGBTQ+ Flair

Playing in Guerneville

The Russian River's biggest vacation spot, **Guerneville** (pronounced *GURN*-vill) only has about 4700 residents, but almost doubles in size on hot summer weekends, when folks come from

GETTING AROUND

West County's winding roads get confusing and there's limited cell-phone service – carry a proper map or download your maps for offline use. The couple of Sonoma County Transit *(sctransit.com)* buses that serve the area (lines 20 from Santa Rosa to Sebastopol, Forestville and the Russian River area as far as Monte Rio; and 28 from Guerneville to Occidental) are very infrequent. On summer weekends and holidays, to avoid parking nightmares take the **Regional Parks River Shuttle** *(parks.sonomacounty.ca.gov; all-day ticket adult/child $5/free)* from El Molino High School in Forestville; it can drop you at Steelhead Beach and pick you up at Sunset Beach if you float down the river (p215).

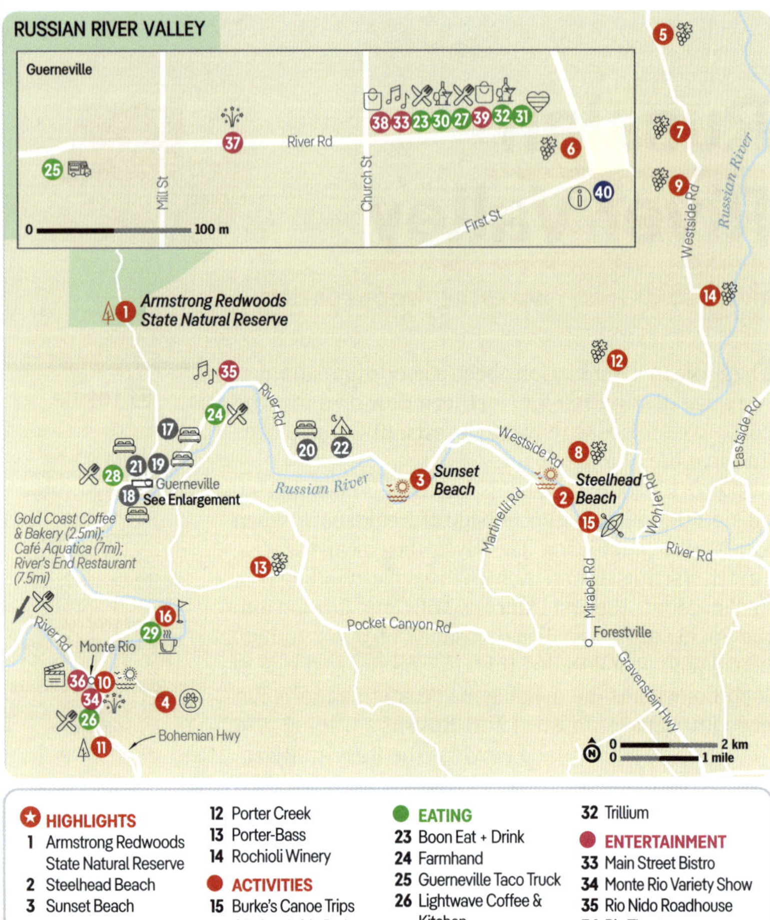

HIGHLIGHTS
1 Armstrong Redwoods State Natural Reserve
2 Steelhead Beach
3 Sunset Beach

SIGHTS
4 Bohemian Grove
5 De La Montanya
6 Equality Vines
7 Flowers
8 Gary Farrell
9 MacRostie
10 Monte Rio Beach
11 Monte Rio Redwoods Regional Park & Open Space Preserve
12 Porter Creek
13 Porter-Bass
14 Rochioli Winery

ACTIVITIES
15 Burke's Canoe Trips
see 26 Creekside Park Skate Park
16 Northwood Golf Club

SLEEPING
17 Boon Hotel + Spa
18 Dawn Ranch
19 Highlands Resort
20 Mine + Farm
21 R3 Hotel
22 Schoolhouse Canyon Campground

EATING
23 Boon Eat + Drink
24 Farmhand
25 Guerneville Taco Truck
26 Lightwave Coffee & Kitchen
see 16 Northwood Restaurant
27 Piknik Town Market
28 Saucy Mama's

DRINKING & NIGHTLIFE
29 Bia Cafe
30 El Barrio
31 Rainbow Cattle Company
32 Trillium

ENTERTAINMENT
33 Main Street Bistro
34 Monte Rio Variety Show
35 Rio Nido Roadhouse
36 Rio Theatre
37 Russian River Pride

SHOPPING
38 Guerneville Bank Club
39 King's Sport & Tackle

INFORMATION
40 Russian River Chamber of Commerce & Visitors Center

all over to hike redwoods, float the river and hammer cocktails poolside. For decades it has been one of the Bay Area's most gay-flavored getaways, and welcomes you to let your hair down and be yourself.

This town is a good time had by all since the 1870s, and it hasn't lost its honky-tonk reputation yet. Just ask burly gay partiers in town in late July and early August for **Lazy Bear Week** *(lazybearweek.org)*, sun-worshiping lesbians in May on

Women's Weekend *(womensweekendrussianriver.com)* and assorted San Francisco scenesters along for the ride. **Russian River Pride** *(russianriverpride.org)* kicks off in September.

Downtown Guerneville is a year-round destination, though, with cafes, indie-maker boutiques, fun casual dining and straight-friendly gay bars like **Rainbow Cattle Company** *(queersteer.com)*, the Guerneville go-to for decades. For a most sedate experience, try wine tasting for a cause at **Equality Vines** *(equalityvines.com; tastings $35)* where proceeds from the wines go toward organizations committed to equality for all.

Gay resorts (which are also typically straight-friendly) include Highlands Resort (p225) and R3 (p225), while the historic Fife's Resort is now Dawn Ranch (p225).

Floating or Paddling Down the River

Goof off with river otters

During summer and fall the absolute best thing to do on the Russian River is to float down it, on a tube or whatever inflatable you can find, with some friends and a flask in hand, passing posing herons. It'll cost you nothing (other than the price of your floaty).

Guerneville's **Johnson's Beach** *(johnsonsbeach.com; parking $10, tube/kayak/canoe rental per day $10/55/65)* is the epicenter of inner tubes, paddleboat rentals and beach concessions, with a campground and cabins to boot. There's also good river access east of Guerneville at **Sunset Beach** *(sonoma-county.org; day-use $12)*, plus sandy beaches and swimming holes downstream toward **Monte Rio Beach** *(mrrpd.org; canoe rental hr/½-day/day $30/45/65)*. You can also do a more organized float with **Burke's Canoe Trips** *(burkescanoetrips.com; canoe rental incl shuttle $95)*.

On summer weekends and holidays, **Regional Parks River Shuttle** *(parks.sonomacounty.ca.gov; day ticket adult/child $5/free)* runs from El Molino High School in Forestville and can drop you at **Steelhead Beach** and pick you up at Sunset Beach. Plan for at least four to five hours – the river is slow-moving – you'll have to do more paddling than you expect, and pack supplies (like drinking water). For picnic supplies, **Guerneville Bank Club** *(guernevillebankclub.com)* and **Piknik Town Market** *(pikniktownmarket.com)* make everything from avocado sandwiches to homemade ice cream. The small farmers market meets on Wednesday afternoons, and there's a Safeway in Guerneville.

In winter, the river can flood during heavy rains, and beach vendors close. But it's a fine time for watching osprey and blue heron ply the moody river mists from the shore.

WHY I LOVE SONOMA COUNTY

Alexis Averbuck, Lonely Planet writer

The final stretch of the Russian River winds by tiny Duncans Mills as the valley broadens out, edged by meadows. Then the terrain rolls into soft coastal hills that change color depending on the season, but there're always grazing cows enjoying the ocean breeze. The view opens wider still at the river's mouth, seals bouncing on the broad beach. It is perfect for a sunset cocktail at River's End restaurant with sheer cliffs and torquing rock towers stretching to either side and the Pacific sparkling in front. I also love to drive the Sonoma coast here, and throw in crab sandwiches at Bodega Bay's Spud Point Crab Company, or have a date night with my peachy husband at Terrapin Creek.

EATING IN GUERNEVILLE: OUR PICKS

Boon Eat + Drink: Tiny, always-packed bistro. Homegrown ingredients for hyperlocal flavor from the chef-owner's Boon Hotel. *4-8pm Wed-Sun* $$

Saucy Mama's: Po'boys, ribs, chicken and catfish at this welcoming southern soul-food place with lashings of sides, at California prices. *4-8pm Wed-Sun* $$

Guerneville Taco Truck: Lines queue for fantastic burritos, quesadillas and tacos. Spice lovers add diablo salsa and jalapeños. *11.30am-9pm* $

Farmhand: Kick back on the river-view deck with fat deli sandwiches or breakfasts (biscuits and gravy…avocado toast) made on the spot. *9am-4pm Fri-Wed* $

FROM 'STUMPTOWN' TO QUEER RESORT

Between the 1840s and 1870s, prospectors stripped the Russian River's redwoods, shipping them to San Francisco to build houses. Guerneville was nicknamed 'Stumptown' for the giant stumps that studded the landscape.

Nature made a comeback, and by the early 1900s there was a new boom: nature tourism. The railroads prospectors used to haul supplies were converted to hauling tourists, who came for cool summers. And a pioneering LGBTQ+ summer resort scene blossomed in Guerneville, still thriving today.

Meanwhile around neighboring Monte Rio, captains of industry, famous performers and US presidents frolicked nude at the secret, 2700-acre, all-male **Bohemian Grove** *(bohemianclub.com)*.

LEANNA RATHKELLY/GETTY IMAGES

Armstrong Redwoods State Natural Reserve

Old-Growth Redwoods

Walk in ancient groves

The oldest tree in Guerneville's magnificent 805-acre **Armstrong Redwoods State Natural Reserve** *(parks.ca.gov; per car $10)* is a true survivor: 309ft high, 1400 years old and named for a lumber baron. Colonel James Armstrong bought these woodlands in 1874 to log, but changed his mind when he saw the old-growth redwoods. Follow the well-maintained, wheelchair-accessible loop trail to take it in.

Famous Redwood Golf Course

Puttin' around in Northwood

Golfers should head to the bucket-list **Northwood Golf Club** *(northwoodgolf.com)*, a gorgeous vintage 1920s Alister MacKenzie–designed nine-hole course in the redwoods. It used to be the course for Bohemian Grove, which was connected by a walking bridge across the river. Now it's open to all. Just beside the course, the **Northwood Restaurant** *(northwoodbistro.com)* serves fabulous breakfasts and Bloody Marys, plus there's a patio beneath the redwoods and occasional live music and karaoke. Neighboring **Bia Cafe** *(facebook.com/BiaNorthwood)* rustles up delish breakfast sandwiches and espresso drinks.

DRINKING IN GUERNEVILLE: COCKTAILS, WINE & MUSIC

El Barrio: Kick back with Guerneville's best craft cocktails: classic mezcal margaritas, seasonal specials or Bloody Marias *4-9pm Wed-Sat, 11am-3pm Sun*

Trillium: Sip wine, beer and cider by the glass or in flights paired with fresh oysters, small plates and tasting boards. *1-9pm Fri & Sat, 5-7.30pm Sun-Tue*

Rio Nido Roadhouse: Bands rock the poolside stage at this kid-friendly roadhouse restaurant, 4 miles east of Guerneville. *noon-9pm Mon-Fri, from 10am Sat & Sun*

Main Street Bistro: Live music is the reason to come here for drinks. Food is pricey for what you get and service uneven. *3-11pm Mon-Thu, noon-midnight Fri-Sun*

Good Times with the Kids

From skate parks to flicks and festivals in Monte Rio

If you're looking for something to do with the kids on land, if you have bikes or skateboards with you, bounce over to **Monte Rio**, where they can hit the **Creekside Park Skate Park** *(mrrpd.org; free)* next to excellent **Lightwave Coffee & Kitchen**. You can also stretch your legs in the 2023-opened 515-acre **Monte Rio Redwoods Regional Park & Open Space Preserve** *(parks.sonomacounty.ca.gov; parking $7)*.

Check the schedule at the **Rio Theatre** *(monteriotheater.com)* to take them for a movie in a repurposed Quonset hut. And if you happen to be in town in June for RioFest *(friendsofmonterio.org)* and July for **Monte Rio Variety Show** *(monterioshow.org)*, they're both super kid-friendly.

Wine Tasting in the Russian River Valley

Idyllic wine road and a hidden winery

The Russian River Valley has become one of California's most distinctive and important wine appellations, and the highest concentration is along **Westside Rd**, between Guerneville and Healdsburg. Take this world-class country drive through redwood hills, sun-drenched vineyards and mossy oaks, even if you aren't a wine taster.

MacRostie *(macrostiewinery.com; tastings from $45)* is tops for gorgeous views and pinots regularly racking up high points from critics. At **Flowers**, *(flowerswinery.com; tastings from $75)* foodie bites and wine pair perfectly, like chardonnay and fennel-pollen-sprinkled *gougères*, and ridge-top pinot noir with black nori.

Step inside the 1930s toolshed at **Porter Creek** *(portercreek vineyards.com; tastings $30)* for sensational, sustainable pinot noir, syrah, viognier and chardonnay – casual wine tasting at its best.

Room for more? Hit the **Gary Farrell** *(garyfarrellwines.com; tastings from $55)*, **De La Montanya** *(dlmwine.com; tastings $30)* and **Rochioli** *(rochioliwinery.com; tastings $25)* vineyards.

One of the region's best hidden wineries is in the hills near Monte Rio: **Porter-Bass** *(porter-bass.com; tastings $25, waived with purchase)*, where mists swirl around redwoods and biodynamic vines yield outstanding vino, poured for you at a wood-plank bar under a walnut tree by the vintner herself, Sue Bass.

RUSSIAN RIVER VALLEY WINES

Nighttime coastal fog drifts up the Russian River Valley, then usually clears by midday. Pinot noir does beautifully here, as does chardonnay, which also grows in hotter regions, but prefers the longer 'hang time' of cooler climes.

Today there are 70-odd wineries spread across 15,000 acres, listed in the handy Russian River Wine Road map (*wineroad.com*). The highest concentration of wineries is along gorgeous Westside Rd, between Guerneville and Healdsburg. Prices are generally far more reasonable than over in Napa Valley.

Guerneville, Monte Rio, Healdsburg and Occidental are the most sensible bases for wine tasting in the Russian River Valley.

EATING IN MONTE RIO & DOWNRIVER: OUR PICKS

Lightwave Coffee & Kitchen: Fresh Mediterranean fare at a relaxed cafe with great coffee alongside the skate park in Monte Rio. *9am-3pm Wed-Mon* $$

Gold Coast Coffee & Bakery: Stop in Duncans Mills for pastries like gooey butterhorns or thin-crust pizza, plus occasional live local music. *7am-6pm* $

Café Aquatica: Jenner's waterfront cafe makes for lazy days sitting at the river-ocean confluence, coffee or crab roll in hand. *8am-4pm* $

River's End: Spectacular ocean views, old-school fully stocked bar and seasonal menus of local fare. Perfect date night. *5-9pm Fri-Tue* $$$

Healdsburg

CULINARY HOTSPOT | CHIC WINE-TASTING | CHEERFUL PLAZA

TOP TIP

Events take place across Alexander, Dry Creek and Russian River Valleys (check *wineroad.com*). **Healdsburg Chamber of Commerce** *(healdsburg.com)* and **Healdsburg Museum** *(healdsburgmuseum.org)*, covering Sonoma County life, offer a wealth of information.

Today Healdsburg has it all – looks, style, taste, plenty of money – but its history is a real-life telenovela. It began with forbidden romance, when rebellious SoCal ('Southern California') teenager Josefa Carrillo fell for wisecracking Massachusetts-born sea captain Henry Fitch. Josefa and Henry planned to homestead a 75-sq-mile ranch on leased Wappo land, but Henry died of pneumonia in 1849, leaving Josefa widowed at age 39, with 11 kids and a not-yet-working ranch. An uninvited guest named Harmon Heald squatted on the property until the US government auctioned it off to bidders, including Heald.

When the dust finally settled in 'Heald's-burg' in the 1860s, a Victorian village flourished around the town's sun-dappled square and ranchlands were planted, with farms and vineyards.

Nowadays Healdsburg is a gourmet magnet, with farm-inspired bistros and tasting rooms for nearby wineries. Or jump north to Alexander Valley and small-town Geyserville and Cloverdale, where country living embraces you in a sense of quiet escape.

GETTING AROUND

The center is easily walkable, and different walking paths crisscross town. Sonoma County Transit *(sctransit.com)* route 67 shuttles around Healdsburg, and bus 60 connects to Santa Rosa and Cloverdale. Some hotels offer shuttles from Sonoma County airport.

Parking *(ci.healdsburg.ca.us/872/Parking)* is easier and cheap or free once you get out of the plaza zone. Since 1976, **Spoke Folk Cyclery** *(spokefolk.com)* has been getting visitors to vineyards on rental bikes. Cycle along vineyard-lined West Dry Creek Rd or **Westside Rd** (p217), where California sunshine and valley mists produce wonderfully nuanced wines. Download bike maps from Spoke Folk or at *ci.healdsburg.ca.us*.

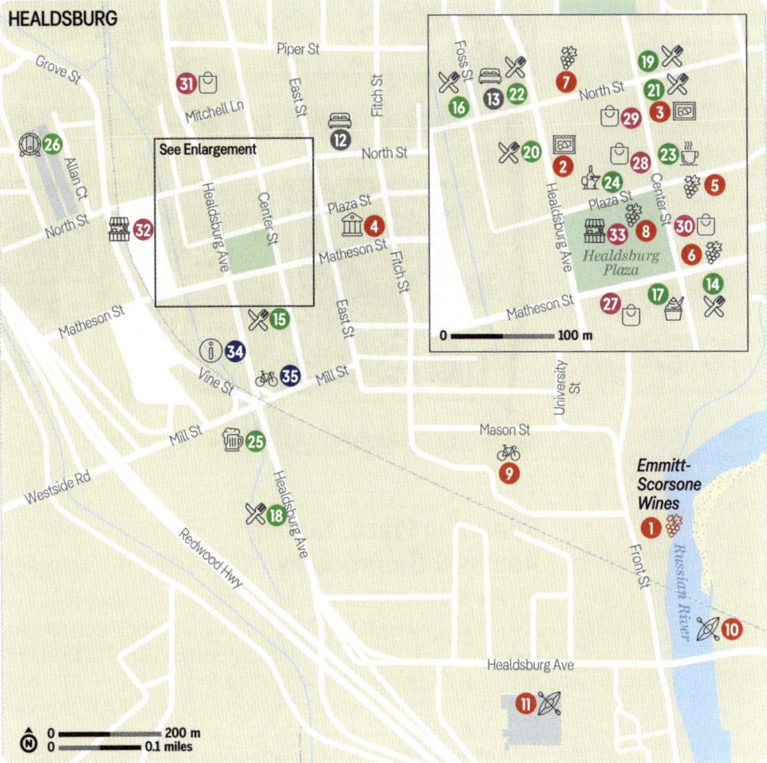

HIGHLIGHTS
1 Emmitt-Scorsone Wines

SIGHTS
2 Erickson Fine Art
3 Healdsburg Center For the Arts
4 Healdsburg Museum
5 Idlewild
6 Lioco
7 Portalupi
see 30 Upstairs Gallery
8 Wine Country Walking Tours

ACTIVITIES
9 Getaway Adventures/ Wine Country Bikes
10 River's Edge Kayak & Canoe Trips
11 Russian River Adventures

SLEEPING
12 Camellia Inn
13 Hotel les Mars

EATING
14 Acorn Cafe
15 Barndiva
16 Little Saint
17 Noble Folk Ice Cream & Pie Bar
18 Quail & Condor
19 SingleThread
20 Troubadour Bread & Bistro
21 Valette
22 Willi's Seafood & Raw Bar

DRINKING & NIGHTLIFE
23 Black Oak Coffee Roasters
24 Duke's Spirited Cocktails
25 Elephant in the Room
26 Young & Yonder

SHOPPING
27 Copperfield's Books
28 Gallery Lulo
29 Jam Jar
30 Levin & Co
31 Modern Antiquarium
32 Saturday Farmers Market
33 Tuesday Farmers Market on the Plaza

INFORMATION
34 Healdsburg Chamber of Commerce

TRANSPORTATION
35 Spoke Folk Cyclery

BEST ACTIVE EXCURSIONS

Getaway Adventures/Wine Country Bikes: From all-ages bike and wine tours to Russian River kayak/bike rides and excursions to the coast/Napa. *getawayadventures.com*

River's Edge Kayak & Canoe Trips: Paddle down Healdsburg's stretch of Russian River, or try stand-up paddleboarding. *riversedgekayakandcanoe.com*

Spoke Folk Cyclery: Rent cruisers, top-end road bikes, e-bikes. Download free ride maps on its site. *spokefolk.com*

Wine Country Walking Tours: Knowledgeable guides lead food and wine pairing tours through some of Healdsburg's best tasting rooms. *winecountrywalkingtours.com*

Russian River Adventures: Paddle on the river/e-bike the vineyards. *russianriveradventures.com*

DANIEL LANE NELSON/SHUTTERSTOCK

Portalupi

Sparkling Plaza, Tasting Rooms & Gastronomy

MAP P219

Parade of sensations

A stroll around Healdsburg's verdant central plaza, lined with cool boutiques, bookstores and tasting rooms will quickly reveal why it's regularly listed in top small towns in America. Central to its offerings are the excellent tasting rooms and farm-to-table fare: an epicure's delight.

Drink all along Northern California's coast from the comfort of your lounge seat at **Lioco** *(liocowine.com; tastings from $30)*, specialist in coastal chardonnays and pinot noirs. At **Idlewild** *(idlewildwines.com; tastings $30)* especially fascinating Piedmontese wines are quietly made by fourth-generation winemaker Sam Bilbro. Also of Italian origin, the wines at **Portalupi** *(portalupiwine.com; tastings from $20)* include unexpected sparkling barbera. The most difficult problem with eating in Healdsburg is choosing where to go. You can splash out on a gastronomic temple like **SingleThread** *(singlethreadfarms.com)*, where edible Sonoma landscape is the first of 11 sensational seasonal courses, ranging from vineyard 'cover crop' grains to forest-floor-foraged morel dashi – a tour de force of nature.

'Healdsburg-inspired' aptly describes Dustin and Aaron, the locally born brothers behind **Valette** *(valettehealdsburg.com)*, and the meals they share with friends and strangers alike. You might spot Dustin at Healdsburg Farmers Market, hauling a wagonful of produce destined for his menus.

Little Saint *(littlesainthealdsburg.com)*, with a delicious plant-based menu, lights up on its free music Thursdays. Any day, slurp ocean-fresh oysters with crisp white wines at **Willi's Seafood & Raw Bar** *(willisseafood.net)*. And what's not to love about **Noble Folk Ice Cream & Pie Bar** *(thenoblefolk.com)*? A dessert dream beyond ice cream – lemon-lavender cupcakes, brownie cubes and raspberry brown-butter macarons are tastier than they'll look on your social media.

Remarkable Produce & Live Music Market Days

MAP P219

Tuesday and Saturday certified farmers markets

On sunny Tuesdays from May to September, the **farmers market** *(healdsburgfarmersmarket.org)* on the Plaza begins with warm hellos from Sonoma County farmers and rolls into inspiring cooking demos and live music, plus seasonal events. Graze regional delicacies, such as Dry Creek peaches, steaming hot samosas, bean-to-bar chocolate, award-winning cheeses and organic Preston olive oil. You can also shop for unique handmade gifts. On Saturdays *(8.30am to 9pm, from April to December)* the **market** sets up in the West Plaza Parking Lot at North and Vine streets, one block west of the Plaza.

Browse Art, Antiques & More

MAP P219

Galleries, shops and bookstores

Healdsburg's center is dotted with crafty shops packed with creative wares and contemporary art galleries, such as **Healdsburg Center For the Arts** *(healdsburgcenterforthearts.org)*, **Erickson Fine Art** *(ericksonfineartgallery.com)*, **Jam Jar** *(jamjargoods.com)* and **Gallery Lulo** *(gallerylulo.com)*.

You probably guessed that Sonoma County barns are full of eccentric collectibles – and here's proof. Thirty local vendors share their obsessions...1930s kitchen canisters, space-themed barware...in 6700 sq ft of warehouse space at **Modern Antiquarium**.

Upstairs Gallery *(upstairsartgallery.net)* sits above family-owned old-school bookstore **Levin & Co** *(levinbooks.com)*. The sign of a healthy creative community? A whole second indie books store: **Copperfield's Books** *(copperfieldsbooks.com)*.

Crushing on Rural Wineries

MAP P222

Dry Creek Valley escape

Hemmed in by 2000ft-high mountains, **Dry Creek Valley** is relatively warm, ideal for sauvignon blanc and zinfandel,

BEST ENTERTAINMENT & FESTIVALS

Tuesdays in the Plaza Concerts: In summer, join **free Tuesday concerts**; food vendors from 5pm, music 6–8pm. *healdsburg.gov*

Farmers Market Concerts: Check website for what's playing at Tuesday's market. *healdsburgfarmersmarket.org*

Healdsburg Jazz Festival: In June, jazz venues include wine-tasting courtyard **Bacchus Landing** *(bacchuslanding.com)*. *healdsburgjazz.org*

Healdsburg Wine & Food Experience: In May, revel in local/international wine and farm-to-table food. *healdsburgwineandfood.com*

Wine & Food Affair: In November, 100 Sonoma County wineries offer a featured dish and wine pairing. *wineroad.com*

EATING & DRINKING IN HEALDSBURG: COOL BAKERIES & CAFES

MAP P219

Quail & Condor: Bakers from SingleThread make superb French-style pastries and bread, a perennial favorite. *8am-3pm Wed-Mon* $

Acorn Cafe: Stop in for coffee and breakfast or gourmet sandwiches, end up people-watching on the Plaza patio. *8am-3pm Mon-Fri, to 5pm Sat & Sun* $$

Troubadour Bread & Bistro: Classic boulangerie: sandwiches by day, pricey bistro with a set menu by night. *7am-4.30pm Tue-Sat, 8am-3pm Sun* $$$

Black Oak Coffee Roasters: Power up before wine tasting with fair-trade, house-roasted coffee made by those who know how. *7am-5pm* $

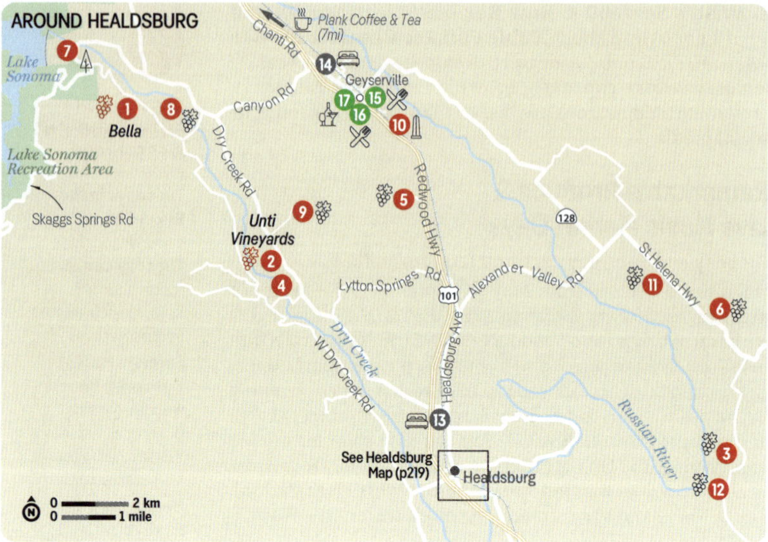

AROUND HEALDSBURG

HIGHLIGHTS
1 Bella
2 Unti Vineyards

SIGHTS
3 Carpenter Wine
4 Dry Creek Valley
5 Francis Ford Coppola Winery
6 Hanna
7 Lake Sonoma Recreation Area
8 Preston Farm & Winery
9 Reeve Wines
10 Sculpture Trail
11 Soda Rock Winery
12 Sutro Wine

SLEEPING
13 Best Western Dry Creek
14 Geyserville Inn

EATING
15 Cyrus
16 Diavola Pizza

DRINKING & NIGHTLIFE
17 Geyserville Gun Club

and in some places cabernet sauvignon. Roll down the valley's undulating country lane – one of Sonoma County's great back roads, ideal for cycling.

The caves at **Bella** *(www.bellawinery.com; tastings from $35)* are as pretty as the name suggests and are impressively hardworking, turning grapes from 105-year-old estate vines into prize zinfandels and syrah. From the tasting-room window at **Unti Vineyards** *(untivineyards.com; tastings $25, waived with bottle purchase)*, rolling vineyards look like sun-drenched Tuscan hills – and that's exactly what you'll taste in your wineglass: organically farmed Mediterranean noble grapes that thrive in these conditions. Dry Creek's best find is **Emmitt-Scorsone Wines** *(emmitt*

DRINKING IN HEALDSBURG: OUR PICKS

MAP P219

Elephant in the Room: Music takes center stage five nights a week at this rollicking pub, walkable to the center. Cover charge on weekends. *1pm-midnight*

Barndiva: Swing in for a predinner cocktail at the bar here, with original concoctions like the Guava Hermosa featuring hibiscus-infused tequila. *5-9pm Thu-Mon*

Young & Yonder: This hip distillery is turning some heads with its takes on absinthe, gin, vodka and bourbon. *2-7pm Fri, noon-7pm Sat, noon-5pm Sun*

Duke's Spirited Cocktails: Creative craft cocktails – once the drink kicks in, so does the dance floor. *4pm-11pm Mon-Thu, 2pm-2am Fri, noon-2am Sat & Sun*

scorsone.com; tastings $25), hidden on a back road, and it does its tastings in town. Upstart cult wine labels Judge Palmer and Domenica Amato are made here as well, you can picnic on-site, and walk-ins are welcome for some weekend hours.

Patio tastings at **Reeve Wines** *(reevewines.com; tastings $50)* let you admire the vineyards and sheep pastures as you sip poetry-inducing rosé of pinot noir and alluring single-vineyard sangiovese. **Preston Farm & Winery** *(prestonvineyards.com; tastings $35)* grows heirloom produce and raises livestock to support an integrated ecosystem – sheep handle weeding, and artichokes and radishes help with pest control. The farm store sells produce and olive oil, while the bar pours citrusy sauvignon blancs.

Geyserville's Wild West Vibes & Pools

MAP P222

Laid-back life and Coppola Winery

As Hwy 101 begins its long journey north from Healdsburg, the valley widens, with pastures and vineyards carpeting the way. Twelve minutes' drive north of Healdsburg, welcome to **Geyserville**, population 830. But where are the geysers? Wander the town's old wooden boardwalk, and you'll find Wild West character and a **sculpture trail**, but no sign of the geothermal wonders that initially attracted visitors in 1847. The hot springs are located underground, and produce 20% of California's renewable energy. To get into hot water, reserve a spot at the vast hilltop swimming pools at the **Francis Ford Coppola Winery** *(francisfordcoppolawinery.com; tastings from $35)*.

Boating, Fishing, Hiking & Biking

MAP P222

The pleasures of Lake Sonoma

A teal lake and wilderness preserve amid golden Sonoma foothills 20 minutes' drive north of Healdsburg, scenic **Lake Sonoma** is the heart of **Lake Sonoma Recreation Area** *(spn.usace.army.mil/Missions/Recreation/Lake-Sonoma)*. In 1983, the US Army Corps of Engineers built Warm Springs Dam for practical purposes, including flood control and irrigation – and the result was this sporting jackpot, with a lake for boating and fishing, miles of trails for hiking and biking, a hillside archery range and a fish hatchery that's helped restore Sonoma's once-endangered steelhead.

BEST ALEXANDER VALLEY WINERIES

Soda Rock Winery: Follow Hwy 128 to this tasting room for excellent California zinfandel. Walk-ins welcome. Down the road, Chalk Hill AVA vineyards flourish at indie, women-run wineries. *sodarockwinery.com*

Carpenter: Try velvety pinots under a sheltering oak with cofounder/sommelier Laura Carpenter Hawkes introducing natural wines with distinct personalities. *carpenterwine.com*

Sutro: Hike the vineyard with fifth-generation winemaker Alice Sutro for chardonnay and cabernets. *sutrowine.com*

Hanna: Taste sunny, rustic, estate-grown chardonnay, zinfandel and cabernet. Also has a vineyard near Sebastopol with tastings. *hannawinery.com*

EATING & DRINKING IN GEYSERVILLE: OUR PICKS

MAPS P219, 222

Cyrus: Who would expect this remote restaurant to have a Michelin star? Exquisite Sonoma County fusion in a modern glass room. *5-9pm Thu-Sun* $$$

Diavola Pizza: A contender for California's most perfectly crispy thin-crust, wood-fired pizza, with house-cured salumi and sausage. *11.30am-9pm* $$

Plank Coffee & Tea: House-roasted espresso drinks and an impressive 50 loose-leaf teas, plus homemade quiche and baked treats. *7am-2pm* $

Geyserville Gun Club: Cocktails and beers on tap meet sake and live music... delish food, too, at this small-town bar. *5-9.30pm Sun-Fri, to 11pm Sat* $$

Places We Love to Stay

$ Budget $$ Midrange $$$ Top End

Napa

MAP P169

Elm House Inn $$ Tidy rooms with generic furnishings in soft pastels a 15-minute walk to downtown. Hot tub.

Napa Winery Inn $$ Request a remodeled room at this good-value hotel north of downtown.

Hotel Indigo Napa Valley $$ Reasonable value, basic 2-story hotel on the suburban strip north of Napa.

Blackbird Inn $$$ Relax in a ruggedly handsome 1902 California Craftsman cottage with eight plush rooms.

Archer $$$ Live like a vintner who's just won Double Gold at downtown Napa's most happening hotel.

Milliken Creek Inn $$$ Understatedly elegant small-inn charm with boutique-hotel service and Napa indulgence.

Yountville

Maison Fleurie $$$ Rooms at this ivy-covered country inn are in a century-old home and carriage house, decorated in French-provincial style.

Petit Logis $$$ Wake to the aroma of croissants from next-door Bouchon Bakery.

Poetry Inn $$$ Contemporary inn with staggering views over Stag's Leap vineyards. Recite sonnets on your balcony.

North Block Hotel $$$ Both sup and stay over at trendy North Block in the village center.

St Helena

MAP P181

El Bonita Motel $$ Free up funds for vintage wines by staying at this affordable vintage motel.

Wydown Hotel $$$ Historic inn redone by a contemporary art collector, with smart rooms and savvy staff.

Harvest Inn $$$ Get in touch with nature at this wooded wine estate, with Tudor-timbered lodges, stone-pillared bungalows, and cedar-shingled cabins.

Calistoga

Bothe-Napa Valley State Park Ritchey Creek Campground $ Wake up in the redwoods, canvas-sided yurt or restored historic cabin.

Aurora Park Cottages $$ This quiet row of sunny yellow immaculate cottages sits back from Calistoga's main road amid trees and flower gardens.

Wine Way Inn $$ This small B&B, set in a 1910-era arts-and-crafts-style house close to the road, has friendly owners.

Meadowlark Country House $$$ Ranch on 20 lush acres with clothing-optional wellness area: hot tub, sauna and pool.

Brannan Cottage Inn $$$ Stay in the iconic 1862 gingerbread cottage of Samuel Brannan, the hustler/entrepreneur who founded Calistoga.

Sonoma Town

MAP P189

Sonoma Creek Inn $ Quirky 16-room motel with retro-Americana decor, including vintage California travel posters and postcard lamps.

Cinnamon Bear Creekside Inn $$ Decent value proposition close enough to the plaza that you could walk.

An Inn 2 Remember $$ Steps from the plaza, this vintage 1910 charmer offers warm welcomes and comfortable lodgings.

Cottage Inn & Spa $$$ Private patios for morning pastries, with a tinkling fountain and on-site spa. What's not to love?

Sonoma Valley

Sugarloaf Ridge State Park Camping $ Lovely hilltop campground near Kenwood, with 48 drive-in sites, clean coin-operated showers.

Glen Ellen Inn & Martini Bar $$ Have a stiff martini then hit the sheets at these welcoming cottages and inn.

Jack London Lodge $$ Sprawl in a spacious, well-kept room with big comfy beds at this mod motel with a pool and hot tub.

Beltane Ranch $$$ African American millionaire civil-rights pioneer Mary Ellen Pleasant built this beautiful ranch in 1892.

Olea Hotel $$$ Relax in impeccable luxury in the oak-blanketed hills of Glen Ellen.

Petaluma to Santa Rosa

MAP P198

Hotel E $ Beaux-arts beauty with signature clocktower on Santa Rosa's Old Courthouse Sq.

Spring Lake Regional Park Campground $ Santa Rosa's 72-acre reservoir, 10 miles of hiking trails, and campsites in the shade of oaks.

Hampton Inn Petaluma $ This boutique-style offering in the gorgeous 1892 Petaluma silk mill is the hippest Hampton Inn you'll ever see.

Gables Wine Country Inn $$$ Friendly Victorian-home B&B draped in antique luxury, with brilliant breakfasts and a verdant spread.

Sebastopol & Occidental

MAP P202

Fairfield Inn & Suites $ Modern farmhouse styling makes this Sebastopol Marriott (the only hotel in town) better than typical chains.

Inn at Occidental $$ Escape the ordinary at this 16-room Victorian inn with heirloom quilts for getting cozy in the redwoods.

Bodega Bay & Coast

Wright's Beach Campground $ Best of the Sonoma Coast State Park, because sites one to 10 are right on the beach. Book well ahead.

Salt Point State Park Campgrounds $ Two campgrounds, convenient for tide-pooling, have sites with cold water. Inland Woodside is protected by Monterey pines.

Bodega Dunes Campground $ The largest campground in the Sonoma Coast State Park with close to 100 sites in high dunes.

Bodega Harbor Inn $ Half a block inland from Hwy 1, this modest, agreeable blue-and-white shingled motel is the town's most economical option.

River's End Inn $$$ Ocean-view cottages have no cell service but do have wi-fi. Many come with fireplaces, decks and breathtaking views.

Timber Cove Resort $$$ Dramatic '60s-modern bluff-top inn refurbished into a luxury lodge. Tinkling piano and crackling fireplace fill the a vast lobby.

Sea Ranch Beach Rentals $$$ Rents out vacation homes exclusively at the Sea Ranch development.

Russian River Valley

MAP P214

Schoolhouse Canyon Campground $ Redwood grove two miles east of Guerneville with well-tended campsites across the road from the river.

Highlands Resort $$ Mellow out in the redwoods at Guerneville's most relaxed LGBTQ+ and straight-friendly resort. Adults only.

R3 Hotel $$ Ground zero for party-all-day LGBTQ+ crowd, Triple R (as it's known) has standard motel-style rooms surrounding a happening bar and pool deck.

Mine + Farm $$$ Modern B&B in a 1906 farmhouse next to Korbel Vineyards and near Sunset Beach.

Boon Hotel + Spa $$$ Sleek retreat, walking/biking distance to Guerneville and Armstrong Woods; 14 spacious rooms feature fireplaces.

Dawn Ranch $$$ Riverside century-old whitewashed cottages let you drift off to the shushing wind in the trees.

Healdsburg & Geyserville

MAP P219

Best Western Dry Creek $ This generic motel has good service and a hot tub. Price is the reason to stay.

Geyserville Inn $ Amid Alexander Valley vineyards walking distance from Geyserville. Request a deluxe room with balcony or fireplace. Pool and hot tub.

Hotel les Mars $$$ Spacious guest rooms have four-poster beds you might find hard to leave, until breakfast arrives at your door.

Camellia Inn $$$ Cheery pink 1871 mansion, with camellia-filled gardens, sociable parlors and upbeat, helpful innkeepers.

JAMES KIRKIKIS/SHUTTERSTOCK

El Bonita Motel

Researched by
Amelia Mularz

North Coast & Redwoods

PEEK BEHIND THE REDWOOD CURTAIN

On California's northernmost coast, curiosity is rewarded with unspoiled beaches, old-world architecture and the world's tallest trees.

Wild is the word that constantly springs to mind when visiting the North Coast. The beaches – hundreds of miles of dune-dotted and driftwood-strewn sand – are notably untamed. Fern- and moss-covered canyons require that visitors play by their rules if they want to have a look (like wading through a creek, as is the case at Fern Canyon in Prairie Creek Redwoods State Park). The forests, often referred to as 'the redwood curtain' because the trees grow so tall and dense, will bring out your wildest urges to hike further, to ascend higher (like taking a canopy-grazing gondola ride at the Trees of Mystery in Klamath) and see more. Then there's the wildlife: the Roosevelt elk you'll catch casually grazing, the elephant seals lazing by a Lost Coast lighthouse and the roughly 330 species of birds that touch down at Arcata Marsh and Wildlife Sanctuary.

Locals here are pretty wild, too. In Eureka, they've preserved a town's worth of Victorian-era architecture and simultaneously pushed the drive-thru experience into the 21st century, offering a way to get your morning java and a joint on the go. But the wildest part of this region is how often you'll find yourself blissfully alone. It's common to pause at one of the state's most awe-inspiring lookout points and realize you have it all to yourself. In those moments you're likely to think, 'Wow, now *that's* wild.'

THE MAIN AREAS

For places to stay in North Coast & Redwoods, see p274

PAOLO TRALLI/SHUTTERSTOCK

Left: Wooden sculpture, Trees of Mystery (p267); Above: Humboldt Redwoods State Park (p254)

Find Your Way

Because the region has hundreds of miles of coastline, tens of thousands of acres of redwoods and vast swaths of vineyards, you could close your eyes, point to any spot on the map and find breathtaking beauty.

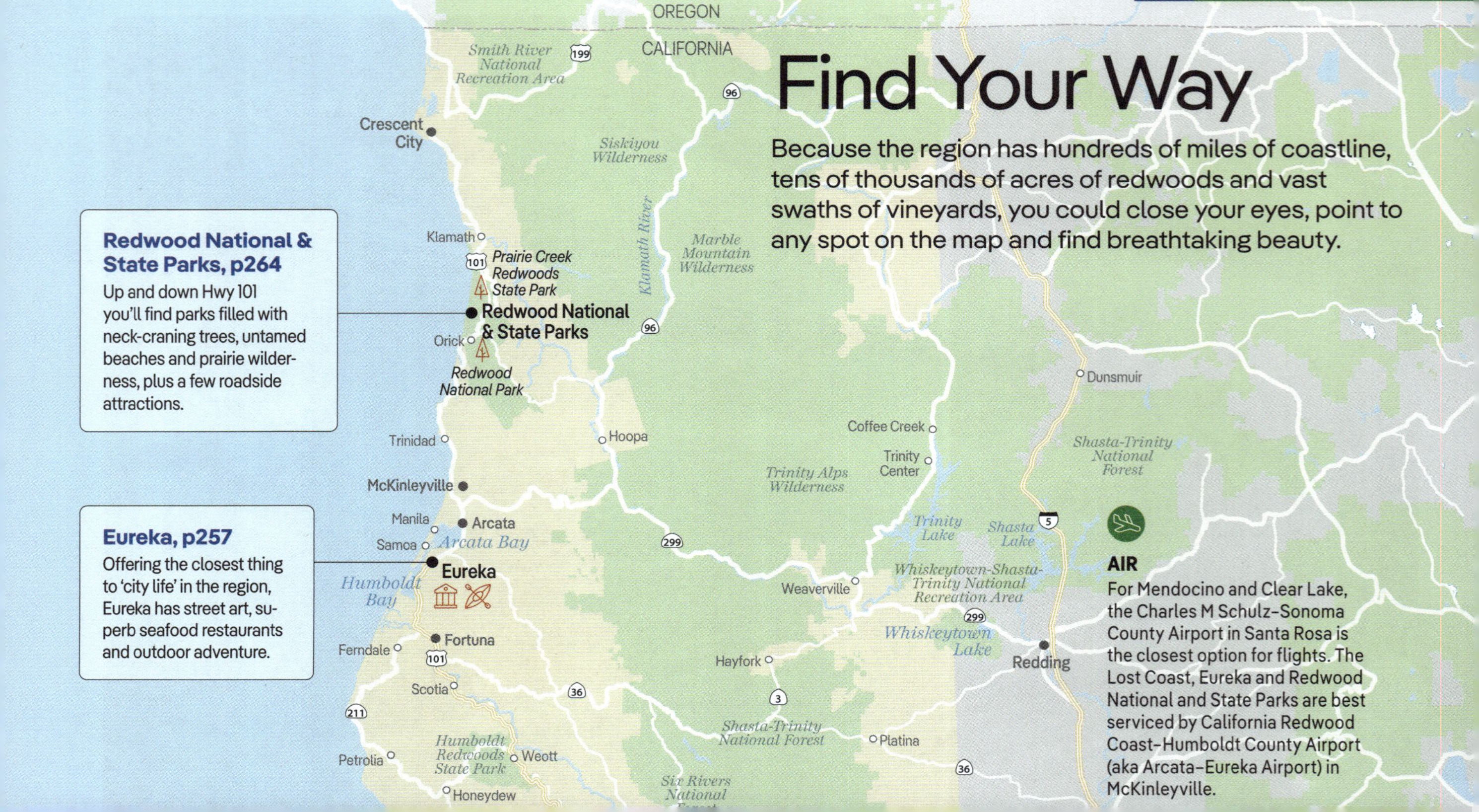

Redwood National & State Parks, p264

Up and down Hwy 101 you'll find parks filled with neck-craning trees, untamed beaches and prairie wilderness, plus a few roadside attractions.

Eureka, p257

Offering the closest thing to 'city life' in the region, Eureka has street art, superb seafood restaurants and outdoor adventure.

AIR

For Mendocino and Clear Lake, the Charles M Schulz–Sonoma County Airport in Santa Rosa is the closest option for flights. The Lost Coast, Eureka and Redwood National and State Parks are best serviced by California Redwood Coast–Humboldt County Airport (aka Arcata–Eureka Airport) in McKinleyville.

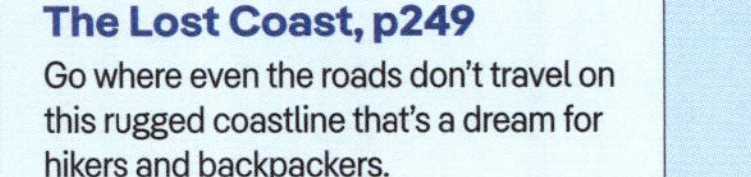

The Lost Coast, p249

Go where even the roads don't travel on this rugged coastline that's a dream for hikers and backpackers.

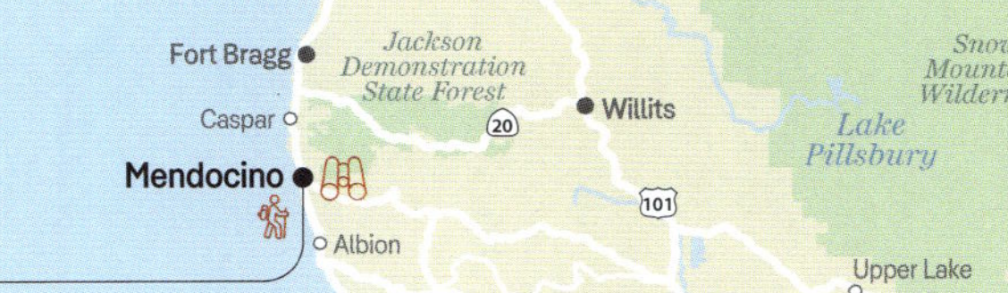

Mendocino, p232

This historic seaside village, dotted with distinctive water towers, is an ideal base for coastal strolls with a side of gallery hopping.

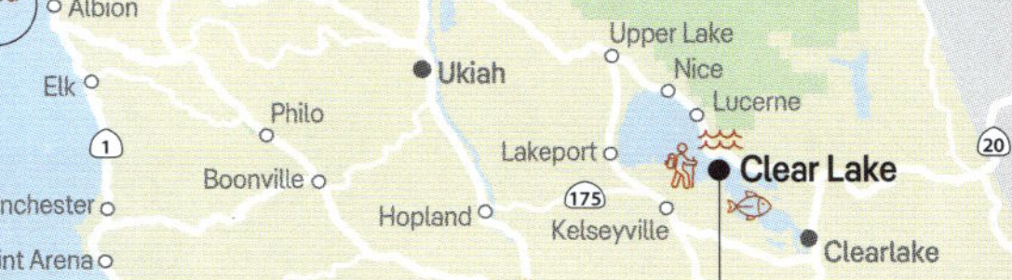

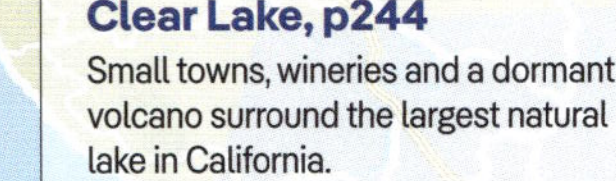

Clear Lake, p244

Small towns, wineries and a dormant volcano surround the largest natural lake in California.

BUS

Those willing to piece together bus travel through the region will face a time-consuming headache, but connections are possible to most towns. Companies include Greyhound, the Mendocino Transit Authority, the Redwood Transit System and Redwood Coast Transit.

CAR

You'll almost certainly need a car to explore this region. Those headed to the far north should take Hwy 101, the faster inland route, then cut over to the coast. Hwy 1 hugs the coast, then cuts inland and joins Hwy 101 at Leggett.

Plan Your Time

Whatever your time constraints, the North Coast is your oyster. Here's how to make the most of your time hiking, paddling, sipping, and oohing and aahing.

GEARTOOTH PRODUCTIONS/SHUTTERSTOCK

Beach, Lost Coast Trail (p252)

You've Got a Weekend

- If you've only got a weekend, hightail it to **Mendocino** (p232), which puts the region's best foot forward. Drive up Hwy 101 and cut through **Anderson Valley** (p242), where travelers can sip excellent wine. Stroll the gorgeous bluff along the **Mendocino Headlands Trail** (p232), dine at one of the many exquisite restaurants and stay in a historic **water tower** (p235).

- The next day, paddle a redwood canoe up **Big River** (p235) and check out the local **art galleries** (p236). Take the long way home on scenic roads, stopping for secluded coves, quiet coastal parks and the majestic **Point Arena Lighthouse** (p240).

Seasonal Highlights

Spring is lovely on the North Coast, as weather warms and wildflowers start to pop. Coastal fog dominates in summertime, harvest is big in the fall and winter is quiet and cozy.

JANUARY

Prime time to spot migrating whales, colonies of elephant seals, monarch butterflies in the trees and hundreds of bird species along the Pacific Flyway.

APRIL

The **Lost Coast** (p249) is covered in wildflowers, including California poppies, lupines and Douglas irises. Low tide, aka peak tidepooling time in **Shelter Cove** (p251) is conveniently midday.

MAY

It's festival season. The **Murder, She Wrote Festival** (p237) comes to Mendocino, the **Pinot Noir Festival** happens in Anderson Valley and the quirky **Kinetic Grand Championship** (p261) hits Eureka.

Your OOO Is Set

- With a week you have time to hike the entire **Lost Coast Trail** (p252), plus tack on a few days for additional exploring (or indulgent recovery). The trail takes two to four days, depending on direction and tidal timing, and includes coastal camping.

- If you're heading south, stick around the end point in **Shelter Cove** (p249) for a couple days and book an oceanfront room with a hot tub. Spend at least one afternoon inland driving the mighty **Avenue of the Giants** (p254), and consider a night in **Ferndale** (p256), California's quaintest town. Shop Ferndale's charming Main St and admire the town's butterfat palaces, perfectly preserved Victorian buildings.

You'll Be Sure to Write

- Eureka! You have discovered a way to escape daily life for over a week and you'll be rewarded with redwoods galore. Start in the town of **Eureka** (p257), easily accessed via the California Redwood Coast–Humboldt County Airport, and spend a couple days **kayaking** (p261) the historic harbor, taking in the **Victorian architecture** (p260) and popping over to Arcata to go **thrifting on the plaza** (p262).

- Head north to hunt for agates on the beach in **Sue-meg State Park** (p272), then check in at a B&B in Trinidad and hike the dramatic **headlands** (p270). Further north, you'll hit **Redwood National & State Parks** (p264), where you'll find days worth of hiking and plenty of opportunities to hang out with the world's tallest trees.

JULY

The **Mendocino Music Festival** (p237), the town's most exciting event of the year, takes place. **Fourth of July** is also a great time to visit, with a parade and lots of live jazz.

AUGUST

Cultural demonstrations, a 5K run, live music and good eats are all part of the fishy fun at the **Klamath Salmon Festival** (p266).

OCTOBER

The **wine regions** celebrate their harvest with food-and-wine shindigs, grape-stomping 'crush' parties and barrel tastings. Some events start in September.

NOVEMBER

In Fort Bragg, the Skunk transforms into the **Mushroom, Whisky and Wine Train** (p240). Rain and fog envelop the coast, and having a wood-burning stove becomes super cozy.

Mendocino

WILD BEACHES | RESTAURANTS | HISTORIC TOWN

GETTING AROUND

Mendocino Village is small and entirely walkable, and you can easily stroll to the Mendocino Headlands from town. But to get to other state parks and area attractions, you'll want a car. If you're flying in, Charles M Schulz–Sonoma County Airport in Santa Rosa is the closest; it's just over a two-hour drive. If you're comfortable going car-free, Mendocino Transit Authority does have a direct bus from the airport to Mendocino once a day.

TOP TIP

Many of the shops, galleries and restaurants in town close for a day or two midweek. Plan your hikes and outdoor activities for those days and save shopping and fine dining for weekends.

A number of North Coast cities have a logging past, but consider Mendocino the connoisseur's historic timber town. Transplants from New England founded the village and lumber mill in 1852, bringing with them architectural influences that can still be seen in the area's Victorian buildings. The logging industry thrived through the turn of the century, but when the mill closed in the 1930s both the town's population and economic stability took a hit. Things turned around with the establishment of the Mendocino Art Center in 1959, revitalizing the town and infusing it with the artistic charm that's now as much a part of its makeup as its logging past. Today, tourism is Mendocino's main industry, and though its population hovers only in the hundreds, nearly 2 million travelers make a pilgrimage each year to shop its exquisite art galleries, dine at its top-tier restaurants and marvel at the views from atop the Pacific-kissed bluffs.

Timber Town Time Machine

Step inside an 1860s house

To get up close and personal with life in a 19th-century logging town – as in peeping at the kinds of products kept in medicine cabinets during the era – head to the **Kelley House Museum** *(kelleyhousemuseum.org; suggested $5 donation)*. William Kelley, a businessman who once owned almost all the land that would become Mendocino, built this historic house in 1861. Today, visitors can wander its bedrooms and see period furnishings and personal effects.

A Diamond in the Bluff

Stroll an extraordinary oceanside trail

If hiking trails were judged by ocean views, the path at **Mendocino Headlands State Park** *(parks.ca.gov; free)* would score an uncontested 10/10. For over two miles in one direction,

SIGHTS
1 Kelley House Museum
2 Mendocino Art Center
3 Mendocino Presbyterian Church
4 Partners Gallery
5 Prentice Gallery
6 The Highlight Gallery

ACTIVITIES
7 Mendocino Headlands State Park

SLEEPING
8 JD House
9 Joshua Grindle Inn
10 MacCallum House
11 Mendocino Hotel and Garden Suites
12 Sweetwater Inn & Spa

EATING
13 Café Beaujolais
14 Flow Restaurant & Lounge
15 Fog Eater Cafe
16 Frankie's
17 Gnar Bar
18 GoodLife Cafe & Bakery
19 Luna Trattoria
20 Mendocino Cafe
21 Patterson's Pub
22 Trillium Cafe

DRINKING & NIGHTLIFE
23 Dick's Place
24 Fog Bottle Shop and Wine Bar
25 MendoVino

SHOPPING
26 Astoria Home Decor & Gifts
27 Gallery Bookshop & Bullwinkle's Children's Books
28 Mendocino Gems
29 Mendocino Jams & Preserves
30 Out of This World
31 Slug Sister Vintage
32 The Study Club

WRECK OF THE FROLIC

In 1850, a ship retired from the opium trade – the *Frolic* – struck a reef near Point Cabrillo (p236), about 3 miles north of Mendocino, and ran aground. Jerome Ford, who came from San Francisco to salvage the cargo, was too late as the Native Pomo had already recovered the Chinese luxury goods onboard. But Ford took notice of the coast's real treasure: the enormous redwoods. He teamed up with entrepreneur Henry Meiggs, who bought a sawmill and had it transported to Big River. During the mill's 50-year run, it produced a billion board feet of timber, which was used to build San Francisco – and then rebuild it after the 1906 earthquake.

MICHAEL VI/SHUTTERSTOCK

Mendocino Presbyterian Church

the trail follows the edge of 70-foot bluffs, meandering through wildflowers on land and past rock formations and dramatic arches in the water. Because the park surrounds the village of Mendocino on three sides, there's plenty of parking near the town's shops and restaurants; the trail is just a short walk away. You'll also find parking areas at several points along the path, meaning you can drop in on those sections without walking the whole thing. If you'd like to hike the full length from east to west, start at **Mendocino Presbyterian Church**, a California Historical Landmark on Church St. The immaculately preserved English Gothic church dates back to 1867 and is built from native redwood, milled right in Mendocino. Or, hike west to east and finish at **Big River Beach**, accessible by way of a staircase down a bluff trail near the church. Cap off the adventure with an oceanside picnic, or simply check out the driftwood that washes up onto the white sand. Depending on the tides, you may even be able to wade out to a sandbar off the shore.

EATING IN MENDOCINO: OUR PICKS

GoodLife Cafe & Bakery: Start the day with a blackberry danish or biscuits smothered in sausage gravy – this really is the good life. *7.30am-2pm* $

Mendocino Cafe: The eclectic menu at this lunch and dinner spot includes a Thai burrito, Indian masala curry and locally caught rockfish. *11am-4pm & 5-9pm* $$

Trillium Cafe: Stop by for fine dining focused on organic seasonal ingredients or order a picnic basket to go. *11.30am-2:15pm & 5-8.30pm Fri-Tue* $$$

Fog Eater Cafe: This cozy vegetarian spot serves southern-inspired recipes for dinner and a full brunch menu on Sundays. *4-8pm Wed-Sat, 10am-2pm Sun* $$

Water (Tower) World

Get to know the town's signature structures

Take one look around Mendocino Village and you'll see why it earned the nickname 'town of water towers.' While about 30 of these elevated tanks still remain, the town once had over 100 of them. Built in the late 19th century, the water towers collected and stored rainwater for year-round use, as the town didn't have a central water system. Get to know a number of these structures on a two-hour water-tower walking tour hosted by a docent from the Kelley House Museum (p232). To step inside one – and simultaneously browse for retro clothes – head to **Slug Sister Vintage** *(slugsistervintage.com)*, located inside a charmingly petite tower. Or you can have a meal at **Flow Restaurant & Lounge** *(mendocinoflow.com)*, which requires climbing the water-tower stairs to reach its 2nd-floor entrance. It's highly recommended for its ocean views.

Finally, if it's R&R in a reservoir that you're after, book an overnight stay. **Joshua Grindle Inn** *(joshuagrindlemendocino.com)*, **Sweetwater Inn & Spa** *(sweetwaterspa.com)*, **MacCallum House** *(maccallumhouse.com)* and **JD House** *(innsofmendocino.com)* all have rooms located in water towers.

Big Adventure on Big River

Paddle a redwood outrigger

Catch a Canoe & Bicycles, Too *(catchacanoe.com)*, located on the Big River at **Stanford Inn** *(stanfordinn.com)*, isn't your average boat-rental business. Sure, they have basic kayaks to borrow, but they really specialize in locally made redwood outriggers. These water craft – which draw inspiration from the redwood vessels made by Native tribes – are steadier and easier to steer (thanks to a foot-controlled rudder system) than common canoes. Rent one for three hours *(adult/child $60/30 per person)* or the whole day *(adult/child $90/45 per person)*. Outriggers can accommodate two to six people, and one design, the Canine Cruiser, is even geared toward pups who want to join for an afternoon of paddling. Additionally, a Catalina Catamaran Canoe fits up to 10 people, with two connected, side-by-side vessels, so you can bring your whole party to the river.

MENDOCINO'S BEST SHOPS

Gallery Bookshop & Bullwinkle's Children's Books: Snag a bestseller, an outdoor guide or a title from a California small press.

The Study Club: Embrace your coastal fantasy life with high-end knitwear, homegoods and beauty products.

Out of This World: Birders, astronomy buffs and science geeks head directly to this binocular, telescope and science-toy shop.

Astoria Home Decor & Gifts: Follow the brick path to this charming boutique stocked with floral fragrances, candles and locally made charcuterie boards.

Mendocino Jams & Preserves: Here's your chance to slip something sweet into your suitcase, like a jar of small-batch wild blackberry jam.

EATING IN MENDOCINO: OUR PICKS

Frankie's: For a casual bite, family-owned Frankie's is the place for falafel, salads and pizza (gluten-free options available). Ice cream too. *11am-8pm Tue-Sun* **$**

Gnar Bar: Get grab-and-go poke, sushi rolls and dumplings at this convenient corner spot. You can even order online. *11am-6pm Wed-Mon* **$$**

Luna Trattoria: Northern Italian cuisine meets the North Coast at this dinner spot with outdoor seating in a charming garden. *5-9pm Tue-Sun* **$$$**

Café Beaujolais: Set in an 1893 Victorian farmhouse, the Café serves French-California dinners and Sunday brunch. *5-9pm Wed-Sat, 9.30am-12.30pm Sun* **$$$**

MURDER, SHE WROTE

Fans of the TV show, which ran for 12 seasons from 1984 to 1996, may spot some familiar sights in Mendocino, which often served as the real-life backdrop for the show's fictional (and crime-riddled) town known as Cabot Cove, Maine. Angela Lansbury, who played the show's protagonist, the mystery writer and amateur sleuth Jessica Fletcher, said that it was more cost effective to shoot in Mendocino rather than in rural Maine.

Blair House, an 1888 Victorian inn on Little Lake St that still welcomes overnight guests, served as the exterior of Fletcher's home. Lansbury also filmed various outdoor scenes around town, including cycling on Ukiah St and chatting with another character on a bluff at Mendocino Headlands State Park.

A Hub for the Arts

Go gallery hopping

Make a pilgrimage to the place that turned this lumber town into an artist enclave: the **Mendocino Art Center** *(mendocinoartcenter.org)*. Visitors are welcome to drop in and wander its gallery, filled with works from local artists, for free from Thursday through Sunday. Don't miss the gift shop, where ceramics, jewelry and T-shirts are for sale. If you'd like to get in on the crafting action, check out the center's calendar for workshops that take place on a single day or over a weekend. Past classes have included throwing large pots on the wheel, punch-needle rug hooking for beginners and screen printing with natural dyes.

If you still haven't scratched your artistic itch, stop by some of the other galleries in town. **The Highlight Gallery** *(thehighlightgallery.com)* has two stories of paintings, ceramics, jewelry and handcrafted wood furniture, while **Mendocino Gems** *(mendocinogems.com)* focuses entirely on jewelry, representing local artisans in addition to featuring their own creations made from precious metals and stones. The smaller yet superbly curated collection at **Partners Gallery** *(partnersgallery.com)* is usually centered around a theme that changes monthly. And speaking of small, if you have limited space in your suitcase but would love to bring home original art to commemorate your time on the coast, **Prentice Gallery** *(prenticefineart.com)* has an impressive array of miniature acrylic-on-canvas paintings.

A Legendary Lens

Take a stroll to Point Cabrillo Light Station

Watch for whales, step inside a historical home, and learn about a lighthouse that's been guiding ships since 1909. It's all at the **Point Cabrillo Light Station State Historic Park** *(pointcabrillo.org; suggested $5 donation)*. The adventure begins on the half-mile stroll from the parking lot to the lighthouse (handicapped parking is available closer to the Light Station in front of the residences). The paved path is lined with whale trivia to get you hyped for the plumes of mist you might see offshore, especially between December and April. Eventually, you'll pass a residence on your right that once served as housing for first assistant lighthouse keepers. Today, it's a museum *(11am-4pm)* with interiors restored to their 1930s glory, so head in for a self-guided tour. You'll also pass

DRINKING IN MENDOCINO: OUR PICKS

Fog Bottle Shop and Wine Bar: A sister spot to Fog Eater Cafe, this cozy cantina offers wine flights, bottles to go and nibbles. *noon-7pm Wed-Sun*

Dick's Place: For nearly a century, this beloved dive bar has toasted tourists and locals alike – just be sure to have cash on hand. *11.30am-2am*

Patterson's Pub: Here's an Irish-style watering hole with almost as many beers on tap as there are water towers in Mendocino. *11am-11pm*

MendoVino: Sample Anderson Valley pinot noirs, sauvignon blancs and chardonnays without leaving town. Flights, glasses and bottles available. *11am-5pm*

LUCKY-PHOTOGRAPHER/SHUTTERSTOCK

Point Cabrillo Light Station

the homes for the head lightkeeper and the second assistant lightkeeper plus a couple cottages – all of these are available for overnight stays from $158 per night. Past the residences is the Marine Science Exhibit, a kid-friendly pitstop with aquariums of tiny marine organisms. Next, you'll reach the lighthouse, which triples as a museum and gift shop. After you've learned about the point's original keepers – the Native Pomo people – head out to the trails along the bluffs and keep your eyes peeled for marine wildlife.

Walk Among Waterfalls

Check out Russian Gulch State Park

The **Fern Canyon Trail** in **Russian Gulch State Park** *(parks.ca.gov; per vehicle $8)*, about three miles north of Mendocino Village, offers a scenic payoff for a relatively low lift from your hiking boots. Follow a flat, 2-mile trail along Russian Gulch Creek until you reach a fork in the road. Head left and it's only about three-quarters of a mile to a 36-foot waterfall. Feeling ambitious? Take the right fork, which is the Falls Loop Trail, and you'll get an additional 1.6 miles of lush forest hiking and eventually end up at the same waterfall.

TOP MENDOCINO FESTIVALS

Mendocino Whale Festival: Come for the whales, stay for the wine. During peak migration in early March, tastings give wildlife watchers another reason to visit.

Murder, She Wrote Festival: Each May, devotees of the TV series converge on Mendocino for walking tours, tea receptions and trivia.

Mendocino Film Festival: Usually spanning a weekend in late May and early June, this event celebrates cinema with dozens of screenings plus live music.

Fourth of July: Independence Day includes a parade plus live jazz on the lawn at the Mendocino Art Center.

Mendocino Music Festival: In July, catch the sounds of bluegrass, big band and Americana with concerts on the coast.

Beyond Mendocino

Tiny towns and big flavor, including plenty of wine, can be found within minutes of Mendocino.

Places

GETTING AROUND

Exploring the area around Mendocino means driving both north and south on Hwy 1, where cell service is limited and rideshare services are even more scarce. You'll need a car. Give yourself plenty of time to reach your destination, as construction can turn stretches of the highway into a one-lane road. There's a good chance you'll stop along the way to take in the coastal views.

As you pull away from Mendocino, you might think you're leaving all the action behind, but you'd be mistaken. Within a few minutes you'll hit Little River, home to the lush Van Damme State Park, followed by art-filled and Michelin-celebrated Elk just a bit further south. North of Mendocino, Fort Bragg is a fun day trip for families, especially little ones obsessed with trains, as well as for anyone who wants to feast their eyes on the astoundingly beautiful Mendocino Coast Botanical Gardens. Inland, there's Anderson Valley, a cool-climate wine appellation known for its award-winning pinot noir and chardonnay. If you're flying out of Sonoma County Airport in Santa Rosa, a stop in Anderson Valley makes sense. You'll pass a number of the area's wineries right on Hwy 29, which is on your way.

Little River

TIME FROM MENDOCINO: **10 MINS**

A Pygmy Forest for all

One of the most accessible hiking trails in Mendocino County is also one of its most unique. The **Pygmy Forest Trail** at **Van Damme State Park** *(parks.ca.gov; per vehicle $10)* is a quarter-mile loop built on a wheelchair-accessible boardwalk over swampy surroundings. You'll see dwarf manzanita, rhododendron, bishop pine and Mendocino cypress, among other petite plants. The area's nutrient-starved soil is the reason for their stunted growth. To head directly to the Pygmy Forest Trail, don't enter through the park's main entrance. Instead, head south on Hwy 1 and take the first left onto Little River Airport Road. In about three miles, you'll see a sign for the parking lot on your left.

For a longer hike, head through the park's main entrance to the **Fern Canyon Trail**, a 5.6-mile round-trip route. Grab a brochure from a box at the beginning of the trail for a self-guided tour that introduces area flora and fauna along the first mile of the path. Afterward, head across Hwy 1 to the exceptionally scenic **Van Damme Beach**, where there's parking, bathrooms and oceanfront lounging.

R ALAN MEYER/SHUTTERSTOCK

Pygmy Forest Trail

Elk

TIME FROM MENDOCINO: **30 MINS**

Michelin-starred dining

In the tiny coastal town of Elk, where the population doesn't even top 300, you can get a meal at a Michelin-starred restaurant. The 20-seat ocean-view restaurant at the **Harbor House Inn** *(theharborhouseinn.com)*, helmed by chef Matthew Kammerer, has earned an impressive two Michelin stars. The lunch and dinner tasting menus change daily, but always focus on hyperlocal ingredients. Make a reservation well in advance, as a table here is one of the hottest for over a hundred miles.

Manchester

TIME FROM MENDOCINO: **45 MINS**

Go horseback riding on the beach

The only thing better than a stroll on a wild Mendocino beach is a horseback ride on a wild Mendocino beach. **Ross Ranch** *(rossranch.biz; rides $70 per person)* leads tours on Manchester Beach and makes the logistics a breeze. Owner Tobi Ross will likely be your guide and is quick to respond to reservation requests. She'll lead you on a 90-minute ride on an unspoiled beach and even volunteer to snap photos of your group on your trusty steeds.

BEST SHOPS BEYOND MENDOCINO

Matson Mercantile: Located inside the early 1900s Elk Garage, this general store has hardware and cute gifts.

Artists' Collective in Elk: Creators from around the coast sell their art here, including paintings, photography, jewelry and pottery.

Lost Coast Found: Locally made pottery, antique home goods and a good selection of vintage clothing. In Fort Bragg.

Lunar Tide: Forgot your healing crystals at home? Grab some quartz and citrine in Fort Bragg, plus a mystical bath bomb.

The Bookstore: Fort Bragg spot for used books and vinyl. Stop in and snag your next beach read.

EATING BEYOND MENDOCINO: OUR PICKS

Little River Inn (p274): Dinner is open to the public at this classic coastal resort. Afterward, grab a nightcap at the ocean-view Whale Watch Bar. *5-8pm* **$$$**

Jumbo's Win Win: This Philo burger joint with soft serve ice cream is the place to be after a day of Anderson Valley wine tasting. *11am-7:45pm* **$**

The Elk Store: Hit up this retro-style general store for all your picnicking needs, including hot and cold deli sandwiches. *11am-5pm Wed-Mon* **$**

The Wharf Restaurant: Watch ships come and go as you dig into pan-seared scallops and fish tacos at this Fort Bragg favorite. *noon-8pm Thu-Tue* **$$$**

TOP SURF SPOTS AROUND MENDOCINO

To rent gear, swing by **Lost Surf Shack** in downtown Fort Bragg.

Smuggler's Cove: Right in Mendocino, just south of the village, Smuggler's Cove has intermediate waves in the winter.

Caspar Beach: Beginners can surf at this beach just 10 minutes north of Mendocino Village. Wear a wetsuit.

Virgin Creek: This Fort Bragg beach is suitable for beginners, and on bigger days can be fun for more experienced surfers.

Point Arena Pier: About 35 miles south of Mendocino Village, this spot is best suited for experienced surfers.

Cooks Beach: Good spot for beginners, but it's over an hour from Mendocino to Gualala.

Point Arena

TIME FROM MENDOCINO: **1 HR**

A classic beacon you can climb

Point Arena Lighthouse *(pointarenalighthouse.com)* is one of the tallest towers in California, and you can climb all 115 feet. Tours *($5, plus a $5 site fee)* include entry to the tower, a brief chat about its history and access to its outer platform (a great place to look for whales). The nearby museum doubles as a gift shop.

Fort Bragg

TIME FROM MENDOCINO: **20 MINS**

Botanicals, bluffs & brew

Spread across 47 acres, **Mendocino Coast Botanical Gardens** *(gardenbythesea.org; adult/senior/child $23/18/8)* is home to a variety of themed gardens (including rose, succulent, magnolias and camellias), four miles of trails, oceanfront vistas and a whale-watching cottage. Feeling inspired by all the botanicals? The gift shop sells gardening gear as well as seeds gathered from the property. **Rhody's Garden Café**, near the garden's entrance, serves coffee, lunch and ice cream (orange cream float!) with a flower-filled view.

Riding retro rails

All aboard for some family-friendly fun. The **Skunk Train** *(skunktrain.com; rides from $50)* dates back to 1885 and gets its name from the stinky fumes these rail cruisers used to emit. But don't worry, the fumes are now substantially reduced. Today, this classic train takes passengers on scenic rides through the redwoods. The 90-minute **Pudding Creek Express**, which includes a stop halfway through the journey so that you can stretch your legs and enjoy a snack under the trees, is perfect for youngsters. Adult passengers can add on a wine package and get a bottle of the train's own Skunk Train Red Cuvée. Keep an eye on the calendar for special events. In November, for example, the Skunk becomes the **Mushroom, Whisky and Wine Train**. Passengers get a lesson from local foragers, in addition to sampling tasty morsels and sips.

A treasure-covered beach

Treasure? Or trash? Well, it's like they say, one person's trash is another's treasure. Starting in the early 1900s, Fort Bragg residents tossed untold amounts of detritus off a bluff and into the surf, expecting it would simply disappear. Instead, the refuse returned to them as sea glass. To this day, you can find these colorful fragments at **Glass Beach**, a popular beachcombing destination. After hunting, head to the nearby **Sea Glass Museum** to get a better understanding of your haul. The exhibit cases include descriptions of what objects may have created each color of sea glass.

JUSTINEMTI7/SHUTTERSTOCK

Mendocino Coast Botanical Gardens

Anderson Valley Tasting Rooms

Napa and Sonoma may get all the attention in California, but that's what makes Anderson Valley even cooler. This under-the-radar gem, on the tail end of a picturesque drive through the redwoods if you're coming from Mendocino, is filled with friendly tasting rooms. In all, it only stretches for about 15 miles along Hwy 128, but the region's 30+ wineries – with notable varietals including pinot noir and chardonnay – are sure to dazzle wine dabblers and experts alike.

Where to sip if you...

Want to be Spontaneous

Navarro Winery No reservations needed at this casual yet widely respected winery. The tasting room has two indoor counters and an outdoor picnic area draped with sweet-smelling wisteria blooms.

Husch Vineyards Reservations are only required for groups of six or more at this tasting room set in a converted pony barn from the late 1800s. The oldest winery in Anderson Valley, Husch is family owned and produces 22 different wines.

Wine bottle, Goldeneye winery

Have Kids in Wow

Meyer Family Cellars Not only are kids allowed here, they'll find some fun on the property's playground while the adults sip pinot noir with notes of pomegranate and blackberry. For older kids, there's an onsite disc golf course.

Foursight Wines In addition to wine tastings, Foursight also offers kid-friendly tours of their lavender field and native plants pollinator garden. Guests can even pick a bundle of lavender to take home.

Are Feeling Hungry

Pennyroyal Farm This sister property to Navarro Winery is a vineyard, creamery and veggie-growing farm. As such, tasting-room guests can purchase small-batch cheeses and farm fare in addition to sampling the wine.

Goldeneye Tasting options here include a seasonal snack, a cheese plate, cheese and charcuterie pairings, or caviar. Be sure to make a reservation – you'll find a link on Goldeneye's website.

Want Something Other Than Wine

The Madrones In addition to two wine tasting rooms, this Mediterranean-style compound also has an apothecary fitting for the Emerald Triangle (the name for the area's cannabis-producing region). Pick up locally grown cannabis and keep an eye out for themed weekends during the spring and summer with farm tours and music.

Gowan's Heirloom Ciders For 150 years Gowan's has been growing apples, and you can sample the fruits of their labor (literally) with a visit to their cider-tasting orchard. Try the cider slushie on a hot day.

Anderson Valley Brewing Company The brewery's Boonville home is a 30-acre kid- and dog-friendly fun zone known as Beer Park. Take your pick from 20 beers on tap, play disc golf and occasionally catch live music.

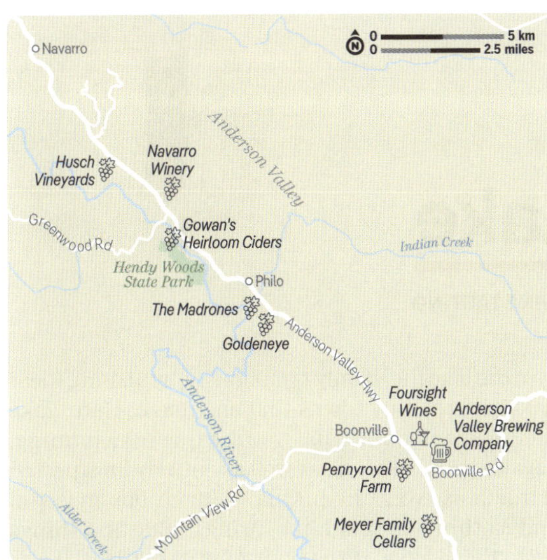

HOW TO

When to go Most tasting rooms are open 11am to 5pm. The Anderson Valley Pinot Noir Festival is held in May; harvest season (Aug-Oct) is another prime time.

Book in advance Check to see if your winery of choice requires reservations, especially for groups of six or more. During harvest months, book well in advance.

Budget Basic tastings run between $10 and $45 per person. You'll pay more for food pairings.

Top tip Buy a bottle to take home, as many wineries here have limited distribution and you likely won't find them elsewhere.

DIY or guided tour?

Having trusted transportation is the most crucial consideration for a day of tasting. If you have a designated driver in the group, the good news is that many of the wineries are located one after another on Hwy 128, so it's not difficult to find them. Coming from Mendocino, you'll hit the area's wine towns in this order: Philo, Boonville and then Yorkville. Plan your tastings accordingly.

If everyone in your party wants to partake in the pinot extravaganza, book a car service. Uber is not readily available for spur-of-the-moment pickups and the wineries aren't walkable from one to the next. Tour Mendocino *(tourmendocino.com)* offers a fully customizable, private all-day experience for up to eight guests *($695 for the van and driver, plus $40 per person)*. The day includes refreshments and lunch as well as visits to three wineries of your choice. They also have a multi-group tour *($175 per person)* with visits to three wineries, all chosen by Tour Mendocino, plus lunch. Another option is Mendo Insider Tours *(mendoinsidertours.com)*, a local transportation company that'll help you craft the wine day of your dreams. They have cars for smaller groups as well as a Sprinter van for parties of six or more. Plus, their knowledgeable chauffeurs can give you tasting-room recommendations along the way.

MICHAEL DEFREITAS NORTH AMERICA/ALAMY

Wine bottles, Navarro Winery

Clear Lake

FISHING | VOLCANOS | WINE TASTING

GETTING AROUND

Having your own vehicle is definitely the way to go. But Lake Transit operates weekday routes between Clearlake and Calistoga. Buses serve Ukiah from Lakeport. Since piecing together routes and times can be difficult, it's best to phone ahead *(707-263-3334)*.

Live the lake life, if only temporarily, by visiting Clear Lake and the tiny towns that encircle it. Here, 'lake life' includes both what you'd expect (swimming, kayaking and fishing), as well as entirely unexpected attractions (volcanic hiking, a lunch box museum and clothing-optional hot springs). But first things first: 'Clear Lake' is the body of water; 'Clearlake' is a town on its southeastern side. The body of water has 100 miles of shoreline and 68 sq miles of surface area. It's actually the largest naturally occurring freshwater lake entirely in California (Lake Tahoe is bigger but straddles Nevada). It's also considered the oldest lake in North America, and dates back 1 to 2 million years, according to geologists. With a 4300ft dormant volcano lording over it and an under-the-radar reputation, Clear Lake is both geographically stunning and easy on the budget.

TOP TIP

When vacationing here in summertime, ask around about the algae situation. Avoid drinking water that has come from the lake and be careful about when and where you (and your pets) go swimming.

Hiking Trails & History

Experience Clear Lake State Park

Dip your toe into Clear Lake, both metaphorically and literally, at **Clear Lake State Park** *(parks.ca.gov; per vehicle $8)*, which has a sampling of what makes the area great. Swim, fish, hike and bike, and get a feel for the lake's Indigenous history by following the moderate half-mile **Indian Nature Trail**, which gives an overview of how the Pomo people used the area's resources. The trail passes through what was once a Pomo village.

Summit a Volcano

Hike Mount Konocti

The fact that Mount Konocti (4305ft) is a dormant volcano is actually only part of what makes it so intriguing. If you follow the Wright Peak Summit Trail – a 6-mile out-and-back route – you'll also spot an off-the-grid early 1900s cabin as well as the wreckage from a tragic 1970 plane crash. The hike begins

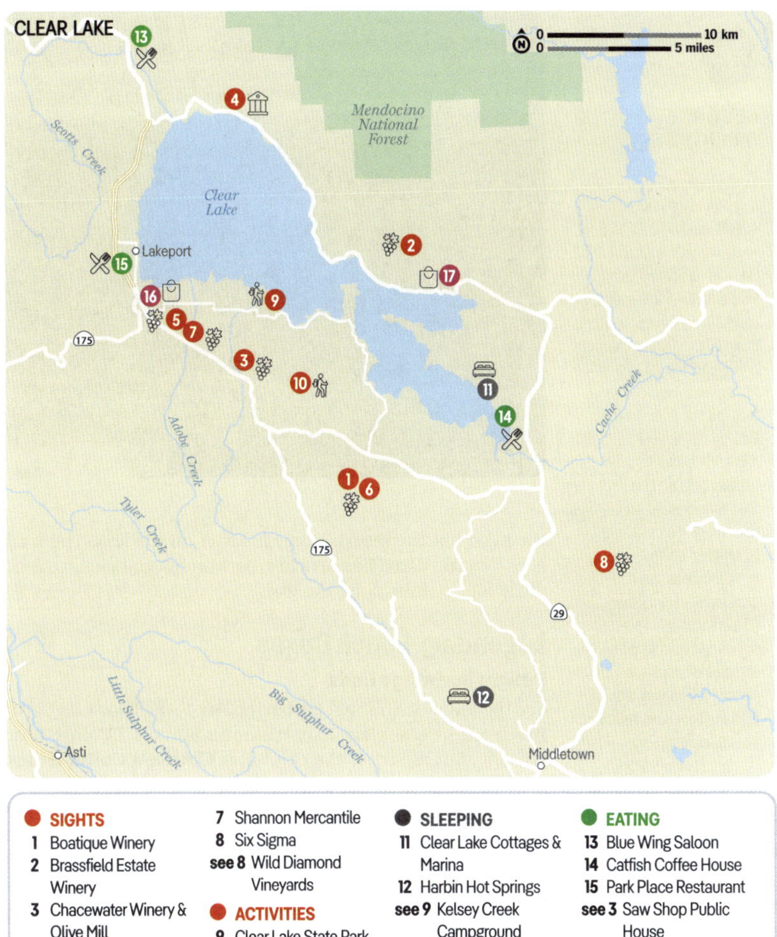

SIGHTS
1 Boatique Winery
2 Brassfield Estate Winery
3 Chacewater Winery & Olive Mill
4 Clarke's Collectibles and Lunch Box Museum
5 Kaz Winery
6 Laujor Estate Winery
7 Shannon Mercantile
8 Six Sigma
see 8 Wild Diamond Vineyards

ACTIVITIES
9 Clear Lake State Park
see 9 Indian Nature Trail
10 Mount Konocti County Park

SLEEPING
11 Clear Lake Cottages & Marina
12 Harbin Hot Springs
see 9 Kelsey Creek Campground
see 3 Suites on Main
see 13 Tallman Hotel

EATING
13 Blue Wing Saloon
14 Catfish Coffee House
15 Park Place Restaurant
see 3 Saw Shop Public House

SHOPPING
16 Clearlake Outdoors
17 Limit Out
see 13 Oliveira's Antiques

at the **Mount Konocti County Park** trailhead *(518 Konocti Rd, Kelseyville)*, where you'll find plenty of parking plus bathrooms. From there, it's a steep climb to the top, gaining 1800ft of elevation. You'll pass Downen Cabin, where the intrepid and peace-seeking Mary Downen lived solo in the early 1900s, about two miles into the hike. The mangled pieces of the white-and-turquoise Navion A aircraft, visible just to the right of the trail, lie scattered just before the peak's summit. At the top, you'll find multiple picnic tables and near-360° views. Of course, you'll get an eyeful of Clear Lake below, and on a clear day you can also spot Mount Lassen and Mount Diablo in the distance. At this point, you're only halfway done with

GETTING ORIENTED

Though tiny, **Kelseyville** (pop 4204), on the southern side of the lake, is likely where you'll spend the most time since it has Clear Lake State Park, the trailhead for hiking Mount Konocti and a number of wineries. Going clockwise around the lake, both **Lakeport**, on the western shore, and the old-timey village of **Upper Lake**, to the north, have charming downtowns. **Clearlake**, off the southeastern shore, is more of an access point for fishing, and **Middletown**, 19 miles south, is home to Harbin Hot Springs, one of California's premier nude-bathing experiences.

the hike, but the return is much easier on the legs. The trail is well marked and has benches, bathrooms and picnic tables at various points along the way.

Legendary Lunch Boxes

Delight in vintage finds

See the Monkees, Vinnie Barbarino, Mr T, the Fonz and Carol Brady all in one place. No, it's not a fantasy TV crossover episode, but a part of the exhibit at **Clarke's Collectibles and Lunch Box Museum** *(retrodeb.com)* in Nice. Part museum, part gift shop, the space allows you to peruse the owner's impressive collection, then shop for vintage finds to keep. Just a few minutes away in downtown Upper Lake, the vintage fun continues at **Oliveira's Antiques**, which has a collection of vintage Western accessories, including hats and jewelry.

An Angler's Paradise

Cast for bass on Clear Lake

Called the bass capital of the West, Clear Lake lures sport fishers from across the country. Largemouth bass make up two-thirds of the fish caught on Clear Lake – crappie, bluegill,

EATING AROUND CLEAR LAKE: OUR PICKS

Saw Shop Public House: Laid-back Kelseyville restaurant with farm-to-table cuisine and delicious cocktails in Mason jars. *noon-8pm Tue-Sat, from 11am Sun* $$

Park Place Restaurant: Lakeport's premier dining venue has classic Italian and American dishes and killer lake views. *11am-7pm Sun-Thu, to 8pm Fri & Sat* $$

Blue Wing Saloon: Cozy up on the heated veranda with casual American fare and live music at this Upper Lake restaurant in the Tallman Hotel. *hours vary* $$

Catfish Coffee House: With a drive-thru window, this is the spot to grab coffee and bagels in Clearlake. *5.30am-6pm Mon-Fri, 6am-6pm Sat, 6.30am-6pm Sun* $

LORI A JONES/SHUTTERSTOCK

Mount Konocti County Park (p244)

carp and catfish make up the remaining third. To get in on the angling action, base yourself at the **Clear Lake Cottages & Marina** *(clearlakecottagesandmarina.com)* in the town of Clearlake. The property has a private launch as well as boat rentals for overnight guests. Book waterfront cottage #27 and you can even fish from your private balcony. Free public boat launches can also be found at various points around the lake. Lakeport, for example, has ramped access on 1st, 3rd and 5th Sts. Also in Lakeport, bait and tackle shop **Clearlake Outdoors** *(clearlakeoutdoors.com)* is a go-to spot for bait and tackle, and **Limit Out** *(limitoutbaitshop.com)* has you covered on the opposite side of the lake, in Clearlake Oaks.

Hippie Hot Springs

Strip down and heat up

Harbin Hot Springs *(harbin.org)* is the oldest hot springs in California, and visiting these clothing-optional baths is practically a rite of passage. There's a youthful, no-frills vibe, and it's also decidedly hippie-dippie (don't be surprised when the bare-chested lady next to you starts chanting mantras). If you're comfortable in the buff, it can be a revelatory experience. The heart and soul of the 1700-acre retreat center is the spring-fed pool area, with eight baths of varying temperatures, plus a sauna and sundeck offering sweeping valley views. Lodging is in creekside caravans, domes or hilltop cottages. Budget travelers can also pitch a tent or sleep in the car and pay for 24-hour access. Day use *($50; not required for overnight guests)* gives you up to six hours to explore the facilities and dine at the organic (and mostly vegetarian) **Dancing Bear Cafe**. All visitors 18 and over, including both overnight and day-use guests, are required to become a member; membership starts at $15 per month.

KELSEYVILLE PEAR FESTIVAL

Held on the last Saturday in September, Lake County's largest one-day event is a real hoot and a showcase of the region's agricultural heritage, including the almighty pear. Think parades, live music and dancing on three stages, a giant decorative pear, a pie-eating contest, a scarecrow contest and plenty of street vendors. There are special exhibits all over town, from a tractor and engine show to a display on the history of Kelseyville farming within the Pear Pavilion. The event has grown from just 1500 attendees in 1993 to more than 10,000 in recent years. The festival's highly appropriate slogan? 'Catch the small-town magic.'

SIP & STAY

If an entire day of wine tasting isn't enough, why not sleep at a winery too? **Boatique** and **Chacewater** have short-term rentals on their property, and **Laujor** has one just above its tasting room. For an even better experience, check out **Bed & Barrel at Stonehouse Cellars** *(stonehousecellars.com)*. Set on 145 acres of secluded countryside, this winery rents a room and a suite within a luxury home, as well as a stylish and cozy three-bedroom ranch. All guests have access to vineyard hiking trails, a pool, a hot tub and a large patio with a BBQ grill. And breakfast is made with farm-fresh local ingredients.

A Wine Country Less Traveled

You're not in Napa anymore

There are some 30 wineries around Clear Lake. All are incredibly welcoming and they typically waive tasting fees if you purchase a bottle. Start your tasting adventure at **Six Sigma** *(sixsigmaranch.com)*, a historic ranch and winery spread across more than 4000 acres in Lower Lake, where you can sip on a full-bodied cab or an earthy tempranillo in the tasting room, mountain bike the ranch's trails and take the excellent vineyard tour in a converted military vehicle. From there, continue south to the nearby **Wild Diamond Vineyards** *(wilddiamond.com)* and its hilltop tasting village, a collection of tables under shade canopies and a refurbished shipping container. The best part: you can sip astoundingly good reds while looking down on Napa (literally).

Hop onto Hwy 29 and start driving toward Kelseyville, where many of the wineries are concentrated. At **Laujor Estate Winery** *(laujorestate.com)*, do the classic tasting and soak up the impressive views from an outdoor fire pit. Then, head over to **Boatique Winery** *(boatiquewines.com)* for more Red Hills AVA sampling, as well as an outstanding view of Mt Konocti and a prized collection of antique wooden boats. Continue on to Kelseyville proper, where **Chacewater Winery & Olive Mill** *(chacewaterwine.com)* offers tastings of organic wine and olive oil. Bring your favorite bottle to the picnic area out back where you can play horseshoes or bocce ball in front of the olive groves.

If you've got even more time, head over to the **Shannon Mercantile** *(shannonfamilyofwines.com)*, a buzzy tasting room with 12 wines on tap, plus picnic areas and cornhole. There's also cult favorite **Kaz Winery** *(kazwinery.com)*, where they're all about blends. Whatever is in the organic vineyards goes into the wine – and they're blended at crush, not during fermentation. Or make a trip across the lake to **Brassfield Estate Winery** *(brassfieldestate.com)*, a stunning Tuscan-style winery in the unique High Valley appellation, surrounded by magnificent gardens.

A Lake County winery

TERRY W RYDER/SHUTTERSTOCK

The Lost Coast

EPIC HIKES | REMOTE BEACHES | TIDEPOOLS

Even in the country's most populated state, you can still find delightful solitude on a wild beach – and the Lost Coast is the place for it. The longest stretch of undeveloped coastline in California is a superlative backpacking destination and a glimpse into California's past, with foggy, windswept coves and rugged 4000ft peaks that plunge into a frothy sea. The coast became 'lost' when the state's highway system deemed the region unruly in the mid-20th century and bypassed it. There is one sizable and difficult-to-reach community: Shelter Cove, perched on a south-facing bluff surrounded by the King Range National Conservation Area. Some folks arrive via the airstrip, while others brave the narrow, curvy road. Once you get there, you'll be rewarded with oceanfront accommodations and endless opportunities to unplug, even if you don't want to bust out your hiking boots.

GETTING AROUND

There's no public transportation on the Lost Coast, but you can book a shuttle service to pick you up from the end of the Lost Coast Trail if you make the multiday journey. We recommend Lost Coast Adventure Tours *(lostcoastadventures.com; per person $98)*, which operates daily shuttles from Shelter Cove to Mattole Beach.

Picnicking with Panoramic Views

Enjoy a DIY outdoor meal

On your way into Shelter Cove, stop off at the **Shelter Cove General Store** *(sheltercovegeneralstore.com)* to grab sandwich supplies, snacks, locally brewed beer or a bottle of wine. Next door, the **Shelter Cove Gift Shop** is one of the few places in town to grab a souvenir or sweatshirt. Take your supplies to either **Abalone Point** or **Seal Rock** for a Pacific-view picnic. Both spots sit on a bluff overlooking the ocean and have picnic tables.

TOP TIP

Visit with the mindset of taking it easy (other than when you're hiking the trails, of course). Shelter Cove is not a bustling city, and restaurant kitchens in town close as early as 7pm. Kicking back and enjoying the natural splendor is the area's big draw.

Urchins & Abalone Galore

Tidepooling in Shelter Cove

Probably the most fascinating (and free!) Lost Coast activity is discovering the diverse and wonderfully weird creatures living in the tidepools. Anemone, urchin, crabs and bright sea stars are all easily visible; these are some of the best pools on the North Coast.

THE LOST COAST

HIGHLIGHTS
1 Lost Coast Trail

SIGHTS
2 Abalone Point
3 Cape Mendocino Lighthouse
see 3 Mal Coombs Park
4 Punta Gorda Lighthouse
5 Seal Rock
6 Shelter Cove Beach

ACTIVITIES
7 Black Sands Beach
8 Deadman's
9 Lost Coast Adventure Tours
10 Mattole Beach Trailhead
11 Shelter Cove Boat Ramp

SLEEPING
12 Inn of the Lost Coast
see 10 Mattole Campground
see 18 Needle Rock Campground
see 17 Tides Inn
13 Usal Beach Campground

EATING
14 Gyppo Ale Mill
15 Mario's Marina Bar
see 9 Mi Mochima
16 Shelter Cove General Store
17 Surf Point Coffee House

SHOPPING
see 16 Shelter Cove Gift Shop

INFORMATION
18 Needle Rock Visitor Center

Start your tidepooling adventure by parking at **Mal Coombs Park**, where you can't miss the **Cape Mendocino Lighthouse** *(capemendocinolighthouse.org; free)*. Originally located about 60 miles north of here, the lighthouse was moved in 1998 for preservation purposes. Today, it's maintained by the Cape Mendocino Lighthouse Preservation Society, who open it to the public as a museum each summer, from Memorial Day to Labor Day.

After giving the historic lighthouse a look, head down the set of stairs to the beach. At low tide, the area looks otherworldly, with exposed rugged black rocks. You may find treasures in the sand, like pieces of petrified wood or dried urchin shells, but climb the rock formations (always keeping an eye on the tide, of course, and peer into the puddles where there's an entire world of living aquatic critters.

Catch a Gnarly Wave

Surfing Shelter Cove

Intermediate surfers looking to ride the swell should give Shelter Cove's most popular wave a go. Set in the town's namesake cove, **Deadman's** is known for long lefts and rights, with the rights being a bit slower. Spring and fall usually provide the best conditions (summer waves tend to be small) since it's southwest facing. And because the coastline here is crescent shaped, the swell ranges anywhere from triple-overhead at Point Delgada to chest-high at the **Shelter Cove Boat Ramp** *(sheltercovefishingpreservation.wordpress.com)*.

Bring your own board and wetsuit (there aren't rentals in town) and prepare for a decent amount of effort to reach Deadman's. You'll have to park at the boat launch and walk over half a mile, passing **Shelter Cove Beach** (the only swimmable beach in town) on your way. Once you get there, be mindful of changing tides, as Deadman's Beach has rocky abutments on either end. Be mindful of the locals too – surf sites have described the vibes as 'intimidating.'

WHY I LOVE THE LOST COAST

Amelia Mularz, Lonely Planet writer

'Hey! Over here!' shouted a local who had joined my mission to spot a sea star in the wild. My excitement nearly sent me tumbling into a frothy puddle of seawater and sea anemone. 'I can't believe this is your first,' she said. 'It's truly a momentous occasion,' I replied, laughing. What I'd intended to be a 10-minute stop at the tidepools below the Mal Coombs Park bluffs in Shelter Cove had turned into a three-hour odyssey. Bounding between black rocks and crouching to peer into entire galaxies of marine life had unleashed a childlike joy that I hadn't felt in years. The Lost Coast is exactly that kind of place: where stopovers become highlights and nature discoveries are somehow deeply personal.

EATING IN SHELTER COVE: OUR PICKS

Surf Point Coffee House: Coffee, housemade pastries and wines to pair with lunch at this bistro with breathtaking views. *7.30am-4pm Fri-Wed, to 4.30pm Thu* $

Mi Mochima: From out of nowhere comes delicious and authentic Venezuelan cuisine: empanadas, arepas and *patacón* sandwiches. *hours vary* $$

Gyppo Ale Mill: California's most remote brewery serves its own lagers, pilsners and blondes. Burgers and wings, too. *5-9pm Mon-Thu, from noon Fri-Sun* $$

Mario's Marina Bar: This local hangout has an ever-changing global menu, killer ocean views from its patio and frequent live music. *hours vary* $$

RON KARPEL/SHUTTERSTOCK

Lost Coast Trail, Punta Gorda Lighthouse in distance

TOP EXPERIENCE

The Lost Coast Trail

The best way to see the Lost Coast is to hike. And while the 24.6-mile Lost Coast Trail between Mattole Beach and Black Sands Beach is a bucket list adventure, it's not for everyone. It requires multiple days, a permit and a shuttle ride back to your car. The good news: there are day hikes along the Lost Coast Trail, too.

DON'T MISS

- Mattole Beach
- Punta Gorda Lighthouse
- Black Sands Beach
- Sinkyone Wilderness State Park
- Bear Harbor

Mattole Beach to Black Sands Beach

This is the whole shebang: the full 24.6-mile Lost Coast adventure. Technically, the Lost Coast Trail extends even further south into Sinkyone State Park (we've included day hikes in that area), but the classic, multiday backpacking experience is this northern section through the King Range National Conservation Area. Because the trail can be dangerous at times, with impassable sections at high tide, going with a group or hiring a private guide is highly recommended. **Lost Coast Adventure Tours** *(lostcoastadventures.com; guided tours from $900)* is a popular and well-respected pick. They offer

PRACTICALITIES

- Day-hiking doesn't require a permit, but overnight trips do. Reserve online at *recreation.gov.*
- Fees: $6 per permit reservation, plus $12 per person area fee.

both north-to-south hikes (five days, four nights) and south-to-north trips (four days, three nights). They provide meals, bear canisters (required for all hikers) and shuttles. If you prefer to go it alone, you can still book a shuttle with Lost Coast Adventure Tours to get you back to your car.

Mattole Beach to Punta Gorda Lighthouse (Day Hike)

No need to pack a sleeping bag for this one. A day hike that starts at the same point as the long-haul trek, this out-and-back route is 6 miles total, traversing sand and coastal shrubbery, with the now-defunct **Punta Gorda Lighthouse** as a turnaround point. From Ferndale, it's about a 75-minute drive along winding, remote roads to the **Mattole Beach Trailhead**. There, you'll find a campground, parking and public bathrooms. Pack a picnic lunch to enjoy at the lighthouse, where you're also likely to see large groups of elephant seals lazing on the sand below.

Black Sands Beach to Gitchell Creek (Day Hike)

If you're staying in Shelter Cove and want to stretch your legs along charcoal-colored sand, this is a convenient choice. Just minutes from the main part of town, **Black Sands Beach** is the southern point of the multiday hike. There's a parking lot and bathrooms near the trailhead, then it's a 7.4-mile out-and-back trek. You'll walk Black Sands for about two miles before passing **Horse Mountain Creek**, at which point the terrain becomes a bit more rocky and trickier to navigate. At your turnaround point, **Gitchell Creek**, you're likely to see overnight campers, as the next 4.5-mile stretch just beyond that becomes impassable at high tide.

Needle Rock to Whale Gulch (Day Hike)

Within Sinkyone State Park, **Needle Rock Visitor Center** *(parking $8)* gives you even more access to coastal hiking. From the visitor center, you can head south to Bear Harbor, or take this 4.6-mile route north. You'll travel grassy sections (with a couple spur trails that lead down to the water), and pass **Jones Beach** before reaching **Whale Gulch**. Wildlife abounds.

Needle Rock to Bear Harbor (Day Hike)

While much of the southern section of the Lost Coast Trail includes forest, this out-and-back 6.2-mile hike, leaving from Needle Rock Visitor Center and heading south, has plenty of ocean views. Tides, though, aren't a concern, as the trail is inland enough that you won't have to battle soaked pathways. The turnaround point, **Bear Harbor**, was once the western terminus of the Bear Harbor Railroad, built in the 1890s. You can still spot rusted rails in the area today.

PUNTA GORDA LIGHTHOUSE HISTORY

Now simply a rest stop for hikers, Punta Gorda Lighthouse was once a functioning beacon for boats. It was first lit on January 15, 1912, and proved difficult to access from the beginning. Lightkeepers had to travel 11 miles by horseback to reach the nearest town, Petrolia, for supplies. In 1951, the Coast Guard abandoned the lighthouse, opting instead for an offshore lighted buoy to warn ships.

TOP TIPS

- Lost Coast Adventure Tour's owner, Blu Graham, offers the following top tips.
- This is one of the most physically demanding coastal hikes in the country, with rugged terrain, deep sand and unpredictable footing.
- Take the weather seriously. Severe storms on the Lost Coast can bring pummeling wind, rain and surf conditions.
- Plan your tidal windows with plenty of buffer time. Don't cut it close; factors to consider include swell size, wind and storm surge.
- Make all arrangements before you arrive. This includes shuttle rides, food, supplies and accommodations. Services are limited here.

Beyond The Lost Coast

Find your way back to civilization and solid footing via an impossibly quaint town or soothing swimming hole.

Places

GETTING AROUND

After traversing the tricky roads along the Lost Coast, you'll be happy to see good ol' Hwy 101 again. A head's up that there's no public transportation around Ferndale, and you also need your own wheels to explore Humboldt Redwoods State Park. Bring a bicycle and you can ride the entire length of the Avenue of the Giants.

If you need extra motivation to get through the full 24.6-mile Lost Coast Trail, let it be this: the nearby settlement of Butterfat City. Technically, that's just a nickname for Ferndale (it's a reference to the town's dairy heyday), but the sentiment remains. Emerge from the coastal wilderness and you'll be treated to good meals and old-school hospitality. Because of its proximity – and the butterfat – Ferndale is the ideal base for exploring the northern portion of the Lost Coast. But if you're heading south, a stop at Standish-Hickey State Recreation Area, near Leggett, and a splash in a swimming hole might be in order. Or, hightail it to the world-famous Avenue of the Giants for even more hiking.

Standish-Hickey State Recreation Area

TIME FROM SHELTER COVE: 1¼ HR

Cool off in a swimming hole

For little more than the price of a fancy coffee drink, you can access one of California's best swimming holes: a dream if you're visiting in the summer. Park in the **Standish-Hickey State Recreation Area** *(parks.ca.gov; per vehicle $8)* and hike about half a mile to the **South Fork of the Eel River**. It's even better if you work up a sweat – that water can be ice cold!

Humboldt Redwoods State Park

TIME FROM SHELTER COVE: 1 HR

Explore the avenue of the giants

Tree huggers, take note: the sprawling redwood groves within **Humboldt Redwoods State Park** *(parks.ca.gov; free)* rival – and some say surpass – those in Redwood National Park, which is a long drive further north. The quickest, easiest way to enjoy the park is to exit Hwy 101 when you see the **Avenue of the Giants** sign and take the smaller, two-lane alternative to the interstate; it's an incredible 32-mile stretch and there are plenty of great stops along the way.

If you're coming from the south, **Stephens Grove** is the first pull-out with truly impressive redwoods, which have

ANNA WESTMAN/SHUTTERSTOCK

Humboldt Redwoods State Park

grown up tall thanks to the nutrient-dense alluvial flat, or flood plain, on which they stand. Parking is easy and there's a short 0.7-mile hike – the **Governor William D Stephens Loop Trail** – that serves as a perfect introduction to the park. If you're interested in a longer hike within lesser-explored territory, drive another 6 miles north to the **Children's Forest**. This is another alluvial flat, and there's rarely anyone here, particularly if the seasonal bridge isn't up over the South Fork of the Eel River. The hike begins at the **Williams Grove Day-Use Area** *(per vehicle $8)*, from which it's a half-mile to the river. After the crossing, the mile-long loop trail brings hikers into a grove that endured a large wildfire in 2003. After about a decade, the resilient forest regained its beauty, and the only evidence of the fire was a burned-up park sign.

Another 10 miles north you'll find **Founders Grove**, the most-visited area of the park thanks to its convenient location beside the Hwy 101 off-ramp. Unless you're dead set on doing the easiest and most popular thing, skip it and instead visit the nearby but lesser-explored **Rockefeller Grove**. Here you can contemplate nature in peace or jump on the **Bull Creek Flats Trail**, a 10-mile hike around what's been called 'the world's tallest forest.'

STORIES OF BIGFOOT

What's with all the Bigfoot stuff?

No doubt you'll notice odes to the hair-covered cryptid all along the Avenue of the Giants. He's been spotted, allegedly, within Humboldt Redwoods State Park. He's also been spotted in Redwoods National Park and Eureka, and cynics might say it's all too convenient for the area gift shops, but maybe the guy just gets around.

Probably the most famous California sighting happened in the town of Willow Creek, also in Humboldt County, but a good 2-hour drive north of the Avenue of the Giants. It's now home to a Bigfoot museum. Closer to these parts, you'll find a dedicated gift shop in Garberville, called Legend of Bigfoot. But Bigfoot tees and plushies also abound on the Avenue itself.

EATING BEYOND THE LOST COAST: OUR PICKS

The Peg House: The burgers, BBQ oysters and blackberry sundaes are standouts, but everything's amazing at this roadside gem in Leggett. *7.30am-7pm* $

Benbow Inn Restaurant: Here's the place to indulge in a fancy meal served in an elegant Garberville dining room. Start with martinis at the bar. *hours vary* $$$

Chimney Tree Grill: Feast on local grass-fed beef burgers, fresh-baked pies and soft-serve ice cream in Phillipsville, on the Avenue of the Giants. *11am-8pm* $

Avenue Cafe: Located on the Avenue of the Giants in Miranda, this cafe cooks up Bigfoot-inspired sandwiches, burgers and pizzas. *11am-8pm* $$

WELCOME TO BUTTERFAT CITY

Ferndale earned the nickname Butterfat City thanks to its history in the dairy biz. In the late 19th century, Danish dairymen brought their trade to town and formed neighborhood creamery cooperatives.

By 1890, there were already 11 creameries in the Ferndale area, and their butter was considered the best in the state. Around this time the town took on another nickname, Cream City.

With the city's creameries making a killing, especially by demanding high prices down in San Francisco, Ferndale prospered and ornate Victorian architecture sprang up all over town. These well-to-do buildings – like the Gingerbread Mansion, which is now a B&B – became known as butterfat palaces.

ADELE HEIDENREICH/SHUTTERSTOCK

The Farmer's Daughter

Ferndale

TIME FROM MATTOLE BEACH: 1¼ HR

Shopping in a Victorian town

Even if you can resist the charm of Ferndale's B&Bs, spending an afternoon here is highly recommended. The town's **Main St** has one-off boutiques and great spots for a casual bite. Fun fact: famed restaurateur Guy Fieri grew up here, so you know the food is good. Plus, Ferndale probably has the most charming public bathroom in the region (a noble distinction). The exterior has Victorian-style decor to match much of the historic architecture in town.

Start off energized by popping into **Main Street Coffee Co** for a Mexican mocha or latte, then head next door to **Sunshine and Fog**, which isn't just the forecast for the day but also a women's boutique. Next, cross the street to the **Ferndale Arts Gallery** *(ferndalearts.com)* to appreciate the area's homegrown creativity. On the next block, **The Farmer's Daughter** specializes in homewares, especially kitchen items like strawberry-print juice glasses and floral tea towels. **The Blacksmith Shop** *(ferndaleblacksmith.com)* celebrates old-school craft with metal arts, including stunning jewelry forged from old coins. And speaking of old school, **Golden Gait Mercantile** *(goldengaitmercantile.com)* has the feel of a retro general store, with candy displayed in barrels, and they even have a small museum onsite that's an ode to general stores of yesteryear. Across the street, **Humboldt's Hometown Store** *(humboldtshometownstore.com)* has gifts from around the county and plenty of Guy Fieri merch.

EATING IN FERNDALE: OUR PICKS

Ferndale Meat Company: Grab sandwiches and chips from this deli counter on your way to Mattole Beach and the Lost Coast Trail. *8am-5pm Mon-Sat* $

VI Restaurant and Tavern: Make like the wealthy dairymen of yesteryear and dine in a Victorian mansion. Ribeye and pork chops are on the menu. *8am-9pm* $$$

Tuyas: Treat all your senses with Mexican cuisine, Spanish wine and art made by locals. *11.30am-8pm Sun-Thu, to 9pm Fri & Sat* $$

The Red Front Store: Ice cream tastes better when you enjoy it on a cow-print bench set along old-timey Main Street. *7am-9pm Mon-Fri, 8am-8pm Sat & Sun* $

Eureka

STREET ART | VICTORIAN ARCHITECTURE | HISTORIC HARBOR

''I have found it!' That's the meaning of the Greek word *eureka*, and what the mathematician Archimedes reportedly shouted after he came to understand the principle of buoyancy as he sank into his bath. It's also California's official state motto and the name of Humboldt County's capital – both fitting applications. In the city of Eureka, you're likely to find plenty of moments of joyful discovery. One of the biggest draws here is the perfectly preserved Victorian architecture that's concentrated in the city's charming Old Town district. Take a brief break from land and hop in a kayak for a tour of Humboldt Bay, where you're likely to make a number of historical discoveries (plus reconfirm the principle of buoyancy). Back on solid turf, you just might discover your new favorite seafood restaurant, as Eureka has plenty of delectable dining options with fish-focused menus.

GETTING AROUND

The Redwood Transit System operates buses between Eureka and cities to the north and south, making stops up and down Hwy 101. For local transportation, the Eureka Transit Service operates buses Monday to Saturday. Both options are $2 per ride.

Humboldt History Lesson

Visit the Clarke Historical Museum

Set in an early 1900s bank, the **Clarke Historical Museum** *(clarkemuseum.org; $10 suggested donation)* covers Humboldt County's past, including the area's Native American cultures, the gold rush, farming traditions and the lumber industry. Peeking into a re-created Victorian-era bedroom is especially fun, as is seeing the museum's 400-pound 'man-eating clam' display. Allot extra time to browse the gift shop, which includes vintage finds.

TOP TIP

For up-to-date happenings around town, check the Lost Coast Outpost *(lostcoastoutpost.com)*. They'll let you know about that night's karaoke event, comedy show or concerts, and also post details of traffic hazards and expected weather conditions.

Not-So-Run-of-the-Mill Millworks

Get hands-on with historic craftsmanship

Part museum, part professional woodworking studio, part center for learning traditional crafts – there's nothing quite like the **Blue Ox Historic Village** *(blueoxhistoricvillage.com; self-guided tour adult/child $15/11; guided tour adult/child $30/15)*. Featured on the Magnolia Network TV show *The*

EUREKA

SIGHTS
1 Clarke Historical Museum
2 Historic Eagle House
3 Morris Graves Museum of Art
4 Romano Gabriel Wooden Sculpture Garden

ACTIVITIES
5 Humboats Kayak Adventures
6 Humboldt Cannabis Tours

SLEEPING
7 Carter House Inns
see 2 Inn at 2nd & C
8 The Pinc

EATING
9 Café Marina & Woodley's Bar
see 2 Gallagher's Restaurant and Pub
10 Jack's Seafood
11 Living the Dream Ice Cream
12 Los Bagels

DRINKING & NIGHTLIFE
13 Lost Coast Brewery & Cafe
see 2 Phatsy Kline's Parlour Lounge
14 The Shanty
15 The Speakeasy

ENTERTAINMENT
16 Kinetic Grand Championship

SHOPPING
17 Dick Taylor Craft Chocolate
18 Eureka Books
see 20 Land of Lovely
see 18 Many Hands Gallery
19 Patricks Candy
20 The Humboldt Mercantile
see 18 The Little Shop of Hers

EATING IN EUREKA: OUR PICKS

Jack's Seafood: Fresh oysters, clam chowder and halibut burgers complement the bay views at this spot right on the boardwalk. *11.30am-8pm* $$

Los Bagels: Try a banana slug-shaped bagel at this totally unique bakery that combines the Jewish deli tradition with Mexican flavors. *7am-3pm* $

Gallagher's Restaurant and Pub: The place for seafarers or anyone who fancies fish & chips with a pint. *11am-8.30pm Tue-Fri, 11.30am-8.30pm Sat, 11am-4pm Sun* $$

Café Marina & Woodley's Bar: Located on Woodley Island, Café Marina is a go-to for a post-paddle sandwich or plate of grilled prawns. *8.30am-8pm* $$

Craftsman, this outpost dedicated to old-school arts has a massive collection of Victorian-era woodworking machinery (still used today), a print shop, craftsman's apothecary (for mixing stains, varnishes, paints and glues) and textile atelier. And that's only what's inside the main building. Outside, guests can explore a skid camp – complete with a bunk house, cook shack and theater – and imagine what it was like to live in the area as a logger in the early 1900s. Keep walking the grounds and you'll also come upon working blacksmithing and ceramics studios, plus meet a horse or two.

If you're happy wandering the property at your own pace, stop by anytime between 9am and 3.30pm from Monday to Friday for a self-guided tour. You're still likely to catch a professional craftsman in action even if you stop by unannounced. Or you can reserve a 90-minute guided tour with either Viviana or Eric Hollenbeck, the founders, who will show you around. For the ultimate experience, book a Blue Ox class *(adult/child from $120/90)*, such as blacksmithing, ceramics or stained-glass making.

Hiking 100 Feet High

Stroll the redwood canopy

At the **Redwood Sky Walk** *(redwoodskywalk.com)* inside Eureka's **Sequoia Park Zoo** *(redwoodzoo.org; adult/child $25/13)*, you can climb up into a redwood grove and explore the ancient giants from 100 feet above the forest floor. The elevated trail is the longest of its kind in the western United States, and the construction of its ascent ramp, launch deck, accessible main loop, nine viewing platforms and optional hanging bridge were all designed by 'en-tree-preneurs.'

Upon entering the zoo, wander past the flamingos on your left and the river otters on your right, and soon you'll reach the ascent ramp, which zigzags at a gentle incline up to the launch deck. From there, the fully accessible main walkways and platforms offer a rare glimpse into a mesmerizing ecosystem: curious barn owls perch in the canopy; gnarled, oversized burls protrude from massive trunks; and from above, you can peer over swirling patches of ferns and bushy red huckleberry.

For the most intrepid visitors, there's the 'adventure leg,' a series of Costa Rica–style hanging bridges that complete the Sky Walk loop. Take your time, watch your footing and relax as you become part of the life in the redwood canopy. If you're feeling hungry afterward, the zoo has an onsite restaurant, the **Evergreen Eatery**, serving sandwiches, pizza and kid-friendly finger foods.

EUREKA'S BEST SHOPS

The Humboldt Mercantile: Snag redwoods tees, hemp hand soap and local hot sauce at this souvenir hotspot.

Many Hands Gallery: Like visiting a few dozen artists' studios in one fell swoop; the gallery stocks ceramics, jewelry and pretty leather journals.

Land of Lovely: Consider a visit here your personal invitation to luxuriate and pick up a new robe, bath soaks and botanical candles.

Eureka Books: Browse new, used and rare books, then have the Zoltar machine in front read your fortune.

The Little Shop of Hers: Find an expertly curated collection of vintage clothes and accessories for both him and her.

EATING IN EUREKA: BEST SWEET TREATS

Dick Taylor Craft Chocolate: Stop by the pretty factory and tasting room for this craft chocolatier based in Eureka. *8am-6pm Mon-Sat, noon-4pm Sun* $

Living the Dream Ice Cream: Cones, shakes and sammiches are all on offer at this perfect spot by the Eureka Boardwalk. *noon-9pm Mon-Thu, to 10pm Fri & Sat* $

Patricks Candy: Since 1941, Patricks has been tempting locals with their creams, chews and nuts – see the saltwater taffy being made. *10am-5.30pm Mon-Fri* $

Ramone's Bakery & Cafe: They roast their own organic coffee and bake decadent desserts, like chocolate silk tarts and cream puffs. *7.30am-5pm Mon-Sat* $

EUREKA'S HISTORIC ARCHITECTURE

This loop will satisfy both your architectural appetite and your actual appetite, as it's bookended by beloved restaurants.

START	END	LENGTH
Los Bagels	Café Waterfront	1½ miles; 2 hrs

Grab coffee to go at ❶ **Los Bagels** (p258), located in an 1877 Italianate building, then head west on 2nd St until you hit the historic ❷ **Eagle House**, originally a hotel, on the corner of 2nd and C Sts.

Looping around, take a left on C St and another left on ❸ **Opera Alley**, where you can enjoy a series of street art murals. At E St, take in the 1911 Classical Revival building that houses the ❹ **Clarke Historical Museum** (p257) on your right. Continue on Opera Alley to see a pretty ❺ **purple Victorian** on your left before the intersection with L St. ❻ **Carter House** (p275) is on the corner of L and 3rd Sts; returning to 2nd St, make a right to reach M St, where you'll see ❼ **The Pink Lady** and ❽ **Carson Mansion**.

Return west on 2nd St. On your right, at 525, you'll pass the former ❾ **Vance Hotel**, an Italianate-style building from 1872, across from a unique purple-and-green building on your left. Now ❿ **The Greene Lily** restaurant, the 1866 Classical Revival building was once the Oberon Saloon. At F St, stop in at ⓫ **Many Hands Gallery** (p259) and ⓬ **Eureka Books** (p259), both in historic buildings, then finish at ⓭ **Café Waterfront**, originally the Wave Saloon, for lunch.

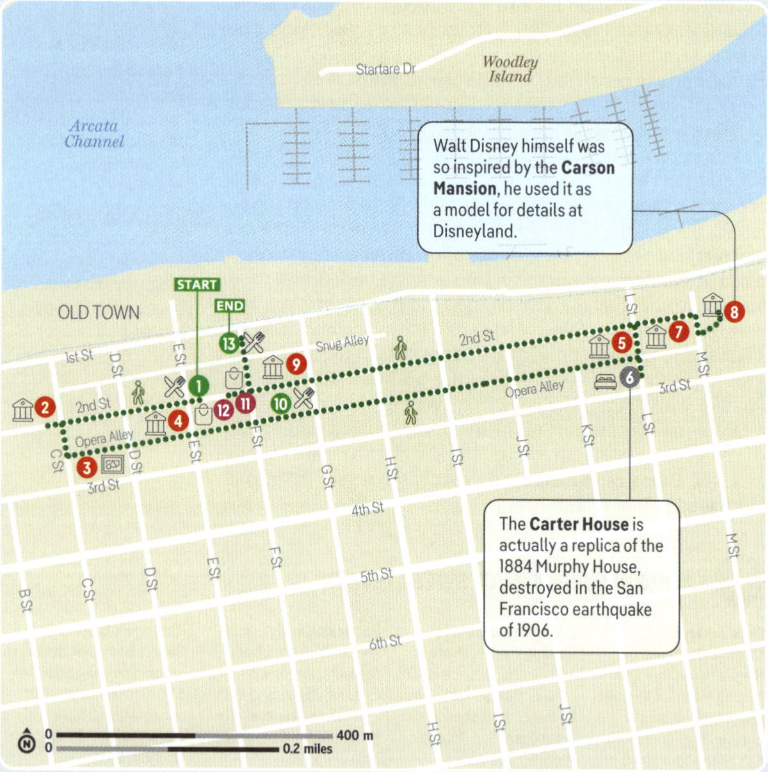

Walt Disney himself was so inspired by the **Carson Mansion**, he used it as a model for details at Disneyland.

The **Carter House** is actually a replica of the 1884 Murphy House, destroyed in the San Francisco earthquake of 1906.

Paddle Through Time

Kayak Humboldt Bay

Get a totally different perspective of Eureka and learn about its rich past on a kayak tour with **Humboats Kayak Adventures** *(humboatskayaking.com; adult/child from $55/45)*. The Humboldt Bay Kayak Eco-Tour includes a cruise to Tuluwat Island, the ancestral home of the Wiyot tribe, and a float past the city's Victorian-era waterfront, with commentary from your guide throughout. Or, go with the Sunset Kayak Tour, which also includes a bit of history but is more geared toward beginners. Single or double kayaks are available, and tours depart from the Woodley Island Marina.

When in Humboldt...

Marijuana tourism

Part of the Emerald Triangle (the cannabis-producing region of Northern California), Eureka has long had a reputation as a weed destination. Though the landscape has certainly changed (many locals say for the worse) with recreational legalization and higher regulatory fees, you can still have a unique Eureka experience. **GR Coffee & Cannabis** has a drive-thru window where you can get java and a joint. If you'd like to visit a working farm, **Humboldt Cannabis Tours** *(humcannabis.com; from $155)* will happily take you.

Murals & Museums

Appreciating Eureka's art

Walk a block in Eureka and you'll experience art in one form or another. The walls are covered in murals (many created by the legendary Duane Flatmo), utility boxes feature paintings and sidewalks are scrawled with poems. The city crackles with creativity and teems with people who love to harness it.

Wander over to the **Romano Gabriel Wooden Sculpture Garden** *(romanogabriel.com)* in Old Town for whimsical outsider art enclosed by aging glass. For 30 years, the wooden characters in Gabriel's front yard delighted locals. After he died in 1977, the city moved the collection here. For those seeking a more traditional setting, the **Morris Graves Museum of Art** *(humboldtarts.org; adult/child $5/free)* is a rotating showcase of works by artists from both the North Coast and around the world.

THE TRIATHALON OF THE ART WORLD

Visit in May and you might see moving sculptures taking to the streets of Eureka. The region's famous **Kinetic Grand Championship** takes place over Memorial Day weekend each year.

The three-day race is a battle of both engineering savoir-faire and artistic flair, as human-powered art vehicles – think five-wheeled bicycles, oversized tortoises and pedal-propelled bananas – traverse sand, street and even Humboldt Harbor. The race starts on the Arcata Plaza, moves to the Eureka waterfront and finishes on Main St in Ferndale, the setting of the event's very first race back in 1969.

DRINKING IN EUREKA: BEST FOR BEER AND COCKTAILS

The Shanty: Popular with hipsters for its pinball, pool and sweet back patio, this is the coolest bar in town. *noon-2am*

Lost Coast Brewery & Cafe: Head to their restaurant on 4th St for craft beers and burgers, or visit the brewery for a tour. *11.30am-9pm Wed-Sun*

Phatsy Kline's Parlour Lounge: Located inside the historic Eagle House, Phatsy's is the place for a fancy cocktail. *4-9pm Wed & Thu, to 11pm Fri & Sat*

The Speakeasy: Squeeze in with the locals at this New Orleans–inspired bar with live blues and a convivial atmosphere. *4-11pm Sun-Thu, to 2am Fri & Sat*

Beyond Eureka

Just outside the city, the hippie college town of Arcata has thrifting fun, good bites, coastal biking and extraordinary birdwatching.

GETTING AROUND

The Arcata and Mad River Transit System is the public bus option in town *($2 per ride)*. Because it's tied to the university, it's primarily a weekday service and only makes limited runs when CalPoly is on break. An even better way to get around town is to test out the Humboldt Bikeshare program, which allows you to reserve bikes through the free Movatic app. There's a sizable network of cycle lanes in Arcata.

Mere minutes to the north of Eureka is the region's most progressive town, Arcata, which earned the nickname Sixties by the Sea as a result of all the countercultural activity that happened here in the 1960s – and still continues to this day. Once called Union, the town played a large part in Northern California's gold rush, acting as a base for supplies. These days, the gold in Arcata might be considered its educational offerings – with the innovative and STEM-focused California State Polytechnic University in town – or its redwood forests and magical marsh. Arcata's grassy central square regularly swells with college students, campers and wanderers, and hosts a farmers market each Saturday that can't be missed.

Arcata

TIME FROM EUREKA: **10 MINS**

Thrifting in Arcata Plaza

An impressive selection of second-hand shops sits just off of Arcata's flower-filled plaza. **Miranda's Rescue Thrift Store** *(mirandasrescue.org)* has weekly sales, and **Vintage Avenger** is expertly curated. **Daydream** *(daydreamarcata.com)* has gently used hiking boots, and at **Eco-Groovy Deals** *(ecogroovydeals.com)* you can pick up a psychedelic tapestry in addition to new-to-you threads. If you're all set clothing-wise, head to **People's Records** *(peoplesrecordsarcata.com)* for vinyl and cassettes or **Tin Can Mailman** *(tincanbooks.com)* for used books.

Bike the Hammond Coastal Trail

If you'd like to give your hiking boots a rest and hop on two wheels, hit the **Hammond Coastal Trail**. The path, which is a mix of asphalt and gravel, runs 5.5 miles from the **Mad River Bridge** in Arcata to **Clam Beach** in McKinleyville. Along the way, you'll wind past coastal pastures, spot remnants of old railroad tracks, cruise within forested tunnels and enjoy views of both the Mad River and Pacific Ocean. Plus, there are convenient stops along the way for a bathroom or snack break. **Hiller Park**, about 1.5 miles in, has bathrooms and picnic tables, and **Murray Rd**, another mile north, has tables, too. If you didn't bring your own bike on the trip, you can rent one (either standard or electric) from **Wildtrail**

WATERSPIX/SHUTTERSTOCK

Lesser yellowlegs, Arcata Marsh & Wildlife Sanctuary

(wildtrailtours.com; standard bike per day from $69; e-bike half-/full-day $80/100), who will even deliver it for free within a 7-mile radius of Arcata. They also offer a two-hour **Hammond Trail Tour** *(standard/e-bike $107/129)*, if you prefer to ride with a guide.

Embark on a bird-watching adventure

The **Arcata Marsh & Wildlife Sanctuary** *(cityofarcata.org)* is an innovative combination: it's both a sustainable wastewater treatment facility and a celebrated birding park. Spread across 307 acres, the area includes freshwater marsh, salt marsh and roughly five miles of paths for walking or cycling. Birding is particularly great here because of its location along the Pacific Flyway – a major migratory route for birds that breed in California, Mexico and South America. If you want to get in on the feathered fun, volunteers lead free guided walks every Saturday, rain or shine, at 8.30am. Open to beginner bird-watchers as well as seasoned seekers, it's the perfect opportunity to get out on the marsh and mingle with nature-loving locals who never miss a week. Meet at the end of South I Street in Arcata (continue past the small parking area to a larger lot). If you see the wooden 'Audubon Nature Walks' sign, you're in the right place.

BIRDING AT ARCATA MARSH

Kathryn Wendel, president of the Redwood Region Audubon Society, gives a season-by-season birding guide.

Spring:
Look for neotropical migrants passing through, including western tanagers and warblers.

Summer:
It's breeding season. Watch for brightly colored orange-and black Bullock's orioles and yellow-breasted chats.

Fall:
From the marbled godwit to the red-necked phalarope, fall is the season for shorebirds, which come to fatten up for their long migration.

Winter:
Look out for waterfowl, including teal, northern shovelers and American wigeon. It's also a great time for raptors, like sharp-shinned hawks and merlins.

EATING & DRINKING IN ARCATA: OUR PICKS

Slice of Humboldt Pie: Expect everything from chicken pot pie to lemon raspberry pie, plus savory empanadas. *10am-9pm Tue-Thu, to 10pm Fri & Sat* $

Tomo Sushi: Located on the plaza within the historic Hotel Arcata, Tomo is the place for maki rolls and teriyaki. *4-8.30pm Mon-Sat* $$

Cafe Mokka: Order an espresso and cozy up next to the fire at Finnish Country Sauna and Tubs. *11am-11pm Sun-Thu, to midnight Fri & Sat* $

SALT: This low-lit, nautical-themed restaurant serves the coastal flavors of Italy alongside craft cocktails. *3.30-9pm Tue-Sun* $$$

Redwood National & State Parks

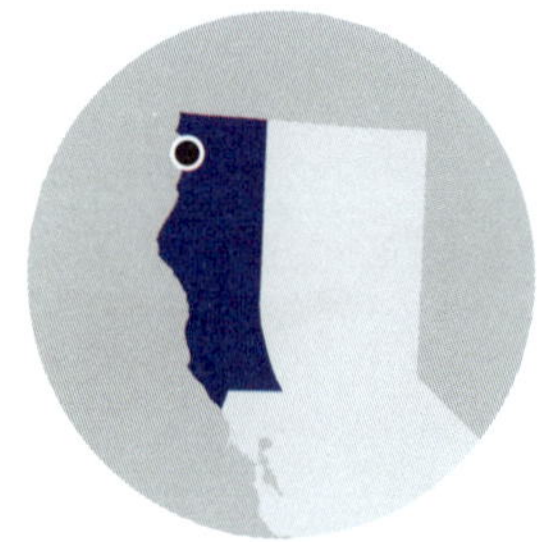

NATURAL WONDERS | HIKING | REVAMPED MOTELS

GETTING AROUND

A car is an absolute must since you'll be logging a lot of miles – plus traversing some pretty remote roads – as you bounce between parks and trails. Word to the wise: try to divide the parks into two sections: southern (Redwood National Park and Prairie Creek Redwoods State Park) and northern (Del Norte Coast Redwoods State Park and Jedediah Smith Redwoods State Park). Group activities accordingly so you don't burn through time (and gas) backtracking multiple times.

TOP TIP

Cell service is extremely spotty in this area, even when you're off the trails and making a pit stop in town. Download trail maps, driving directions and a good podcast or two for offline use.

Waterfalls, fern-covered canyons, rugged ocean coastline and, oh yes, the world's tallest trees...It's all part of the experience in this unique four-in-one park system. Located in the upper reaches of California's Pacific Coast, the area is maintained through a partnership between the National Park Service and California State Parks. That means that in addition to Redwood National Park, this northern natural wonderland also includes three state parks (from south to north): Prairie Creek Redwoods State Park, Del Norte Coast Redwoods State Park and Jedediah Smith Redwoods State Park. Because it's not your typical national or state park, there aren't gated entrances to the area (with two exceptions). Instead, the parks sit along a 50-mile driving route on Hwy 101. To experience them all, use Orick as your gateway town in the south, and Crescent City as the gateway or terminus in the north. Then all you have to do is make many, many stops in between.

Prairie & Redwoods from the Road

Take a scenic drive

Get warmed up for all the natural beauty you'll experience by taking in your surroundings on a picturesque drive. About two miles north of Orick, in **Redwood National Park** *(nps.gov/redw)*, **Bald Hills Road** is a winding jaunt over hills and alongside prairies, with an occasional lupine superbloom. The **Newton B Drury Scenic Parkway**, a 10-mile stretch in Prairie Redwoods State, is just as the name suggests – an extraordinarily scenic route through untouched ancient redwood forests. And **Howland Hill Road** is a 10-mile, unpaved stunner through the towering ancient redwoods of **Jedediah Smith Redwoods State Park** *(parks.ca.gov)*.

HIGHLIGHTS
1 Prairie Creek Redwoods State Park
2 Redwood National Park

SIGHTS
3 Bald Hills Road
4 Enderts Beach
5 Gold Bluffs Beach
6 Howland Hill Road
7 Jedediah Smith Redwoods State Park
8 Trees of Mystery

ACTIVITIES
see 7 Boy Scout Tree Trail
9 Fern Canyon Loop
10 Lady Bird Johnson Grove
11 Newton B Drury Scenic Parkway
12 Redwood Yurok Canoe Tour
13 Simpson-Reed & Peterson Loop
14 Stout Grove Loop
15 Trillium Falls Loop

SLEEPING
16 Elk Meadow Cabins
see 5 Gold Bluffs Beach Campground
see 21 Historic Requa Inn
see 14 Jedediah Smith Redwoods Campground
see 8 Motel Trees
see 20 Roosevelt Base Camp

EATING
17 Chart Room Restaurant
see 12 Country Club Bar & Grill
18 Hiouchi Cafe
19 Kin Khao Thai & Sushi Bar
see 20 Mojo Pizza
20 Orick Market
see 19 SeaQuake Brewing
21 The Historic Requa Inn

ENTERTAINMENT
see 12 Klamath Salmon Festival

INFORMATION
see 19 Crescent City Information Center
see 14 Hiouchi Visitor Center
see 14 Jedediah Smith Visitor Center
22 Prairie Creek Visitor Center
23 Thomas H Kuchel Visitor Center
see 12 Yurok Country Visitor Center

YOU'RE IN YUROK COUNTRY

With 6500 enrolled members, the Yurok Tribe (which means 'downriver people') is California's largest Native American group. Historically, they've been celebrated as expert basket weavers, canoe makers and fishers, and the traditions continue to this day. The tribe even hosts an annual **Klamath Salmon Festival** each August. In addition to supporting the tribe by hiring Yurok people as outdoor guides, consider purchasing their locally made handicrafts. You'll find dangly earrings made from pieces of abalone shell, and long beaded necklaces strung with pine nuts and tubular dentalium shells. Resembling miniature elephant tusks, these shells were once used as currency. One great place to shop is the **Yurok Country Visitor Center** in Klamath.

GERRY MATHEWS/SHUTTERSTOCK

Paul Bunyan and Babe the Blue Ox statues, Trees of Mystery

Just Bluffing

Hit the beach

If you're looking for beaches within the parks, **Gold Bluffs Beach** fits the bill in the southern section. Drive right up and bring your pup (though keep him or her on a leash) and take in the tide. Part of **Prairie Creek Redwoods State Park** *(parks.ca.gov)*, this wild coastline got its name for the gold that was once discovered in the area. Gold Bluffs Beach is open for day use and also has an overnight campground. The area can get quite busy, as the start of the popular one-mile Fern Canyon Loop Trail (p268) is nearby. Note that an entry permit is required from May 15 through September 15; reserve online at redwoodparksconservancy.org/fern-canyon. Throughout the year, there's a fee of $12 per car to access the beach, unless you have a state or national park pass.

In the northern section of the parks, just south of Crescent City, **Enderts Beach** is the place to be. There's no entry fee and the drive from Hwy 101 is much shorter than to Gold Bluffs, but getting to the sand does require a half-mile hike.

EATING IN THE NORTHERN PARKS: OUR PICKS

Chart Room Restaurant: Up in Crescent City, this harborside spot has views of sea lions and top-notch chowder. *11am-7pm Wed, Thu & Sun, to 8pm Fri & Sat* $$

Kin Khao Thai & Sushi Bar: Traditional Thai dishes and maki rolls hit the spot at this Crescent City eatery. *hours vary* $$

SeaQuake Brewing: Pizzas, burgers and beer, of course, are all on tap at this Crescent City brewery. *11.30am-8pm Sun-Thu, to 9pm Fri & Sat* $$

Hiouchi Cafe: A breakfast and lunch spot in Hiouchi, near Jedediah Smith Redwoods State Park. The cafe will gladly pack you a meal to go. *7am-2pm* $

One important note: neither of these beaches are suitable for swimming, as currents are extremely strong. But Enderts does have the best tidepooling within the park's boundaries.

Family Fun in the Forest

Visit Trees of Mystery

Disneyland may have Mickey and Minnie, but **Trees of Mystery** *(treesofmystery.net; adult/child $30/15)*, something of a nature-focused amusement park, has Paul Bunyan, Babe the Blue Ox and the redwood tree itself. It's not technically part of the national or state park systems, but it does lie along the parks' corridor so you're likely to pass by as you drive through the town of Klamath – and a stop is highly recommended. The park itself is a nature trail with attractions along the way, including intriguingly shaped redwood trees, a series of aerial suspension bridges in the canopies and a gondola ride to a scenic lookout. At times it's cheesy, but it's also the delightful kind of roadside attraction that feels straight out of a different era. And in fact, Trees of Mystery has been family-owned and operated since 1946.

After completing the trail, browse souvenirs in the massive gift shop (they have a good selection of books on local history and hiking, in addition to Paul and Babe salt and pepper shakers) and wander through the attached museum. Called the **End of the Trail Collection**, the museum has free admission and is filled with Native American artifacts as well as jewelry for purchase. If you'd like to make a full weekend of the experience, there's a retro roadside motel across the street, **Motel Trees** (p275) *(moteltrees.com)*, and a restaurant called **Forest Cafe** *(forestcafe.net)*.

Ride a Redwood down the Klamath River

Take a Yurok canoe tour

If you're going to visit Yurok Country, experience it the traditional Yurok way – by floating the Klamath River in a handcrafted vessel. June through August, visitors can book a two-hour **Redwood Yurok Canoe Tour** *(visityurokcountry.com; adult/child $150/100)* and ride in one of three dugout redwood canoes, the traditional boats of the Yurok people, the Native Americans who have been living along the Klamath for centuries. Along the ride, your guide will introduce the river's history as well as its unique geography and wildlife.

MAGNIFICENT ROOSEVELT ELK

Roosevelt elk roam the coast and forestland, and encountering these majestic creatures is as cool as it is worrisome, particularly during the August to October mating season. Bulls can weigh up to 1000 pounds and do damage with their antlers and legs, while cows with calves can also become aggressive.

Human–elk conflict has been on the rise in Northern California, and scientists are making a concerted effort to study the elk in hopes of identifying solutions. Protect both yourself and the elk by staying at least 75 feet away. They can run at speeds of up to 40mph, which is considerably faster than Olympic sprinter Usain Bolt (28mph).

EATING IN THE SOUTHERN PARKS: OUR PICKS

Orick Market: Grab snacks, picnic supplies and marshmallows for your campfire at this convenience store located right off Hwy 101 in Orick. *10am-9pm* $

Mojo Pizza: In the same parking lot as Orick Market, this food truck serves wood-fired pizzas sure to satiate the hungriest hikers. *11am-7pm Mon-Sat, from noon Sun* $

The Historic Requa Inn: Scarf down a plate of pancakes with a side of Klamath River views. *8-10am Apr-Oct, 8.30-9.30am Nov-Mar* $

Country Club Bar & Grill: This Klamath eatery has everything you'd want from a roadside stop: burgers, beer and a jukebox. *noon-8pm Wed-Mon* $$

HELP ME PICK:

Redwood National & State Parks Hiking Trails

Trying to choose a hiking trail at a national or state park can be overwhelming, so imagine what happens when you combine four parks into one. To help you make sense of the options, we've selected six all-star trails that meet specific criteria. As a reminder, tackling the southern half of the park system before moving north (or vice versa) makes logistics easier, so we've noted in parenthesis where each trail lies.

Where to hike if you...

Want Something Quick

Fern Canyon Loop (south)
There's nothing quite like this Prairie Creek canyon trail, which follows a stream surrounded by towering fern-covered walls that once served as a backdrop for *Jurassic Park: The Lost World*. The loop is only a mile, though you should allot at least 30 minutes to drive the windy gravel road (Davison) from Hwy 101 to the trailhead parking lot. Tip: wear water shoes or bring a backup pair of sneakers. Your feet will get wet.

Simpson-Reed & Peterson Loop (north) Hike two trails in under an hour at Jedediah Smith Redwoods. Combining these two short loop trails creates a 0.8-mile hike through a redwood grove that's suitable for just about any ability level. You'll start on Simpson-Reed Trail and keep veering left to add on the Peterson Loop portion of the walk. Eventually, you'll return to the Simpson-Reed Trail to finish the hike.

CAVAN-IMAGES/SHUTTERSTOCK

Fern Canyon Loop

Have Kids in Tow

Lady Bird Johnson Grove (south) This 1.4-mile hike in Redwood National Park is the ideal length for little ones. There are a number of benches where you can stop for a rest. Or give your kids a history lesson: the trail gets its name from the former first lady Claudia Johnson, whose husband, President Lyndon B Johnson, signed the bill to create this park in 1968.

Stout Grove Loop (north)
First-time hikers will feel a major sense of accomplishment when they finish this 0.6-mile loop in Jedediah Smith Redwoods. The extraordinarily picturesque surroundings – redwoods soaring above a lush forest floor – will have them permanently hooked on the great outdoors.

Hope to See a Waterfall

Trillium Falls Loop (south)
At only 2.7 miles and with a trailhead that's right off Hwy 101, this Prairie Creek path also qualifies for the quick and kid-friendly categories. The scenic and soothing falls are located in the first half-mile of the walk, so you could do the hike as a short out-and-back.

Boy Scout Tree Trail (north)
You'll have to put in a little more work to see the falls along this trail in the Jedediah Smith Redwoods, but it's worth it. The total out-and-back distance is 5.6 miles; Fern Falls is the turnaround point. Your muscles will stay active, with intermittent climbs, occasional sets of stairs and a few bridge crossings.

STEPHEN MOEHLE/SHUTTERSTOCK

Trillium Falls

HOW TO

When to go Spring is a favorite time to visit, with wildflowers in bloom and smaller crowds than summer. However, summer has drier conditions.

Book in advance Some sites, like Tall Trees Trail and Gold Bluffs Beach (which includes the Trillium Falls Loop), require advance permits during summer.

Fees There's no general entry fee for Redwood National and State Parks, though some day-use areas, including Gold Bluffs Beach *($12)*, do have fees.

Top tip Be sure to have cash on hand, as Gold Bluffs Beach kiosk only accepts cash and checks.

Visitor centers and campgrounds

Multiple parks means multiple visitor centers – five in total – which is extra convenient for getting additional details from park experts when you're on the ground. All of the visitor centers have maps. **Thomas H Kuchel Visitor Center**, located in Orick, is the furthest south. Then comes **Prairie Creek Visitor Center** at the southern end of the Newton B Drury Scenic Parkway. The **Crescent City Information Center** is located at park headquarters, then comes **Jedediah Smith Visitor Center** and the **Hiouchi Visitor Center**, both in Hiouchi. The latter has exhibits about local Native art and culture.

Want to spend the night in the parks? Camping is the only way to do so, as you won't find any hotels within the parks' boundaries. Take your pick between four developed campgrounds and seven designated backcountry options. The developed campgrounds, managed by the state parks, all have bathrooms, food storage lockers, firewood for sale and potable water, and two have year-round cell reception. Be sure to reserve your campsite in advance *(reservecalifornia.com)*, especially during the busy summer season. For the backcountry campgrounds, you'll need to request a free permit online anytime between 160 days and 24 hours in advance. These campgrounds still have some amenities, but they don't have drive-up access – instead, you have to hike to your site.

Beyond Redwood National & State Parks

Find more state parks, plus a charming town perched before a jaw-dropping headland and dramatic offshore rock islands.

Places

Trinidad p270
Sue-meg State Park p272
Humboldt Lagoons State Park p272

GETTING AROUND

As with the redwood parks area, you'll be spending the majority of your time cruising Hwy 101, so a car is definitely necessary. The good news: cell reception here is better than it is further north, so you should be okay with pulling up directions on your smartphone. If you need to gas up, do so around Trinidad.

Just south of Redwood National and State Parks, you'll find the perfect seaside village of Trinidad, a magical beach peppered with semi-precious pebbles in Sue-meg State Park, and the kayaking and bird-watching paradise that is Humboldt Lagoons State Park. While this area is big on beauty and adventure, it covers a relatively small stretch off of Hwy 101. From Trinidad in the south to Humboldt Lagoons in the north, the driving time is less than 20 minutes (and the lagoons are only about 25 minutes from Eureka/Arcata airport). That makes this area a nice stop-off either before or after you've explored the redwoods in the northernmost part of the state – though you'll still get to ogle more of the towering trees here.

Trinidad

TIME FROM ORICK: **20 MINS**

Take in Trinidad's coast

To get the lay of the land, head out on a hike at Trinidad Head, which soars 358ft above the Pacific Ocean. The **Trinidad Head Loop** is a scenic 1.4-mile stroll that offers views of partially submerged rock formations, wildflowers, an 1871 lighthouse and maybe even whales during migration season (December through April). The path is paved. For parking, follow Lighthouse Road down toward the ocean and **Trinidad State Beach** *(parks.ca.gov; free)*. Grab a spot in the lot on your right (Bay St, on the left, leads to the town's harbor and pier). The loop's trailhead is on the southern side of the parking lot up a series of steps.

After your hike, stroll over to the beach, which makes the perfect spot for a post-walk picnic. Or, grab breakfast or lunch at **Seascape Restaurant** *(seascapetrinidad.squarespace.com)* at the pier. It's open daily from 8am to 4pm, serving locally smoked salmon, bay oysters and microbrews from the area.

NAERADNUOVO/SHUTTERSTOCK

Trinidad State Beach

Shopping in Trinidad

Shopping in this tiny town isn't an all-day affair, but you'll find a few cute shops with totally unique souvenirs. Within minutes of rolling into town from the Hwy 101 exit, you'll come upon a group of stores on your right, just off of Main St. **Windandsea** *(windanseajewelry.com)* specializes in handcrafted jewelry, with earrings, cuffs and pendants made from abalone shells. They're also your go-to spot for stuffed banana slugs, glow-in-the-dark Trinidad tees and wind chimes. **Sea Around Us**, in a distinct building with weathered-wood shingles, is the place for crafters: get beads made from abalone, pine nuts and dentalia to string your own creation. The shop has been family-owned for three generations. Next, there's **Trinidad Trading Company** *(trinidadtrading.com)*, where you'll find hand-blown glass goods and Pacific Coast–inspired stationery. They also have locally made abalone baubles and wire-wrapped agate rings, which might make you feel better if you strike out at **Agate Beach** (p272).

Eating in Trinidad

Once you've worked up an appetite, **Trinidad Bay Eatery** *(trinidadeatery.com)* is the place to indulge in heaping portions of chowder (voted the best in Humboldt), served in sourdough bread bowls or with a side of garlic toast. Anything from their selection of melts or the seafood platter are solid choices, too. They're open for lunch and dinner, though you're likely to find long waits on weekend evenings in the summer.

For something casual and quick, **Headies Pizza & Pour** *(headiespizzatrinidad.com)* serves individual slices and full pies. Their menu constantly changes, so stop in to see what flavorful combinations they're sliding into the oven that day (gluten-free and vegan options available).

ALL ABOUT ABALONE

Primarily found in Pacific regions like California and Japan, these marine mollusks usually clamp tightly to rocky surfaces, feeding on algae that floats by. Their shells provide protection from predators, and the interior is the part that's prized for its iridescent kaleidoscope of colors.

Additionally, abalone meat, which is rich in protein, has long been savored in various cultures, including Japanese and Native American. In fact, up until recently, Californians on the North Coast still took part in recreational abalone diving. But because of declining populations, due to a combination of factors, including overfishing and climate change, abalone hunting has been on pause since 2017. Empty abalone shells, however, are fair game for beachcombers.

ALWAYS THERE

If you have an old map, you might notice a state park that seemingly no longer exists: Patrick's Point. That was the name of Sue-meg State Park until 2021, when the California State Park and Recreation Commission voted unanimously to change it.

The name Patrick's Point came into use after an Irish settler named Patrick Beegan spent time in the area briefly in the 1850s. He was accused of killing a Native American boy and fled, yet the name stuck. Nearly a century later, the name has reverted back to what the Yurok people have used since time immemorial – Sue-meg, which means 'always there.'

Sue-meg State Park

TIME FROM ORICK: **25 MINS**

A rockhounding haven

Anyone that appreciates a treasure hunt, both kids and adults included, will enjoy a visit to **Agate Beach**. This 2-mile stretch of sand gets its name for the semi-precious agate stones you may find scattered about. You'll find other types of pretty pebbles, too – including jade and jasper – all polished by the mighty Pacific. In addition to rockhounding, visitors can explore tidepools and keep their eyes peeled for whales and sea lions. To access the area, leave your car in the Agate Beach Campground lot and follow the designated trail down toward the water, winding past wildflowers and coastal shrubbery. It's only about a 0.3 mile-walk, but the trail descends 200 feet and is steep. Hold on to the hands of little ones and be sure to bring a bag or bucket for all your treasures.

Humboldt Lagoons State Park

TIME FROM ORICK: **10 MINS**

Lagoon hopping

The largest lagoon system in the US, **Humboldt Lagoons State Park** *(parks.ca.gov)* is home to four landlocked bodies of water. From south to north, they are: Big Lagoon, Dry Lagoon, Stone Lagoon and Freshwater Lagoon. If you'd like to take a dip, **Big Lagoon** has shallow spots where the water temperature is suitable for swimming in the summer. **Dry Lagoon**, as the name implies, isn't quite a bountiful body of water – it's more marshy than a lake. Decades ago, farmers drained it for growing crops, which didn't work out. Today, there's excellent bird-watching in the area.

If you're a diehard lagoon lover and want to spend the night, **Stone Lagoon** has a unique boat-in-only campground with six sites. To rent a kayak *(from $40)*, head to the Stone Lagoon Visitor Center, just off Hwy 101. You're also welcome to bring your own kayak and launch it near the visitor center. **Freshwater Lagoon** also has a boat launch on its northwest side. Swimming and fishing are popular activities here. If you'd like to angle for largemouth bass, catfish, cutthroat trout and stocked rainbow trout, be sure to get a California fishing license in advance.

VIVEK SEKAR/GETTY IMAGES

Humboldt Lagoons State Park

Places We Love to Stay

$ Budget $$ Midrange $$$ Top End

Mendocino

MAP P233

The Mendocino Hotel and Garden Suites $ Established in 1878, this character-filled place is a relic of the Old West.

Mendocino Grove $$ This glamping gem by the sea has safari-style tents and elegant bathhouses.

MacCallum House $$ A historic landmark, the main house has 19 unique rooms, some with claw-foot soaking tubs.

JD House $$ Enjoy breakfast delivered to your door at this hotel decked out in nautical style and surrounded by an English garden.

Stanford Inn $$$ A solarium-enclosed pool, organic gardens and a widely celebrated vegan restaurant are all part of the experience at this superlative resort.

Little River

Van Damme State Park Campground $ Three miles south of Mendocino, this campground gives you easy access to the Fern Canyon Trail and a scenic beach.

Little River Inn $$$ All rooms here have ocean views, and many also have fireplaces and hot tubs. There's also a golf course on the grounds.

Elk

Elk Cove Inn, Restaurant & Spa $$ A romantic escape set in a 19th-century Craftsman with ocean views, a rooftop deck and a beachfront gazebo.

Harbor House Inn (p239) **$$$** Home to a Michelin-starred restaurant, Harbor House also features traditional guest rooms in the main building and standalone cottages.

Anderson Valley

Hendy Woods State Park Campground $ Open to camping year round, Hendy Woods has 92 sites spread across two campgrounds, plus four cabins in Cabin Colony.

The Boonville Hotel and Restaurant $$ Take your pick between 17 unique rooms, then stay on the property for a multicourse meal with a regularly changing menu.

The Madrones (p242) **$$$** A destination for wine and cannabis, the Madrones is a Mediterranean compound with guest accommodations, two tasting rooms, an apothecary and restaurant.

Fort Bragg

Beachcomber Motel and Spa $$ Located near Glass Beach, Beachcomber has rooms with hot tubs and fireplaces, plus a large communal deck with grills.

Noyo Harbor Inn $$$ This luxury hotel is set in a historic Arts and Crafts mansion; rooms feature stunning woodwork.

Clear Lake

MAP P245

Kelsey Creek Campground $ Snag a lakeside site at this year-round campground inside Clear Lake State Park.

Harbin Hot Springs (p247) **$** Located in Middletown, this clothing-optional compound has camping, cottages and unique dome-style stays.

Clear Lake Cottages & Marina (p247) **$$** This is the ultimate retreat for fishing fans in the town of Clearlake, with boats to rent, a launch and guest cottages.

Tallman Hotel $$ Here's an elegant Upper Lake hotel featuring a shady garden, walled-in pool, brick patios and classy porches.

Suites on Main $$ A collection of bright, contemporary suites with full kitchens, the property has a backyard garden and views of downtown Kelseyville.

The Lost Coast

MAP P250

Mattole Campground $ At the northern point of the Lost Coast Trail, this campground is just steps from the beach and has 27 sites.

Usal Beach Campground $ Inside Sinkyone Wilderness State Park, this is a somewhat lawless Lost Coast campground that's accessed from the south via Hwy 1.

Needle Rock Campground $ Another option inside Sinkyone Wilderness State Park, with 10 basic sites and a cozy barn.

Tides Inn $$ Perched above Shelter Cove's tidepools, the squeaky-clean rooms here offer excellent views.

Inn of the Lost Coast $$$ Rooms have ocean-facing balconies and kitchenettes; one suite even has a hot tub and sauna.

Ferndale

Gingerbread Mansion $$ Stay in one of the most iconic Victorian mansions on the North Coast. The rooms are just as exciting as the inn's exterior.

Victorian Inn $$ Situated in an old bank on Ferndale's main drag, the Victorian has period-style wallpaper and funky antiques.

The Shaw House $$ Bring your whole crew for a stay at California's oldest B&B – the family suite has three beds, a fireplace and claw-foot tub.

Eureka

MAP P258

The Pinc $ Stay in Eureka's iconic Pink Lady mansion – some (more budget-friendly) rooms have shared bathrooms.

Inn at 2nd & C $$ This glorious historic hotel has been tastefully restored to combine Victorian-era decor with every possible modern amenity.

Carter House Inns $$ Choose a room in the Hotel Carter, Carter House, Carter Cottage or Bell Cottage and enjoy free wine on arrival.

Arcata

Hotel Arcata $ Anchoring the plaza, this renovated 1915 brick landmark has friendly staff and comfortable, old-world rooms.

Front Porch Inn $$ This boutique oasis has elaborate themed rooms and a magical outdoor bathhouse with private soaking tubs surrounded by moss- and fern-covered walls.

Redwood National and State Parks

MAP P265

Gold Bluffs Beach Campground $ Within Prairie Creek Redwoods State Park, sleep within easy reach of a secluded beach and Fern Canyon.

Jedediah Smith Redwoods Campground $ Stay in the main loop, outer loop or redwoods cabin area, with cabins that sleep up to six.

Motel Trees $ Kiddos will be excited about the views of the jumbo Paul Bunyan statue across the street at Trees of Mystery.

Roosevelt Base Camp $$ Fitting for a classic road trip, this amenity-filled stay (popcorn in your kitchenette and wood by the firepit) is in a refurbished 1950s motel.

Historic Requa Inn $$ Every room at this 100-year-old inn has a Klamath River view. One room is the town's former post office.

Elk Meadow Cabins $$$ These spotless and bright cabins have equipped kitchens and elk on the lawn. Bonus: they're sandwiched between two redwood parks.

Trinidad

Trinidad Bay Bed & Breakfast $$$ Hospitality is king at this B&B perched above Trinidad Bay. Gourmet breakfasts and cozy rooms with ocean views.

Lost Whale Inn $$$ High above the crashing waves north of Trinidad, this spacious, modern and light-filled B&B has stunning views.

Sue-meg State Park

Agate Beach Campground $ Calling all rockhounding fans: Sue-meg has a campground and cabin area at the entry point for Agate Beach.

Abalone Campground $ As Sue-meg's largest campground, Abalone is your best bet for finding a site during peak times.

MICHAEL VI/SHUTTERSTOCK

Carter House Inns

For places to stay in the Northern Mountains, see p311

MICHEAL LEE/SHUTTERSTOCK

Above: Bumpass Hell (p293), Lassen Volcanic National Park; Right: Mt Shasta (p284)

Researched by
Celeste Brash

Northern Mountains

CALIFORNIA'S UNSUNG MOUNTAIN PARADISE

Vast forests, lofty peaks and high deserts delight, with the surreal, pyramid-shaped Mt Shasta winking at you around every turn.

'Hidden California' gets bandied around casually, but the northeastern corner of the state really does seem forgotten. Prepare yourself for something completely different from the sunny West Coast clichés: vast expanses of wilderness – some 24,000 protected acres – divided by rivers and dotted with cobalt lakes, horse ranches and alpine peaks. Further east is a stretch of shrubby high desert cut with amber gorges, caves and dramatic light that's a photographer's dream. The topography resembles the older mountains of the Rockies more than the relatively young Sierras. The towns are tiny but friendly, with few comforts; come to get lost in vast remoteness. Even the two principal attractions, Mt Shasta and Lassen Volcanic National Park, remain relatively uncrowded at the peak of summer.

You'll want a car out here to explore the interstates and country roads, places where you can drive for hours without seeing another soul – or a gas station (fill up when you can). Wonders like McArthur-Burney Falls and Lava Beds National Monument are far from everything, but worth the trip. Or base yourself at Mt Shasta or Lassen Volcanic National Park where there are enough hiking trails to fill several months, plus lakes, biking and fishing. Spiritual seekers will be drawn to Shasta's mountain magic and counterculture vibes. Load up on crystals and try to find a vortex.

CARRIE EPLEY/SHUTTERSTOCK

THE MAIN AREAS

MT SHASTA REGION
Mountain vortexes to lava tubes.
p282

MT LASSEN REGION
Fantastic volcanic landscapes.
p292

REDDING & SHASTA LAKE
Houseboating and camping.
p303

Find Your Way

I-5 divides the better-known mountain areas to the east from the lesser-visited forests, small towns and lakes to the west. Hwy 89 is the principal route to get around Mt Lassen.

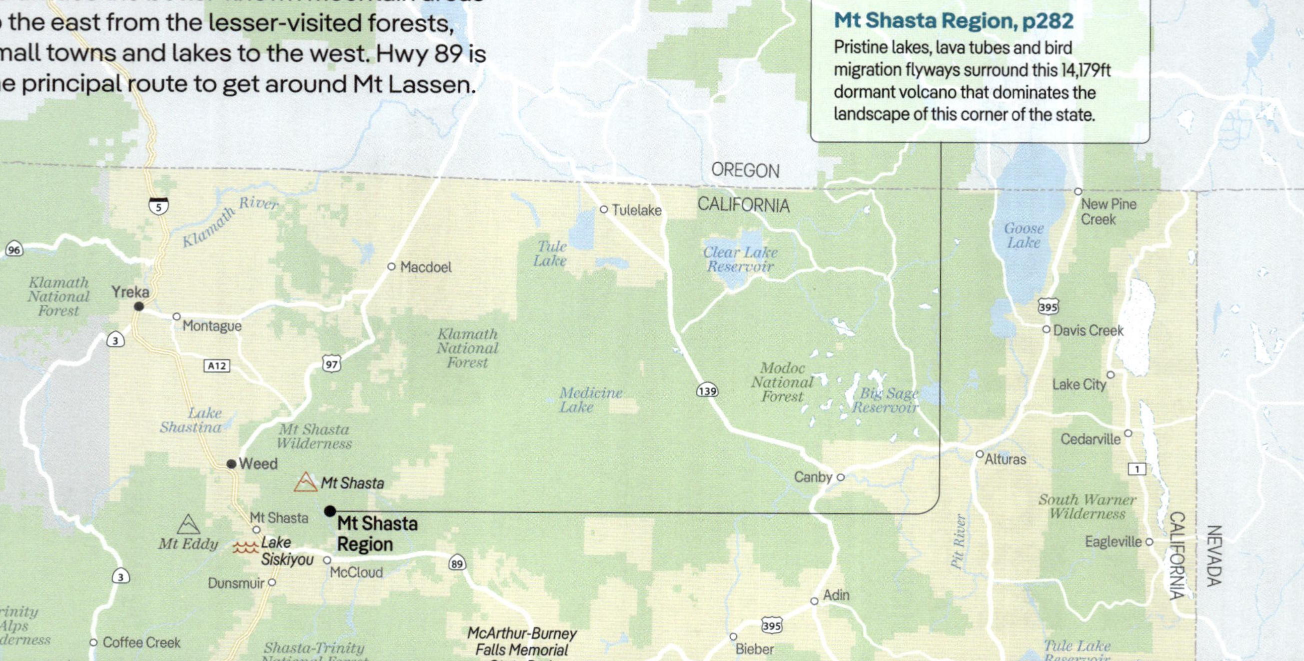

Mt Lassen Region, p292

Head here for volcano-laced hiking, through bubbling mud pots and sulfuric ponds. Winter heralds snowshoeing, sledding and skiing in spectacular scenery.

Redding & Shasta Lake, p303

Rent a houseboat or take a day trip to the massive Shasta Caverns to discover California's largest reservoir.

TRAIN

Amtrak stops in Redding, Dunsmuir, and Klamath Falls, Oregon. The latter is a good jumping-off point (you'll need a car from here) for Lava Beds National Monument and Tule Lake.

BUS

Long-distance buses like Greyhound ply I-5, but you'll have to navigate small local services with limited schedules to get elsewhere.

CAR

The Northern Mountains are heaven for road-trippers. Even the interstates lead through incredible scenery and tiny towns. Roll into campsites and pitch a tent, or stop at motels on a whim.

Plan Your Days

This is road-tripping Shangri-la, where you can stop at mountain lakes, pitch a tent, hike to incredible vistas and see a plethora of wildlife.

SUNDRY PHOTOGRAPHY/SHUTTERSTOCK

Lassen Peak (p292), Lassen Volcanic National Park

If You Only Do One Thing

- Magnificent **Mt Shasta** (p284) is just off I-5 (you'll see it for miles before you reach it), so there's no excuse not to pull into Mt Shasta City, then drive as far as you can up the mountain – in summer you can get up to 7800ft and in winter 6950ft.

- Wherever you end up, take as long a hike as time allows and enjoy the incredible scenery of this forested, dormant volcano. On your way out, you might be inspired to shop for a **crystal souvenir** (p282), eat at one of the town's enticing **restaurants** (p284) or even stay the night to soak up the mountain energy. **Lake Siskiyou** (p287) is only 5 miles from town and is perfect for a summer dip.

Seasonal Highlights

The main season runs May–October. Many services close during colder months. Lakes are warmish July–September; winter snow sports are best December–March.

FEBRUARY

The best months for winter sports, with the deepest snow base for snowshoeing, Nordic and downhill skiing, plus a good chance of blue skies. Ice skate in Shasta City or take a snowmobile tour.

APRIL

Songbird and waterfowl numbers peak (up to 10,000 swans!) around **Tule Lake** (p290) and the main breeding period begins near the end of the month for epic bird-watching. Meanwhile, it's bald-eagle nesting season at **Shasta Lake** (p303).

MAY

A great month for offseason road-tripping; visitation at the national parks is still low. Many services begin opening at the start of the month and most are open by the last week. The weather can be cool to warm, but pleasant.

Three Days to Travel Around

- From the Bay Area, head first to **Lassen Volcanic National Park** (p292) and spend a day driving the park and hiking to the bubbling and bright 'mini Yellowstone' **Bumpass Hell Trailhead** (p293).

- The next day take back-road Hwy 89 for incredible views of Mt Shasta and detour to the impressive **McArthur-Burney Falls Memorial State Park** (p288). Spend the night in tiny, charming **McCloud** (p286), where you can start or end the day with a forest stroll.

- Spend day three exploring **Mt Shasta** (p284), either hiking on the mountain or relaxing and swimming in **Castle Lake** (p287). Don't miss strolling the town of Mt Shasta too, with its new-age shopping and mellow vibe.

If You Have More Time

- Follow the three-day itinerary, taking more time in the national park and on **Mt Shasta** (p284), then take Hwy 97 east from Weed to **Tule Lake** (p290) for a day or more of canoeing and oohing and aahing over bald eagles, waterfowl and osprey.

- From here it's only 12 miles to the fantastic **Lava Beds National Monument** (p289), where you could spend a few days exploring caves, above-ground lava-scapes and Native American historical sites scrawled with petroglyphs.

- Then loop back via Yreka and down Hwy 3 through mountains and charming small towns to **Weaverville** (p309) and **Redding** (p303). In summer, plunge in to **Trinity** (p310) or **Whiskeytown Lake** (p307), cast a line in **Lewiston Lake** (p309) or pitch a tent in the vast wilderness.

JUNE

Scenic, pre-summer-rush hiking, with lingering mountain snow, gushing waterfalls and blooming wildflowers in the lowlands. Farmers markets open up for fun shopping around the region.

JULY

Summer is in full swing and the **High Sierra Music Festival** (p302) rocks the town of Quincy. Lakeshores and the national park can be busy. Expect fun July 4 parades and fireworks in all the towns.

AUGUST

It's hot outside, perfect for family camping, paddleboarding and kayaking around Lake Siskiyou or motorboating and fishing on Lake Almanor. Sundays mean free live-music performances in Mt Shasta's Shastice Park.

OCTOBER

Leaves begin to turn, with foliage peaking mid-month on Mt Shasta and Lassen Peak; warm days and cold nights. Halloween means pumpkin patches and small-town celebrations.

Mt Shasta Region

ALPINE HIKING | SPIRITUAL ADVENTURES | WINTER SPORTS

TOP TIP

There are great views of Mt Shasta from I-5, but leaving the interstate and driving east will afford even better angles. Be sure to account for the time you'll need to pull over again and again to take in all the majesty and snap photos.

GETTING AROUND

This region is best explored by car in order to get to all the remote roads, trailheads and campsites. However, the Amtrak Coast Starlight Train stops in Dunsmuir and Greyhound buses stop in Weed. You could catch local bus services to get around from either of these towns, but schedules are erratic and you won't have the freedom to get to into the wilderness, which is what the whole place is about.

'Lonely as God and white as a winter moon,' wrote poet Joaquin Miller about this lovely mountain. The sight of it is so awe-inspiring that the new-age claims about its power as an energy vortex sound plausible, even after a first glimpse.

There are a million ways to explore Mt Shasta and the surrounding Shasta-Trinity National Forest: take scenic drives or get out and hike, mountain bike, raft, ski or snowshoe. Around the mountain sit four excellent little towns: Dunsmuir, Mt Shasta City, McCloud and Weed. Each has a distinct personality, but all hold a wild-mountain sensibility and first-rate amenities. Find the snaggletoothed peaks of Castle Crags just 6 miles west of Dunsmuir.

A long drive northeast of Mt Shasta and a world away, the eerily beautiful Lava Beds National Monument is a blistered badland of petrified fire. The contrasting wetlands of Klamath Basin National Wildlife Refuge lie just west.

Crystal Shops & Vortex Tours

MAP P285

A mystical energy center

Mt Shasta is considered a power center, where mythical ley lines cross, producing a high concentration of electromagnetic energy on par with Stonehenge, Machu Picchu and the pyramids of Giza. Whatever you believe, there's no denying that the mountain exudes intense beauty and majesty. If you want to explore the mountain's mysticism, **Mt Shasta City** is where to start. Within the town's tiny grid of streets you'll find six crystal shops, each different from the next. The **Crystal Room** *(thecrystalroom.store; 11am-6pm),* is the biggest, with myriad rooms and museum-grade pieces with prices to match. **Soul Connections** *(soulconnectionstore.com; 10am-6pm),* just around the corner, has books, candles and sage sticks alongside a good selection of crystals. Cross the street to **Crystal Keepers** *(crystalkeepers.net)* in one large room, featuring accessible pricing and

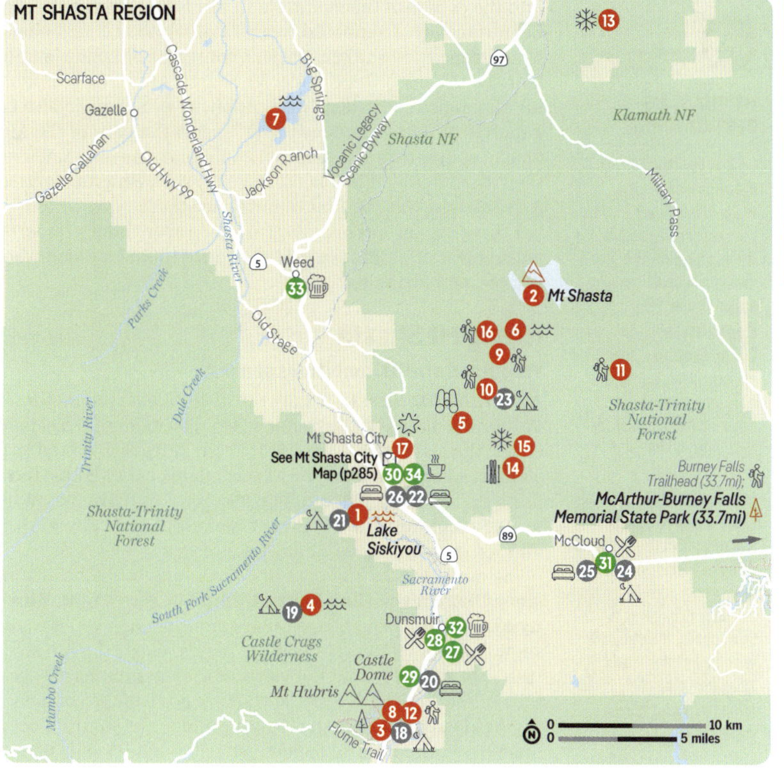

★ **HIGHLIGHTS**
1 Lake Siskiyou
2 Mt Shasta

SIGHTS
3 Castle Crags State Park
4 Castle Lake
5 Everitt Vista Point
6 Helen Lake
7 Lake Shastina
8 Vista Point Trailhead

ACTIVITIES
9 Avalanche Gulch
10 Bunny Flat
11 Clear Creek Trailhead
12 Crags Trail Trailhead
13 Fun Factory Rentals
14 Mt Shasta Nordic Center
15 Mt Shasta Ski Park
16 Sierra Club Horse Camp
17 Siskiyou Ice Rink

SLEEPING
18 Castle Crags State Park Campground
19 Castle Lake Campground
20 Jubilee Railroad Resort
21 Lake Siskiyou Beach & Camp
22 LOGE Mt Shasta
23 Lower Panther Meadows
24 McCloud Dance Country RV Park
25 McCloud Hotel
26 Strawberry Valley Inn

EATING
27 Bee Kind Bakery & Cafe
28 Cornerstone Bakery & Café
29 Dining Car at Jubilee Railroad
30 Lily's
31 Sage Restaurant

DRINKING & NIGHTLIFE
32 Dunsmuir Brewery Works
33 Mt Shasta Brewing Company
34 Seven Suns Coffee & Cafe

personal care from the friendly staff; it's open 10am to 6pm. Our favourite is **Crystal Matrix** *(crystalmatrixgallery.com; 10am-6pm Wed-Mon)* hidden on the next block, which feels more like a rock-hound shop, with a kind and intuitive owner who knows his stuff.

Crystals in hand, sign up for a **Vortex Tour** (plan a few weeks ahead in summer). These tours are generally one-on-one and the guide will lead you to various vortexes on the mountain, where you'll meditate with the goal of being led

MT SHASTA'S BEST CAMPING

Lower Panther Meadows: Fifteen walk-in, summer-season tent sites are the highest on the mountain and have spectacular views.

Castle Lake Campground: Only six primitive, summer campsites are found here, about a quarter mile below the lake, but they are very special indeed.

Lake Siskiyou Beach & Camp: On the shore of Lake Siskiyou, this sprawling, family-friendly place has a summer-camp feel, with swimming and boat rentals.

Castle Crags State Park Campground: Campsites are shady, pretty and have plenty of amenities.

McCloud Dance Country RV Park: With campsites under the trees and a small creek, this is a good option for families. The view of the mountain is breathtaking.

into the depths of the mountain to meet the Lemurians. The Lemurians are a supposed race of tall white or blue beings who escaped the sunken, ancient continent of Lemuria and founded the city of Telos under Mt Shasta. Anything goes, but it's all happening in deep meditation, so what you believe is a matter of faith. The tours often end at the base of the Mt Shasta summit trail, a spot that could make anyone feel like they're surrounded by magic. Ashalyn with **Shasta Vortex Adventures** was the first to introduce these types of tours, but there are several operators around town and it's important to meet or at least email in advance to find a guide who you feel comfortable with.

Hiking Mt Shasta

MAP P283

Woodland strolls, ambitious summit

At 14,179ft, **Mt Shasta** is only the fifth-highest mountain in California, but its beauty is unrivaled. The mountain has two cones: the main cone has a crater about 200yd across and the younger, shorter cone on the western flank, called **Shastina**, has a crater about half a mile wide. You can drive part way up the mountain via the Everitt Memorial Hwy (Hwy A10) and see exquisite views at any time of year.

The moderate 3.5-mile out-and-back hike to the beautiful stone 1922 **Sierra Club Horse Camp** hut leaves from **Bunny Flat** (6940ft) and is open year-round, though you'll want snowshoes in winter. It's popular for a reason: the forested trail isn't too steep and the views of the mountain are spectacular. Bunny Flat is also the starting place of the challenging **Avalanche Gulch**, the easiest route to the summit, best done between May and September. Although it's only about 10 miles round-trip, the vertical climb is more than 7000ft, so acclimatizing to the elevation is critical – many hikers overnight at **Helen Lake** (10,443ft). This route requires crampons, an ice axe and a helmet, all of which can be rented locally. Rockslides, while rare, are also a hazard. If you want to make the climb without gear, the only option is the **Clear Creek Route** (10 miles round-trip), which leaves from the east side of the mountain. In late summer this route is usually manageable in hiking boots, though it could also be done as an overnight hike. Novices or those wanting to climb the more technical Cascade Gulch or West Face Gully routes should contact the **Mt Shasta Ranger Station** *(fs.usda.gov; 8am-4pm Mon-Fri)* for a list of available guides.

The section of highway beyond Bunny Flat is only open when it's snow-free (mid-June to October). This road leads to

EATING IN MT SHASTA REGION: RESTAURANTS

MAPS P283, P285

Bistro 107: Get excellent burgers and hearty hot sandwiches at this homey yet classy little joint. *11.30am-9pm Fri-Tue* **$$**

Hari On Shri Ram Indian Cuisine: The most authentic and delicious Indian food for hundreds of miles, served with a smile. *noon-3pm & 5-9pm Wed-Mon* **$$**

Lily's: Great American breakfasts plus Asian or Mediterranean-touched salads, fresh sandwiches and good, square meals. *8am-2pm & 4-8pm Wed-Sun* **$$**

Crave: Street tacos, sandwiches, barbecue, vegetarian...it's all good. Setting is basic but comfy and friendly. *11.30am-8pm Tue-Sat* **$$**

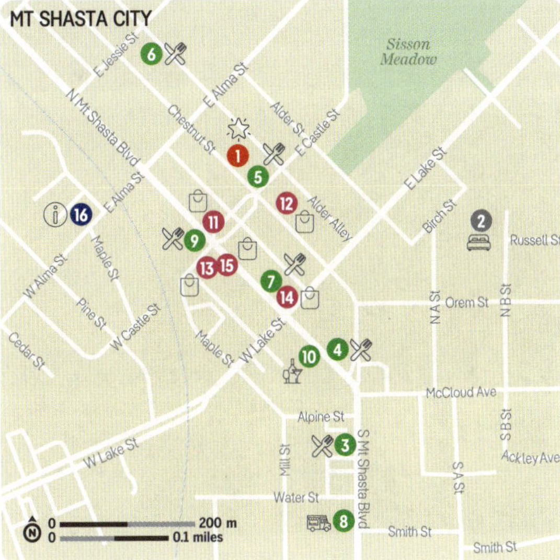

Lower Panther Meadows, where short trails connect the campground to a Wintu sacred spring in the upper meadows near the Old Ski Bowl (7800ft) parking area. Several other gorgeous trails leave from here, including a 7-mile downhill jaunt to Bunny Flat. Shortly after Panther Meadows is the highlight of the drive, **Everitt Vista Point** (7900ft), where a short interpretive walk leads to a stone-walled outcrop affording exceptional views of Lassen Peak to the south, the Mt Eddy and Marble Mountains to the west and the whole of Strawberry Valley below.

There's a charge to climb beyond 10,000ft: a three-day summit pass costs $25; an annual pass is $30. Contact the ranger station for details. You must obtain a free wilderness permit any time you go into the wilderness, whether you're on the mountain or in the surrounding areas.

Small-Town Bliss

MAP P283

Outdoor fun, great food

The small towns surrounding Mt Shasta and Mt Shasta City are not only excellent bases for outdoor fun; they also hold some of the region's best dining. Little **Dunsmuir**, a railroad stop with an adorable historic downtown, has cafes, restaurants,

EATING IN MT SHASTA REGION: QUICK EATS & COFFEE

MAPS P283, P285

Poncho & Lefkowitz: Surrounded by a picnic table or three, this classy, wood-sided food cart turns out juicy Polish sausages, tamales and burritos. *11am-4pm* $

Yak's Shack: Massive, wacky burgers, outdoor seating plus an attached ice shop in Mt Shasta. There's a second Yak's off I-5 near Dunsmuir. *7am-8pm* $

Seven Suns Coffee & Cafe: This snug, very local hangout serves organic, locally roasted coffee and light meals. *6am-2pm* $

Berryvale Grocery: Natural groceries plus a sandwich counter, perfect for grabbing lunch for the trail. *8am-8pm* $

FREEING THE KLAMATH RIVER

In 2024 the state of California returned 2800 acres of land – located around 30 miles northeast of Yreka – to the Shasta Indian Nation *(shastaindiannation.org)*. The Shasta and Klamath Peoples lost their last holdings in the region and were displaced in 1911 when the Copco No 1 Dam was constructed as part of the Klamath Hydroelectric Project. In December 2024, the dam was destroyed (along with three others, as part of the Klamath River Renewal), freeing the Klamath River for spawning salmon and for the Shasta Indian Nation to return home. Within weeks of the dams' destruction, Chinook salmon were observed spawning in the area.

galleries and a spirited artistic community. **Weed** has suffered some serious fire damage over the years, but you can still get an 'I love Weed' T-shirt or stop for a craft brew at the excellent **Mt Shasta Brewing Company** *(mtshastabrewingcompany.com; noon-8pm)*. Tiny **McCloud** is a scenic hamlet with excellent hiking, fishing and a snow park at its doorstep. The 1916 refurbished jewel, the **McCloud Hotel** *(mccloudhotel.com)*, has both fine dining and more casual fare.

Hiking in Castle Crags State Park

MAP P283

An exceptional peak

The spectacular, soaring spires of granite at **Castle Crags State Park** *(parks.ca.gov; vehicle day use $10)* rise to an elevation of over 6500ft. Best views are from **Vista Point** (a 0.25-mile walk from the parking lot), where you can also start the strenuous 2.7-mile **Crags Trail**. This longer hike rises through the forest past the Indian Springs spur trail, then clambers to the base of Castle Dome. You're rewarded with unsurpassed views of Mt Shasta, especially if you scramble the last 100yd or so up into the rocky saddle gap. The park

EATING AROUND SHASTA CITY: OUR PICKS

MAP P283

Dining Car at Jubilee Railroad: Classy California cuisine in newly remodeled train dining cars make for a memorable meal. *8am-9pm* $$$

Sage Restaurant: Swanky McCloud venue with locally sourced meats and veg dishes prepared with Californian-Mediterranean flair. *5-8pm Fri-Tue* $$$

Cornerstone Bakery & Café: Best breakfasts and lunches around – all the Benedicts are excellent and the biscuits are legendary. *7.30am-2pm Thu-Mon* $$

Bee Kind Bakery & Cafe: Adorable cafe with delectable baked goods and coffee, light meals and a sunny back garden to enjoy it in. *8am-2pm Wed-Sun* $

SIMONE HOGAN/SHUTTERSTOCK

Lake Siskiyou

also has a number of more gentle trails; 8 miles of the Pacific Crest Trail passes through the park.

Mountain Lake Majesty

MAP P283

Relax by the water

There are a number of pristine mountain lakes near Mt Shasta, some of which are only accessible by dirt roads or hiking trails. The closest, largest and busiest lake to Mt Shasta City is lovely **Lake Siskiyou**. There's a huge campground here where you can join the family revelry, splashing around, sunbathing (in summer) and making new friends. Another 7 miles up in the mountains, southwest of Lake Siskiyou, lies quieter and more remote **Castle Lake**, an unspoiled gem surrounded by granite formations and pine forest. Try your luck hiking in a quarter mile to nab a free, primitive campsite in the conifers. Then swim, fish and chill; in winter, folks ice-skate on the lake. **Lake Shastina**, near Weed, is great for paddling a kayak or canoe when its calm, or windsurfing when the regular winds here pick up. It has an extraordinary view of Mt Shasta.

OVERTOURISM AT BURNEY FALLS

These stunning, remote falls became Instagram famous during the COVID-19 pandemic and afterwards, bringing a massive visitor increase, peaking at over 350,000 annual visitors in 2023. Now on summer days, the parking lot fills, two-lane Route 89 gets backed up for miles and many hopeful selfie snappers are turned away once the park reaches capacity. As the second-oldest state park in California, this once sleepy spot was not prepared for its popularity and was forced to close in early 2024 due to trail damage caused by excessive use. It quietly reopened at the end of 2024. If you're visiting May–September, check the park website *(parks.ca.gov)* for conditions or prepare for a possibly frustrating day.

DRINKING IN & AROUND MT SHASTA: OUR PICKS

MAPS P283, P285

Pipeline Craft Taps & Kitchen: Lively gastropub; indoor/outdoor seating right in Mt Shasta. Excellent craft brew selection and food to match. *11am-9pm* $$

Dunsmuir Brewery Works: Come for the exceptional beers brewed in-house and stay for the food; from steamed mussels to elk burgers. *11am-8pm Wed-Sun* $$

Mt Shasta Brewing Company: Try a tasty Lemurian Lager or the rich, easy-drinkable Hazy IPA alongside pub food like bratwurst and wings. *noon-8pm* $$

Clandestino: Spanish wines, tapas and beer in an intimate yet convivial space. *4-7pm Tue-Sat* $$

SÁTTÍTLA HIGHLANDS NATIONAL MONUMENT

To be or not to be. In January 2025, at the very end of his term, President Biden designated this 224,676 acres of land on the Modoc, Shasta-Trinity and Klamath national forests as the US' newest National Monument. When we visited later that year, park officials were unsure that the designation will stick. The monument's center is **Medicine Lake Volcano**, a dormant volcano roughly 10 times the size of Mt St Helens in Washington. Unexplored lava tubes, threatened wildlife such as the Sierra Nevada fox, at least 16 species of rare plants and 20 species of fungi and a deep cultural importance to the region's Native Peoples are a part what makes this place worthy of protection.

STEPHEN MOEHLE/SHUTTERSTOCK

Burney Falls

View Wondrous Burney Falls

MAP P283

Take a misty stroll

Worth the 41-mile detour from McCloud, **McArthur-Burney Falls Memorial State Park**'s *(parks.ca.gov; parking $10)* centerpiece 129ft falls are fed by a spring that flows year-round at the same temperature, a nippy 42°F (5.5°C). It might not be California's highest waterfall, but it may be the most beautiful (Teddy Roosevelt considered it the eighth wonder of the world). Clear water surges over the top and also from springs in the waterfall's face. Hiking trails include a portion of the Pacific Crest Trail, but it's the 1.3-mile **Burney Falls Trail Trailhead** that you shouldn't miss. It's an easy loop for families and allows close-up views of water rushing right out of the rock.

Top Shasta Winter Activities

MAP P283

Snowshoe, ski and ice skate

There's no end of winter fun around Mt Shasta. For pristine snowscapes, try snowshoeing on trails leaving from Castle Crags State Park (p286) or the Bunny Flat Trailhead (p284) on Mt Shasta. For more excitement, ski, snowboard or sled at family-friendly **Mt Shasta Ski Park** *(skipark.com)*. You can also cross-country ski on the scenic, groomed trails of **Mt Shasta Nordic Center** *(mtshastanordic.org)*, take a thrilling snowmobile tour with **Fun Factory Rentals** *(funfactory rentals.com)* or ice-skate at **Siskiyou Ice Rink**, right in the heart of Mt Shasta City. Locals love to go ice fishing for trout at **Castle Lake**. You can rent most gear in Mt Shasta City at **Fifth Season Sports** *(thefifthseason.com; 9am-6pm)*.

Beyond Mt Shasta Region

From caving to bird-watching, this remote corner of the state is worth the long drive.

One of California's most remote areas holds two special places that would be overrun by tourists were they closer to, well, anything. Lava Beds National Monument is a remarkable 47,000-acre landscape of lava flows, craters, cinder cones, spatter cones, amazing lava tubes and petroglyphs. More than 800 caves have been found in the monument and they average a comfortable 55°F (13°C) no matter the season. Only a 15-minute drive away, the Klamath Basin Wild Refuge is where you can drive, canoe or hike to gaze on a spectacular array of birdlife. This network of lakes extends over the Oregon border and is a key nesting and resting area on the Pacific Flyway.

Places

Lava Beds National Monument p289

Klamath Basin Wildlife Refuge p290

GETTING AROUND

You'll need your own wheels to get around the national monument and wildlife refuge. Klamath Falls in Oregon is the closest real town (about an hour by car) and it's possible to base yourself here. Be aware that FS-97, FS-49 (to Medicine Lake) and FS-10 (to Tionesta) leading into Lava Beds National Monument are not maintained and may be closed November to mid-May. Check the park website *(nps .gov/labe)* for current conditions.

Lava Beds National Monument

TIME FROM MT SHASTA: 1¾HR

Caving at Lava Beds National Monument

A wild landscape of charred volcanic rock and rolling hills, this remote national monument is reason enough to visit the region. Off Hwy 139, immediately south of Tule Lake National Wildlife Refuge, **Lava Beds National Monument** *(nps.gov/labe; parking $25)* is roughly 90 miles northeast of Mt Shasta City. Spending a day or two exploring the two dozen or so caves open to the public here will be unlike any other caving experience you've ever had, simply because of the sheer variety.

Every cave is unique and the short, one-way **Cave Loop** drive provides access to many of them. **Mushpot Cave**, the one nearest to the visitor center, has lighting and information signs and is an easy, beautiful introductory hike for all levels. More challenging options include the naturally lit **Sunshine Cave**; the rugged, lava-formation-filled **Hercules Leg Cave**; the azure-hued **Blue Grotto**; and the truly spectacular **Golden Dome Cave**, with its ceiling covered in hydrophobic bacteria that sparkles like gold. Good brochures with details of each cave are available from the visitor center; staff will also inform you which are currently open. **Symbol Bridge Cave**,

CAPTAIN JACK'S STRONGHOLD

Captain Jack, a Modoc Native also known as Chief Kintpuash, used a naturally formed fort in Lava Beds National Monument as a stronghold after returning with his band of around 160 people to their ancestral homeland at Lost River in 1873. For about half a year, just over 50 Modoc warriors were able to hold off the US Army, which sometimes numbered as many as 300 soldiers. Eventually, the Army cut off access to the nearest water supply, the group was defeated and Captain Jack surrendered. He was executed in 1873 and the surviving Modoc were relocated to a reservation in Oklahoma.

reached via an easy 0.8-mile hike, is rarely visited and is filled with paintings and petroglyphs, likely from early traveling Native Americans on vision quests.

Rangers at the **visitor center** loan mediocre flashlights (and sell helmets and kneepads in the summer) for cave exploration and lead summer interpretive programs, including campfire talks and guided cave walks. Better is to have your own headlamp with extra batteries. Wear good shoes, long sleeves (caves can get cold) and do not explore the caves alone.

Hiking at Lava Beds National Monument

Lava Beds National Monument has volcanic thrills above ground as well. The landscapes were dramatically painted by ancient, fiery eruptions. There's little shade, so it's best to avoid hiking midday.

At the center of the monuments, the unmissable tall black cone (5253ft) of **Schonchin Butte** rewards hikers with magnificent vistas from a lookout, after a steep 0.75-mile trail. But the best walk in the park is your choice of two self-guided routes along the **Stronghold Trail** (0.5 mile to 1.5 miles) that wend through the labyrinthine landscape of **Captain Jack's Stronghold**. Then don't miss a drive to the far northeastern end of the monument to stroll **Petroglyph Point** (0.25-mile hike), where Modoc carved the patterned petroglyphs thousands of years ago. There's also a short trail at the top of the hill with amazing views over the plains and Lower Klamath Lake.

Klamath Basin Wildlife Refuge

TIME FROM MT SHASTA: 1½HR

Bird-watching in a magical habitat

The **Klamath Basin Wildlife Refuge** *(fws.gov; entry free)* straddles the Oregon–California border, providing habitats for a stunning array of birds migrating along the Pacific Flyway. Some stop over only briefly; others stay longer to mate, make nests and raise their young. Spying them is an intensely magical experience, regardless of the time of year you visit.

Grab a map at the **visitor center** *(9am–4pm)* and head off on a self-guided driving tour that will take you to some of the best viewing points. For even better views from the water, try out the self-guided canoe trails in the **Tule Lake** *(fws.gov; free)* refuge, which is usually open from July 1 to September 30; canoes are available for free at the visitor center. Canoe trails in the **Upper Klamath** *(fws.gov; free)* refuge are open

EATING AROUND LAVA BEDS NATIONAL MONUMENT: OUR PICKS

Polar Bear: Classic, cute and friendly burger joint in Merrill, Oregon; with good-quality food. *10am-8pm Mon-Sat, to 6pm Sun* $

Lulu's: Cheerful burger and ice-cream shop in Tulelake, run with love. *11am-6pm Tue-Sun* $

Mike & Wanda's Family Dining: Diner-style place: sandwiches, steak and chicken dishes and classic American faves. *11am-8pm Wed-Fri, to 2pm Tue* $

Jalapenos Taco Shop: Merill, Oregon food truck with cheap, big and delicious burritos and tacos to take away. *9am-7pm Thu-Tue, to noon Wed* $

Klamath Basin Wildlife Refuge

year-round, with rentals available at **Rocky Point Resort** *(rockypointoregon.com)*.

What you see will depend on the season. The spring migration peaks during March, when over a million birds may fill the skies. In April and May, songbirds, waterfowl and shorebirds arrive, some to nest while others stay to build up their energy before continuing north. In summer, ducks, Canada geese and other waterbirds nest here. The fall migration peaks in early November. In and around February, the area hosts the largest wintering concentration of bald eagles in the lower 48 states, with 1000 in residence (but you should only expect to see a few at a time). Eagles prey on migrating geese and yes, seeing one catch a goose can be quite dramatic.

Tule Lake (in California) and Upper Klamath across the border in Oregon are all about 85 miles northeast of Mt Shasta City.

WWII INTERNMENT CAMPS

From 1942 to 1946, the area around Tule Lake held one of the largest incarceration camps of Japanese-Americans who were brought here after being forcibly removed from their homes during WWII. At its peak, 18,789 people were imprisoned here. The camp was the last of its kind to close after the war. The jail at **Tule Lake Segregation Center**, in the town of Newell, can be visited by reservation from May to September.

Camp Tule Lake, visible from the roadside and 8km west of Tulelake City, held German and Italian prisoners of war from 1944 to 1946. These prisoners, unlike the Japanese-Americans, were allowed to roam freely and worked on local onion and potato farms.

Mt Lassen Region

GEOTHERMAL HIKES | LAKESIDE RELAXATION | WINTER ADVENTURES

TOP TIP

Trails like Lassen Peak or Kings Creek Falls can still be snow-covered well into June or even July. Bring micro-spikes or trekking poles early in the season and check trail status. Always be prepared for windy conditions!

GETTING AROUND

You'll definitely want a car to explore this area. From Lassen Volcanic National Park you can take one of two very picturesque routes: Hwy 36, which heads from Redding east past Chester, Lake Almanor and historic Susanville. Hwy 89 leads southeast to the cozy mountain town of Quincy; or north, as part of the spectacular Volcanic Legacy Scenic Byway, to Mt Shasta via McCloud.

The dramatic crags, volcanic formations and alpine lakes of Lassen Volcanic National Park are surprisingly untrammeled when you consider that they are only a few hours from the Bay Area. Snowed in through most of the winter, the park blossoms in late spring. While it's only 50 miles from Redding and thus close enough for a day trip, to do it justice you'll want to spend a few days exploring the area along its scenic, winding roads. The park is surrounded by the vast Lassen National Forest, which is so big that it's hard to comprehend: it covers 1.2 million acres of wilderness in an area called the Crossroads, where the granite Sierra, volcanic Cascades, Modoc Plateau and Central Valley all meet. At the mountain's base lies the summer playground of wooded Lake Almanor, where you'll find lodging, a few restaurants and amenities. Sadly, you'll still see plenty of scorched areas from the 2021 Dixie Fire.

Hiking Lassen Volcanic National Park

Lava-formed fiery landscapes

The smoldering terrain within this 106,000-acre **national park** *(nps.gov/lavo; entry per vehicle $10 Dec-Apr 15, $30 Apr 15-Nov 30)* stands in stunning contrast to the green (though partially charred by fire) conifer forest that surrounds it. That's in summer; in winter, tons of snow ensures you won't get too far inside its borders without the appropriate gear and some serious motivation. There are several lakes here; those at higher elevations can stay partially frozen, even in summer.

Lassen Peak, the world's largest lava-dome volcano, is the park's superstar, rising 2000ft over the surrounding landscape to 10,463ft above sea level. Classified as an active volcano, its most recent major eruption was in 1915, when it spewed a giant cloud of smoke, steam and ash 7 miles into the atmosphere. The national park was created the following year to protect the newly formed landscape. Some places destroyed by the blast, including the ominous-sounding Devastated Area

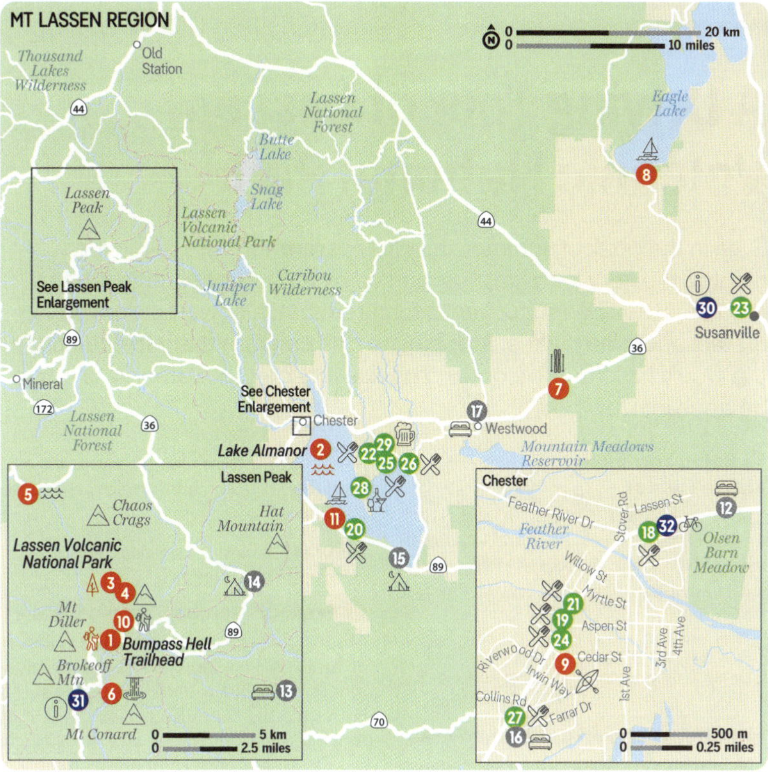

MT LASSEN REGION

HIGHLIGHTS
1 Bumpass Hell Trailhead
2 Lake Almanor
3 Lassen Volcanic National Park

SIGHTS
4 Lassen Peak
5 Manzanita Lake
6 Mill Creek Falls

ACTIVITIES
7 Coppervale Ski Hill
8 Eagle Lake Marina
9 High Elevation Kayak Rentals
10 Lassen Peak Trailhead
11 Major's Outpost

SLEEPING
12 Bidwell House B&B
13 Drakesbad Guest Ranch
14 Lassen Volcanic National Park Campgrounds
15 Rocky Point Campground
16 Timber House Lodge
17 Walker Mansion

EATING
18 Aslan's Mediterranean Grill
19 Bing's Lake Almanor Bistro
20 Carol's Prattville Cafe
21 Cravings
22 Il Lago Pizza & Pasta
23 Lassen Ale Works
24 Pine Shack Frosty
25 Red Onion Grill
26 Sandpiper
27 Timber House Brewery

DRINKING & NIGHTLIFE
28 Sugar Pine Lounge
29 Waganupa Brewing

INFORMATION
30 Eagle Lake Ranger District
31 Kohm Yah-mah-nee Visitor Center

TRANSPORTATION
32 Bodfish Bicycles & Quiet Mountain Sports

northeast of the peak, are recovering impressively, though forest fires have done more recent damage. Lassen Peak and Mt St Helens (1980) were the only two volcanoes to erupt in the lower 48 in the 20th century.

Exploring some of the 150 miles of hiking trails is a highlight here. If you only do one hike, make it **Bumpass Hell**, a moderate 1.5-mile trail and boardwalk that leads to an active

(continued on p296)

ROAD TRIP

A Driving Tour of Lassen Volcanic National Park

Even in the peak of summer, this route is rarely busy. In a fuming display, the fiery landscape is marked by roiling hot springs, steamy mud pots, noxious sulfur vents, fumaroles, lava flows, cinder cones, craters and crater lakes. Stopping to hike can turn this into a multiday trip (you'll have to drive out and back every day), but otherwise it can be done in a few hours.

1 Kohm Yah-mah-nee Visitor Center

About half a mile north of the park's southwest entrance, this handsome **center** (p297) is the perfect starting place, with educational exhibits, a gift shop, cafe and toilets.

The Drive: Turn left out of the parking lot and drive 1 mile till you see steam rising from the rocks.

2 Sulfur Works Hydrothermal Area

The best roadside place to see geothermal action, **Sulfur Works** has bubbling mud pots, hissing steam vents, fountains and fumaroles. You can hike 1 mile to the Ridge Lakes from here.

The Drive: The next 5 miles winds through some of the best vistas in the park.

3 Brokeoff Volcano Scenic Vista

This big parking lot hosts a beautiful **view** of Brokeoff Volcano, Mt Conard and Diamond Peak, but a better reason to stop is to hike the 1.5 miles to park highlight Bumpass Hell, or to picnic by Emerald Lake or Lake Helen, both right off the roadside.

DANITA DELIMONT/SHUTTERSTOCK

Chaos Crags

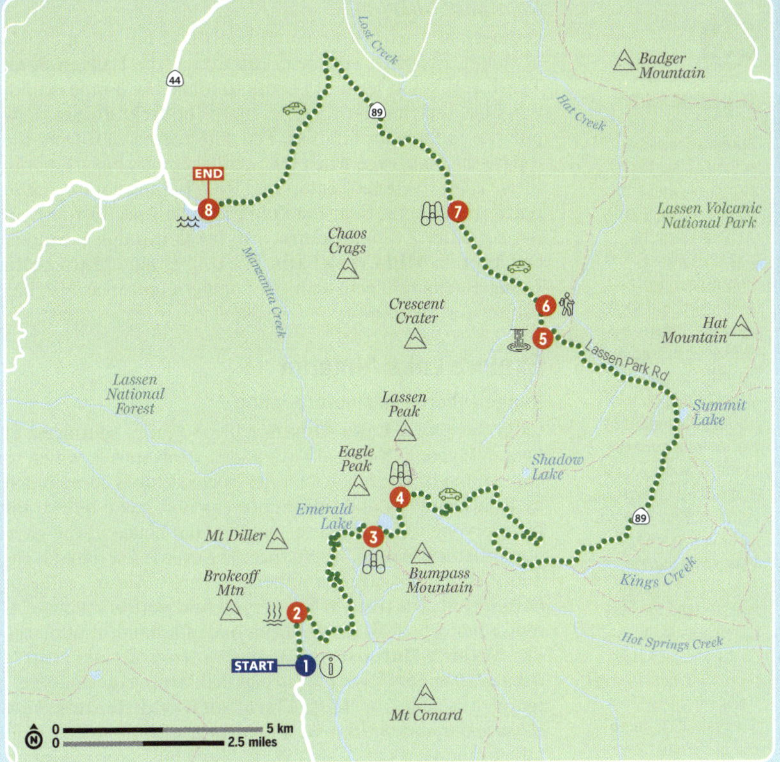

The Drive: In just over a mile turn into the parking lot; Lassen Peak looms on your left.

4 Lassen Peak Scenic Vista

Even if you're not going to take the 5-mile trail to the peak, the sight of the rocky slopes up close is awe-inspiring.

The Drive: There are several places to stop over the next 11 miles, including Kings Creek Meadow and Summit Lakes; both were partially burned in the Dixie Fire.

5 Hat Creek Meadow

This spot is one of the best for fall foliage and there's a dreamy 1.25-mile walk to **Hat Meadows** and a gorgeous waterfall.

The Drive: It's a quick half mile to your next stop on the right.

6 Devastated Area

This 0.25-mile loop is fascinating and includes interpretive panels and remnants of the 1915–16 eruption. A highlight is the 30-ton 'Hot Rock' that flew here from the vent of the volcano during the eruption.

The Drive: The scenery becomes lusher over the next 7.5 miles. Make a quick stop at Emigrant Pass, once plied by covered wagons.

7 Chaos Crags

This giant field of rock rubble is the result of a massive slide in the 1660s. It's worth pulling over and gazing out at the weird and wild terrain.

The Drive: It's about a mile through light forest to your final stop.

8 Manzanita Lake

The northwest park entrance is home to Loomis Museum (May–October) and a 1.8-mile loop around **Manzanita Lake** (p296), where there are kayak rentals in summer. Just across the road is the smaller Reflection Lake, which has great views of Lassen Peak.

THE DIXIE FIRE

Burning nearly 1 million acres, 1329 structures and entire communities, this 2021 catastrophe was the largest single-source wildfire in California's recorded history and the second largest overall. Caused by a tree falling on a power line, the blaze lasted for over three months. Some 73,240 acres of Mt Lassen National Park burned, including Warner Valley and Juniper Lake on the eastern side and the Summit Lakes area in the north. The park has reopened most hiking trails, but the vistas over a never-ending sea of burned trees are a stark reminder. It's best to check in at the visitor center for updates on what trails are open and any dangers (falling branches etc) that might be present in affected areas.

(continued from p293)

geothermal area, with colored pools and billowing clouds of steam. Experienced hikers can attack the **Lassen Peak Trail**; it takes at least 4½ hours to make the 5-mile round-trip hike, but the first 1.3 miles up to the **Grandview** viewpoint is suitable for families. The 360-degree view from the top is stunning, even when the weather is a bit hazy. Early in the season, you'll need snow- and ice-climbing equipment to reach the summit. Near the Kohm Yah-mah-nee Visitor Center, a gentler 3.8-mile return trail leads through meadows and forest to **Mill Creek Falls**. The trail around **Manzanita Lake**, an emerald gem near the northern entrance, also has fishing and swimming.

Explore Lake Almanor

Rugged shores and motorboating

Calm, turquoise **Lake Almanor** lies 40 miles southwest of Lassen Volcanic National Park and is a top spot in which to base yourself. The lake's 52 miles of coastline is surrounded by lush meadows and tall evergreens and has a quiet spot for everyone. Pitch a tent or book a lake house in the ritzy northeastern section, where there are even a few gated communities. On the rugged southern end are miles and miles of nothing but pine trees. Wherever you find yourself, plunge in, rent a motorboat or Jet Ski from one of a handful of places like **Major's Outpost** *(majorsoutpost.com; Jet Ski rentals from $120 per hr)*, go stand-up paddleboarding or canoeing – rentals available from **High Elevation Kayak Rentals** *(highelevationkayakrentals.com; 3hr kayak rentals from $70)* – and take in the views of Lassen Peak. Many businesses close up from October through April but in summer the lake is abuzz with action. Properties are continually being developed all around the shores, so it seems the word is getting out about this once-secret spot.

Cool Off at Eagle Lake

Summer getaway

Those who have the time to get all the way out to **Eagle Lake**, California's second-largest natural lake, are rewarded with a blue jewel on the high desert plateau. From late spring until fall, this lovely spot, about 15 miles northwest of **Susanville**, is a fantastic, off-the-beaten-path place to cool off, swim, fish, boat and camp. On the south shore, you'll find a 5-mile, paved

EATING IN CHESTER: OUR PICKS

Cravings: City-worthy coffee and cooking (breakfast and lunch) with small-town smiles and service. *8am-2pm Thu-Mon* $$

Bing's Lake Almanor Bistro: Modern Chinese plus some Japanese and American faves in a spick-and-span diner-style setting. Also hearty breakfasts. *9am-8pm* $$

Aslan's Mediterranean Grill: Lovingly prepared Turkish food, from kebabs and shawarmas to hummus and Greek salad. *11am-9pm* $$

Pine Shack Frosty: Classic burger and milkshake joint, to eat-in or takeout, perfect after a long hike. *11am-5pm Thu-Sun* $

ALISSA_555/SHUTTERSTOCK

Lake Almanor

recreational trail that weaves through pine trees and is great for walking, biking or casting a fishing line (there's excellent trout fishing). Keep your eyes peeled for bald eagles. There are several busy campgrounds here, administered by **Eagle Lake Ranger District** and the Bureau of Land Management *(blm.gov)*. **Eagle Lake Marina**, close by, has shower and laundry facilities and can help you get out onto the lake with a fishing license. The water level has been dropping here over several years of drought but began to make a comeback in 2025. It's still plenty deep for recreational activities!

Winter Fun

Sled, ski or snowshoe

Winter is magical around Mt Lassen and there's no shortage of activities to keep the blood pumping. A great place to start is the **Kohm Yah-mah-nee Visitor Center**, which has several sledding hills to choose from. People out here can get pretty wild, so start on the smaller slopes before joining the scrum. For a more peaceful experience, try snowshoeing. Joining a ranger-led walk in the park is a good idea if you're new to the sport – these are usually available from January through March and snowshoe rental is included. Alternatively, there

THE STATE OF JEFFERSON

Welcome to the State of Jefferson. The name comes from Thomas Jefferson, who once envisioned a separate republic on the West Coast. You'll notice billboards and bumper stickers ('Jefferson: A State of Mind') endorsing the proposed 51st state and as you travel the two-lane blacktop in Northern California and southern Oregon, they start to make more sense. For one, these folks are mostly conservatives surrounded by a sea of Democrats.

The State of Jefferson was originally proposed in 1941 by a band of well-armed locals, who were irate about terrible road conditions. Today, Jefferson encompasses over three million people across some 30 counties. You can tune into regional news by listening to Jefferson Public Radio *(ijpr.org)*.

EATING AROUND LAKE ALMANOR: OUR PICKS

Il Lago Pizza & Pasta: Buzzing pizza and Italian-food place in Westwood with a popular bar. *11.30am-8pm Tue-Sat* $$

Carol's Prattville Cafe: Find big breakfasts, burgers and pie at this homey old-style place, in Prattville at the southern end of the lake. *7.30am-2pm Tue-Sun* $$

Red Onion Grill: Delicious Italian fare in a casual setting in Westwood. *5-8.30pm Wed-Sun* $$

Sandpiper: In Hamilton Branch, east of Westwood, this is the best food in the region from fire-roasted chicken to vegetarian dishes. *5-8.30pm Thu-Sun* $$$

WHY I LOVE THE MT LASSEN AREA

Celeste Brash, Lonely Planet writer

Some of the earliest photos of me are as a cowboy-hat-toting toddler at my aunt's house in Susanville. Whenever I come back to these mountains and lakes, it feels like coming home. I love the freshness of the clear rivers, the pine smell in the mountains and the untarnished kindness in the small towns. Mt Lassen's geothermal features never cease to amaze and entertain. I was sad to still see so much scorched land on this trip, but the regrowth and resilience of nature and the communities make one believe in miracles. Visiting the region is one way to help Lassen get back on its feet.

SUNDRY PHOTOGRAPHY/SHUTTERSTOCK

Kohm Yah-mah-nee Visitor Center (p297)

are several great snowshoe trails from the visitor center that you can do on your own, featuring wintry white mountain views; rentals are available in Redding or at **Bodfish Bicycles & Quiet Mountain Sports** in Chester.

About 20 miles east of Chester, the family-friendly **Coppervale Ski Hill** *(facebook.com/p/Coppervale-Ski-Area-Page)* is run by Lassen College. Ski or snowboard the eight well-groomed trails, try out the half-pipe, or skip the hills altogether and go cross-country skiing. Check its Facebook page for opening hours that change with snow conditions.

EATING & DRINKING IN THE LASSEN REGION: OUR PICKS

Timber House Brewery: Reserve in advance at this uberpopular, modern mountain lodge-style brewery and restaurant in Chester. *11am-9pm Thu-Mon* $$

Waganupa Brewing: In Lakeview, the beer here is brewed from snowmelt from the surrounding volcanos. *3-8pm Fri-Sun* $$

Lassen Ale Works: Great beer alongside fish and chips as well as steaks in a super-cool, renovated 1862 saloon; located in Susanville. *noon-8pm Wed-Sun* $$

Sugar Pine Lounge: In Westwood at the golf course, with great cocktails and a friendly band of regulars. *2.30-8pm Thu-Sun* $$

Beyond Mt Lassen Region

This is backcountry at its finest: little known, little trodden and filled with glorious mountain scenery, kind folks and outdoor activities.

The gold rush–era region of Plumas County was named for the Feather River that flows through it (*plumas* means 'feathers' in Spanish). Located at the far north of the Sierra Nevada, it holds over 100 lakes. This is an all-season outdoor paradise, with hiking, rafting, skiing, fishing and more, serviced by the friendly and pretty mountain town of Quincy.

The county seat is Susanville, which has good facilities and some mountain-biking options (the spectacular 25.4-mile Bizz Johnson Trail ends here), but little else. Several small towns in the county were destroyed by the 2021 Dixie Fire and you'll still see plenty of regrowing forests as well as new housing construction.

Places

GETTING AROUND

The one-hour drive south on Hwy 89 from Chester, along the shores of Lake Almanor and through the towns of Greenville and Crescent Mills (that are recovering from the Dixie Fire), then along the Feather River to Quincy, is dreamy. Truckee, close to Lake Tahoe and I-80, is a little over 60 miles south of Quincy if you continue on Hwy 89.

Bucks Lake

TIME FROM CHESTER: **1HR20MIN**

Chill out by the water

This clear mountain **lake** is cherished by locals in the know. Surrounded by pine forests, the lightly developed banks are like a deep breath of fresh air. Set up camp or check into a woodland cabin, then just chill out. Take a leisurely swim in summer, drop a line for some trout, or rent a canoe or paddleboard to cruise around. Need more exercise? The region is lined with beautiful hiking trails, including the Pacific Crest Trail, which passes through the adjoining 21,000-acre **Bucks Lake Wilderness** in the northwestern part of Plumas National Forest. In winter, the last 3 miles of Bucks Lake Rd are closed by snow, making it ideal for cross-country skiers. It's about 90 miles southwest of Lassen Volcanic National Park, via the white-knuckle Bucks Lake Rd (Hwy 119).

HOW TO ENJOY LASSEN'S DARK NIGHT SKIES

Make a night-vision flashlight: If you don't have a specialty night-vision red light, cover a small flashlight with red tape or lightweight cloth so that it doesn't disrupt your night vision.

Stargaze: This area's exceptional lack of light pollution offers a prime opportunity for viewing the Milky Way and other celestial wonders.

Go for a night hike: At full moon there's usually enough light to see without a flashlight. At other times let your eyes adjust to the darkness – you will often need less light than you think.

Look for nocturnal wildlife: Owls, bats, deer and fireflies are common suspects that you might encounter.

Lassen National Forest

TIME FROM CHESTER: **45MIN**

Hit the trails

Plumas National Forest *(fs.usda.gov)* has 460 miles of trails, ranging from a brutal 120-mile section of the famous Pacific Crest Trail to ambitious day hikes (the 12-mile **Spencer Meadows National Recreation Trail**) and just-want-to-stretch-the-legs-a-little shorter jaunts (the 3.5-mile **Heart Lake National Recreation Trail**). Near the intersection of Hwys 44 and 89 is the most spectacular feature of the forest: the pitch-black 600yd **Subway Cave** lava tube. Other points of interest include the 1.5-mile volcanic **Spattercone Crest Trail**, **Willow Lake** and the 900ft-high, 14-mile-long **Hat Creek Rim** escarpment.

For those seeking to get far off the beaten track, the **Caribou Wilderness** and the **Thousand Lakes Wilderness** are high-altitude gems, while **Ishi Wilderness** (named after Ishi, the last surviving member of the Yahi people), is at a much lower elevation.

Plumas-Eureka State Park

TIME FROM CHESTER: **1½HR**

Gold-mining history

This lightly restored historic mining area, now a **state park** *(parks.ca.gov; vehicle pass $10)* is 5 miles outside of the tiny, planned community of **Graeagle** and is a great place to learn about the area's rich gold-mining history. Start in the museum (open May–September) to peruse displays on mining and tough, often snowbound pioneer life, before crossing the parking lot to the museum trail. Walk up the gentle slope to see old equipment from a panning area and other various stops with information panels, till you reach the big **Mohawk-Stamp Mill**, where ore was crushed to recover gold, at the top (about 0.25 mile). During peak summer months there are sometimes blacksmith demonstrations and docents on hand to bring the area more alive.

There are a few other short hikes in the park if you want more exercise, including the shady, 6.2-mile out-and-back **Jamison Creek Trail** to **Grass**, **Rock** and **Jamison Lakes**; there's good swimming and this trail connects to some of the other Lake Basin trails. Easier are the 4.3-mile out-and-back, valley view hike to **Eureka Lake** or take a flat 1.6-mile jaunt around reedy **Madora Lake**, that's filled with birdsong.

Lake Basin Recreation Area

TIME FROM CHESTER: **1½HR**

Mountain lakes galore

This glorious **area** *(fs.usda.gov; vehicle pass to most areas $10)* has the scenic beauty of the Sierra Nevada without the crowds – although word is getting out and summer weekends can get busy. There are 20 lakes and over 30 miles of trails,

HONGIRRIS/SHUTTERSTOCK

Plumas National Forest

most dog-friendly, so you could easily fill a few days here exploring, swimming and fishing (bring your own equipment). Top day hikes include a quick but rewarding 1.1-mile out-and-back walk to 176ft
the 3.4-mile **Smith Lake Loop** around the tranquil, clear, trout-filled lake; and more challenging 4.7-mile **Long Lake Loop** for spectacular lake views. The biggest lake in the area is popular **Gold Lake**, which has a boat ramp, a 37-site **campground** *(recreation.gov; sites per night $25)* and plenty of opportunities for cooling off in the clear water.

Mountain biking is also possible, especially for more advanced riders looking for an adventure. If you're too short on time for a good hike, you can drive the 15-mile **Gold Lake Highway** that links the towns of Graeagle and Basset to take in the stunning mountain scenery.

In general, Gold Lake Hwy, hiking trails and campgrounds are only open from late May to October.

Quincy

TIME FROM CHESTER: **1HR**

History lessons with snacks

Aside from being an excellent base for hiking, fishing, river floating and more in the **Plumas National Forest** *(fs.usda.gov; vehicle pass $5)* and Feather River area, idyllic **Quincy** is a

EATING IN QUINCY: OUR PICKS

Grandma Jane's Place: Like a cozy living room, serving savory and sweet treats, such as calzones and macarons. *6am-noon Tue-Sat* $

Morning Thunder Café: Homey and hip, this is the best place in town for breakfast and the vine-shaded patio is a lovely way to start the day. *6.30am-2pm* $$

Quintopia Brewing Co: Crowd-pleasing beers; even better paired with a bar snack like lemon, garlic, Parmesan fries. *4-9pm Wed-Thu, noon-9pm Fri-Sun* $$

Sage & Salt Fusion: Healthy Asian-inspired bowls, pizza, salads, great cocktails. An eclectic selection of teas and more. *11am-9pm* $$

ROCK OUT AT THE HIGH SIERRA MUSIC FESTIVAL

If you're lucky enough to be in Quincy at the end of June or early July, check out the **High Sierra Music Festival** *(highsierramusic.com)*, a four-day family-fun extravaganza (camping included) that brings a five-stage smorgasbord of art and music from a spectrum of cultural corners (indie rock, classic blues, folk and jazz). Past acts include Thievery Corporation, Lauryn Hill, Primus, Ben Harper, Ziggy Marley and Neko Case. Sure, a curmudgeonly local might call it the Hippie Fest, but it's pretty tame in comparison to some of Northern California's true fringe festivals. If you plan to attend, reserve a room or campsite a couple of months in advance.

DAVIDRH/SHUTTERSTOCK

Plumas County Courthouse

lovely little artist-and-student town to explore in its own right.

Just about everything you need is on or close to two one-way streets: Main St, with traffic heading east; and Lawrence St, with traffic heading west. Jackson St runs parallel to Main St one block south and is another main artery, making up Quincy's low-key commercial district.

Start with a leisurely visit to **Plumas County Museum** *(plumasmuseum.org; 10am-4pm Tue-Sat)*, a multistory old-timey place. Peruse hundreds of historical photos and relics from the county's pioneer and Native Maidu days, its early mining and timber industries and the construction of the Western Pacific Railroad. The 1921 **Plumas County Courthouse** *(9am-3pm Mon-Fri)* across the street is worth popping into to see enormous interior marble posts and staircases and a 1-ton bronze-and-glass chandelier in the lobby. Then wander through town, checking out the handful of art galleries before stopping into **Quincy Provisions** for excellent baked goods and coffee; or craft beer and pub food at **Quintopia Brewing Co**.

Quincy is 71 miles southeast of Lassen Volcanic National Park.

Redding & Shasta Lake

RIVER WALKS | HOUSEBOATS | LAKESIDE CAMPING

North of Red Bluff, the dusty central corridor along I-5 starts to give way to panoramic mountain ranges on either side. Redding, with its hot and congested downtown that blends to open space along the scenic Sacramento River, is the last major outpost before the small towns of the far north and the surrounding lakes make for easy day trips or overnight campouts. If you get off the highway – like, way off – this can be an exceptionally rewarding area of the state to explore. A surge of good eating and drinking spots in Redding makes it an excellent pit stop for a meal if you're taking a long road trip on the interstate. And if you stay the night, Redding has a handful of excellent craft breweries, wineries and the Cascade Theater, a 1935 art deco gem that hosts some up-and-coming top-tier bands.

TOP TIP

Packers Bay is the best area for leg-stretcher hikes, with easy access off I-5, but the prettiest trail (outside of summer months when it's intensely hot) is the 7.5-mile loop known as the Clikapudi Trail. To get there, follow Bear Mountain Rd several miles until it dead-ends.

GETTING AROUND

To really explore you'll need your own car. Shasta Lake has a mix of paved and rugged, unpaved road that does not circle the entire lake. Redding is a transportation hub along busy I-5, with an Amtrak station, Greyhound bus station and a small regional airport that runs commercial flights to cities that include San Francisco, Los Angeles, Seattle and Denver.

Houseboating on Shasta Lake

Cruise a forested coastline

Shasta Lake is known as the 'houseboat capital of the world,' and with good reason: the water reaches 78°F (26°C) in summer and there are 365 miles of shoreline to putter along. All you need is a driver's license to rent a boat and you'll get to pilot one of the many vessels gliding through the water at a reasonable 15mph. Pack your own supplies and enjoy lazy evenings cooking for yourself beneath the star-filled sky. There are many levels of luxury, but most houseboats require a two-night minimum stay. Reserve as far in advance as possible, especially in summer.

While some will be happy to float and swim at leisure, there are also several destinations to explore, including the famous Lake Shasta Caverns (p305), waterfalls like **Little Backbone Creek** (don't miss the natural waterslide), the **Shasta Dam** and any number of hiking trails.

And while you're out on the water, be sure to keep an eye peeled for wildlife: this massive lake hosts the largest reservoir populations of ospreys and bald eagles in California.

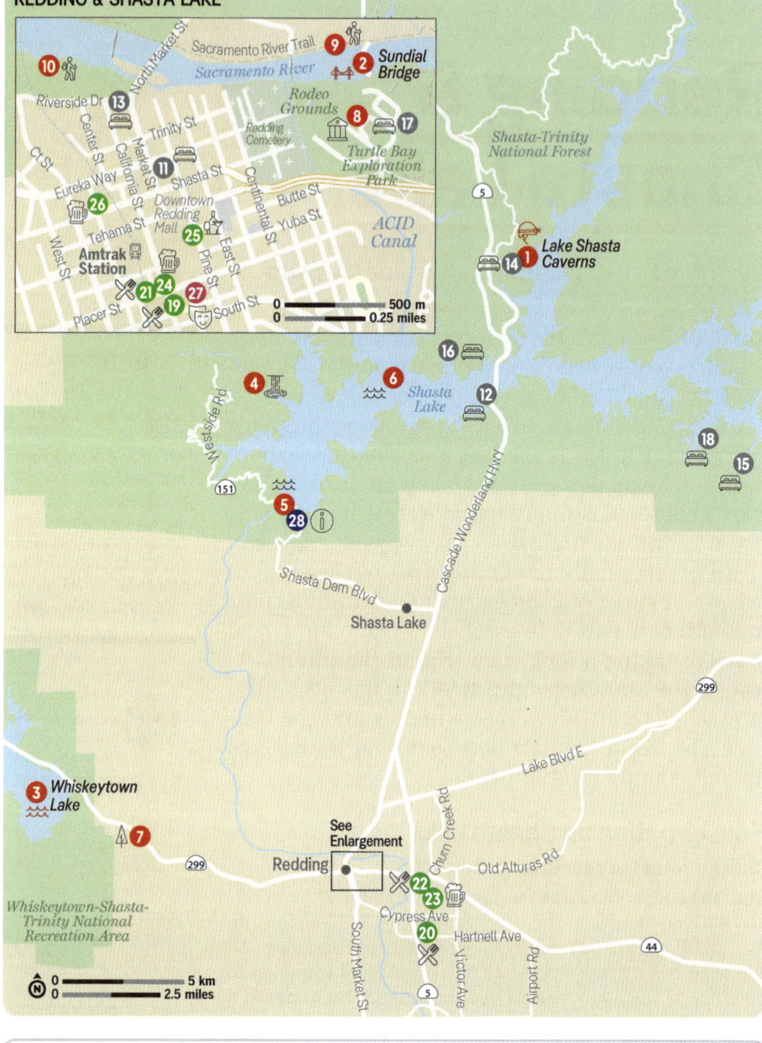

HIGHLIGHTS
1 Lake Shasta Caverns
2 Sundial Bridge
3 Whiskeytown Lake

SIGHTS
4 Little Backbone Creek
5 Shasta Dam
6 Shasta Lake
7 Shasta State Historic Park
8 Turtle Bay Exploration Park

ACTIVITIES
9 Redding Trails
10 Sacramento River Trail

SLEEPING
11 Americana Modern Hotel
12 Bridge Bay Resort
13 Desmond House
14 Holiday Harbor
15 Jones Valley Resort
16 Shasta Marina at Packers Bay
17 Sheraton Redding Hotel at the Sundial Bridge
18 Silverthorn Resort

EATING
19 Jack's Grill
20 Luna's Latin-Asian Fusion
21 Park
22 Wilda's Grill

DRINKING & NIGHTLIFE
23 Fall River Brewing
24 Final Draft Brewing Company
25 Westside Tap & Cork
26 Woody's Brewing Co.

ENTERTAINMENT
27 Cascade Theater

INFORMATION
28 Shasta Dam Visitors Center

Ospreys are best seen from March to October and peak in May and June, which is their nesting season. Look for bald eagles (white head, brown body) year-round, who nest primarily in tall coniferous trees. If you're lucky, you might see one swoop down to catch a fish or even a waterfowl. Other birds to look out for are double-crested cormorants, western grebes and mallard ducks. On land, look for acorn woodpeckers, quails and wild turkeys.

Get Deep at Shasta Caverns

Underground geological wonderland

Located high in the limestone megaliths at the north end of Shasta Lake are the impressive **Lake Shasta Caverns** *(lake shasta caverns.com; 2hr tours adult/child $44/26)*. Tours through the many chambers dripping with massive formations operate daily and include a boat ride across Shasta Lake. Guides are fantastic and will help you spot bald eagles en route to the caves, as well as answer all sorts of geeky geology questions within the caverns. Once inside, it's a one-hour meander along lighted trails and some 600 steps, passing a wondrous array of formations, including waterfall-like curtains of limestone, impressively large stalactites and stalagmites, Jurassic fossils and coral-like helictites. Bring a sweater, as the temperature inside is 58°F (14°C) year-round. On Friday and Saturday evenings in summer, the company also runs sunset buffet dinner cruises on the lake. Call and check what's on, particularly in winter, since the website schedule can be misleading.

Explore Shasta State Historic Park

Ghosts of the past

This **state park** *(parks.ca.gov; admission $3; accessible 10am–4pm Thu–Sun)* 6 miles west of Redding on Hwy 299, preserves the ruins of an 1850s gold-rush mining town called Shasta – not to be confused with Mt Shasta City. When the gold rush was at its heady height, everything and everyone passed through this Shasta. But when the railroad bypassed it to set up in Poverty Flats (present-day **Redding**), poor Shasta lost its raison d'être. The 1861 courthouse is now a **museum**, housing an amazing gun collection, gallows out back and spooky holograms in the basement; it's a thrill ride. Afterwards, pick up walking-tour pamphlets from the information desk and follow trails to the beautiful **Catholic cemetery**, brewery ruins and other historic sites.

SHASTA LAKE HOUSEBOAT RENTALS

Shasta Marina at Packers Bay: One of the biggest outfits, but maintains great service. Also has good smaller motorboat, kayaks and stand-up paddle board rentals.

Holiday Harbor: A reliable choice, with a camping and RV (recreational vehicle) park plus stand-up paddleboard rentals near the busy marina.

Bridge Bay Resort: This friendly resort has a lakeside lodge, serves American fare and libations at waterfront Huff's Restaurant and rents small fishing and leisure crafts.

Jones Valley Resort & Silverthorn Resort: These joint-run marinas are located on the secluded eastern part of the lake and have a good selection of small watercraft rentals. Silverthorn Resort also has waterfront cabins.

EATING IN REDDING: OUR PICKS

Wilda's Grill: Hot dogs with crazy toppings, healthy falafel and Buddha rice bowls. *11am-7pm Mon-Sat* $

Luna's Latin-Asian Fusion: Creative, delicious creations like shrimp tempura tacos, Korean marinated burgers plus equally interesting cocktails. *4-9pm Mon-Sat* $$

Park: Rotating collection of food trucks, assortment of lawn games and live music on warm weekends. Regular carts: crêpes and pizzas. *6-10pm Thu-Sat* $$

Jack's Grill: Regulars line up to get the best steaks around at this dark cavern of a restaurant. No reservations. *4-10pm Mon-Sat* $$$

THE DAM AT SHASTA LAKE

On scale with the enormous natural features of the area, the colossal 15-million-ton **Shasta Dam** (p303) is second in size only to Grand Coulee Dam in Washington state and second in height only to Hoover Dam in Nevada.

Built between 1937 and 1949, its 487ft spillway is nearly three times as high as Niagara Falls. Woody Guthrie wrote 'This Land Is Your Land' here while he was entertaining dam workers. The **Shasta Dam visitor center** offers a 21-minute video shown on request and self-guided walking tours across the vertiginous top of the dam are available from 6am to 10pm daily. It's located at the south end of the lake on Shasta Dam Blvd.

EWY MEDIA/SHUTTERSTOCK

Sundial Bridge

Discover Local Nature via the Sundial Bridge

An architectural wonder

Resembling a beached cruise ship, the shimmering-white **Sundial Bridge**, designed by renowned Spanish architect Santiago Calatrava, spans the bucolic shores of Sacramento River and is one of Redding's marquee attractions. The bridge and partially working sundial attracts visitors from around the world, who come to marvel at this unique feat of engineering and artistry. Stroll across the bridge for a surprisingly glamorous selfie against its silhouette.

The bridge also connects with 80 miles of trails in the **Redding Trails** network, which loops through parks, along rivers and up hills for strolling, hiking and mountain biking. The star is the paved **Sacramento River Trail**, which meanders for 17 miles along the river all the way to Shasta Dam. You can easily turn this into a shorter loop by crossing the river and turning around after 5.5 miles.

At the other end of the bridge, a glass-deck pedestrian overpass connects to the **Turtle Bay Exploration Park** *(admission adult/child $22/16; 9am-5pm)*, an artistic, cultural and scientific center for all ages. Don't miss the arboretum gardens, a butterfly house (open seasonally) and a 22,000-gallon, walk-through river aquarium full of regional aquatic life.

DRINKING IN REDDING: OUR PICKS

Fall River Brewing: Best beers around. Bring your kids if you have them and expect to mingle with locals. *noon-8pm*

Woody's Brewing Co: Open since 2015, has great beers plus food menu – from burgers and salads to crunchy tater tots. *11am-9pm Tue-Sun*

Final Draft Brewing Company: Industrial-style brewpub with vats on display. Try beer styles you won't find elsewhere in Redding. *11am-9pm*

Westside Tap & Cork: Several wineries have tasting rooms in Redding but this is a good stop to sample a variety of them plus local beers. *4-9pm Tue-Sun*

Beyond Redding & Shasta Lake

The sunbaked lowlands of Redding blend into mountains, lakes and wild rivers dotted with eclectic towns.

Here are some of the most rugged towns and wilderness areas in California – just difficult enough to reach to discourage big crowds. The Trinity Scenic Byway (Hwy 299) winds spectacularly along the Trinity River and beneath towering cliffs as it makes its way from the plains of Redding to the coastal redwood forests around Arcata on the coast. It cuts through some of the northern mountains' most pristine wilderness and passes through the vibrant gold-rush town of Weaverville. Heavenly Hwy 3 heads north from Weaverville through the Trinity Alps – a stunning granite range dotted with alpine lakes – past the shores of Lewiston and Trinity Lakes, over the Scott Mountains and finally into mountain-rimmed Scott Valley.

Places

GETTING AROUND

Hwy 3 can be an interesting alternative to I-5 but it can become impassible in winter due to snow. Take off-the-beaten-path Trinity Scenic Byway (Hwy 299) from Redding, via Weaverville, to Eureka (about three hours) for spectacular forest and Trinity River views. From Eureka you can head up or down Hwy 1 for a whole other coastal redwoods adventure.

Whiskeytown Lake National Recreation Area

TIME FROM REDDING: **20MIN**

Lake with a historic twist

Sparkling **Whiskeytown Lake** *(nps.gov/whis; vehicle pass $25)* takes its name from an old mining camp. In the 1960s, a new 263ft dam was built, the few remaining buildings of the original Whiskeytown were relocated and the camp was submerged beneath the rising waters.

Just 15 minutes from Redding, the lake's serene 36-mile forested shoreline is the perfect place to camp while enjoying nonmotorized water sports. On the western side, the Tower House Historic District contains the **El Dorado** mine ruins and the pioneer **Camden House**, open for summer tours. On the southern shore of the lake, **Brandy Creek** is ideal for swimming; on the northern edge of the lake, **Oak Bottom Marina** rents boats. The 1.2-mile hike to roaring **Whiskeytown Falls** follows a former logging road and is a good choice if you're only making a quick stop. Camp at tightly packed **Oak Bottom Campground** near the shore for longer stays.

Trails and campsites are open, but the area is still recovering from the 2018 Carr Fire that burned virtually all of the

HIDDEN HIGHWAY 3 ROAD TRIP

Drive way off the beaten path on this rarely used, scenic alternative to I-5 that links Yreka to Weaverville.

START	END	LENGTH
Yreka	Weaverville	104 miles; 6hr

Start in historic Yreka, just south of the Oregon border, stopping to learn about Native peoples at the ❶ **Siskiyou County Museum**. Drive southwest on Hwy 3, through postcard-worthy farmlands toward Fort Jones. The one-road main street holds stops for coffee or burgers, as well as tiny, brick ❷ **Fort Jones Museum**. Back on the road, it's 12 miles of increasingly mountainous scenery to the adorable town of ❸ **Etna**, a favorite overnight spot for long-distance hikers on the Pacific Crest Trail. Stop at Farmhouse Bakery for coffee and delicious breads, grab a microbrew at legendary Etna Brewing or nab a table at Denny Bar Co Distillery.

At ❹ **Callahan**, 12 miles on, veer right following signs to Weaverville. The road steepens through serpentine cliffs and ponderosa pine forests to stunning views over Scott River Valley and mountains. The Pacific Crest Trail crosses the highway at ❺ **Scott Mt Summit**. The road descends, winding through forest and along Scott Mt Creek and ❻ **Trinity River**.

Turn into the small vacation-rental hamlets of ❼ **Coffee Creek** or ❽ **Trinity Center** where you'll find old-fashioned general stores. It's 29 miles from Trinity Center to Weaverville, partly skirting pretty ❾ **Trinity Lake** (p310), a local favorite fishing spot in summer.

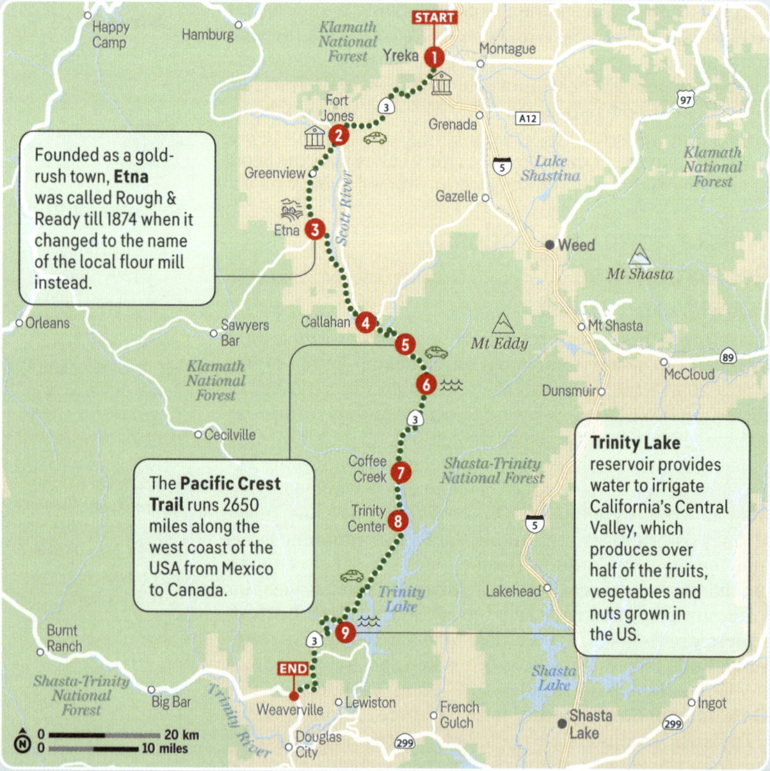

Founded as a gold-rush town, **Etna** was called Rough & Ready till 1874 when it changed to the name of the local flour mill instead.

The **Pacific Crest Trail** runs 2650 miles along the west coast of the USA from Mexico to Canada.

Trinity Lake reservoir provides water to irrigate California's Central Valley, which produces over half of the fruits, vegetables and nuts grown in the US.

recreation area. However, it's a surprisingly beautiful time to visit, with lush regrowth contrasting with the sienna-colored charred trees. The visitor center has knowledgeable staff that can answer your questions and let you know more about the area's recovery.

Weaverville

TIME FROM REDDING: **50MIN**

Chinese heritage and a gold-rush community

Roughly an hour's drive west of Redding, **Weaverville** is the place to learn about Northern California's original Chinese immigrant community. The walls of the 1874 **Weaverville Joss House State Historic Park** *(parks.ca.gov; tours $4)* basically talk – they're papered with 150-year-old donation ledgers from the once-thriving community: first gold prospectors and, later, workers who built so much of Northern California's infrastructure. The blue-and-gold **Taoist temple** is the oldest in California that's still in use and contains an ornate alter a more than 3000 years old, which was brought here from China. Next door to the Joss House you'll find gold-mining and cultural exhibits, plus vintage machinery, memorabilia, an old miner's cabin and a blacksmith shop. The adjoining schoolhouse was the first to teach Chinese students in California. Don't miss the tours that depart hourly from 10am to 4pm, Thursday to Sunday.

Lewiston Lake

TIME FROM REDDING: **50MIN**

Reel in trophy trout

The narrow 9-mile **Lewiston Lake** connects Trinity Lake with Trinity River and offers sublime fly-fishing. If you didn't bring a rod or if you're new to the sport, hook up with a guiding service like **Trinity River Adventures**, which will ferry you through the slow-moving, marsh-lined channels in the search for several species of trout, many weighing 4lb or more. Aside from the plentiful fish, this is a serene alternative to the other lakes in the area because of its 10mph boat speed limit. Early in the evening you may see ospreys and bald eagles diving for their dinner. Even if you're not fishing, head to the **Trinity River Fish Hatchery**, where juvenile salmon and steelhead are held before being released into the river. The only marina on the lake, **Pine Cove**, has free information about the lake and its wildlife, boat and canoe rentals and guided off-road tours.

THE KLAMATH KNOT

A conglomeration of coastal mountains – **Klamath** and **Siskiyou Mountains** – gives this region the nickname 'the Klamath Knot.' Coastal temperate rainforest gives way to moist inland forest, creating a diversity of habitats for many species, some found nowhere else in the world. Around 3500 native plants live here. Local fauna includes northern spotted owls, bald eagles, tailed frogs, several species of Pacific salmon, wolverines and mountain lions. One theory for the extraordinary biodiversity of this area is that it escaped extensive glaciation during recent ice ages. This may have given species refuge and longer stretches of favorable conditions during which to adapt. To learn more, read David Raine Wallace's 1983 cult classic memoir about hiking here, *The Klamath Knot*.

EATING & DRINKING IN WEAVERVILLE: OUR PICKS

Mamma Llama: Delightful coffeehouse that also serves breakfast, light meals and microbrews. *8.30am-2pm Mon-Fri* **$**

Crocket's Up North: Gourmet grilled cheese sandwiches, homemade soups, an ice-cream parlor plus a mercantile and outdoor seating. *9am-9pm* **$$**

Trinity County Brewing Co: Seven-barrel brewery and pub serves 10 craft beers alongside food made with local ingredients. *11am-8pm Wed-Sun* **$$**

Tangle Blue Saloon: Pizzas, burgers, salads, a lively bar, indoor and outdoor seating and line dancing on Friday nights. *11am-2am* **$$**

A QUIET, WATERY WORKHORSE

Lewiston Lake isn't a true lake – it's a bypass in California's sprawling water system. Water released from Trinity Dam flows through this constructed channel before reaching the Lewiston Powerhouse, which supplies electricity to the Trinity River Fish Hatchery (built in 1963 to compensate for lost spawning habitats). Surplus energy is sold to PG&E. Around 90% of the water is then diverted into Whiskeytown Lake, which eventually flows to the Sacramento River. That water is destined for irrigation canals that supply farms throughout the Sacramento and San Joaquin Valleys. The remainder returns to the Trinity River. The result? A consistently cold reservoir: ideal trout habitat and a vital link for hydropower, irrigation and fisheries.

MICHAEL VOROBIEV/SHUTTERSTOCK

Trinity Lake

The adorable town of **Lewiston**, 40 minutes west of Redding, is little more than a collection of rickety historic buildings beside the Trinity River; the lake is about 1.5 miles north of town. It's worth stopping here to peruse antiques at the photogenic **Country Peddler**, or stop to eat, drink or stay the night at the quirky **Old Lewiston Inn**.

Wine tasting at Trinity Lake

Placid **Trinity Lake**, California's third-largest reservoir, sits beneath dramatic snowcapped peaks, 6 miles north of Lewiston Lake. **Trinity Center**, its main town, is another 30 miles away. In the off-season it's serenely quiet, but in the summer, multitudes come here for swimming, fishing and other water sports. Even if you're just driving through, it's worth detouring to the little-known, utterly picturesque **Alpen Cellars**. Specializing in riesling, Gewürztraminer, chardonnay and pinot noir, the vineyard is open for tours, tastings and picnicking on its idyllic riverside grounds.

Places We Love to Stay

$** Budget **$$** Midrange **$$$ Top End

Mt Shasta Region

MAPS P283, 285

Strawberry Valley Inn $ Cozy, well-run motel in Mt Shasta with B&B-like touches and, fittingly, good included breakfasts.

LOGE Mt Shasta $$ Dorms, gear lockers, shared bathrooms and covered campsites geared toward social, active folks.

Jubilee Railroad Resort $$ Located about 2 miles south of Dunsmuir. Visitors can spend the night inside refitted vintage railroad cars and cabooses or camp in the forest.

Shasta Mountain Inn Retreat & Spa $$$ Victorian B&B with incredible views, gardens and a spa; walking distance to Mt Shasta town.

McCloud Hotel (p286) **$$$** This grand hotel opened in 1916 and has been a destination for Shasta's visitors ever since. It has been restored to luxurious standards.

Lava Beds National Monument

Indian Well Campground $ Forty-three first-come, first-served campsites are available here, half a mile from the monument.

Winema Historic Lodge $ Fifteen basic yet homey rooms plus RV hookups, between Klamath Basin National Wildlife Refuge and Lava Beds National Monument.

Wild Goose Lodge $$ In Merrill, Oregon, 9 miles out of Tulelake, this is a good-value motel with country charm and you'll meet a posse of local quilters.

Mt Lassen Region

MAP P293

Rocky Point Campground $ Many of these sites are tent-centric and more tranquil than the others surrounding Lake Almanor.

Lassen Volcanic National Park Campgrounds $ The park has seven developed campgrounds that are open between late May and late October.

Walker Mansion $ Quaint B&B with restaurant serving high tea. Also a country mercantile on-site.

Timber House Lodge $$ Every room is uniquely themed and comfortable at this hopped-up motel in the center of Chester.

Bidwell House B&B $$ The historic summer home of pioneers John and Annie Bidwell has classic accommodations that come with all the modern amenities.

Drakesbad Guest Ranch $$$ Stay in bungalows or pitch a tent then enjoy a hot-springs-fed swimming pool and horseback riding and hiking in the national park.

Quincy

Quincy Featherbed Inn $ The five rooms and two cottages in this Victorian-decorated gem in the historic part of Quincy are the best value in town.

Quincy Courtyard Suites $$ Beautifully renovated suites in the 1908 Clinch building, overlooking Quincy's main drag.

Greenhorn Guest Ranch $$$ Think of this place as the cowboy version of the getaway resort in *Dirty Dancing*.

Redding

MAP P304

Americana Modern Hotel $ Very central motel completely remodeled in 2019, with mid-century modern style.

Desmond House $$ A pretty Victorian house filled with antique furniture; it's close to town with views of the river.

Sheraton Redding Hotel at the Sundial Bridge $$$ This luxurious hotel is ideally located at the Sun Dial Bridge and the Turtle Bay Exploration Park.

Weaverville & Around

Old Lewiston Inn $ This 1862 rambling, ramshackle hotel has small, rustic rooms with quilts, historic photos and river views.

Whitmore Inn $$ Classic Victorian B&B with a wraparound deck on the edge of downtown Weaverville.

Indian Creek Lodge $$ Comfy fishing lodge located 8 miles southeast of Weaverville along the banks of the Trinity River.

Van Ness Ave., California
59
& Market
Streets
Van Ness Ave., California
30
& Market
Streets

TOOLKIT

The chapters in this section cover the most important topics you'll need to know about in San Francisco and Northern California. They're full of nuts-and-bolts information and valuable insights to help you understand and navigate San Francisco and Northern California and get the most out of your trip.

San Francisco's cable cars (p56)

CANADASTOCK/SHUTTERSTOCK

Arriving

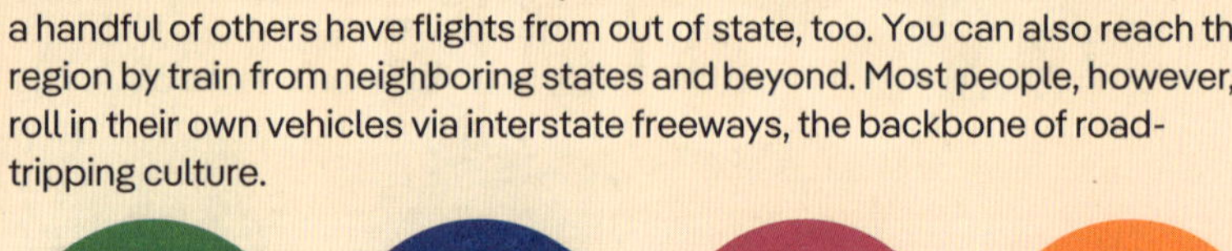

Northern California's two main airports are San Francisco and Oakland, and a handful of others have flights from out of state, too. You can also reach the region by train from neighboring states and beyond. Most people, however, roll in their own vehicles via interstate freeways, the backbone of road-tripping culture.

Easy Visas

Check *travel.state.gov* for rules for the US Visa Waiver Program (VWP), whereby citizens of 42 countries can stay up to 90 days with an approved passport and Electronic System for Travel Authorization (ESTA).

Complex Visas

Regulations for visas change regularly. For up-to-date information about requirements and eligibility, check the visa section on the US Department of State website or contact a US embassy in your home country.

Cell Phones

Foreign phones usually work in Northern California. Buy prepaid SIM cards locally or get an e-SIM. Coverage can be spotty in remote areas such as the far northern coast and in the mountains.

Wi-fi

Wi-fi is nearly ubiquitous in the state that is home to Silicon Valley. Free networks abound in civic centers, restaurants, cafes, hotels and more.

Public Transportation from Airport to City Center

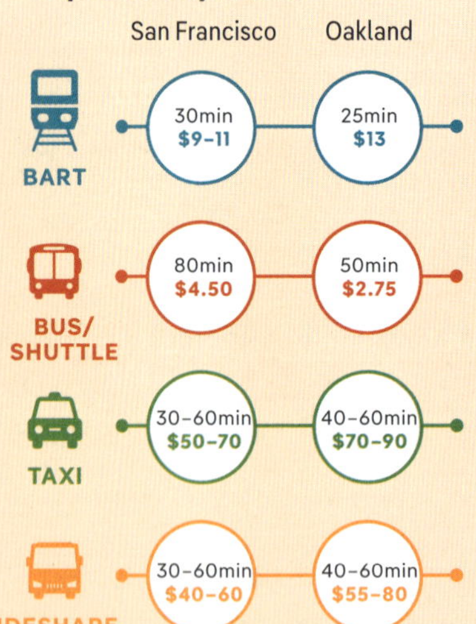

THE SCENIC WAY TO CALIFORNIA

Four Amtrak routes serve California from the rest of the USA. Each offers superb scenery. From Seattle and Portland, the *Coast Starlight* serves Sacramento and the Bay Area en route to Los Angeles. From Chicago and Denver to the Bay Area, the *California Zephyr* traces the route of the first Transcontinental Railroad as it enters the state at Truckee high in the Sierras. Also from Chicago, the *Southwest Chief* reaches LA via the beautifully stark desert as does the *Sunset Limited* from New Orleans, Houston and Tucson. Within Northern California, the *Capital Corridor* connects San Jose, Oakland and Berkeley with Sacramento.

FROM LEFT: FUSE/GETTY IMAGES, CHIMPINSKI/SHUTTERSTOCK

Getting Around

While the car is king in Northern California, there are many regional options to get around by train, ferry, bus and trail.

TRAVEL COSTS

Car rental
Per day $35–160

Gas
$5/gallon

EV charging
$0.45/KWh

Train ticket from Oakland to Los Angeles
From $55

Car Hire

There's no inherent advantage between airport and city location rates for rental cars. Both vary widely depending on season and demand. Don't rent a car if all you'll do is park it in the pricey hotel garage – for example, ride BART into San Francisco, then get a one-day rental for Napa.

Road Conditions

After years of neglect due to fractured state finances, California's voters approved an extra gas tax which is funding repair, rebuilding and construction of roads statewide. You may get caught in work-related delays. But the result is that road conditions in the state are rapidly improving.

TIP

Download the **Caltrans QuickMap** *(quickmap.dot.ca.gov/QM/app.htm)* app, which shows road conditions statewide.

ROAD HABITS

Californians spend a lot of time in their cars – 97 hours a year is the Bay Area average. Certain rules and habits are enshrined in the state's road culture that may not be immediately apparent to visitors. On scenic and mountainous roads, pull over so that residents can whizz past. Motorcycles are allowed to ride between cars on freeways. It's called lane-splitting. Car-pool lanes are tightly regulated. If you have the correct number of passengers, use them and fly past traffic.

DRIVING ESSENTIALS

Drive on the right.

Speed limit is usually 65mph on freeways, 55mph on two-lane highways and 35mph in cities.

.08

Blood alcohol limit is 0.08%.

Bus, Train & Ferry

Northern California has more public transit than many think. The Bay Area region is well covered with a dense network. Whether it's a ferry to Sausalito or a SMART train to Santa Rosa, the ride is part of the adventure. Amtrak's regional trains are fast and reasonably frequent.

Public Transit Tickets

In the Bay Area use the Clipper Card app. It lets you ride the various forms of transit in the region, including many neighboring bus systems, like Napa, with a tap of your phone. Refill its stored value online or just use your phone's payment options.

Plane

Californians use planes the way people in other places use trains. The environmental cost aside, service between the state's 12 major airports and numerous smaller ones is frequent and cheap, especially for tickets bought ahead. One downside is that, barring a clear day and a window seat, you miss the scenery.

Money

CURRENCY: US DOLLAR ($)

Credit & Debit Cards

Visa and Mastercard are accepted everywhere, American Express and Discover less so. Regular visitors from abroad will cheer that the US has finally fully adopted chip-and-pin systems for cards, although some small businesses have not. Debit cards may require extra security checks at gas stations, rental car counters etc.

Digital Payments

After a surprising lag compared with Europe and Asia, the home to Apple and Google has finally caught up with digital payments. Residents commonly pay for everything with a tap of their phone and can go weeks without ever using cash. (Save $1 bills for the tip jars in coffee bars etc.)

Taxes & Refunds

California state sales tax (7.25%) is added to the retail price of most goods and services (groceries are exceptions). Local sales taxes may add on up to 3%. Tourist lodging taxes vary statewide, but average 10.5% to 14% in major cities.No tax refunds are available to international visitors.

HOW MUCH FOR A...

Beach parking
Free–$15

Bridge toll
$9

Driving Hwy 1
Free

ATM fee
$3.50

HOW TO... Save Some Dollars

If you're sticking to Northern California, the national parks are affordable (eg Point Reyes is free and Redwood National and State Parks just has nominal day use fees). If you're traveling more broadly, an **America the Beautiful Pass** *(store.usgs.gov/pass)* costs $80 and grants unlimited entry to all US national parks – 28 of which are in California – plus national wildlife refuges and more. It can usually pay for itself after visiting three parks.

LOCAL TIP

Most passes for California's 280 state parks *(parks.ca.gov)* are best for year-round residents, but some like Senior Golden Bear Pass are good outside of summer. Without a pass, for the parks that charge, do like many residents: park outside and walk in.

WHAT TO TIP

Tipping is *not* optional: it's part of the workers' wages.

Bartenders 15% to 20% per round, minimum $1 per drink.

Concierges Nothing for simple info, up to $20 for securing last-minute restaurant reservations etc.

Hotel bellhops $2 or $3 per bag, minimum $5 per cart.

Housekeeping staff $2 to $4 daily.

Parking valets From $2 to $5 when your car keys are handed back.

Restaurant servers 15% to 25%

Counter service Optional. Generally 10%, $1 or nothing.

Taxi/rideshare drivers 10% to 15% of the fare, rounded up to the next dollar.

Accommodations

Unique Accommodations

With its many beautiful destinations and innovative spirit, Northern California has hundreds of cool, unique accommodations. Find solitude at a mountain campsite or feed all your desires with decadent city luxury. Aside from the usual motels and hotels, there are offbeat options like retro motels, vacation rentals right on the beach, campsites perched in dramatic locations and myriad forms of glamping.

Retro Motels

The humble motel has revitalized over the last few years, with many tired models receiving makeovers that have given them a second act. Designed with an eye to the mid-century aesthetic and consciously addressing contemporary needs, these roadside spots are hot little properties that can be stylish but affordable options. Look for brilliantly restored neon signs.

Estate Wineries

Immerse yourself in a wine country retreat with views of vineyard rows. Go big at a high-end chateau, complete with spa treatments and South of France ambience, or choose from a wide range of more low-key winery digs. Northern California's wine regions aren't limited to Napa and Sonoma Counties, and accommodations styles can be as individual as their winegrowers and makers.

Glamping

Northern California may not have invented glamping, but it has perfect backdrops and set pieces for the concept. Iconic national parks and private entities alike have placed canvas safari tents and yurts in pristine settings like Bothe-Napa Valley State Park. Outside of the mountains, much of Northern California maintains a fairly temperate climate (pack warm gear for winter), making glamping a realistic option.

HOW MUCH FOR A NIGHT IN...

a hotel
$100–300 and up

a hostel
from $40

a campsite
$25–45 and up

Sleep in the Trees

Commune with the redwoods in a treehouse. Widely viewed on Instagram, human-size nests and birdhouse-clad pods are some of the more feral-feeling luxury aeries you can settle into for the night. Some meet the definition of shelter better than others, so check details, weather reports and your comfort zone before committing. Confirm basic details such as sanitation and water availability.

VACATION RENTAL LIMITS

Vacation rentals are a charged topic in Northern California. In a state with a catastrophic shortage of affordable housing, any housing stock removed from availability for the locals provokes strong reactions. Once affordable rural areas have become weekend retreats for the urban affluent, forcing residents who work in the shops and cafes to scramble for housing they can afford. In wealthy areas, residents have grown weary of beach houses turned into party pads for tech bros. In response, cities and towns statewide have imposed limits on vacation rentals, especially ones listed on Airbnb.

CLOCKWISE FROM TOP LEFT: RUSLAN IVANTSOV/SHUTTERSTOCK, GIVAGA/SHUTTERSTOCK, SOMCHAI SOM/SHUTTERSTOCK

Family Travel

Northern California is a tailor-made destination for family travel. Kids will enjoy places like SF's Exploratorium or activities like crossing the Golden Gate Bridge. Then take 'em into the greater outdoors – from seal-studded beaches to misty redwood forests and four-seasons mountain playgrounds.

Prams, Strollers & Babies

Urban areas are great for strollers, but if you plan on enjoying the great outdoors, child carriers are definitely a better option. Some attractions offer rental strollers. Basics are available in supermarkets and drugstores 24/7, while organics and specialty items can be found at higher-end supermarkets, big-box stores and boutiques. Bathrooms with changing facilities are common, as are family bathrooms.

Dining Out

Casual eateries typically have high chairs and children's menus available. More clever eateries won't just cut down on portions for small-size diners but will offer special kid-tested items so that everybody at the table feels special. Roadside restaurants on tourist routes often have extra inducements for families to stop such as playgrounds, amusing displays or a chance to pet a winsome barnyard animal.

San Francisco Play

The city is a mind-bending classroom for kids, especially at the interactive **Exploratorium**, multimedia **Children's Creativity Museum** and ecofriendly **California Academy of Sciences** in Golden Gate Park. Or simply take them out and run at **Ocean Beach** and **Crissy Field**.

Car Travel

Any child under the age of eight must be buckled up in the car's back seat in a child or infant safety seat; children under two must be in a rear-facing safety seat – reserve one ahead when renting a car. Bring in-car distractions for inevitable traffic delays.

KEEPING COSTS DOWN

Much of Northern California is not cheap. Cost-conscious families need help avoiding sticker shock.

Children's discounts are available for everything from museum admission and movie tickets to bus fares. In hotels and motels, look for 'kids stay free' and/or 'free breakfast' promotions. Motels are cheaper on average, most have two queen- or king-size beds, and many have fridges and microwaves.

If you're visiting parks, carry a cooler in the car and have a picnic to avoid expensive and often junk-foodie roadside options.

From endless beaches, mountains and urban parks, some of the most family-friendly activities in Northern California are free.

KID-FRIENDLY PICKS

Fort Bragg Skunk Train (p240)

Munch popcorn chugging through Mendocino countryside.

Chabot Space & Science Center (p135)

Space out with planetarium and galactic thrills.

Point Cabrillo Light Station State Historic Park (p236)

Family fun with whale trivia, aquariums and a lighthouse.

Children's Fairyland (p135)

Old-school kids' playland on Lake Merritt in Oakland.

Lava Beds National Monument (p289)

Explore cinder cones, lava flows, caves and lava tubes.

Safari West (p187)

Jeep around a wildlife reserve with giraffes and wildcats (overnight, too).

Paddle an outrigger on the Big River Estuary

Row a redwood double outrigger canoe outside of Mendocino.

Health & Safe Travel

INSURANCE

Travel insurance to cover theft, loss and medical problems is essential, especially for international visitors. Domestic visitors should confirm they have proper coverage for injuries or maladies. Some policies do not cover 'risky' activities such as diving, motorcycling and skiing, so read the fine print. Trip-cancellation insurance can be a worthwhile expense, too.

Earthquakes

Earthquakes happen all the time, but most are so tiny they're undetectable. If you're caught in a serious temblor:

- Stay in an open outdoor space.
- If indoors, get under a desk or table or stand in a doorway.
- Protect your head and stay clear of windows, mirrors or anything that might fall.
- Don't head for elevators or run into the street.

Wildfires

The wildfire season gets ever-longer (at least June through November). Fires limit access to roads and parks, and can cause vacationers and residents to flee for their lives. The smoke can also be thick, a special hazard for those with breathing issues. Of late, fires have affected Los Angeles, Napa and Sonoma Wine Country, Lake Tahoe and all the national forests.

MARIJUANA

Cannabis is legal in California for medicinal and 21-plus recreational use. Shops sell myriad forms of marijuana. Driving under the influence is illegal.

WILDFIRE DANGER RATINGS

Low (Green) Control of fires is generally easy.

Moderate (Blue) Fires can start from accidental causes.

High (Yellow) Fires can start easily from most causes.

Very High (Orange) Fires start easily and spread rapidly.

Extreme (Red) Fires start quickly, burn intensely and are hard to control.

Smoking

Smoking (tobacco, marijuana, vapes, anything) is prohibited inside all public buildings, including airports, malls, stadiums and transportation stations. No smoking is allowed inside restaurants, although lighting up may be tolerated at outdoor patio or sidewalk tables (ask first). As of 2024 hotels no longer have smoking rooms. In some areas you can't smoke outside near a business.

THOUSANDS WITHOUT HOMES

Despite billions spent annually to combat California's homelessness crisis, the number of people living on the streets keeps inexorably growing. You'll see unhoused people in large cities and small towns, living in tents, under tarps, in battered RVs etc. Solving the causes, which include housing costs, mental health and substance-abuse problems, seems an elusive goal.

Food, Drink & Nightlife

When to Eat

Breakfast Usually 7:30am–11am. Residents often grab this meal on the go, except on weekends.

Brunch 11am–3pm weekends. Often boozy.

Lunch Generally served 11:30am–2:30pm. Lunch out tends to be for social or business purposes. Alcohol is less consumed than in Europe.

Dinner 5pm–9pm

MENU DECODER

Californian casual Few restaurants require more than a dressy shirt, slacks and shoes that aren't flip-flops. At most places, T-shirts, shorts and sandals are fine.

Corkage You can bring your own wine to most restaurants; a 'corkage' fee of $15 to $30 usually applies.

Entree Always confusing to non-Americans – the word for the main course.

Heirloom Trendy term for types of produce meant to evoke varieties grown in the past.

Split-plate If you ask the kitchen to divide a plate between two (or more) people, there may be a small split-plate surcharge.

Vegetarian and vegan Travelers with food allergies or dietary restrictions are in luck – vegetarian and vegan fare is routine in California and many restaurants are used to catering to specific dietary needs.

Where to Eat

Whether you're into fine dining or searching for the ultimate surf-shack taco, California will spoil you. Make reservations online at least a month ahead for top tables.

Cafes and diners Historically, diners were often called 'coffee shops.' Hours vary, but expect breakfasts and comfort food.

Farmers markets Vendors selling superb local produce and prepared foods.

Food trucks Get fresh, imaginative food to go, often in a parking lot.

Destination dining Top restaurant in a high-end hotel or wine country resort.

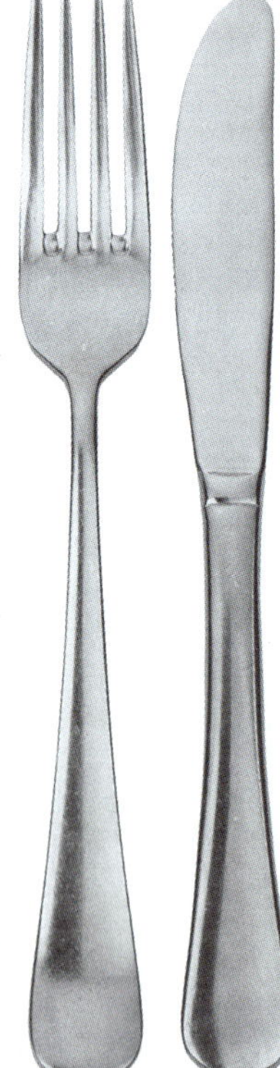

HOW TO... Tips & Tricks of Northern California Dining

Northern Californians love to swipe right with restaurants, especially places deemed new and unmissable. It's essential to reserve a table as far in advance as possible at restaurants with buzz or perennial popularity. Hot tables in a trend-loving place like Napa Wine Country will be booked up weeks in advance.

Destination restaurants like the **French Laundry** have become tick boxes for some diners whose main interest is bagging another famous meal. An entire market has been created for secondary sales of table reservations – people pay hundreds of dollars for a booking. Trust us, there's always a fine alternative restaurant.

How to tip (p316) is already a minefield for non-Americans not used to the practice. Now some restaurants in the Bay Area have introduced mandatory tip fees. But they often leave the door open to additional tipping (!). So inquire if the waitstaff will actually get the 'service fee.'

SERGIY KUZMIN/SHUTTERSTOCK

HOW MUCH FOR A...

Coffee
$3–7

Glass of local wine
$8 and up

Craft beer
$7–10

Burrito
$9–12

Bowl of cioppino
$30–50

Dungeness crab sandwich
$18 and up

California sushi roll
$9.50

Cup of artisanal ice cream
$5.50

HOW TO... Eat & Drink Like a Northern Californian

Start your morning with a coffee. Some have it black, others add something like oat milk or various flavorings. Breakfast might be a Greek-style yogurt or something simple from an artisan bakery; fare like omelets and hash browns is saved for a special occasion or weekend brunch.

Lunch can easily be from a food truck; Mexican food trucks or 'taco trucks' are the most popular, often superb and relatively cheap, but there're plenty of other types, too. Lunch might also be something light like a sandwich or salad. And while many tend to ignore this, ubiquitous fast-food joints prove that all Northern California meals aren't created healthy.

After-work drinks outside on a patio at a brewery or bar are popular year-round. Sure, sometimes temperatures might get down into the 50s, but that's what overhead heaters are for.

Dinner at home might feature whatever is fresh at the local farmers market (many are open year-round). Favorite dining-out choices are Japanese, regional Chinese, Vietnamese, Italian, the catch-all Mediterranean (which is a lot like Californian!), regional Mexican (of course), other Central American cuisines and regional American. A trendy cocktail and/or a local wine is a favorite accompaniment. Restaurants are uniformly casual and many feature year-round outside dining.

Bars tend to close early, so even in San Francisco, the streets are quiet by midnight.

Food Trucks

California has about 1000 food trucks (p33) operating across the state. Some are found in clusters, others operate alone. Some are in the same spot every day, others move around. Sample widely!

WINE TASTING 101

Clutch your wallet The days of free tastings are long gone at the vaunted vineyards of Napa and Sonoma Counties (and elsewhere), where a 45-minute tasting costs $30 or more. At many Napa Valley wineries, it's much more.

Swirl Before tasting a just-opened bottle of wine, swirl your glass to oxygenate the wine and release the flavors.

Sniff Dip your nose (without getting it wet) into the glass for a good whiff. This sniff prompts your senses and salivary glands to fully appreciate the wine.

Swish Take a swig, and roll it over the front of your gums and sides of your tongue to get the full effect of complex flavors and textures on all your taste buds. After you swallow, breathe out through your nose to appreciate the finish.

If you're driving or cycling, don't swallow Sips are hard to keep track of at tastings, so perfect your graceful arc into the spit bucket.

Take it easy There's no need for speed, even if the winery seems to be hurrying you along. Plan to visit three wineries a day maximum.

No need to buy No one expects you to buy, especially if you're paying to taste or take a tour – but it's customary to buy a bottle before winery picnics, and tasting fees are sometimes refunded with purchases.

Join the club? Many wineries push their own 'wine clubs' with promises of free future tastings and discounts of bottles. Before plunking down the dough, ask yourself: 'Will I ever come here again?'

Responsible Travel

Climate Change & Travel

It's impossible to ignore the impact we have when traveling; Lonely Planet urges all travelers to engage with their travel carbon footprint, which will mainly come from air travel. While there often isn't an alternative, travelers can look to minimize the number of flights they take, opt for newer aircrafts and use cleaner ground transportation, such as trains. One proposed solution – purchasing carbon offsets – unfortunately does not cancel out the impact of individual flights. While most destinations will depend on air travel for the foreseeable future, for now, pursuing ground-based travel where possible is the best course of action.

The **UN Carbon Offset Calculator** shows how flying impacts a household's emissions.

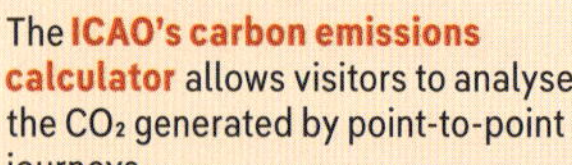

The **ICAO's carbon emissions calculator** allows visitors to analyse the CO_2 generated by point-to-point journeys.

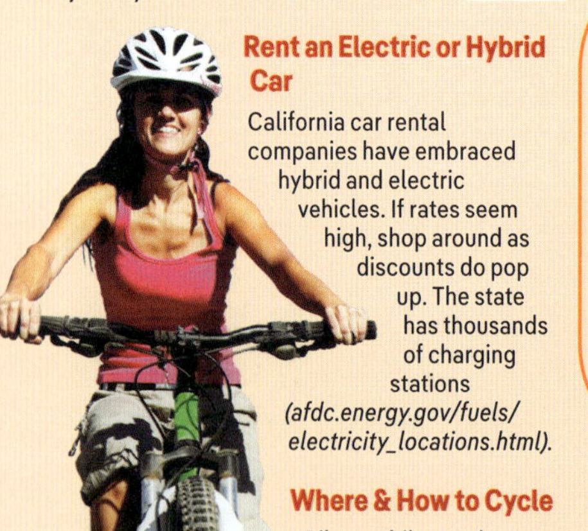

Rent an Electric or Hybrid Car

California car rental companies have embraced hybrid and electric vehicles. If rates seem high, shop around as discounts do pop up. The state has thousands of charging stations *(afdc.energy.gov/fuels/electricity_locations.html)*.

Where & How to Cycle

Bikes, e-bikes and e-scooters are easily rented at all of Northern California's main tourist areas. CalBike *(calbike.org)* has dozens of links to online and downloadable maps of bike routes, lanes and paths.

California's near-permanent drought means that everybody can help save water, including visitors. The state has a list of easy things we all can do to reduce our use; see *saveourwater.com*.

A thicket of federal and state regulations governs California's fishing industry. Learn about the most sustainable seafood to buy at *seafoodwatch.org* or learn sustainable practices and fish with **Sea Forager Expeditions** in San Francisco.

SAVE ON PLASTICS

Bring a reusable water bottle with you and skip plastic drink bottles. If you're given a plastic straw (banned in many parts of Northern California), rinse and reuse it.

TRAIN IT!

Within California, Amtrak is excellent, timely and efficient, often faster than clogged freeways. Don't forget regional rail and metro like Marin and Sonoma Counties' SMART train and the San Francisco Bay Area's Caltrain and BART.

Sustainable Wineries

Northern California has scores of wineries committed to sustainable practices – important, given the amount of water, pesticides and herbicides that others can use. Check out the following places:

Napa Valley (p174) Matthiasson Winery, Pride Mountain Vineyards, Grgich Hills Estate, Cakebread Cellars, Cliff Family Winery, Bennett Lane Winery, Joseph Phelps and Tres Sabores.

Sonoma County (p174) Preston, Porter Creek, Nalle, Quivira, Ridge Vineyards – Lytton Springs, Littorai and Truett-Hurst.

Anderson Valley (p242) Goldeneye.

Clear Lake (p244) Six Sigma, Chacewater and Kaz Winery.

Trinity Lake (p310) Alpen Cellars.

Northern California has great drinking water and many water fountains have spigots for refilling water bottles easily.

Help the beaches: adopt any trash you see as your own and toss it – works elsewhere too!

Get Cash for Containers

Look for 'CA CASH REFUND' or 'CA CRV' on beverage containers sold in California (although not wine bottles). Refunds range from 5¢ to 10¢. Find recycling points to collect the cash at *calrecycle.ca.gov*.

Combat Overtourism

Crowds during high season at popular spots like the Golden Gate Bridge, Muir Woods, Lake Tahoe and Big Sur impact the environment and cause friction between residents and visitors. Visit in low season or join local initiatives for giving back, such as Sonoma County Tourism Cares *(sonomacounty.com/partners/sctourism-cares)*, or take a cooking class at **Sonoma Family Meal**.

Emissions

Driving between San Francisco and LA emits about 150kg of carbon dioxide for an average-size car and 20kg for an e-vehicle; flying emits 160kg per passenger, bus emits 20kg per passenger and train 40kg. Calculate your trip at *native.eco/for-individuals/calculators/#Travel.*

RESOURCES

greenbusinessca.org
Search for green businesses by categories.

happycow.net
Vegetarian and vegan restaurants in California and beyond.

parksconservancy.org
Join a beach cleanup around San Francisco.

CLOCKWISE FROM TOP LEFT: JASON FINN/SHUTTERSTOCK, ROBCOCQUYT/SHUTTERSTOCK

LGBTQ+ Travelers

Inclusivity tends to be the norm in Northern California, and its embrace of all things LGBTQ+ is cause for admiration and ridicule in other parts of the USA. But it's a large and diverse region in terms of demographics and culture. So though it's largely progressive, attitudes do vary: to generalize, the rural and mountainous areas can be less tolerant.

Queer Havens & Hazards

Many places in Northern California are queer-friendly but the following are at another level. San Francisco's nationally iconic neighborhood called the Castro District (p99) was the home of the rainbow flag, and the Mission is now a hub for lesbian and transgender folks. The Russian River's Guerneville (p213), a long-running gay getaway, is tops for river and redwood escapes.

Be careful in the rural north and mountainous areas. Even the cities can be conservative. College towns are better. The recent national political climate has also made people's conduct more uncertain.

NOTABLE TIMES FOR LGBTQ+ TRAVEL

There's no bad time for LGBTQ+ travel in Northern California, but some months are famous for special events. First, of course, is June, when Pride events and fabulous parades fill San Francisco (p41) with Soul of Pride, too, as well as smaller cities like Santa Rosa (p206). The Russian River holds **Women's Weekend** in May, Lazy Bear Week in late July/early August and Pride in September.

Get Married in California

Though it's legal across the USA, many LGBTQ+ couples prefer to marry in a state known for its queer welcome. In California, you needn't be a citizen or take a blood test. Just fill out a form at a county clerk's office, pay a fee and get a license. Then get hitched!

DISCOVER LGBTQ+ HISTORY

In San Francisco, visit the Leather & LGBTQ (p64) and Transgender Districts. You can also book guided tours like Cruisin' the Castro *(cruisinthecastro.com)*. The Cal Migration Museum *(calmigration.org)* walking tours include one in the Castro, and if you're traveling to LA, download the free Pride Explorer *(thelavendereffect.org/pride-explorer)* app.

LGBTQ+ RESOURCES

Advocate *(advocate.com/travel)* News, LGBTQ+ travel features and destination guides.
Damron *(damron.com)* Long-running, advertiser-driven gay travel guides and app.
Out Traveler *(outtraveler.com)* Free online magazine articles with travel tips, destination guides and resort reviews.
LGBT National Help Center *(lgbthotline.org)* Counseling, information and referrals for people of all ages; special resources for youths.
Strut *(sfaf.org)* San Francisco clinic for inclusive sexual health services.

LGBTQ+ Employment Rights

The California Fair Employment and Housing Act makes it illegal for an employer to fire, demote, fail to hire, fail to promote, harass or otherwise discriminate against anyone because of their sexual orientation, gender identity and/or gender expression.

Accessible Travel

California leads the way on accessibility in the US. More populated areas of Northern California are reasonably well equipped for travelers with disabilities, although older properties may have limitations.

Park Passes

US residents with a permanent disability qualify for a free lifetime pass, which waives entry fees to all national parks. California State Parks' disabled discount pass ($3.50) gives 50% off parking and camping fees.

Trains

In the Bay Area, BART is fully wheelchair accessible; Caltrain has four minor stations that are not accessible. In the North Bay, Sonoma-Marin Area Rail Transit (SMART) trains and stations are all accessible. Amtrak requires advance notice for accessibility service.

Buses

Public transit buses are all wheelchair accessible by law. Ramps that deploy automatically when the bus is lowered to the curb are the norm. The driver may have to assist with securing wheelchairs once inside the bus.

AIRPORT

California's airports comply with accessibility laws. Assistance is available through your airline.

Beach Accessibility

California lags behind the EU in providing accessibility for all on its beaches, which are mostly left in a natural state and don't include ramps into the water. However, the California Coastal Commission does provide a useful resource of over 100 beaches with available wheelchairs designed for use on the sand. These devices can be reserved and are free to use; some are motorized. See the CCC *(coastal.ca.gov/access/beach-wheelchairs.html)* website for full details.

RESOURCES

Access Northern California *(accessnca.org)* Extensive links to accessible-travel resources, including outdoor recreation opportunities, lodgings, tours and transportation.

California State Parks *(parks.ca.gov)* Searchable online map and database of accessible features at state parks.

DISABILITY RIGHTS

The US Department of Justice *(ada.gov)* enforces the Americans with Disabilities Act (ADA). It makes this statement on its comprehensive website: 'Disability rights are civil rights.' The Act covers many areas of public life including employment, transportation, accommodations and telecommunications.

Accommodations

Hotels built since 1993 must meet modern accessibility requirements. Major chains usually have rooms adapted for accessibility needs, but you should book in advance and double-check they have what you require. Holiday rentals and vintage properties may not be accessible.

Outdoor Safety

California's great outdoors is mostly safe, but there are a few warnings to heed and precautions to take to ensure you avoid danger.

Mountain Lions

Attacks on humans by mountain lions are rare, but can be deadly. If you encounter a mountain lion on a hiking trail, stay calm, pick up small children, face the animal and retreat slowly. Make yourself appear larger by raising your arms or grabbing a stick. If the lion becomes menacing, shout or throw rocks at it. If attacked, fight back aggressively.

Snakes & Spiders

Snakes and spiders are common throughout California, not just in wilderness areas. There are many more species than just the rattlers seen in Westerns. Always look inside your shoes before putting them on when camping. Snake bites are rare, but occur most often when a snake is stepped on or provoked (eg poked with a stick). Antivenom is available at most hospitals.

Sharks & Jellyfish

Despite the hype, sharks are not a big concern in the ocean off Northern California. Since records were kept in 1851, only 25 people have been killed by sharks in California. The many species of jellyfish in the Pacific are worth your concern, however. Several come equipped with poisonous stingers which – while not deadly – can cause extreme pain. Check the water to see if there are jellyfish.

Sneaker Waves

One of the biggest causes of death along the California coast are sneaker waves. These dramatically larger waves suddenly appear and wash people off the rocks or sand. If you're not swimming, keep a good distance from the water and never turn your back toward the water. Most Northern California beaches do not have lifeguards. Your safety is entirely left up to you.

What to Pack on Hikes

Wear quick-drying (synthetic or woolen) clothing and carry a waterproof wind layer. Bringing the 10 essentials *(americanhiking.org/10essentials)* is recommended, especially in remote areas.

BEAR SAFETY

The California grizzly bear (as seen on the state flag) is long extinct, but forests are still home to countless black bears. They can be attracted to campgrounds: never leave food unattended or in a car, and always use bear canisters.

If you encounter a bear, don't run. Speak in a calm voice to show you're human ('Hey, bear' is popular), and slowly back away to at least 100m. Black bears are not aggressive by nature and will try to avoid confrontation. Keep kids and dogs near. Some national parks ban bear spray.

DON'T FEED THE ANIMALS

Never feed or approach wild animals, not even harmless-looking critters – it causes them to associate humans with food, which can lead to negative animal-human interactions. Also, many birds and mammals carry diseases that can be transmitted through bites.

DOODLING POE/SHUTTERSTOCK

Nuts & Bolts

OPENING HOURS

Businesses, restaurants and shops in tourist areas may close earlier and on additional days during the winter off-season (November to March). Standard hours include:

Banks 9:30am–5pm weekdays

Bars 4pm–2am

Restaurants 11am–3pm and 5:30pm–10pm daily; some open later Friday and Saturday

Shops 10am–7pm Monday–Saturday, 11am–6pm Sunday (many open later)

Toilets

Free public restrooms are easy to find inside shopping malls, public buildings, libraries, gas stations and some transportation hubs, as well as at parks and beaches.

Weights & Measures

Imperial (except 1 US gallon equals 0.83 imperial gallons)

Water

Tap water in Northern California is good quality and is safe to drink. (San Francisco's comes mostly from snow melt and is excellent.)

GOOD TO KNOW

Time zone
Pacific Standard Time (GMT/UTC minus eight hours)

Country calling code
1

Emergency number
911

Population
40 million

Electricity

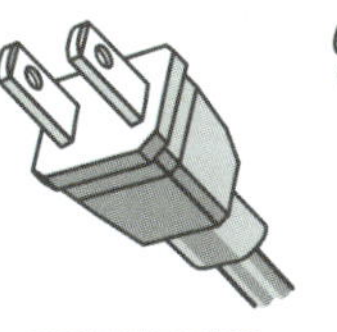

Type A
120V/60Hz

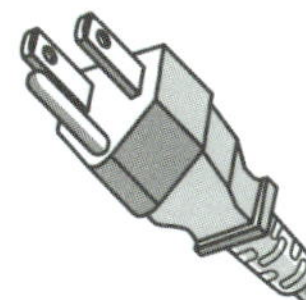

Type B
120V/60Hz

PUBLIC HOLIDAYS

On the following holidays, banks, schools and government offices (including post offices) are closed, and transportation, museums and other services may operate on a Sunday schedule. Holidays falling on a weekend are usually observed the following Monday.

New Year's Day January 1

Martin Luther King Jr Day Third Monday in January

Presidents' Day Third Monday in February

Cesar Chavez Day March 31

Memorial Day Last Monday in May

Independence Day July 4

Labor Day First Monday in September

Veterans Day November 11

Thanksgiving Day Fourth Thursday in November

Christmas Day December 25

STORYBOOK

Our writers delve deep into different aspects of Northern Californian life.

Pigeon Point Light Station (p159)

GARY C TOGNONI/SHUTTERSTOCK

A HISTORY OF NORTHERN CALIFORNIA IN 15 PLACES

On a Pacific island ruled by Amazon queen Califia, women warriors wear golden armor and ride dragons – recognize the story? Today the heroine of Garci Rodríguez de Montalvo's 1500 Spanish novel, an ancient version of Hollywood superhero Wonder Woman, is better known as the namesake of California. Who can resist a place like this? By Alexis Averbuck

FIVE HUNDRED NATIVE American nations called this land home for some 15,000 years before 16th-century European arrivals gave it a new name: California. Spanish conquistadors and priests came here for gold and God, but soon relinquished their flea-plagued missions and ill-equipped *presidios* (forts) to Mexico. Their main lasting legacy was the near-extermination of the region's Indigenous peoples.

The unruly territory was handed off to the US in the Treaty of Guadalupe Hidalgo mere months before gold was discovered in 1848. A virtual flood of prospectors and settlers washed over California in a short time – the first of many such influxes. Generations of California dreamers have made the trek to these Pacific shores for gold, glory and self-determination, making homes and history on America's most fabled frontier.

The Golden State has surged ahead to become the world's fourth-largest economy, much of that fueled by successive booms in the last 100 years: Hollywood, aerospace, computers, the internet. But like a kid that's grown too fast, California still hasn't figured out how to handle such rapid growth, including housing shortages, traffic gridlock and breathtakingly high costs of living. Even so, today Northern California flaunts its international status and is taking leading roles in such global issues as environmental standards, online privacy, AI, marriage equality and immigrant rights.

1. Lava Beds National Monument

19,000 YEARS OF CIVILIZATION

Human settlement began in the area now known as Northern California as early as 19,000 years ago. These Indigenous people passed knowledge of hunting grounds and turf boundaries from generation to generation in at least 100 distinct languages. In Lava Beds National Monument is a sacred area for the Modoc people, one of the 500 Indigenous groups that have been identified so far. The centerpieces are ancient petroglyphs carved thousands of years ago.

By 1870, California's Indigenous population would be decimated by 90%, due to introduced European diseases, conscripted labor, violence, marginalization and hunger in their own fertile lands.

For more on Lava Beds National Monument, see p289.

2. Mission San Francisco Solano

MISSIONS AND GENOCIDE

For the glory of God and its tax coffers, in 1769 Spain decided to establish missions across California that would be self-sustaining and run by local converts. Franciscan friar Junípero Serra established Mission San Diego de Alcalá in 1769. Another 20 missions followed, eventually reaching Sonoma's Mission San Francisco Solano, built in 1823 by Native American conscripts. And, like the others, it was never a big success. Native Californians balked at life as slaves, and many died due to European-introduced diseases, including measles and smallpox. In 1821 Mexico (which included California) won its independence from Spain and the mission system soon collapsed.

For more see p190.

3. Alamo Square's 'Painted Lady'

WHERE AMERICAN CALIFORNIA BEGAN

In 1846 Mexico and the US went to war. Meanwhile, legions of Americans were already arriving in California, lured by its obvious bounties. When Mexico ordered them out in 1846, they declared independence and raised the US flag. Mexico could not compete and hostilities ended with the Treaty of Guadalupe Hidalgo, in which Mexico ceded much of its northern territory (including Alta California) to the US.

Today Alamo Square, in San Francisco, is home to the famous 'Painted Lady' Victorian mansions. Built in 1857, these are some of the finest examples of houses built soon after California became a US state.

For more on Alamo Square, see p82.

4. Jack London Square

GOLD! GOLD! GOLD!

John Sutter and James Marshall built a sawmill in the Sierra Nevada foothills in 1847, and a few months later Marshall saw something glittering in the American River. When San Francisco tabloid publisher Sam Brannan heard gold flakes has been discovered, he published the rumor as fact, figuring it might sell some newspapers. It did. Word spread, gold fever swept the world and thousands of people poured into California in 1849. In San Francisco's Devil's Acre neighborhood and in Oakland's Jack London Square (where a replica of the writer and adventurer's cabin stands), he and miners drank and gambled away their finds.

For more on Jack London Square, see p133.

Jack London Square (p133)

BONDROCKETIMAGES/SHUTTERSTOCK

5. Angel Island Immigration Station

WEST COAST PORT OF ENTRY

Denied gold rush mining claims, many Chinese prospectors opened service-based businesses that became the basis for the Chinatowns once found in nearly every California city and town. However, discriminatory Californian laws restricting housing, employment and citizenship for anyone born in China were codified with the 1882 US Chinese Exclusion Act, which remained US law until 1943.

One legacy of the law can be found on Angel Island in the San Francisco Bay Area, where the Immigration Station operated from 1910 to 1940. At this detention center for Chinese immigrants, many were cruelly held for long periods before ultimately being sent back to China, leaving only mournful graffiti behind.

For more on Angel Island, see p123.

6. San Francisco's Dolores Park

REFUGE FROM EARTHQUAKE FLAMES

California's 'robber barons' (Leland Stanford et al) built Nob Hill mansions in San Francisco with their fortunes. The City by the Bay dominated the West Coast and attracted notables such as William Randolph Hearst, who took over his first newspaper here in 1887. But San Francisco's grand ambitions came crashing down on April 18, 1906, when earthquake and fire reduced the city to rubble. With flames destroying what the shaking didn't, thousands – including many from Nob Hill – escaped the inferno in Dolores Park. Cross 20th St to the fire hydrant (still painted golden) that saved the neighborhood, and take in the view of the city's skyline today.

For more on Dolores Park, see p90.

7. Longshoremen's Union Hall

THE RISE OF 'LEFT COAST' POLITICS

While San Francisco was rebuilt at a rate of 15 buildings a day, political reformers set to work on city, state and national policies, one plank at a time. Mexico's revolution from 1910 to 1921 brought a new wave of migrants and revolutionary ideas, including ethnic pride and worker solidarity. As California's ports grew, longshoremen's unions coordinated a historic 83-day strike in 1934 along the entire West Coast that forced concessions for safer working conditions and fair pay. San Francisco's Longshoremen's Union Hall, a mid-century example of the union's might, would go on to be the site of Bill Graham's 1960s Trips Festival.

8. Golden Gate Bridge

SYMBOL OF HOPE

At the height of the Depression in 1935, some 200,000 farming families fled the drought-struck Dust Bowl on the Great Plains and headed to California, where they found scant pay and deplorable working conditions. California's artists alerted middle America to the migrants' plight, from Dorothea Lange's haunting documentary photos and John Steinbeck's harrowing fictionalized account in his Pulitzer Prize–winning novel *The Grapes of Wrath* (1939), to federally funded Works Progress Administration (WPA) murals by 26 local artists in Coit Tower. Built from 1933 to 1937, the Golden Gate Bridge was a symbol of ingenuity and hope rising in this difficult time.

For more on the Golden Gate Bridge, see p54.

9. Tule Lake Segregation Center

CALIFORNIA'S CONCENTRATION CAMPS

In the 1930s, Japanese Americans had thriving farms and businesses across California. Many others were jealous of this success, and people like William Randolph Hearst sought political power by fueling ethnic hatred and division. After the attack on Pearl Harbor by Japan on December 7, 1941, sparked the US' entry into WWII, Hearst and company saw their chance: they would stop opposing the policies of the normally progressive President Franklin Roosevelt. In return, he'd allow nearly 120,000 Japanese Americans to be rounded up and sent to concentration camps scattered across desolate corners of the west, including the largest at Tule Lake Segregation Center in the furthest northern reaches of the state.

For more on Tule Lake Segregation Center, see p291.

10. Rosie the Riveter WWII Home Front National Historic Park

ALL HANDS ON DECK

No place better symbolizes the win-at-any-cost WWII war effort than the old Kaiser shipyards on the San Francisco Bay in Richmond. From 1942 until 1946, a whopping 747 ships were built here – an extraordinary accomplishment, made more so because much of the vast workforce had been marginalized before the war: women and African Americans. The societal changes caused by this upheaval of the social order are still felt today, as detailed at the Rosie the Riveter WWII Home Front National Historic Park. Meanwhile, names like Douglas and Lockheed created the Southern California aerospace industry, which fueled California's first postwar boom.

For more on the park, see p144.

Rosie the Riveter sign (p144)

EWY MEDIA/SHUTTERSTOCK

11. City Lights Bookstore

HOWL FOR FREEDOM

The Navy discharged WWII sailors for insubordination and homosexuality in San Francisco, as though that would teach them a lesson. Instead, San Francisco became an outpost of free speech and free spirits, and everyone who was anyone got arrested here – including dancer Carol Doda for going topless, comedian Lenny Bruce for dropping F-bombs onstage, and City Lights Bookstore founder Lawrence Ferlinghetti for publishing Allen Ginsberg's epic poem *Howl*. Doda won and kept dancing for 45 years, Bruce was posthumously pardoned, and City Lights continues to celebrate its landmark 1957 free speech victory by publishing fresh verse and provocative prose.

For more information on City Lights Bookstore, see p71.

12. Golden Gate Park

TURN ON, TUNE IN, DROP OUT

The Summer of Love really started on January 14, 1967, in San Francisco's Golden Gate Park, when Human Be-In blew minds, gave Timothy Leary a stage and celebrated all things psychedelic. Free speech was the mantra and Haight-Ashbury became the place to be.

Passions soon turned to racial injustice and the Vietnam War. Starting with UC Berkeley, college campuses across California and the US were roiled by unrestrained, at times violent, protests. Yet the social upheavals also jump-started the careers of California's 'law and order' politicians Ronald Reagan (who was elected governor in 1966) and Richard Nixon (elected US President in 1968).

For more on Golden Gate Park, see p106.

13. West Oakland

HOME OF THE BLACK PANTHERS

Soon after Cesar Chavez and Dolores Huerta formed United Farm Workers (UFW) in 1962 to champion the rights of immigrant laborers, bringing the issues of fair wages and pesticide health risks to the nation's attention, the Black Panther Party for Self-Defense began its revolutionary campaign for African American rights. Bobby Seale and Huey P Newton started the group in 1966 with headquarters at 1048 Peralta St in West Oakland, promoting popular programs like breakfast and lunch for children and free health clinics. The group fought against police brutality and advocated for reparations, concerns that are still present today.

For more on West Oakland, see p134.

14. GLBT Historical Society Museum

THE ROAD TO MARRIAGE EQUALITY

San Francisco Supervisor Harvey Milk became the first openly gay man elected to public office in California in 1977. He lived in the Castro, now home to the GLBT Historical Society Museum. Milk sponsored a gay rights bill before his murder by a political opponent in SF's iconic City Hall.

In 2004, then-mayor Gavin Newsom ordered marriage licenses to be issued for same-sex couples, a first in the US. However, in 2008 California voters narrowly passed a proposition defining legal marriage as between man and woman. California courts ruled it unconstitutional, and in a surprise decision, the US Supreme Court upheld marriage equality in 2013. The museum covers this battle and much more.

For more on the GLBT Historical Society Museum, see p101.

15. Apple Park

FAKE IT TILL YOU MAKE IT

At the 1977 West Coast Computer Faire, 21-year-old Steve Jobs and Steve Wozniak introduced the Apple II, a personal computer with unfathomable memory (4KB of RAM!) and microprocessor speed (1MHz!). But the question remained: what would ordinary people do with all that computing power?

The rest, of course, is history. What's now known as Silicon Valley has spawned countless millionaires and products that have changed lives worldwide. Boom-and-bust cycles are the norm, which is worth remembering as you navigate the antiseptic minimalism of the visitor center at Apple Park, the hubristic bunker of the multi-billion-dollar corporate headquarters in Cupertino.

For more on Apple Park, see p149.

MEET THE CALIFORNIANS

Expect a friendly, smile-filled welcome paired with a sense of self-reliance and independence. It's the expression of a live-and-let-live ethos. Alexis Averbuck introduces her people.

COMPARED WITH THE rest of the US, many of us see our state as a laid-back, free-thinking multicultural society that gives everyone a chance to live however we like.

Indeed, many powerful movements that have changed the world began here. Chicano pride, Black Power, the Farm Workers movement and LGBTQ+ pride all built political bases here. In 2017, then-governor Jerry Brown signed a law making California a sanctuary state, thereby preventing local law enforcement from aiding federal authorities in detaining undocumented immigrants.

That's for good reason. Throughout California's history, immigration has been a core aspect of the state's very existence. California had a thriving Indigenous population for over 10,000 years, but Native Californians were decimated when California was colonized by Spain, Mexico and even Russia, before becoming a US state. Today, around 11 million Californians are immigrants. One of every four people who have immigrated to the US are in California, with about 46% coming from Asia and 38% from Latin America.

The idea of California lives in world lore and some stereotypes are not strictly wrong. For example, nearly 68% of Californians do live in coastal areas (much of which are protected by the California Coastal Commission). And yes, the Cali self-help and new-agey movements have been successfully pioneered and marketed here since well before their 1970s heyday. Similarly, SoCal's movie and music industries are wildly influential – though nowadays, Silicon Valley and the state's powerful tech industry jockey for the title of top influencer.

But life here is not charmed. The rising cost of housing has reached a crisis level leading to a huge spike in homelessness. Eight of the 10 most expensive US housing markets are in California and buying or even renting a home these days is out of reach for many Californians. The home-ownership rate has dropped to 55%, down from a 60.7% peak in 2006. The high cost of living is also prompting more middle- and low-income Californians (especially millennials) to migrate to other states with more affordable pastures and if you're a Californian aged 18 to 24, there's a more than a 50% possibility that your roomies are your parents.

It's also true that Californians drive a lot. We commute an average of 29 minutes each way to work. But at least Californians are zooming ahead of the national energy-use curve in smog-checked cars and buying more hybrid and fuel-efficient cars than any other state. In 2022, Governor Gavin Newsom signed into law some of the most sweeping measures to hasten the use of clean energy and protect us from polluters, though in 2025 the Trump administration endeavored to roll these back. Generally, we always back initiatives that promote a clean environment – keeping California a progressive oasis in our rough-and-tumble national politics.

Big as a Nation

With almost 39.5 million residents, California is the most populous state in the US. It also has the fourth-largest economy in the world. It's ripe for jokes about seceding from the nation.

TYPICAL CALIFORNIAN?

I grew up in Oakland, a child of two people with wildly different backgrounds. My mother's family has been here for seven generations. One of my ancestors on her side was among the first female Spanish-land-grant-holders in the Los Angeles area. She in turn married a German immigrant. My father's family arrived from Eastern Europe via NYC to East LA (Boyle Heights, to be specific) in the 1940s. They were Jewish communists who were persecuted during Joseph McCarthy's Red Scare. Proof that California's institutions are actually not always tolerant. My parents were both teachers and during my youth we spent many years living overseas, speaking other languages, but always returned to Oakland.

California is a land of immigration, innovation and change and my family history is as multivalent as many people here. So, really, all it shows is that the only thing typical in California is that there is no such thing as a typical Californian.

Boudin Bakery, San Francisco
PACK-SHOT/SHUTTERSTOCK

BREAD CULTURE IN THE BAY AREA

A bevy of bakers is drawing people from near and far to revel in the rich culture around artisanal bread. By Lisa Park

HEAD OVER TO Acme Bread Company in Berkeley any day of the week and you'll find a line of customers that's sometimes 30-plus deep, eagerly waiting to get inside. Hand-drawn signs touting savory creations such as 'hella wet levain' and 'multigrain spelt' border the bakery's picture window, which offers a tantalizing glimpse of the arts-and-crafts loaves that have earned Acme accolades and a devoted following. Meanwhile, the yeasty aroma of freshly baked bread keeps customers enthralled until it's their turn to pick and choose from crusty baguettes, buns, rounds and rolls – like a kid in a candy store.

Not too shabby for a bakery that's been around for over 40 years. But Acme's not alone when it comes to getting this kind of steadfast attention. Artisanal bakeries across the San Francisco Bay Area are drawing big crowds and fostering communities keen on indulging their appetite for – and love of – handcrafted, high-quality bread.

Artisanal Bread's Ups & Downs

Bay Area breadmaking goes back to the mid-1800s when Isadore Boudin of Boudin Bakery used a sourdough starter given to him by a gold miner to create his classic French bread. While the rest of the country moved toward ultra-processing bread post WWII (using commercially made cake yeast and chemicals such as emulsifiers to speed up production), Boudin Bakery resisted. Staying true to old-world traditions, it still makes bread with just flour, water and salt, using the same starter or mother dough from 176 years ago.

Even as Boudin flourished, many artisanal bakeries gave way to large, industrial operations mass-producing cheap, bland, chemically enhanced white bread. It wasn't until the 1970s when a new breed of bread makers, including Zen monks, hippies and counterculture kids, decided they'd had enough of Wonder Bread. They started making bread the old-fashioned way – kneaded and shaped by hand then baked in wood-fired ovens – fusing classic techniques focusing on texture and flavor development with modern values emphasizing good, clean and nourishing food.

Over the next few decades, bakers at Tassajara, Cheeseboard Collective, Acme, Semifreddi's and the San Francisco Baking Institute (SFBI) each had a hand in 'laying the groundwork for people to enjoy arts-and-crafts style bread,' says Miyuki Togi, SFBI baking instructor. Their success helped elevate people's appreciation for, as Togi explains, 'handmade bread that takes time and is made with care.' And it also helped make artisanal bread accessible – via storefronts, restaurants and grocery outlets – throughout the Bay Area.

JUNE
SEPTEMBER
NOVEMBER

Tartine's Outsize Impact

Then along came Tartine in the early aughts. Its novel bakes experimenting with longer fermentation, higher hydration, whole grains and a super-dark crust blew the Bay Area bread scene wide open. The now-famous brand snagged the ultimate endorsement from New York Times food writer Mark Bittman who called Tartine his 'favorite bakery in the United States.'

Artisanal bakeries inspired by Tartine's spirit of innovation and excellence started popping up all over the Bay, each investing the time and resources toward creating delicious, nutritious bread. Consider San Francisco favorite the Mill, whose owner and head baker Josey Baker specializes in freshly milled (in house, no less) whole-grain sourdough breads that need up to 40 hours to complete – 'because good things take time,' according to Baker on his website.

At Fournée Bakery in Berkeley, the mission is to 'make the best possible product consistently using the best possible ingredients sourced from local farms and purveyors.' Meanwhile, Mountain View–based the Midwife and the Baker is all about cultivating 'craft and community,' baking only with organic flour and seeds from sustainable farms to create quality products for its customers.

'THERE'S A REAL SYMBIOTIC RELATIONSHIP BETWEEN MAKING BREAD THAT'S BEAUTIFUL AND HAVING PEOPLE WHO VALUE YOU AND THE ART OF BAKING.' AZIKIWEE ANDERSON, RIZE UP BAKERY FOUNDER

Tartine Bakery
GADO IMAGES/ALAMY

Love for Craft & Community

With Tartine's meteoric rise, 'customers got more serious about what they were looking for in bread,' says Togi. In addition, 'people in the Bay Area are more open to paying more for better quality food. So they don't mind paying more for a loaf of really good bread from a small bakery.'

Theo Dolarian, fellow SFBI baking instructor and Mill alumnus, agrees and adds that 'people are also more open to new flavor profiles. They will try different things... The wonderful thing about the San Francisco Bay Area is that if there's a style of bread you're interested in, there's a place that does it and probably does it really well.'

Case in point: home-based-project-turned-growing-commercial-operation Rize Up Bakery, whose inventive sourdough breads – ube, masala and K-pop (aka gochujang) – have struck a resounding chord. Says founder Azikiwee Anderson (who was previously a chef), 'the only reason I get to innovate is because I have customers who care enough to support what I'm doing. There's a real symbiotic relationship between making bread that's beautiful and having people who value you and the art of baking.'

Adds Anderson, Rize Up is a reflection of the San Francisco Bay Area, 'where there's a lot more we than I. Breadmaking is about being part of a community of different cultures. It's about representing and including those cultures so that they feel seen and cared about.'

'When you ask me what makes bread culture in the Bay Area special, I really do think it's the community. We're part of something bigger. And when you're surrounded by people who care and are down to do the hard work, that makes our bread untouchable.'

Baking is a labor of love for the craft and for the community, says Anderson, whose North Star questions include things like: 'Would you stand in line for our bread? Would you buy it special to share at a dinner? When you bite into it, do you do a little happy dance? Does it talk to your soul?'

Yes, yes and so much yes.

THE CLIMATE CRISIS

California is on the leading edge of the global climate crisis, facing both the repercussions and the need to pioneer initiatives to fight back.

ALTHOUGH THE WHOLE world is facing up to the reality of the climate crisis, California is especially vulnerable to its effects. The challenges – wildfires, swings between drought and floods, plus rising seawater levels – are a continuous threat to life, property and landscapes.

The State of Things

According to the California Environmental Protection Agency's Office of Environmental Health Hazard Assessment (OEHHA; *oehha.ca.gov*), annual air and ocean temperatures have been rising since records began in 1895. This has been scientifically proven to be due to human activity. Average temperatures have risen by 2.5°F and the rise is accelerating rapidly: it's projected to increase by another 4.4°F to 5.8°F degrees by 2050. It's most noticeable in Southern California and more than half of the 20 warmest years in California have occurred after 2000.

Warmer seas mean rising sea levels and this is a huge problem for coastal populations in a state where more than

Death Valley National Park

STEVEN GROUP/SHUTTERSTOCK

26 million people live near the sea. Authorities are fast-tracking the expensive work of 'coastal armoring,' and California has already spent billions of dollars improving seawalls and fortifying wetlands. Not only has the sea risen by six inches since 1950, but the rise has accelerated to a pace of one inch per decade.

Extreme Weather Events

Rising tides and rising temperatures are also causing an increase in extreme weather events. The Indicators of Climate Change in California report (2022) warned that weather extremes are getting more intense and less predictable – which plays dangerously into California's seasonal wildfires.

AUTHORITIES ARE FAST-TRACKING THE EXPENSIVE WORK OF 'COASTAL ARMORING,' AND CALIFORNIA HAS ALREADY SPENT BILLIONS OF DOLLARS IMPROVING SEAWALLS AND FORTIFYING WETLANDS.

Cyclone, Capitola
ROSANGELA PERRY/SHUTTERSTOCK

The 2020 wildfire season broke records when more than 6565 sq miles burned; 2024 saw the state's fourth-largest fire, the Park Fire; and 2025 started as a brutal year with the Palisades Fire. The world watched as Los Angeles burned: decimating Pacific Palisades, Malibu and Altadena. Though Californians are fighting back and CAL FIRE has put in place an expanding network of high-tech cameras in fire-prone areas (speeding up firefighting responses) and scientists are harnessing AI to model wildfire behavior, the human capacity to curb Mother Nature is limited.

You also can't ignore the extreme smoke pollution hanging thick in the air during large fires. On September 9, 2020, the infamous 'orange sky day,' San Francisco Bay Area residents woke to a sun that never appeared, so thick was the smoke brought in by high winds.

Speaking of winds (which also exacerbate fires)...El Niño and La Niña wind changes and weather events like atmospheric rivers, which bring intense rainfall, mean more Californians than ever are at risk of experiencing floods and landslides. The impact of the climate crisis on Californians intersects with racial and economic inequalities. A study by UC Irvine showed that Black and low-income households in the Los Angeles Basin are at the greatest risk of impact by flooding – up to 79% higher risk than white residents.

Lessons from California's First Nations

Climate change isn't the only accelerant of California's worsening wildfires; forest management also holds a key. In 2022, the Wildfire and Forest Resilience Task Force (*wildfiretaskforce.org*) announced a plan to expand the use of 'beneficial fire,' a concept passed down through generations of Native American people.

A UC Berkeley study showed that the Klamath Mountains forests have doubled in size since the native Karuk and Yurok tribes were able to steward the land. These original custodians carried out controlled burns to prevent overgrowth and keep the forest floors in healthy balance. Europeans, in contrast, carried out extensive logging, followed by replanting trees close together. Much modern forest management has focused on preventing burns, the end result is an overgrown carpet of forest and undergrowth that can carry fires over a devastatingly wide area. CAL FIRE and other organizations now manage prescribed burns.

San Francisco skies glow orange from wildfires in 2020
LARRY ZHOU/SHUTTERSTOCK

The Impact of Tourism

When visitors encounter California's natural splendor and learn about the state's complex environmental challenges, an uncomfortable truth arises. The fragile beauty that draws around 270 million visitors to California in a single year is at the mercy of their behavior. At popular destinations like Big Sur and Lake Tahoe, where overtourism has caused soil erosion and other problems, many blame social media for having popularized the areas' photogenic locations.

Sustainable Futures

Fortunately, California has an extensive set of programs to encourage sustainable travel (*travelmattersca.com*). The National Park Service is increasingly shifting to renewable or alternative energy sources, with some parks heading toward carbon-neutral status. One example is the Golden Gate National Recreation Area (the USA's most visited park in 2024) which buys 100% renewable electricity for park operations. Winter sports giant Vail Resorts has committed to achieving carbon-neutral status by 2030, while the SIP (Sustainability in Practice) certified program highlights increasing numbers of wineries (p323) using sustainable practices.

California may be at the sharp edge of climate change, but it's also mounting some of the most robust measures to meet these challenges. The state has been reducing its greenhouse gas emissions since 2007 (except for a hiccup during the COVID-19 pandemic). The state enacted regulations banning the sale of new fossil-fuel-powered cars from 2035, but this was blocked by the Trump administration in May 2025. Legal battles will ensue.

CALIFORNIA MAY BE AT THE SHARP EDGE OF CLIMATE CHANGE, BUT IT'S ALSO MOUNTING SOME OF THE MOST ROBUST MEASURES TO MEET THESE CHALLENGES.

There are also efforts to harness California's abundant sunshine for solar power. Rooftop solar alone won't meet the population's energy needs, but devoting land to this use is hotly debated. Wildlife conservationists want solar sites in the cities, far from protected land, meanwhile urban dwellers want the sites far from view.

Many more hurdles lie ahead, but the urgency of California's climate crisis, mixed with its cutting-edge technology and research, are equipping the state for a fight.

Learn more about how to be a responsible visitor on p322.

Desert Sunlight Solar Farm, Mojave Dessert

THE DESERT PHOTO/SHUTTERSTOCK

INDEX

A

Map Pages **000**

Map Pages **000**

Map Pages **000**

Map Pages **000**

'San Francisco (p41) is the threshold between fact and fiction, past and future, body and soul.'

ALISON BING

'Mendocino Village (p232) was saved from economic disaster by artists in the 1960s. Today it feels simultaneously suitable for a well-journeyed sea captain and a bohemian poet.'

AMELIA MULARZ

FROM LEFT: GJEE/SHUTTERSTOCK, HY-DP/SHUTTERSTOCK

Mapping data sources:
© Lonely Planet
© OpenStreetMap http://openstreetmap.org/copyright

THIS BOOK

The 4th edition of Lonely Planet's *San Francisco & Northern California* guidebook was written and researched by Alexis Averbuck, Alison Bing, Celeste Brash, Amelia Mularz and Ryan Ver Berkmoes. The previous edition was written by Alison, Celeste, Helena Smith, Brett Atkinson, Sara Benson, Nate Cavalieri, Michael Grosberg, Ashley Harrell, Josephine Quintero and John A Vlahides. This guidebook was produced by:

Destination Editor Melissa Yeager

Production Editor Katie Connolly

Image Editor Compton Sheldon

Cartographer Julie Dodkins

Coordinating Editor Gabrielle Innes

Assisting Editors Nigel Chin, Paul Harding, Anne Mulvany, Karyn Noble

Cover Researcher Rhianydd Hylton

Thanks Imogen Bannister, Michelle Bennett, Dylan Lalanne-Perkins, Kellie Langdon, Ailbhe MacMahon, Darren O'Connell, Charlotte Orr, Lisa Park, Margot Seeto, Saralinda Turner

Paper in this book is certified against the Forest Stewardship Council™ standards. FSC™ promotes environmentally responsible, socially beneficial and economically viable management of the world's forests.

Published by Lonely Planet Global Limited
CRN 554153
4th edition - Jan 2026
ISBN 9781787016071
© Lonely Planet 2026
10 9 8 7 6 5 4 3 2 1
Printed in China